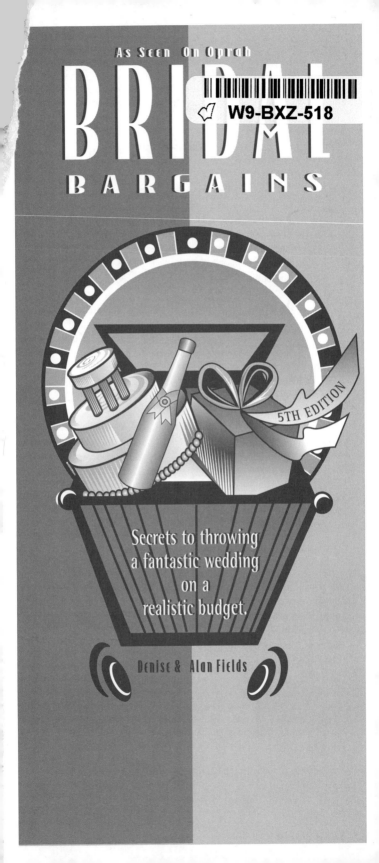

As Seen On Oprah

BRIDAL
BARGAINS

5TH EDITION

Secrets to throwing
a fantastic wedding
on a
realistic budget.

Denise & Alan Fields

II

The Copyright Page and Zesty Lo-Cal Recipes

French horn, electric guitar and samples by Denise Fields
Drums, stand-up bass, and spelling mistakes by Alan Fields
Additional percussion and backing vocals by Ben & Jack Fields
Backing vocals on "Bridal Magazines" by Sting and Ric Ocasek
Piano solo on "Wedding Cakes" by Randy Newman

Cover, interior design and cello by Epicenter Creative, Boulder, CO
Index and cowbell by Doug Easton
Actual heartfelt gratitude to our distributor, PGW
Thanks Mark, Heather, Charlie, John, Kathy, Olu and all others
Special thanks to Kirstin Bock, our invaluable helper.

This book was written to the music of the Barenaked Ladies,
which probably explains a lot.

Alan Fields appears courtesy of Howard & Patti Fields.
Denise Fields appears courtesy of Max & Helen Coopwood.
Denise & Alan wishes to thank their sons, Ben & Jack for their funkiness.
More thanks to the Salt Lick, Amy's Ice Cream and IronWorks BBQ.

Published by Windsor Peak Press, 436 Pine Street, Suite 7000, Boulder, CO, 80302. To order this book, check your local bookstore or call (800) 888-0385. Or send $14.95 plus $3 shipping to Windsor Peak, 436 Pine Street, Suite 7000, Boulder, CO, 80302. Quantity discounts are available.

Questions or comments? Feel free to contact the authors at (303) 442-8792; e-mail at authors@BridalBargainsBook.com; or write to them at the above address. More information on books by Windsor Peak Press and updates to this book are posted on our web page at www.windsorpeak.com.

Library in Congress Cataloging in Publication Data
Fields, Denise
Fields, Alan
    Bridal Bargains: Secrets to Throwing a Fantastic Wedding on a Realistic Budget/Denise and Alan Fields. 3rd Edition. Includes index.
    1.   Wedding—United   States—Planning.   2.   Consumer education—United States. 3. Shopping—United States.
ISBN1-889392-02-2   93-093752 LIC

    Distributed to bookstores by Publisher's Group West, 1-800-788-3123

Version 5.0

OVERVIEW

Your Wedding teaches you how to find the best deals on bridal apparel for the bride and the wedding party. Then, you learn how to shop for your ceremony site, wedding flowers, and invitations. Each chapter gives you in depth money-saving tips and shopping strategies.

Your Reception shows you how to save money on everything from catering to entertainment. Our chapter on wedding photography gives you nine creative ways to save money plus eleven important questions to ask any photographer. You'll also learn how to find the best deals on wedding cakes and wedding videos.

Learn about Canada's most popular bridal gown designers, a web site to search for reception sites and other Canadian tips and advice.

An easy-to-use directory with every phone number and web site address mentioned in this book.

Contents

Chapter 3

Chapter 4

Chapter 5

Chapter 6

Part II: Your Reception

Chapter 7

ICONS

 What are You Buying?

 Sources

 Brides in Cyberspace: What's on the Web?

 Getting Started: How Far in Advance?

 Step-by-Step Shopping Strategies

 Questions to Ask

 Top Money-saving Secrets

 **Myths**

 Hints

 Pitfalls to Avoid

Aaaaaaigh!!! So, you're engaged? Well, fasten your seat belts! Soon you will travel through a bizarre and crazy world, where the boundaries of good taste and sane thought are only fuzzy lines. Yes, you've done it now. You have entered the WEDDING ZONE.

See, that's why we are here. We're sort of your tour guides through this wondrous journey of things bridal and ideas nuptial. Of course, right off the bat, you will probably notice a basic difference between this and all those other wedding books—this book contains actual COMMON SENSE.

Sure, we know we're going out on a limb here but what the heck? Why not write a book you can actually use to plan your wedding? Hey, it's the least we can do. At this point you may have a question: so, who are you guys? Let's put that into bold type.

So Who Are You Guys?

When we got engaged, the first thing we did was trot down to our local bookstore. There has got to be a book that will help us survive this process, we thought. What we wanted was a consumer guide that would show us how to plan a wonderful wedding without spending an amount equivalent to the Federal Deficit. From recently-married friends, we heard all the horror stories—that wasn't going to happen to us. We would find out how to shop, what questions to ask and how to avoid scams and frauds. A small request, we thought.

Ha! All we found were etiquette books last revised when Eisenhower was president. Plenty of bridal books wanted to tell us what was "proper," what was "socially acceptable" and what was "never to be done except under threat of death." Gee, that's nice, we said, but what we need is help with the money thing, not useless etiquette.

So we left the bookstore with our heads down. Now what? Then the idea hit us: hey, why can't we write this book? There must be a few other engaged couples going through this needing practical advice too.

To make a long story somewhat shorter, we were right. In the past 12 years, we have "mystery shopped" over 1000 wedding businesses, from bridal shops to caterers; photographers to bakeries. From these anonymous visits, we learned a lot about planning a wedding. We realized there are tricks to spotting a truly talented wedding photographer or finding a bakery that creates the best wedding cakes. At the same time, we learned how to identify dishonest merchants who will try to rip off brides with dubious products or inferior service.

We first took those experiences and wrote six regional guides to planning a wedding for cities in the Southwest. But we didn't stop there. For this book, we spent 12 years interviewing bridal professionals and wedding "experts" across the country. We then spoke to hundreds of engaged couples, carefully documenting problems and challenges they had encountered planning their weddings. When you read this book, you not only get our opinions but the wise advice of many recently married couples who have gone before you.

Of course, we are not wedding consultants or planners. We don't own a farmhouse in Connecticut and decorate it with gold-dipped walnuts and cut-up credit cards. Nope, we're just normal folks (well, as normal as two people can be and still live in Boulder, CO). We see our role as consumer activists, working to educate brides on how to be smart shoppers. Believe it or not, this is a full-time job—we write and research about the wedding biz for a living.

If you find this book helpful, please recommend it to your friends. If they can't find it at a local bookstore or library, call us toll-free at (800) 888-0385. Or email us at authors@BridalBargainsBook.com. Also feel free to write to us at 436 Pine Street, Suite 7000, Boulder, CO 80302. We value your opinions, comments and experiences—we plan to revise this book with future editions so please feel free to contact us.

The four truths about weddings you won't read in etiquette books

1 **So you think your wedding is for you and your fiancé?** Ha! Forget it. Unfortunately, weddings often become less a celebration of marriage and more like a huge social torture test for the participants. Parents, and even some brides and grooms, are frequently guilty of turning weddings into spectacles to impress their friends or business associates. Money can become the sticking point since whoever pays for the wedding may feel a divine right to influence the proceedings with their own tastes.

Sometimes, parents and relatives try to make your wedding into the wedding they never had (and always dreamed of). Your friends may be guilty of pressuring you to make your wedding fit some predetermined mold. Put another way, while you may be the stars of the show, you and your fiancé may not be the wedding's directors, producers or choreographers.

Recognize this fact early and learn to negotiate without giving ultimatums. Yes, it is YOUR day, but remembering that others (parents, friends, relatives) are on the stage with you may prevent excessive bloodshed.

2 **Weddings always end up twice as large as originally planned.** If only we had a dime for every couple we met who said "all we wanted was a small, intimate wedding and what we got was a huge affair for 500 guests." A wedding often takes on a life of its own, expanding into a hideous creature several times larger than you ever imagined.

This process usually begins with what we call Guest List Inflation. Here the guest list grows because each family simply must invite personal friends, close business associates and people whom they haven't seen in fifteen years. The main problem: adding to the guest list has a direct, negative impact on your budget.

Several weddings have nearly unraveled when families have insisted on inflating the guest list without offering to help pay for the additional cost. We suggest you and your families be allowed to invite a certain number of guests each. Any invites beyond those targets must be financed by the offending party. Careful negotiations are often necessary to avoid open warfare on this point. Good luck.

3 **Perfect weddings don't exist in the free world.** No matter what anyone tells you, understand that the "perfect wedding" is an impossibility on planet Earth. That's because weddings always involve human beings who, on the whole, tend to be less than perfect creatures.

Now, we know everyone tells you that you must have the perfect gown, perfect flowers, perfect cake unless you want to catch the Bridal Plague and die an agonizingly painful death. Don't listen to these demons. Instead, we suggest you aim for a "fantastic" or "wonderful" wedding. Or even just a fun wedding!

Since it's impossible to perfectly script something as complex as a wedding, we say why try? Attendants will miss cues, things will go wrong—if you need any proof of this just watch any of those "outrageous and shocking home video" shows. Ever wonder why so many of those clips are of weddings? Hmmmmm.

Aiming for a wonderful wedding will also give you another benefit—you will probably be able to maintain your sanity.

4 **The "wedding industry" isn't as innocent as it looks.** You might think the wedding industry is a collection of sweet old ladies whose only desire is to help young couples in love, but the reality is quite the opposite. Instead, think of the bridal biz as a group of cut-throat small business persons who, in some cases, will do anything for a sale.

Newspaper columnist Dave Barry once wrote that the motto of the wedding industry is, "Money can't buy you happiness, so you might as well give your money to us." Quite true. Weddings are big bucks.

According to the latest research, over $20 billion dollars will be spent this year by couples tying the knot. That's billion with a "b." And that's just the wedding and reception—add in another $19 billion on gifts and $8 billion on honeymoons and you've got a $47 billion bridal juggernaut we like to call the Wedding Industrial Complex. Scary fact: the wedding industry dwarfs many other businesses, including the breakfast food biz (a paltry $16 billion in Fruit Loops and the like) or the record industry ($15 billion in CD sales).

And you can bet your bridal veil that the industry knows EXACTLY how lucrative all these "I Do's" can be. To illustrate this, check out what the publisher of *Bride's* magazine told a trade journal about the wedding industry: "Never before in a woman's life, and never again, is she going to be worth this much money to a marketer. There is no price resistance and she is completely open to new brands," *Bride's* publisher cackled, adding that the internal tag line for *Bride's* is "Where Love Meets Money."

Of course, we're not against folks trying to make a buck. Hey, sell a quality product or service at a fair price and make a profit—that's America. Yet what makes wedding planning so crazy are bridal merchants who view brides and grooms as automatic cash machines. Other wedding vendors seem at war with their customers, as odd as that seems. Take bridal dress retailers—please! As you'll read in the next chapter, these stores are incredibly inventive at separating brides from their money, generating a huge volume of complaints from consumers.

Why do some bridal merchants and vendors think engaged couples are an easy mark? That's because weddings are a one-shot deal. There are no repeat customers (except if you are, say Elizabeth Taylor or Larry King). Unlike other industries that rely on repeat customers, wedding merchants know you won't be stopping by next month to buy another bridal gown, cake or ice sculpture. And with a fresh crop of new brides and grooms each year, some sleazy merchants can continue their rip-offs and scams with little fear of getting busted.

So, the mission for this book is to teach you how to separate the good guys from the scamsters out there in wedding land. Yes, there are ethical and honest bridal professionals out there that charge a fair price. Just be aware the wedding business is just that—a business, where folks are trying to make a buck while you tie the knot.

The Goal of This Book: To help you save money and still have a fantastic wedding!

Consumer justice doesn't have to be a somber topic. Getting a great bargain should be fun. Outfoxing dishonest merchants should be a joyful experience. That's why we try to keep our perspective about this wedding stuff, and we urge you to do the same. Not maintaining your sense of humor during wedding planning may be hazardous to your health. That's why we've liberally sprinkled what could loosely be described as "humor" throughout this book.

In each chapter we give you Pitfalls to Avoid. As you learn about these bridal scams and wedding frauds, realize that just because you are a bride does not mean you have to be a victim. By using our consumer tips, you can protect yourself from losing hundreds, if not thousands, of dollars and have a good time doing it!

This book is for brides and grooms who want to hire professionals for their wedding. This book doesn't teach you how to sew a bridal gown or give you a recipe for a wedding cake. Instead, we'll show you how to get a nationally-advertised designer gown at a 20% to 40% discount. We'll also show you the secrets to finding an affordable baker, photographer and DJ.

There's no advertising in this book?

There are no paid advertisements in this book. Furthermore, no company paid any consideration or was charged any fee to be mentioned in it. The publisher, Windsor Peak Press, derives its sole income from the sale of this book and other consumer guides. As consumer advocates, the authors believe this policy ensures objectivity. The opinions expressed in this book are those of the authors.

So, how much does a wedding cost anyway?

Unless you are a Certified Public Accountant, you may not be inclined to use the words "fun" and "exhilarating" to describe setting the budget for your wedding. As you might expect us to say, however, this is a critical (albeit painful) part of the planning process.

Whether you're spending $100 or $100,000 on your wedding, every bride and groom has a limited amount of money to spend. This means you'll have to make tough choices regarding how you want to allocate your limited resources. In Appendix A, we provide an in depth look at setting a budget. Hopefully, this will help make this process easier.

So, how much does a wedding cost? Here are the average costs for a formal wedding for 175 guests. Chart A lists the actual costs, while Chart B is a pie chart to show you the biggest expense areas.

At this point you might be packing up to catch the Greyhound to Vegas, but we say "Whoa!" Weddings do NOT have to be that expensive. Let's put that into bold caps: YOU DO NOT HAVE TO GO BANKRUPT TO HAVE A BEAUTIFUL WEDDING. Of course, that's the whole point of this book and we'll spend the next 300 pages or so showing you how to cut the cost without compromising on the quality of your wedding.

AVERAGE WEDDING COSTS

ITEM	$ AMOUNT	% OF TOTAL
APPAREL		
BRIDAL GOWN	$800	
HEADPIECE, VEIL	175	
ALTERATIONS, ACCESSORIES	315	
GROOM'S TUX RENTAL	100	
APPAREL SUB-TOTAL	**1390**	**7%**
RINGS		
ENGAGEMENT RING	3000	
WEDDING RINGS	1000	
RINGS SUB-TOTAL	**4000**	**20%**
MUSIC		
CEREMONY MUSIC	150	
DJ AT RECEPTION	400	
MUSIC SUB-TOTAL	**650**	**3%**
MISCELLANEOUS		
MARRIAGE LICENSE	30	
ATTENDANTS GIFTS	320	
OTHER STUFF	450	
MISC. SUB-TOTAL	**800**	**4%**
CEREMONY SITE AND OFFICIANT	200	1%
FLOWERS	900	5%
CAKE	525	3%
RECEPTION/CATERING	8,400	42%
PHOTOGRAPHY	1,500	8%
VIDEOGRAPHY	1,000	5%
INVITATIONS	390	2%
LIMO	190	1%
TOTAL	**$19,945**	**100%**

(BASED ON INDUSTRY ESTIMATES FOR 175 GUESTS)
NOTE: PERCENTAGES DO NOT ADD UP TO 100% DUE TO ROUNDING.

CHART B: BREAKDOWN OF AVERAGE WEDDING COSTS

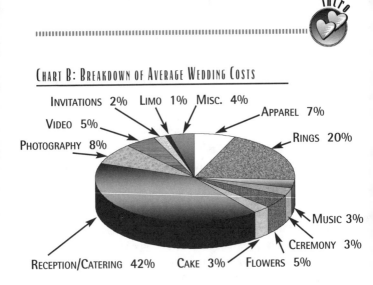

INVITATIONS 2% LIMO 1% MISC. 4%
VIDEO 5%
PHOTOGRAPHY 8%
APPAREL 7%
RINGS 20%
MUSIC 3%
CEREMONY 3%
RECEPTION/CATERING 42% CAKE 3% FLOWERS 5%

Of course, where you get married will dramatically impact your wedding costs. Heck, even the cost of a marriage license can vary widely, from a piddling four bucks in Massachusetts to over $80 in California and Florida.

If you are a bride-to-be in the largest metro areas like New York City or Los Angeles, you may be looking at the above numbers and laughing (or crying). That's because many items there cost at least two to three times the average. Keep this in mind throughout the book when we quote "average prices." (See Appendix A: Setting the Budget for average New York City wedding costs).

And to be fair, we should note that we left some costs out of the above chart. Wedding favors (a little tchotchke given to each guest) are a regional tradition, common in some areas but not seen in others. Couples spend $240 on average on favors. Another expense we didn't put here: the honeymoon, which can run $3000 to $5000 depending on the where you go.

What about bridesmaids dresses and groomsmen formalwear rentals? Those costs aren't in the above table because they are typically paid by each attendant. Of course, if you intend to help out a bridesmaid by paying for her gown, start adding to your budget accordingly. In a similar vein, the rehearsal dinner ($750 on average), ceremony programs ($75), hair and make-up for the bridal party ($200 or more) are optional items that some couples put in their budgets.

Of course, averages are just that—averages. Walk into any bridal dress shop and you'll notice gowns can be $1000, $2000 or more. The same goes for many other wedding items . . . you can quickly spend many times the average in a flash. For example, that $1000 tab for a wedding video assumes single-camera coverage—add another $800 or $1000 if you want two or three cameras capturing your wedding and reception.

In each chapter, we'll discuss what "average" means for everything from flowers to invitations.

The Five Fields' Commandments for Bridal Bargains

We went up the mountain and came down with these five commandants for brides on a budget. Please repeat after us:

1 **The Budget is King.** Set a budget and stick to it like a duck on a June bug. Yes, that means making hard choices . . . like whether you really need an orchid corsage for the wedding cake knife—but, hey, we'll try to point out where to put your money. And where not to waste it.

2 **Daylight Savings Time.** Timing is everything—and the same goes for weddings. Everyone wants to be married in the peak wedding months of June and August. Do your budget a favor and get hitched in an off-month like October, November, January, February or March. Remember it is also cheaper to get married in the "daylight"—brunch or afternoon weddings are always less than evening bashes.

3 **Plan Ahead.** Do the math—each year 2.4 million couples will tie the knot . . . but there are only 52 Saturdays each year. The best bargain sites and merchants always book up early. Give yourself plenty of time to comparison shop, get competitive bids and ferret out sales.

4 **Undress the Dress.** If you pay full retail for a bridal gown, please give us your street address so we can come over to your house and whack you on the head with this book. Seriously, we found TWO DOZEN ways to slash that dress bill, from bargains on eBay, special designer sales and outlets to mail order catalogs that can slash your dress bill by 30% to 50% or more.

5 **Cut the Cake—and other frills.** Brides and grooms pile on the sweets at receptions, but can guests really wolf down a wedding cake, groom's cake AND a dessert table? And do you really need a six-tier confection that looks like a chandelier when a simple cake will do? The same goes for other ridiculous bridal items: wedding favors (guests don't need another dust collector), engraved invitations (other options look just as good at half the cost), exotic flowers at the ceremony (guests spend much more time at the reception).

Getting Set, Getting Organized

Start the process of wedding planning on the right foot by getting organized. And no, this doesn't mean you have to buy the $50 "bridal organizers" that the wedding industry hawks. We received several great suggestions about how to get organized from our past readers. For example, one bride suggested going down to a local office supply store and buying a plain accordion file for all the contracts, proposals and receipts every bride collects. The unglamorous brown file was a mere $5—significantly less than the $35 price for a "bride's" accordion file advertised in a bridal magazine with taffeta fabric and a satin bow.

Another bride organized her wedding using a three-ring binder. She hole punched all the contracts and bought pocket inserts for her receipts, photos and fabric swatches. Total cost: $4 to $5. If you bought a similar product specially designed for brides with lacy inserts and full color photos, you'd spend as much as $50.

Regardless of the method you use to organize your wedding, keeping all your receipts and contracts in one place is vitally important. Also, make copies of any written correspondence (emails, faxes, letters) you have with the businesses you hire. Even keep a telephone log of your phone conversations.

Although chances are your wedding planning will be a smooth process, if any problems do crop up, you'll be glad you spent the time and money to be so well organized.

The Bridal Clock

"I'm late! I'm late for a very important date!" said the rabbit in *Alice in Wonderland*. At times, as you plan your wedding, you might feel a bit harried yourself.

Of course, the first real crisis of any engagement is the realization that you must accomplish 1.6 million things in about 13 seconds in order to get to the church on time. The second crisis is wondering which of those 1.6 million things you should do *first*.

To solve this problem, we have invented our BRIDAL CLOCK, which is displayed below. Think of the numbers of the clock as the sequence of events in the wedding planning process. At high noon is your wedding.

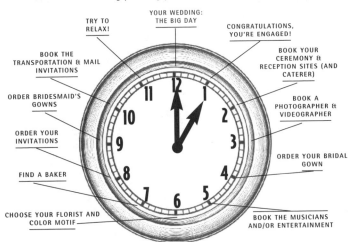

Start with reserving your ceremony site (two o'clock). Next, find and book a reception site and caterer. From there, shop for your wedding gown . . . and so on.

In each chapter in this book, you'll find specific advice on how much time you need to order everything from invitations to a wedding cake. Of course, the BRIDAL CLOCK gives you a general sense of how far you've gone—and how much further you need to go until the bewitching hour.

As a side note, you'll notice we did not organize this book in the same order as the Bridal Clock. For simplicity's sake, we divided the book into two sections—the wedding and the reception.

To be fair, we should also note that many of the bargain tips and advice in this book may require advance planning—it can take up to six months to order a gown through a discount mail-order service, for example. What if you've just got a few months (or weeks) before your wedding, can you still save money? Of course. Each chapter of this book contains cost-cutting alternatives anyone can use, no matter how much time you have before you walk down the aisle.

What's new in this edition

So, what's changed with the fifth edition of *Bridal Bargains?* As always, we just couldn't leave well enough alone. New to this book, you'll find sections on gift registries and honeymoons, with tips on the best travel bargains and more. How can you hurricane proof your honeymoon? We'll discuss that, along with dirt-cheap e-fare honeymoons and more.

In our chapter on wedding dresses, you'll notice new web sources for

---

REAL WEDDING TIP

Objects are closer than they appear

What? You want to get married in just three months? If you read most bridal publications, you'd think it was violating the laws of physics to tie the knot without *years* of planning. Not true, says one bride who recently emailed us:

"Everyone told us that four months was an impossible length of time for planning a wedding. . . it is not only possible, it's a reality. It's amazing (and disgusting) to me that a store will tell you that shoes or dresses or whatever will take four months to order. Upon learning that your wedding is sooner than that, they make a call and lo and behold that item is in stock and today is your lucky day because it can be here in ONE WEEK! From sixteen weeks to one week in five minutes . . . amazing! I know it's true, because it has happened to us more than once, in more than one store and with different items."

The lesson: don't give up. You CAN plan a wedding with short notice, no matter the lead time.

discount gowns as well as helpful charts that help you compare designers at a glance. We'll cover the new trend of designer-owned "factory stores" and the latest bargains with bridesmaids dresses from department stores and mail-order catalogs. And we didn't forget the guys—this edition includes a beefed up section on tuxedos with more tips, advice and bargains.

The Internet is still a hot place for bargains; this time out, we add more bargain sources on the 'net for everything from invitations to flowers. You'll read about bargains on eBay for gowns and wedding items, as well as new web sites that are hooking up with photographers to showcase your wedding pictures online. In videos, we'll discuss the trend toward wedding DVD's and some pitfalls that accompany this hot new technology.

In other news, this edition of Bridal Bargains includes new advice on how to rent a tent, as well as bargains on chair covers. We'll also cover the latest wedding cake trends, including pitfalls with that new Martha Stewart-inspired fondant cake look.

Finally, you'll see more bargain tips in each chapter, from photography to catering. We've added 60-plus pages of deals and steals on every topic in the book. And, for you Canadian brides, you have your own section of *Bridal Bargains*, complete with reviews of Canada's best bridal gown designers.

Bridal Bargains Hall of Fame

When it comes to bargain shopping, many of our readers have earned their black belts. While we write about saving money for a living, we are constantly amazed at the bargains our readers discover. Here's a list of our all time favorites, the Bridal Bargains Hall of Fame:

♥ THE $47 VERA WANG BRIDAL GOWN. Karin Srisilpan of San Francisco found the deal of a lifetime at a Bay Area bridal outlet—a Vera Wang bridal gown in excellent condition for a mere $47. Original price: $6000. Karin found this steal at Jeremys (2 South Park, 415-882-4929), a designer outlet that gets bridal gown samples from tony department stores from time to time. We'll talk about more about bridal outlets and special "secret" sales by big bridal designers where you can save 50% to 75% off retail in Chapter 2.

♥ TAKE ME OUT TO THE . . . WEDDING? Here's a bargain idea that's definitely out in left field—literally. Lisa Touye of New York City was aghast at the cost of wedding receptions in the Big Apple, where $150 per-plate dinners are considered "routine." Her solution: get married at Shea Stadium during a Mets game. She rented the Left-Field Terrace, a luxury box that seats 144. For $44 per person, her guests had a choice of two entrees, dessert, wedding cake, beer, wine, soda and the "best hot dogs we've ever had." Sure, she also had to pay for tickets to the game ($19 per guest), but hey, they also got to take pictures down on the field before the game and the bride's and groom's names were flashed on the Diamond Vision screen. Instead of a guest book, guests autographed baseballs for the couple. For more info, contact the Mets' Coordinator of Group Sales (718) 565-4332. More reception bargain ideas are in Chapters 7 and 8.

♥ **25 ROSES FOR $14.** Ever wish you had a friend in the wholesale flower business? Check out 2G Roses, a California flower wholesaler who ships nationwide (800) 880-0735, www.freshroses.com. A reader in San Francisco discovered this bargain and we have to agree—these are great deals! Besides roses, 2G sells a wide variety of other flowers, all shipped FEDEX overnight to insure freshness. They have complete wedding packages starting at just $100, or buy a la carte (enough roses, greens and filler for a bride's bouquet, just $25). Check out Chapter 5 "Wedding Flowers" for more details on this best buy.

♥ **A LIMO DEAL TO DIE FOR.** We've got to hand it to Stephanie Kampes of Drexel Hill, PA. She discovered that funeral homes rent out limos at HALF the cost of regular limo companies (see the Etcetera chapter for more).

♥ **EZ Bowmaker.** This simple $10 device enables you to make professional-looking bows for pew decorations, table centerpieces and more. Why pay a florist hundreds of dollars when you can do it yourself for pennies? Made by EZ Bowz (call 800-311-6529 or 865-453-3060 for a store near you), the EZ Bowmaker is available in craft stores like Michaels (800-MICHAELS, www.michaels.com). Another similar item: **Miracle Bow.** This $5 barrette (made by Offray & Sons, call 301-739-6314 for store near you, web: www.offray.com) comes with four-step instructions for making ribbon bows for headpieces. Attach a piece of veiling to the Miracle Bow and you've got a complete headpiece and veil look for a fraction of retail. We've got more floral cost-cutters in Chapter 5.

♥ **Wedding Invitations CD-ROM Kit.** Wedding invitations can cost hundreds of dollars—and sometimes take weeks to order. But if you've got a PC and desktop printer, you can whip up wedding invitations in just minutes. This CD-ROM software package spits out perfect etiquette invites that can be printed on a home laser or inkjet printer. For a mere $20, the kit also includes heavy stock paper for 25 invitations and 50 accessory folders (such as thank you notes). The PC-only program is made by American Pad & Paper (call 800-621-3684 for a dealer near you) and is available in office supply stores like Staples. We've got more on this best buy in Chapter 6.

Find a bargain you think belongs in the Hall of Fame? Contact us at (303) 442-8792 or via email at authors@BridalBargainsBook.com.

1

Your
Wedding

Wonder how you can save 20% to 70% off those fancy designer bridal gowns? We'll show you how, plus teach you 17 steps to buying the right dress. Then you'll learn 23 valuable money-saving tips. Finally, we'll expose how dishonest bridal shops rip-off brides, while we teach you how to outfox them. Last but not least, we'll take a candid look at the country's biggest bridal designers, rating them on price and quality.

The Bridal Gown. Nothing symbolizes a wedding more than the bridal gown. Prospective brides are taught from birth to fantasize about this ultimate dress, sparkling with beads, sequins and pearls delicately sewn onto French lace. Of course, the designers who make those gowns are well aware of this—their ads are laced with references to "fairy-tale" weddings and "storybook" brides.

Okay, I admit to falling into this fantasy stuff head first when I was a bride. But, hey, how often do you get to wear a piece of clothing that costs $1000? Finding the right bridal gown (at a price that doesn't resemble the federal deficit) is the overriding priority for many brides. And why not?

As it turns out, however, bridal gown shopping often turns into the ultimate battle between women and the evil apparel industry. This is the Olympics of shopping.

Thanks to a host of tricks, scams and outright rip-offs in the bridal apparel business, buying a bridal gown is perhaps the most perilous and tricky task in this journey we call wedding planning. You didn't expect this to be easy, did you?

In this chapter, we explore the reasons why buying a bridal gown generates the biggest number of complaints from engaged couples. We'll teach you how to find the gown that's just right for you and how not to get ripped off doing it.

Where do brides buy bridal gowns? According to a magazine survey, 70% of all brides purchase a gown at a bridal shop, a specialty store or off-the-rack chain that focuses on bridal and formal apparel. Another 12% purchase a dress from a department store, while 10% have a gown sewn by a professional or friend. Other brides wear a gown that was a family heirloom (2%), borrow or rent a dress (2%), or buy through a discount service or mail order (3%).

In this section, we will focus on buying a bridal gown from a traditional bridal shop. Of course, there are several little-known but quite fascinating alternatives to this route. We'll discuss them later in the chapter.

What Are You Buying?

At the simplest level, you are buying a dress. But not just any dress. This is a darn *expensive* dress. The average bridal gown costs $800 in most stores, no matter where you live. Many of the premium designer gowns sell for much more, topping $1000 and even $2000.

So what do you think you should get for $800? Well, before you answer this question, we ask you to shift your mind into BRIDAL MODE. That's because if you think in the REAL WORLD MODE you're going to be in for a shock. For example, if we gave you $800 and told you to buy a nice party or cocktail dress you'd expect a few things for that amount of money. Fine fabrics like silk? Sure. Quality construction with a lining and finished seams? Why not. How about sewn sequins and detailing? Hey, you'd expect that for $800! Right?

Well, BRIDAL MODE isn't like that. For $800, you'll see plenty of dresses with synthetic fabric, shoddy construction with unfinished seams and no lining. Want a sophisticated gown made of silk with a splash of delicate embroidery? Sadly, dresses like that are often way over $1000.

Frankly, we can't figure out why this is. Perhaps the entire bridal apparel industry (from the powerful designers to the lowly local bridal shops) thinks that when women get engaged they collectively lose all common sense. Like zombies, brides are supposed to walk into bridal shops and plunk down a cool $1000 for a gown they wouldn't even consider buying for $300 if they saw it at a department store.

As a side note, don't forget that the bridal gown is just the beginning. There are many "hidden costs" when buying a bridal gown—you'll also need undergarments, a slip, shoes and the ubiquitous headpiece and veil. If you think bridal gowns are overpriced, wait until you see the prices for accessories. The "average" headpiece and veil runs $175 (although many top $200), while you can add another $400 for other accessories (see below). Hence, the total ensemble may cost you over $1300. Below is a break-down of extra costs:

And those figures are just averages. Alterations can be much more expensive than $75 (roughly the national average). We've received mail from brides who report that in major cities, bridal shops are now charging exorbitant "flat fees" for alterations—$150, $200 and even $250. While that figure covers any changes to the gown, brides who

Hidden Gown Costs

(Sample figures for a typical gown—and those necessary extras)

Gown	$800
Rush Charge	50
Alterations	75
Pressing	50
Delivery to ceremony	50
Crinoline/Slip	45
Bra	30
Headpiece/Veil	175
Shoes	60
Jewelry	25
Gloves/Stockings	30
Total	**$1390**

(Note: in the introduction for this book, we say the average cost of the bride's ensemble is $1290. That's because we don't count two of the above items—the rush charge and delivery to the ceremony, since those are charges most brides don't incur).

merely need a minor nip and tuck get socked for the full fare. On the other hand, some shops throw in free alterations and a pressing if you spend a certain amount of money in the store. (More on alterations later in this chapter).

Even if you pay the average for these items, it's amazing how an $800 gown can turn into a $1390 total tab in a hurry. Of course, you don't have to pay that much. Order early (at least six months before the wedding) and you won't pay the rush charge. You can save big bucks by borrowing a crinoline/slip, forget the special delivery to the church (carry it yourself), and buy shoes, jewelry, and other accessories at discount stores. More on money-saving strategies later in this chapter.

We should also note that most shops require a 50% deposit on all special orders. (We'll explain later why most gowns are special-ordered instead of bought off-the-rack.) That can be a sizable financial hit several months before the wedding. The balance is due when the dress comes in. The exception to the half-down rule: some discounters (both online and mail order) require payment in full when you order. This certainly requires more of a leap of faith on the consumer's part, but the discount (20% to 30% off retail) may make this deal attractive.

Sources to Find a Bridal Shop

Finding a bridal shop is easy. Finding a *good* bridal shop is somewhat more challenging. Beyond the basic sources, there are four important ways to locate local shops:

♥ **BRIDAL MAGAZINES.** The major bridal magazines are literally plastered with ads from apparel manufacturers. On the page next to the dress, you can often find a list of shops that carry the designer. Just look for your city and bingo! There will be at least one candidate for your search. (A few caveats: some ads don't list any local shops. Others have incomplete listings—some local stores may carry the dress, but are not listed in the ad). Before you put much stock in magazines, however, read our article on them later in the chapter.

♥ **FRIENDS.** Ask everyone you know if they know someone who was recently married. Call several brides and drill them on their experiences. Any shops they recommend? Any shops you should avoid like the plague? Listen carefully to their advice—we know one couple who was repeatedly warned by friends *not* to buy at a particular shop. They bought there anyway, and, wouldn't you know, fell victim to a scam and lost $500.

♥ **THE 'NET.** Surf the web to find local bridal shops, some of which have established sites that tout their stores. Find them by accessing gown designers' web sites that have store locators or check out the "generic" wedding web sites for links. More on this later.

♥ **THE BETTER BUSINESS BUREAU.** Check to see if any shops you have heard about have a record of complaints. Any complaint (even if the company resolved it) is a big, red flag.

Brides in Cyberspace: What's on the Web?

The sheer volume of gown info on the web is mind boggling. Here are two of the best places to go, plus some other general ideas on using the web in your gown search.

The Wedding Channel's Sketchbook Search
Web site: www.weddingchannel.com, go to "Fashion"
What is it: The best organized gown picture database on the web.
What's cool: The nifty "Sketchbook Search" (see Figure 1 on the next page) lets you zero in on a dress with particular attributes (nine categories—sleeve length, waistline, bodice, etc). Don't know a jewel neckline from a bandeau sleeve? No problem. Just roll your mouse over each word and a cool sketch pops up. Of course, you can just look up dresses

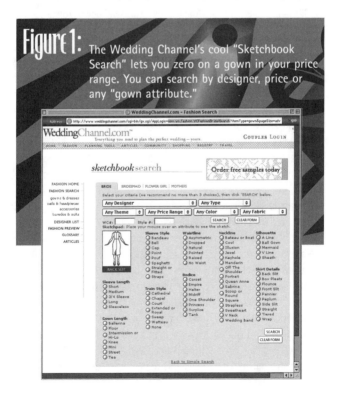

Figure 1: The Wedding Channel's cool "Sketchbook Search" lets you zero on a gown in your price range. You can search by designer, price or any "gown attribute."

by designer, price range and fabric. The Wedding Channel's designer list isn't as extensive as the Knot's (see below), but still includes some heavy hitters—and fortunately omits quite a few of the Knot's obscure, hard-to-find designers.

Needs work: Prices are omitted from some gowns and others have bogus (or missing) style numbers. Also, the Wedding Channel has fewer gown pictures than the Knot (see below).

The Knot's Bridal Search

Web site: www.theknot.com

What is it: The Mother of all bridal gown sites.

What's cool: Part of the Knot's web site, Bridal Search is an incredible treasure trove of gown info—20,000 dress pictures from over 100+ designers. Want to search by designer? Price range? Size? You can do that, or sort gowns by silhouette, train style/length, neckline or sleeve. In short, you can customize a search for exactly what you want. Best of all, it's free.

Needs work: Well, the Knot isn't perfect. First, the gown pictures have no style numbers, so you don't know exactly WHICH gown you've fallen in love with. (Of course, you could still use the pictures to get quotes from discounters—it'll just require some detective work on their part). Second, while price is one search criteria, it's a *range*, not the exact price. And it's a BIG range—the Knot says "moderately expensive" gowns run anywhere from $1500 to $3000. (We'd call that DAMN expensive). Critics also point out that many of the gowns pictured on the site are discontinued (that is, no longer in production). The Knot does try to track which styles are actively in production, but apparently falls behind in this task. Another major caveat: the Knot doesn't tell you whether you are looking at a major gown designer or a very small dressmaker. Apparently, the Knot will let any gown maker with a sewing machine in the back of their garage advertise their gowns on the site. As a result, it is easy to fall in love with a gown that is sold in just three shops nationwide (or worse, only at the designer's "studio" which turns out to be a double wide trailer in North Dakota).

Romantic Headlines

Web site: www.romanticheadlines.com

What it is: The Amazon.com of bridal headpieces and accessories.

What's cool: This site (see Figure 2) features the largest collection of headpieces for sale on the Internet. Dallas-based Romantic Headlines can custom design a headpiece, hat or veil with material to match your bridal gown . . . or you can choose from one of 600 pre-made styles. Want a tiara? They've got 95 pictured. And the prices are excellent. Rhinestone tiaras are $35 to $65, while crystal ones are $70 to $100—that's HALF or more off what most retail stores charge. Regular headpieces with veils are a bargain at about $100. Or just buy the veil itself (plain or pearl-edged,

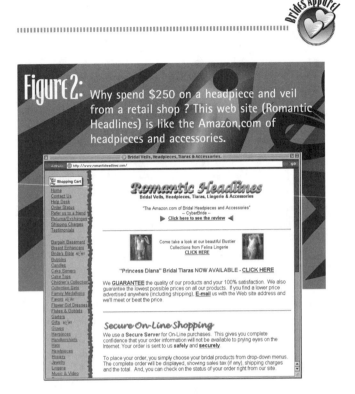

Figure 2: Why spend $250 on a headpiece and veil from a retail shop? This web site (Romantic Headlines) is like the Amazon.com of headpieces and accessories.

in a variety of lengths) from $12 to $40. We also liked their "bargain basement" with veils on combs for as little as $35. You can order on-line with a credit card via their secure server and the site also sells bridal accessories, shoes, lingerie, hosiery and jewelry.

Needs work: It would be nice if you could search for headpieces by price. Instead, you have to wade through page after page of options at varying prices. Romantic Headlines has added a slew of bridal accessories to their site in recent months; now they sell candles, cake tops, favors, garters and more. As a result, the site is becoming a bit cluttered with a long navigation list in a purple frame that shows the categories. The site could use a bit more organization to make it more navigable.

Other sites: Of course, Romantic Headlines isn't the only site to sell headpieces and veils online. **Veils A La Mode** (web: www.veilsalamode.com) sells tiaras for just $30 to $40 and various other headpieces at very affordable prices. If you want, you can buy just the veil for $35 to $55 for cathedral length (the price depends on the edge finish). Those prices are fantastic savings over retail shops, where headpieces and veils can run $200 or more.

A reader recommends **August Moon Designs** (web: www.bridalstuff.com) for their affordable headpieces and veils—she bought one for just $79 from the site and was very pleased with the quality and customer service.

Games That Bridal Shops Play

(Not all bridal shops are guilty of the following dishonest practices. However, after personally visiting over 250 bridal shops and researching this topic for over ten years, we have encountered several disturbing practices of which you should be aware.)

Once you decide which shop carries the type of gowns you want, the fun begins! It's time to hit the streets! Before you go, realize that once you step inside some bridal shops, you are entering the DARK AGES OF CONSUMERISM. For whatever reason, many bridal shops exist in a time and space where their owners think they're exempt from such silly concepts as Honesty and Ethics. Let's take a look at the appalling tactics that some shops use to confuse you, the consumer.

1 Mystery Gowns. Many bridal shops rip the tags out of their sample dresses to keep you from knowing who designed and manufactured the gown. When asked, these shop owners simply refuse to tell brides who made the dresses. Why would they do this? We've interviewed many shop owners who basically admit they do it to prevent brides from price shopping their dresses. Hey, they argue, if we tell you the designer, then you'll go down the street to our competitor and get the dress at a discount.

We say this is a bunch of bull. What the shops are trying to do is keep you ignorant. All designers are not equal, some offer better quality work than others. Keeping the designer from you is a sneaky way for them to pass off an inferior gown as "comparable" to a premium design.

What is most perplexing about this deceptive practice is the fact that most brides find out about the shop from a designer's ad in a bridal magazine. Designers spend millions trying to get brides to recognize their brand name and for what? To have their retailers tear out the tags is stupid, especially under the guise of stopping "price competition."

Not only is it stupid, it's also illegal. A federal law called the Textile Fiber Products Identification Act of 1963 requires all apparel (yes, even bridal) to be properly labeled. This must include the name of the manufacturer (or their "registered number" assigned by the Federal Trade Commission, 202-326-2222) as well as the fiber content and country of origin. Both federal and state laws forbid the removal of these tags. Sadly, many bridal shops openly and flagrantly violate this long-standing consumer law.

There is a one big loophole in the label law, however: shops can remove manufacturer's tags as long as they substitute their own tags with the store name and the required information (fiber content, country of origin, care instructions). For imported gowns (the vast majority of all gowns sold in the US are made overseas), this store tag must be sewn into the garment. While this sounds like a big loophole, we've noticed many stores don't even bother to replace tags. They just rip out the designer tags and slap a hang tag that omits all the required information.

You can read more about tag requirements at the Federal Trade Commission's web site at www.ftc.gov. The FTC has a special publication entitled "Wedding Gowns Labels: Unveiling the Requirements" at http://www.ftc.gov/bcp/online/pubs/buspubs/wedgown.htm.

What if you encounter a shop that rips tags and won't reveal info on the dress as required by law? First, file a complaint with the FTC. The FTC's web site (www.ftc.gov) has a quick and easy link to do this at www.ftc.gov/ftc/complaint.htm. The FTC will only take this problem seriously if they receive a good number of complaints from brides. Second, post a message on this to our web site, BridalGown.com. Go to "Real Brides Say" and either send us an email or post your story to our message boards. This will warn other readers about such shops.

So, why all the fuss about tags? Without it, you can fall victim to a series of consumer scams we've documented:

♥ **PRICE GOUGING.** By hiding the manufacturer's name, you cannot tell whether you're looking at a designer original . . . or a cheap knock-off made by a copy house. With 200 manufacturers of bridal apparel sold in North America, there is a WIDE difference in quality of construction, fabric and detailing. We think you have the right know what you are buying. Tag-ripping bridal shops sometimes try to gouge unsuspecting brides on price—we've seen cases of retailers trying to pawn off a $700 dress for over $1200.

♥ **FABRIC FRAUD.** With the fiber content label torn from dresses, it's hard to say whether the dress you're looking at is silk or polyester. In recent years, many new synthetic fabrics have come on the market that mimic the look and feel of silk. While these fabrics have creative names ("silky satin," for example), they are all polyester or blends. Unscrupulous retailers try to pass off these fabrics as silk.

♥ **SWEATSHOPS AND SLAVE LABOR.** Most bridal gowns sold today are made overseas, typically in Asia. A handful are still sewn in the U.S., Canada or Europe—these gowns are generally perceived to be of higher quality. When the bridal shop removes a gown's tag that indicates the country of origin, you don't know whether the dress is hand-crafted in the USA . . . or mass-produced in a sweatshop in China.

So, what happens when you ask a bridal retailer point blank "Who makes this gown?" Well, some refuse to tell you anything. Others say they'll happily tell you the brand . . . AFTER you place down that hefty

50% deposit (which is non-refundable, of course). You'd be offended if you ran into the same practice in an appliance or electronic store, but for some reason bridal retailers think they can get away with it. (Memo to Gloria Steinem: note that while shops rip out bridal gown tags, the men's tuxedo section has LOTS of tags).

What about style numbers? Well, while federal law prevents the removal of manufacturer, fiber content and country of origin tags, *there is NO requirement to reveal a gown's style number* (a unique number assigned to each dress). Often, bridal shops will tag their dresses with secret codes, not the actual style numbers.

Are designers upset about retailers that rip out their names from their gowns? Well, yes and no. Some designers (Demetrios/Ilissa, for one) have sent letters to their retailers warning them to not rip tags. Other designers could care less. Why? Most bridal gown makers are just concerned with selling samples into bridal stores; they could care less what the retailers do with the gowns after they get them (as long as they pay their bills, of course).

Top 7 Most Outrageous Excuses For Why Bridal Shops Rip Tags

Our email box is always stuffed with brides' gown tales. As a public service, we have been cataloging the most creative excuses used by bridal retailers as to why they rip tags out of their bridal gowns—and as a result, can't tell you who makes your dress. Yes, these are actual words uttered by retailers to consumers:

1. "The tags are removed to protect the feelings of brides since dress sizes are larger than those in street clothes."

2. "Bridal gown manufacturers forbid us to tell you who makes which dress. So, it's out of our hands."

3. "It's in the computer and that's down, so we don't know."

4. "Designers don't put tags in dresses for copyright purposes (to keep their gowns from being copied) and shops can't do anything about that."

5. "Only the store's buyer knows who makes each dress and she's not telling."

6. "All our dresses are made exclusively for this store in the Orient, so there are no brand names."

7. "We don't know who makes which dress, but if you pay us a 50% non-refundable deposit, we can find out!"

The bottom line: you're probably going to encounter this problem when you gown shop. We found three out of four bridal shops rip tags and violate federal label laws. This happens in both big and small cities, from some of the country's biggest gown sellers in New York and LA to the smallest town in Alabama. Yes, the FTC did try to crack down on this practice in 1999, sending letters to offending shops warning them to stop. They didn't. And the FTC hasn't done anything about it since.

Solution: Find a few dresses you like in a bridal magazine. Then walk into the shops listed in the ads and ask to see those specific dresses. If the salespeople say they don't know who makes which gowns, don't believe them. Before you walk out, you may mention to the salesperson that they just lost a big sale.

2 **Nickel and dime charges.** As if bridal gowns weren't expensive enough, some independent bridal retailers have started to add a series of questionable "fees" and "charges" to inflate your final bill. Here's a samples:

♥ TRY-ON FEES. Hard to believe, but some shops actually charge their customers to try on their dresses! One shop charges their brides $50 for an hour of dress up! Other shops only sock out-of-town brides with such fees (they figure in-town brides are more likely to buy). How can they tell you are from out of town? These retailers force all brides to register before browsing the racks—and the registration card asks for your address (age, blood type, etc). While try-on fees are typically deducted if you make a purchase, we can't think of any better way to drive brides to chain stores than such bogus fees.

♥ SHIPPING AND HANDLING. More mom-and-pop shops are slapping brides with shipping and handling fees for any special order. Bridal gown? $10 to $20 in shipping charges. Bridesmaids $5 to $10 EACH. Veils, headpieces, shoes and anything else is $3 to $5. We could understand shipping fees if these items were shipped to your home, but that's not the case in Bridal World. Here, retailers charge you shipping to have an item sent from their supplier to the BRIDAL STORE. Then you have to go pick it up! Even more deceptive: shops that claim these shipping charges also cover "insurance." "What girl doesn't want insurance against damage," one retailer told us, bragging that their customers have never questioned this. The only problem: ALL retailers must deliver you a gown free from damage, if you special order brand new merchandise. If UPS damages your gown, the shop has to make it good, whether you paid for "insurance" or not.

♥ ACCOUNTING SURCHARGES. A Jacksonville, FL bridal shop charges brides a $10 "accounting surcharge" for special orders that are not paid in full at the time of ordering. Never mind that the industry standard for special orders is almost always half down with the balance due when the goods are delivered. (Yes, there are exceptions, but more on this later). Either shops should do the standard half-down deal or require payment up front—surcharges for those who don't pay in full are ridiculous. Another questionable accounting charge: credit card surcharges. Some shops tack on another $2 to $5 for orders paid by credit cards (especially if the order is paid by phone for bridesmaids, for example). Credit card companies and some states expressly forbid surcharges on such purchases.

♥ **PENALTY FEE.** Yes, you can save money by ordering a gown mail-order or online, but beware the penalty box when it comes to alterations. In order to punish brides who bought from discount sources, bridal retailers add special "penalty fees" and surcharges to do alterations on such gowns. Some shops boost their alterations rates 15% to 50% over regular fees or others add a flat $10 to $100 extra charge to alter any dress not bought in their store.

♥ **LIGHT BULB FEE.** Just kidding—but will it be long before some bridal retailer decides to charge brides $20 to use the light bulbs in their dressing rooms so you can see that gown during a try-on?

Why do shops try to zap brides with all these bogus fees? Because they know MOST brides only look at the price of the gown, not the charges for all those little "extras."

We find these nickel and dime charges offensive since they are RARELY disclosed to the bride until the order is written. That way brides will fall in love with a gown before they are hit with the shipping fees, accounting charges and whatever bogus fee a retailer can dream up.

The obvious defense against this is to ask about any extra charges up front, before you start trying on gowns. Yes there are some "legitimate" extra charges—fees for larger sizes, rush delivery, etc. (more on these later). But be careful that your local bridal retailer doesn't try to sneak in some bogus fees onto the final bill.

3 **The Big Fuss.** No matter what gowns you try on, the salesperson who helps you will invariably gush and say something like *"That dress is sooooo beautiful!"* Sometimes I wonder if I tried on a gown made out of potato sacks, the salesperson would say something like *"Wow! That natural look! It's so you!"*

As you might have guessed, most salespeople at bridal shops work on commission. Hence, it's to their advantage to get you to buy any gown, preferably an expensive one. The pressure to buy can get even more intense at designer "trunk shows" (see the box on page 30 for more details).

Some salespeople go overboard, taking advantage of brides-to-be by playing on their emotions. For example, at one store we visited, the salespeople couldn't stop complimenting how wonderful one particularly expensive designer gown looked on me. One salesperson came up to me and asked if she could take my picture for "an album of all their brides." After the picture, the salespeople put the camera down and helped me back in the dressing room. That's when Alan looked at the camera and noticed that it didn't have any film! Later we visited the same store again and saw no picture album. The whole "schtick" was a clever ploy to convince me to buy that dress. A word to the wise: don't get caught up in all the false flattery that will be heaped on you by the bridal shop.

In this section, we should also point out a darker side of the "big fuss"—shops that try to pressure brides into thinking their "dream dress" will be GONE if they don't order RIGHT NOW! Listen to what one bridal shop said about this, in a post we intercepted off a retailer-only chat board: "I have been telling my brides when they find their dream dress to buy it now. They won't find anything they like better and will just keep second guessing themselves.   If they wait to order, the dress just might not be available.   Create urgency and doubt....if you wait....you may not get your dream gown. Tell them stories of disappointed brides who waited. Ask for the sale...and pray!"

Brides have told us they have been pressured to buy their gown TODAY! Or else the gown will be discontinued and gone FOREVER! Or else the special MONSTER sale we have today will be history! In some cases, shops request a "small deposit" to hold the gown—and retailers promise such deposits are refundable if you change your mind. The sleaziest shops then change *their* minds and try to keep the deposit if brides try to back out of the deal.

The point: yes, dresses DO get discontinued. But not overnight—no dress deal is so good you can't even sleep on it (or take a day or two to compare prices online). Don't wait forever (several weeks or months is courting disaster), but don't be pressured either into making a snap decision. Any dress deal you can't sleep on is no deal at all.

To avoid pressure from shops, bring ONE trusted friend or relative with you whose opinion you value—this ensures a more objective critique. Another tip: consider leaving your wallet at home. That way you're not tempted to rush into a dress decision (and non-refundable deposit) in the heat of the moment.

4 False Discounts. In what is a patently illegal practice, many shops mark their gowns over suggested retail and then offer you a "discount." Gee, thanks! For example, we visited one shop that was offering a 10% discount off all special-order gowns. One gown we saw had a price tag of $1100—we later learned the suggested retail for the gown was just $1000. Their big 10% discount knocked $110 off the gown, bringing the price down to $990. The real discount was just $10 off the real retail price—a puny 1%.

Solution: Find the actual retail price for your dress. Our free dress web site (BridalGown.com) includes dress descriptions and prices for many major bridal designers. You can also get a price quote from any of the gown discounters reviewed later in this chapter or on our site BridalGown.com.

5 Killer Mark-ups. The profit for bridal shops doesn't stop at the 100% mark-up they charge on gowns. Alterations are also a big profit center, averaging $50 to $200 per gown. Euphemistically called "custom fitting," alterations to make the gown fit perfectly add insult to

Designer Trunk Shows: Tips & Traps

Bridal gown designers do have something in common with rock stars—occasionally, both go on tour. For dress makers, these tours include personal appearances at various bridal shops where they are the stars of "trunk shows." But just what the heck are these trunk shows and are they any benefit to you, the bride?

Trunk shows are "limited time" events where designers will show off their complete collection of gowns at a bridal retail shop (or department store). Brides can meet one-on-one with the designer and discuss the right dress for them.

The key advantage for consumers is obvious: for once, you can see a designer's ENTIRE line of dresses. Stores can only stock a limited number of gowns; trunk shows give you the whole perspective. Another big plus: face-to-face meetings let you ask designers about possible changes to a dress. The result is a customized dress that's right for you.

Of course, that's the upside. Here are some traps to look out for, plus some general tips on getting the most out of trunk shows:

♥ UNDER PRESSURE. Trunk shows typically last only two to three days (say, Thursday to Saturday). After that, most of the gowns are gone. If you want to go back next weekend and show the dress to your mom, tough luck. As a result, you feel tremendous pressure to make a quick decision. The best advice: shop extensively before you go to a trunk show. That way you know whether a "here-today, gone-tomorrow" dress is the right one . . . or you need to keep looking.

injury when it comes to your gown budget.

Accessories are another big profit area. Shops sell everything from bras, shoes and slips to ring pillows, garter belts, and champagne glasses at steep mark-ups. Veils and headpieces are extraordinarily expensive—some top $200 or $300 for a simple fabric-covered comb and spritz of tulle. Shops regularly take a veil that costs $39 wholesale and mark it up to $149—then they might offer a 10% discount if you buy during today's special sale. See the chart on the next page for comparisons of accessory costs between the full price retailer, discount Internet sources and David's, a national chain of bridal dress superstores.

Solution: Bridal shops aren't the only places that sell alterations and accessories. Those same white dress shoes can be found at an outlet store for 50% less. As we'll discuss later, craft stores carry affordable bridal accessories at prices way below those charged by bridal retailers.

♥ **FORGET DISCOUNTS.** Given all the hoopla surrounding trunk shows, some brides think that gowns will be discounted. Forget it. The gowns are almost always sold at full retail. The best you can hope for is to negotiate for changes to a dress without any additional charges.

♥ **PLAN IN ADVANCE.** Designers typically visit a city only once a year. Miss that one weekend and you're stuck. The best advice: call the designer's phone number (listed in their ads or later in this book) and get their trunk show schedule. Most designers know by October their travel schedule for the following year. Another idea: some bridal magazines list upcoming trunk shows in their calendar section.

♥ **MAKE AN APPOINTMENT.** Some designer trunk shows can be mobbed. The best advice is to make an appointment in advance. Typically, you will be given an hour or two time slot to try on gowns.

♥ **BE PREPARED.** Just in case you decide to order a gown at a trunk show, make sure you're prepared. In order to take correct measurements, you should bring any special undergarments or shoes you plan to wear on your wedding day.

Which designers do trunks shows? The most common road warriors include Christos, Jim Hjelm, Lazaro, Janell Berte, and Galina (see later in this chapter for designer-by-designer reviews). We've also noticed several of the smaller designers do trunk shows as well.

Price Comparison

We found wide differences in prices when shopping for bridal accessories in stores and online.

	Shoes	Veil	Purses	Gloves	Slips	Bras
Davids*	$36	80–185	18	24	49–59	29
'Net**	30	30–50	25–35	20	40–55	20
Retail	70	100–250	45	30–50	65	40

Notes:
Shoe prices are for a satin pump with a 1 3/4" inch heel.
Veil price is for a headpiece and veil.

*David's is a chain of bridal superstores reviewed later in this chapter.
**The following Internet sources were used for price selections.
  Shoes: www.discountdyables.com
  Headpieces: www.romanticheadlines.com
  Purses: www.discountdyables.com
  Gloves: www.bridalgloves.com
  Slips: www.trousseaux.com
  Bras: www.barenecessities.com

6 **Elusive Exclusives.** Some bridal designers occasionally give one shop in a city an "exclusive" over certain dresses. These dresses are termed "confined," and you can't find them anywhere else in town. Or can you? Many bridal shops skirt these exclusive rules by a process called "transshipping."

We visited several shops that told us they can order any gown we want, even if they don't carry it in their store. How do they do this? Transshipping—bridal retailers will order gowns for other shops, even if they are NOT authorized dealers for that particular designer.

Is transshipping illegal? No, there is no law that forbids this practice. However, bridal designers HATE transshipping (which lets retailers skirt their minimum stock requirements) and a few force their dealers to sign agreements saying they will not transship. These agreements are widely ignored by retailers.

Why does transshipping happen to begin with? Most bridal shops are small in scale and can only stock ten to 12 lines of bridal apparel.

But there are over 200 apparel designers out there, and odds are a customer may want a dress they don't carry. Instead of losing the sale, the shop places the order through back-door channels. By the way, shops often add a small mark-up for the trouble of ordering a dress from another shop.

By limiting the distribution of certain dresses (or entire lines), designers hope to stop the discounting of their gowns. However, designers also need to sell dresses to make a living—and restricting the sale of a dress design to one shop in a city doesn't make financial sense.

In fact, that's why we've noticed many designers talk out of both sides of their mouth when it comes to this issue. While they rail against the evils of transshipping and discounting (keeping their retailers happy), the apparel designers then quietly sell to transshippers. Others turn a blind eye to discounting since, of course, they end up selling more dresses and making more profit.

The latest twist to this debate involves the internet. Designers once could control their distribution by just selling to a few small shops, who sold gowns in their local markets. Yet that all has gone out of the window with the internet—now, shops can market their goods world-wide, if they wish.

To stop this, some designers have issued "no 'net" policies, forbidding their dealers from selling online. Among the biggest designers to do this include Mon Cheri and Alfred Angelo. Of course, manufacturers once again cheat on this—many (including Angelo) quietly sell to dot-coms while officially banning the process. Crazy, eh?

What does this mean for you the consumer? Be careful of bridal shops or web sites that promise they can get in "any dress you want." Call the designer to see if the shop is an authorized dealer. Check with past client references and the Better Business Bureau to make sure the shop has fulfilled its previous promises. The bottom line: that "exclusive" dress may not be that exclusive. Don't be fooled into thinking it can't be found from another source.

7 **Service? What service?** The debate over the internet versus Main Street usually breaks down to one central point: do you want the absolute rock bottom lowest price? Or are you willing to pay a bit more to get service from a locally owned business?

The usual implication here is the local merchant has a large staff standing at the door, waiting to greet you and lavish attention on you as they search to find the "perfect gown" in your budget range. Or at least that's the way bridal magazines make it sound.

Flash forward to reality: service even at "full service" bridal shops can often be, well, lacking. As one bride wrote in a bridal chat group, "Are these folks who write for bridal magazines on crack or am I living in the wrong city? I've been to SEVERAL bridal salons and literally at each one, some salesperson doesn't even ask my name, takes me to a room, brings in 3-4 winter gowns (outdoor July wedding) and leaves me alone to find my way into the big dress by myself (isn't it like crawling head first into a white sleeping bag?) Then the salesperson stops by 40 minutes later to see which one I want to buy. Meanwhile, I'm clipping this damn dress myself to keep it from falling off of me and talking to myself in the fitting room to keep myself from dying of boredom. What's the deal?"

The sad truth: just like many other retail industries today, service at bridal shops has sunk to new lows. We find this especially ironic in light of the ongoing debate about the internet and mail order gown sources. Retailers can't expect brides to pay full price when they get non-existent service; no wonder many brides are abandoning independent retailers to order online or even (gasp) shop chains like David's.

Yes, not all retailers have let service slip. Yet, shops that truly service the bride seem to be more the exception these days than the rule.

Getting Started: How Far in Advance?

Most brides are surprised when they learn how far in advance they must place an order for their gown. In general, most bridal gowns are not bought off-the-rack. You try on sample dresses and then "special order" the gown in your size. It's the special order nature of bridal apparel that takes so long—the *average* dress takes ten to 14 weeks to arrive (yes, that's three months). And ordering is just the beginning. When you add in time for shopping, alterations and other necessities, you quickly realize it's best to order your dress five to nine months before the wedding. Let's take a look at the five stages of buying a bridal gown.

REAL WEDDING TIP

Where's your mother?

A bride in Chicago wrote about the way she was treated at local bridal shops:

"Having been through this quest for a gown over the past month, I am completely amazed and shocked at the bridal industry and some of the tactics I experienced. I am a 34 year old professional and I was often treated like a child. One shop asked me where my mother was and why she didn't come with me to pick out my dress. Frankly, my mother hasn't picked out my clothes for me since I was 7."

The British Double Standard

Flip through any US bridal magazine and you'll see lots of dress ads but little else—NO style numbers, prices or other info. But you'll note the same gown makers have a double standard for Europe. US manufacturers like Mon Cheri, Alfred Angelo and Jasmine will advertise in British bridal magazines like *Wedding & Home* . . . and, lo and behold, the same gown ads include style numbers and prices! Why this is OK for Britain and Europe, while a no-no for the US and Canada? It's a mystery to us.

1 **Shopping.** Hey, don't forget that you need time to look for the gown that is just right for you. Sure, you can do this in as little as one day, but most brides we have interviewed said they took two to three weeks. That's because it takes time to visit a handful of the area's best shops and more time to make a final decision.

2 **Ordering.** Once you place your order, the shop sends it to the manufacturer. Each dress designer has different delivery schedules—some are as quick as six weeks, while others are six months. That's why it's important you know the designer of the gown in order to make sure the gown will arrive in time for your wedding—see the reviews of designers at the end of this chapter for the scoop. Some manufacturers offer "rush service," but the extra fee for this may bust your budget.

3 **Alterations.** After the gown comes in, leave another month for alterations. Some shops may be able to do "rush" jobs but the quality may be rushed too. You may have several time-consuming "fittings," appointments with the seamstress where you inch closer and closer to getting the gown to fit just right.

4 **Portrait.** In some areas, brides have a formal portrait taken before the wedding which is displayed at the reception. In order to have enough time to view the proofs and get the final print framed, most photographers suggest doing the portrait four to six weeks before the wedding. That means the dress has to be altered and ready to go at that time.

5 **Safety Zone for Mistakes.** Yes, mistakes can happen, especially with gowns. Apparel is most prone to problems since there are more people involved in this process than any other. Orders can be botched at several points between the store and the manufacturer. Leaving time (perhaps two weeks) in your schedule to correct problems is prudent.

Whoa! That's a lot of time! The time guideline we recommend is at least six months. If you want an elaborate designer gown, allow for even more time. However, don't panic if your wedding is around the corner. Look for our TOP MONEY SAVING TIPS later in this chapter—many of these strategies can quickly unite you with a gown.

Does the process of special-ordering a gown sound like too much hassle? There is good news: several "off-the-rack" stores have sprung up in recent years that enable you to walk in and walk out with a bridal gown in your size. More on these later.

Step-by-step Shopping Strategies

♥ **Step 1:** After you've set the date, sit down with your fiancé to talk about your wedding. The key decision is how formal you want the event to be. Now, the bridal magazines have all kinds of crazy rules to tell you what to wear for each formality degree but just remember this: your gown should reflect your ceremony and reception. The gown that is perfect for an intimate garden ceremony held in the afternoon probably won't work at an evening ceremony for 200 close friends at a big church with a sit-down dinner reception following.

♥ **Step 2:** Now that you have an idea of how formal your wedding is, look through those magazine ads for bridal designers. Which gowns

---

Just what the heck is 'couture' anyway?

In the world of fashion, "couture" clothing (in French, literally meaning *sewing* or *seam*) typically describes a designer's most expensive line of personally-designed garments. Unlike less-expensive "ready to wear" and "bridge" lines, couture clothes are only sold in a handful of stores to a very moneyed crowd. So, what does couture mean in bridal? Absolutely nothing. Bridal apparel makers have so misused and abused the word "couture" that they slap it on any expensive dress (say, over $1000). To us, a couture bridal gown would be personally designed by a famous designer and then hand-crafted by a seamstress in the U.S. or Canada. In bridal, however, couture dresses have no special pedigree and are often made in assembly-line fashion. To add insult to injury, some bridal retailers slap extra alteration fees on "couture" dresses (sometimes $200 to $250 for a simple nip and tuck). Are these dresses any more difficult to alter than a $500 gown? Nope, some shop owners just think if you spend $2000 or $3000 on a dress, you can be socked with overpriced alterations.

---

intrigue you? Which ones make you sick? Key on the elements of the dresses—the silhouettes, the necklines, waistlines, train length, amount of lace, etc. A caveat: take these ads with a grain of salt. All of them feature anorexic models with Barbie doll figures. What looks good on you (a real bride in the real world) may be vastly different that what you see in the magazines. Keep an open mind.

♥ **Step 3:** Before you head out to local bridal shops, ask your ceremony site coordinator if there are any restrictions on the amount of skin you can show in the sanctuary. Some churches frown on low-cut, off-the-shoulder or strapless gowns. Determining what's appropriate before you fall in love with the "wrong" gown is prudent. If you are determined to wear that bare look, consider ordering extra fabric to make a shawl or shrug to wear for the ceremony. Another note of caution: beware of sheath or mermaid-style gowns if you have to kneel during the ceremony. Most of these gowns don't have slits in the back, making kneeling next to impossible. One option is to have your seamstress add a slit in the back (look inside the gown to make sure a back seam is available).

♥ **Step 4:** Listen to the advice of recently-married friends and acquaintances about local bridal shops. Their insights on selection, service and prices may be valuable. Using our other sources mentioned above, draw up a list of three to five stores that offer the gowns you want. Don't forget that a store's service (how you're treated when you come through the door) is almost as important as the selection of dresses.

♥ **Step 5:** In addition to the stores on your list, visit a store or two that sells expensive dresses. Why? This is the best way to educate yourself about quality bridal gowns. Expensive gowns (over $1000 or even $2000) feature quality construction, luxurious fabrics and exquisite detailing. Then, when you hit the discounters, warehouse stores and outlets, you can tell what's quality—and what's not. You won't be fooled by gowns marked "sale $490, originally $1000," when the fabric and construction indicate the original price should have been much less. Besides, trying on those fancy gowns is fun.

♥ **Step 6:** Back to reality. It's time to go shopping for real. Try to visit the stores on your list on any day *other* than a Saturday. Weekends at bridal shops are crazy—everyone tries to shop on Saturday. If you can go during the week (some stores are open in the evening), you'll find better service, less-crowded dressing rooms, etc. Call ahead—some shops require an appointment. (Worse still, some shops charge brides without appointments "try-on fees" to discourage walk-ins). Go with just one other person (your mom, a friend, even your fiancé) whose opinion you value. Remember to wear undergarments similar to what you plan to wear under your bridal gown; and have your hair in a similar style as what you plan for the wedding. Skip the makeup and lipstick, since that can damage sample gowns.

♥ Step 7: When you visit the shop, be prepared to answer a few questions. The first is probably the most critical: how much do you want to spend? We recommend fibbing here. Most salespeople will try to "up-sell" you slightly, so we recommend you under-estimate your price range by 10%. If you really have budgeted about $1000 for a gown (not including alterations, headpiece/veil and any accessories), tell them you want to spend $800 to $900. Undoubtedly, they'll show you a few dresses closer to $1000.

♥ Step 8: Next you'll be asked about your wedding date and how formal your wedding will be. We recommend fudging about your wedding date—push it forward about three to four weeks. For example, if your real wedding date is June 15, tell the shop the "big day" is May 15. This insures that your gown will arrive (and any potential problems will be fixed) in time. The wedding date will also help determine whether you'll want long or short sleeves, for example. Also, they'll ask you what "style" of gown you prefer: Ballgown or sheath-style? Sleeves or sleeveless? Long train or no train? Obviously, you won't know all the answers but try to give the salesperson an idea of your preferences. Some shops now put pictures of the gowns they stock in big binders—you're suppose to look through these pictures to pick styles you like before hitting the racks. (A side note: this shouldn't surprise you, but the gowns' manufacturer/designer names are carefully omitted from these pictures).

♥ Step 9: Keep an open mind. Try a few different styles, with a friend (your mom, a bridesmaid, etc.) taking notes on which gowns you like the best. Be careful of "gown overload:" trying on too many gowns in one day can confuse you, blending into a blur of lace and sequins. Our advice: don't try on more than five gowns at each shop. Besides you'll become exhausted.

♥ Step 10: Narrow down your choices to two or three gowns. Make an appointment with the same salesperson you talked with on your first visit. Now, it's decision time! Don't be rushed into a snap decision. Compare prices with discounters, both online and mail order (see later in this chapter for sources). If you decide to order from a local retailer, be sure to confirm any extra fees for your gown purchase (protective gown bag? Pressing? Shipping?). Get a written estimate for alterations BEFORE you commit to the purchase.

QUALITY: GOOD VS. BAD

Walk into any bridal shop and you'll be greeted by a seat of white. This dress is $500; this other one is $900. How about gowns for $1500? What's the difference? The proof is in the details. The more expensive gowns have better fabric, finished seams and built-in crinolines. The following chart summarizes the difference between good and bad quality when it comes to bridal gowns:

	GOOD	POOR
BEADING	SEWN-ON	GLUED-ON
SEAMS	NO VISIBLE THREADS	THREADS SHOW THROUGH SEAMS
INSIDE OF DRESS	COMPLETELY LINED; FINISHED SEAMS	UNLINED; UNFINISHED SEAMS
FABRIC	SILK OR HEAVY WEIGHT SATIN	FEELS LIKE YOU CAN TEAR IT
SEWING	BUILT-IN PETTICOAT OR SLIP	LAYERS SEWN TOGETHER IN SAME SEAM
HEM	HERRINGBONE-TYPE HEM	A SIMPLE STRAIGHT STITCH HEM
COMFORT	DRESS IS COMFORTABLE TO WEAR	SCRATCHY LACE OR ITCHY DETAILING

♥ **Step 11:** Congratulations! You've selected your bridal gown! Now, before you put down that hefty 50% non-refundable deposit, ask the bridal shop the questions we list later in this chapter. Get measured (bust, waist, hips and from the base of your throat to the hemline) with a vinyl tape measure and ask to see the manufacturer's sizing chart. Given your measurements (and remember your bust measurement is *not* your bra size), select the gown size that corresponds to the *largest* of your measurements. Remember you can make a gown smaller but you can't easily expand it. It's important that *you* make the decision of what size to order—don't let the bridal shop make it for you. We'll explain why later in our PITFALLS section.

♥ **Step 12:** If you're unsure whether the shop is an authorized dealer for the gown you want, call the manufacturer (many designers' phone numbers are printed later in this chapter). Most manufacturers will tell you if the shop is a legitimate re-seller for their gowns. If the shop won't tell you the manufacturer of the gown, we suggest you go elsewhere. If the manufacturer tells you the shop is not an authorized dealer, the shop may be sewing counterfeit gowns or transshipping the gowns from another source. Ask the owner about this and if you don't get a straight answer, go elsewhere. Don't worry: you may be able to get the dress from another, more honest shop even if the first shop claims they have an "exclusive."

An exception to this rule: many discount mail order and warehouse companies are not "official" authorized outlets, according to public statements by bridal manufacturers. While the discounters often purchase gowns through legitimate channels, the designers don't want to admit that they're selling to them.

♥ **Step 13:** When you place an order, get a receipt with the price, color, size, manufacturer, style number, and most importantly, the promised delivery date. Also, listed on the ticket should be any special-order requests (some dresses can be ordered on a rush basis, with changes to the fabric, lace or detailing, etc.). All these requests cost extra. If the store recommends a size for you, write on the ticket "Store recommends size." Then, if the gown comes in needing extensive (and expensive) alterations, you're in a better negotiating position. When you place your order, also get a written estimate on alterations. Be sure you ask about the store's refund policy, as well as any extra charges for pressing and so on.

♥ **Step 14:** One to two weeks after you place the order, call the bridal shop for a "confirmed shipping date." The shop usually receives this date from the manufacturer after it places the order.

♥ **Step 15:** Starting two weeks before your dress is due in, call the bridal shop to confirm the date your dress will actually arrive. Delays at the factory (imported lace arriving late, a larger number of back-orders) can delay the delivery of your gown, as well as the bridesmaids'. Bridal shops are usually aware of such delays. Calling ahead will help avoid surprises.

♥ **Step 16:** Hooray! The dress has arrived! Now, inspect the dress carefully *before* you pay the final balance. Gowns have been known to come in with flaws, stains, tears—you name it. Don't rely on the bridal shop to inspect the dress for you (many let problems slip through the cracks). Also, confirm the size of the dress by actually trying it on (or measuring it). Incorrect sizing is a major problem with some manufacturers. Remember if you pay for the dress, sign a receipt and walk out the door with the gown, you are accepting the dress as is. If you don't inspect the dress, take it home and THEN discover a problem, the shop may say "tough luck."

What if you order a gown from the 'net or mail order? Make sure you IMMEDIATELY inspect the dress and try it on. Any problem should be promptly reported to the gown seller. Most 'net and mail order gown sellers refuse to accept a claim for damage after a certain number of days.

♥ **Step 17:** Alterations. Whether you have the shop or an outside seamstress alter the gown, give the alterations person a firm deadline. Be sure to confirm the experience level of the seamstress—how familiar are they with bridal fabric? How long have they been altering gowns? See our PITFALLS for more advice on alterations.

Questions to Ask a Bridal Shop

1 **Who is the manufacturer of this dress?** As we previously mentioned, some shops try to hide this from you. Even though they have torn out the tags from the dress (in an illegal effort to keep you from comparison shopping), you can still ask them about who makes the dress. This is important for several reasons. First, you can determine if the store is an authorized dealer for the gown by calling the manufacturer. Second, you know what you are buying— some designers offer better quality than others. If the shop refuses to tell you, or if the salesperson says they just "don't know," go elsewhere.

2 **How long will it take to get the dress in?** A critical question since the delivery times for different manufacturers vary greatly. If you choose to fudge your wedding date (moving it forward a few weeks from the actual date), be careful here. If you move the date up too early, the shop may not be able to order the dress in time for the early date. In general, it takes ten to 14 weeks to special order a typical bridal gown, although some designers take as little as six weeks and others six months.

3 **What are your payment policies?** Can I put the deposit on a credit card? How about the final balance? This is a very important point as you'll learn in our next section. Also, confirm the store's refund policy. Nearly all bridal shops have a "no refunds" policy on special-order dresses—even if the wedding is called off or postponed. Read the receipt (or contract) carefully before you sign. Note: some shops are requiring final payment to be made in cash. If this is the case, be sure everything is perfect before leaving the shop with any merchandise.

4 **Can I have a written estimate for alterations?** Before you order, get this in writing. Remember that you do not have to use the store's in-house alterations department (even though they will strongly encourage you to). Quality alterations are extremely important—we've seen too many unskilled seamstresses (many at bridal shops) botch alterations. Whomever you decide to hire, try to meet the seamstress who will alter your gown. Ask them about their experience with bridal gowns. How long have they been doing this work? Have they ever worked with the fabric and lace on your dress before? If you detect any problems here or can't get a written estimate, consider hiring another seamstress.

5 **What free services are available?** Some stores throw in a free "steaming" with all bridal gown orders. Other freebies might include free alterations, delivery to the ceremony site and even wedding coordination (especially when you place a large order with the shop). Some of these services might be offered quietly. Ask and ye shall receive.

6 **Are there any extra fees for special orders?** As we mentioned earlier in this chapter, some independent bridal retailers are slapping their customers with all manner of bogus fees and charges. Many such charges aren't disclosed until after you've whipped out the credit card to place an order. So, it would be wise to ask if you will be socked for another $20 for shipping or any other creative "fee." Ask for the TOTAL for your order (gown? Extra size fee? Rush charge? Alterations? Shipping?) to make sure you are getting a good deal.

CONSUMER WARNING

Use Credit Cards Instead of Cash For All Deposits. Here's a little consumer tip that can protect you from getting ripped off by unscrupulous bridal shops: use your credit card (instead of cash or a check) to pay for a bridal gown. Most consumers do not realize that a special federal consumer protection law protects all deposits and payments made with credit cards. The law, called Federal Regulation C, entitles consumers to receive refunds if the merchandise delivered doesn't live up to what's promised.

Specifically, the law says that if you have a problem with the quality of goods or services that you purchased with a credit card and you have tried in good faith to correct the problem with the merchant, you may not have to pay the bill. (As a side note, this only applies to purchases over $50 and if the purchase was made in your home state or within 100 miles of your mailing address). Note: this protection does not apply to debit cards or cash advance checks that some credit card companies send their customers.

So what does that mean for you? Well, let's suppose two brides put $500 deposits on the exact same dress at BRIDAL SHOP XYZ in their town. One bride puts the deposit on her MasterCard (or any credit card) and the other writes a check. Delivery will take four months.

Let us tell you that four months may not seem like a long time to you but it's an ETERNITY to retailers. Much can happen in four months. In fact, BRIDAL SHOP XYZ has now gone out of business. The owner of the shop has left town without a trace. So what's happened to our two brides? Well, the bride who put the deposit on her credit card will contact the bank that issued her card and, most likely, she will receive a full refund.

And what happens to the other bride who paid with a check (or cash)? Her $500 is probably lost forever. Sure, she can sue the owner in small claims court—if she can find the owner. She can also report the incident (which is technically theft) to the local authorities. But, if the shop owner has left town, the bride may never see her money again.

Does this sound far-fetched? Well, it happens more often than you think. In one city we researched, for example, no less than ten bridal shops went out of business in just three years! While four closed "responsibly" (they stopped taking deposits and turned their special orders over to other shops in town), the other six bridal shops did not. Their owners took deposits until the day they closed and then quickly left town. We know dozens of brides who lost hundreds of dollars in deposits because they paid cash (or by check) instead of with a credit card.

In 1992, a couple who owned a chain of Detroit area bridal shops was indicted on 60 counts of fraud in a "bridal scam." Over 5000 brides were bilked out of $1 million in deposits when the chain failed to deliver dresses. This happened AGAIN in 2000 in Detroit when another bridal retailer closed suddenly, leaving brides without dresses. And this isn't just a Detroit problem: sources in the bridal industry tell us not a week goes by when there isn't a shop somewhere in the country that closes and takes brides' deposits.

According to several credit card-issuing banks we've talked to, deposits paid with credit cards for bridal apparel (or any wedding-related purchase) are protected by Federal Regulation C. Be aware that the rules apparently vary slightly with each issuing bank. One bank we talked to had a requirement that complaints be filed within 60 days of the purchase. The fact that a deposit isn't really a "purchase" clouds the issue somewhat. Another bank told us they would refund money to a bride under a scenario like the one above even if more than 60 days had elapsed from the date the deposit was processed.

What if you've already paid the bill? You still may be able to get a refund—contact your card-issuer for more info. What if the shop only takes cash or checks? Go elsewhere. Most bridal shops take credit cards.

Now we are not telling you this to scare you. The odds of you getting ripped off by a dishonest bridal shop are not great, but . . . BE CAREFUL! This advice applies to other deposits too, not just gowns. If you can, don't pay for any other "wedding" deposits (the cake, flowers, photographer, etc.) with cash or a check. A WORD TO THE WISE: USE YOUR CREDIT CARD.

Top Money-saving Secrets

1 **Purchase a gown through the mail.** Most brides don't realize they can order nationally-advertised gowns from bridal brokers at a substantial discount from retail. These brand-new gowns, discounted 20% to 30% off retail, are shipped directly to you, cutting out the middlemen. For more information on one of the most popular discounters, see our review of Discount Bridal Service (DBS) later in this chapter. Another great mail-order source: JCPenney's bridal catalog (800) 527-8345 (web: www.jcpenney.com) features affordable bridal gowns from Sweetheart and Alfred Angelo for $130 to $450. (Penney's prices aren't discounted but are generally more affordable to begin with). Also available: bridesmaids gowns ($89 to $178), flower girl dresses, headpieces, shoes and other accessories.

2 **Order from a 'net discounter.** We found several web sites that sell brand new, name-brand gowns at 20% to 40% off retail. You can email for a price quote, surf weekly specials and (in some cases) check out gown pictures on-line. See the Best Buy section later in this chapter for specifics.

3 **Go for a heavily advertised designer.** If you want to order a dress from a mail-order or on-line gown discounter, pick a gown from a designer that heavily advertises in bridal magazines. Why? It's

Top 10 Gown Advertisers

Here is our list of the top ten bridal gown advertisers. We compiled this list by counting the ad pages placed by designers in the February (or Spring) 2000 issues of the following publications: *Bride's, Modern Bride, Martha Stewart Living: Weddings, Bridal Guide, Elegant Bride, Demetrios For the Bride.* We picked this issue because it's the most read (and most advertised in) issue of the year. Here's the list:

Demetrios	Moonlight
Alfred Angelo	Mori Lee
Mary's	Eve of Milady
Diamond	Monique
Jim Hjelm	Bianchi

For more information on these designers, see their individual reviews later in this chapter. Note: omitted from this list is David's, an off-the-rack discounter that advertises heavily but only sells their own private label dresses.

easier to find a picture of such dresses. Once you know where (and when) a dress was advertised, it's much simpler to get a discount quote. Conversely, pick an obscure designer that rarely advertises and it's darn difficult to price shop. See the box on the previous page for a list of the Top 10 bridal gown advertisers.

4 One word: eBay. Yes, you can use web auction goliath (Figure 3, web: www.ebay.com) to buy bridal gowns—and headpieces, veils, shoes, tuxes and just about anything else bridal you can think of. Pop the words "bridal gown" into eBay's front page search function and you'll find 100 to 200 items up for auction on average. See the Real Wedding Tip on the next page for reader success stories with eBay.

5 Haggle. How can full-price bridal retailers compete with discounters? It's simple: many quietly match prices quoted by mail order and web discounters . . . if you ask. These "no frills" discount packages typically offer 20% to 30% discounts if you forgo some of the extra perks shops offer (free pressings, gown bags, etc.). The rub: most of these discount deals are completely unadvertised. You have to ask. Also: beware of hidden charges that can turn a discount deal into a bum steer. See the box on page 46 for more on this tip.

Figure 3: Over 500 wedding gowns were for sale when we popped into eBay recently. Readers tell us they find some incredible bargains here.

6 Go "off-the-rack." Chains like David's (reviewed later in the Best Buy section of this chapter) offer a wide selection of moderately priced gowns with in stock sizes 2 to 24. Most David's gowns sell for $450, about half the national average. It isn't that David's gowns are such tremendous bargains quality-wise, but the store offers a wider selection and price range than specialty stores. Of course, David's isn't the only player in the off-the-rack bridal store business. In Texas and Oklahoma, BridesMart (web: www.bridesmart.com) has 20 locations in major cities, while Group USA (reviewed later in the designer section) boasts 25 stores mostly in outlet malls.

REAL WEDDING TIP

eBay Success Stories

Our readers have been unanimous in their praise of 'net auction house eBay (www.ebay.com). Here are some of their success stories:

A reader in Florida writes: *"I found my dress on eBay, at a great bargain (I got a $1300 silk dress for only $138!) Granted, many of the dresses on eBay are hideous and should be burned but you can find something nice if you look closely and search well. You can also find veils, shoes, crinoline slips, tuxedo items and other items there."*

A reader in Louisville, KY agrees: *"My biggest bargains, thus far, have been found on eBay. I was able to find an Eden silk dress, brand new (but discontinued) for $87, and it is exactly what I wanted! I found my best friend's headpiece for less than half of the price she saw it for at a salon. And I found my little dyable flats for $9 (including shipping!)."*

Ditto for this reader: *"One of my co-workers found a $3300 Christian Dior gown for just $99. Another friend snagged a Bianchi silk gown (originally $1600) for just $85."*

If you want to buy a gown on a 'net auction, here are some tips:

1. eBay isn't the only ball game in town. Yahoo!, MSN, OnSale and Amazon run auction sites. Cast a wide net for bargains.

2. Avoid the tragedy of a missed auction. Most auction sites have an email notification service that clue you in to new auctions. eBay's is called "Personal Shopper" and Onsale.com's is "My Deals." You can even track auctions across several sites with web sites like Itrack.com.

3. Use plastic. If possible, never use cash or a check to pay for that

7 **Check the classifieds.** We've found some incredible bargains listed right in the Sunday classifieds. Why? Sometimes weddings are canceled or postponed. In other cases, recent brides who need extra cash are willing to part with their gowns. Most of these gowns are in excellent shape; some have never been worn before! Best of all: the prices we've noticed are often 50% or more off retail. And sometimes you can haggle an even lower price. Of course, you'll need to carefully inspect the gown before buying. Other items available through the classifieds: accessories like crinolines or full slips.

---

winning bid. Instead, whip out the credit card. As we discussed earlier in this chapter, credit cards offer a strong measure of consumer protection against fraud—and that applies to online auctions as well.

4. Watch out for subtle clues. Worried that "dream bargain" of a bridal gown will really be a trashed sample? Be careful to pour over the descriptions of items with a fine tooth comb. Often sellers will leave subtle clues that an item may not be brand new.

5. Know thy seller. Look at the seller's feedback—most auction sites like eBay track feedback on how sellers have conducted themselves on the site. With one click, you can hear what previous customers say about their experiences with the trader. Most sellers try to jealously protect those good ratings—and hence may try to fix any problem you have with the merchandise before you tell the world the seller is a crook.

6. Consider an escrow service. Two web sites (I-Escrow.com and TradeSafe.com) offer a measure of protection. You send your money to the escrow service, who doesn't release it to the seller until you receive the merchandise and (hopefully) approve of the condition. Yes, escrow services charge a fee (usually 5%) of the transaction for this effort, but it might be worth investigating.

7. Realize some gown auctioneers are actually bridal shops. eBay isn't just for individual sellers; many bridal retailers have jumped on the bandwagon too. Some are desperate to unload their discontinued samples at bargain prices. Yes, some of these dresses can be steals but be careful—a sample may be trashed from multiple try-ons (try to see detailed pictures of the gown before bidding). And don't think you are safe when buying from an individual—remember that a gown can be altered significantly from its original size. Ask the seller about this issue before bidding.

Is a 'no frills' deal right for you?

"I found a bridesmaids dress at a local shop for $235. Then I priced it for $171 (including shipping) from a 'net discounter. To my surprise, the shop said they'd match the price—but we'd have to do a 'no frills' contract. All orders must be paid up front and the shop won't do the alterations. Is this a real deal?"

Yes, it is. Many retail shops have adopted so-called no-frills (or no-service) deals to compete with discounters. In short, the retailer matches the discount price. What's the catch? You don't get any of the "frills" from the shop. These include a variety of freebies that shops offer their full service customers, like payment plans, complimentary gown storage, free garment bags, pressings, etc. Some shops refuse to do alterations on no-frills orders . . . which is not always a bad thing, since independent seamstresses probably charge less anyway. It's just more of hassle to have it done elsewhere. While we applaud this move by retailers (not all brides need or want these extras anyway), watch out for hidden charges. We've seen shops charge no-frills customers exorbitant fees for items like garment bags ($15 for a bag that costs the store $2), pressings ($50 to $150), etc. One shop in Connecticut shamelessly tries to pressure brides into abandoning a no-frills deal by pointing out all these inflated charges.

8 **Consider "custom-designing."** If you want a gown that costs over $1000, consider having a local seamstress create a copy of the original. We've seen several beautiful gowns that were custom-designed by talented seamstresses. Why is this a money-saving tip? Well, first a seamstress can often buy the fabric at wholesale (or at a discount from retail). Second, there are no costly alterations—your gown is made to fit. Through several fittings, you can watch the gown take shape and make suggestions along the way. Certainly the labor costs for an expert seamstress can be substantial, but the results can be striking. Total savings here will vary but we priced one exquisite silk Jim Hjelm gown at $2700 retail which cost only $1400 to reproduce with a local seamstress. The best deals on custom-designed gowns would be on dresses that would retail for $1000, $2000 or more—seamstresses can usually replicate these dresses for far less than what you'd pay in a store. On the other hand, budget polyester gowns that sell for $500 in stores would be hard to duplicate with a seamstress for less money.

9 **Hit Filene's Basement sale.** Can you buy a $3000 designer bridal gown for just $249? You might if you can brave Filene's Basement sale in Boston. Four times a year in Boston this sale prompts a stampede of brides who strip the racks of designer gowns in mere seconds. Call the stores directly for the latest schedule (617) 542-2011 and read the box "The Running of the Brides" later in this chapter for more information on this amazing event. Of course, Filene's isn't the only company to offer special gown sales. Priscilla (the designer reviewed later in this chapter) has an annual factory sale in May with 400 gowns on sale for $300 to $800, which is 50% to 75% off retail. Call Priscilla (617) 242-2677 for sale details, times and location. Designer Vera Wang also has frequent sample sales in New York, held twice a year at the Hotel Pennsylvania in February and September.

10 **Sew it yourself.** If you have a flair for sewing (or know a good friend who does), consider making your gown yourself. Patterns for bridal gowns are readily available at local fabric shops. One such store pointed out to us that the exact materials (fabric, lace, pattern) to make a popular designer dress would cost $225. The retail of this dress was $995—not counting an extra $100 for alterations. One note of caution: sewing with bridal fabric is challenging so be careful if you go this route.

Fabric Sources

Need a source for bridal fabric or trim? Here are some of the sources our readers have cited:

♥ Hyman Hendler & Sons (212) 840-8393 sells fabric and ribbons from both domestic and European sources.
♥ Dulken & Derrick (212) 929-3614 sells silk flower trim for gowns.
♥ Greenberg & Hammer (800) 955-5135 has notions and dress-making supplies in their mail order catalog.
♥ Our readers have also recommended: David's Textiles (800) 548-1818; Minnetonka Mills (800) 328-4443; The Fabric Mart (800) 242-3695; Fabric Depot (800) 392-3376; McGowen's (908) 965-2298; Milliners Supply (www.milliners.com) and Vogue Fabric's "Designer Cut" (847) 864-1270.

For further reading: *Bridal Couture: Fine Sewing Techniques for Wedding Gowns & Evening Wear* by Susan Khalje (Krause Publications, $29.95 US, $37.50 Canada, in bookstores or call 800-258-0929) is an excellent resource for brides who want a custom bridal gown. Even if you don't want to make a dress yourself, the book includes extensive information on fabrics, laces and proper construction techniques.

11 **Buy a "sample" gown.** Bridal shops often sell their "samples" throughout the year at substantial discounts from retail. Most gowns are marked down at least 50%, some even more. Since many shops sell most of their gowns by special order, they need these demonstrator samples to entice orders. What happens when a gown is discontinued or they need more room for new styles? It's sale time! Check your local paper since some shops have big sample sales throughout the year. However, most shops have a rack of discounted "sample" gowns year-round. Before you use this tip, read our PITFALLS section for special tips on buying a sample dress.

12 **Wear your mom's dress or borrow a friend's gown.** You'd be surprised how inexpensively a seamstress can restore a vintage gown. Even if you spend $100 to $200 to have the gown altered or jazzed up, this will be much less than buying a gown at retail. Borrowing a gown from a friend is another great money-saving option. Total savings = $800 or even more!

13 **Order a bridesmaid's or less formal gown.** Most brides don't realize that many bridesmaids' gowns can be ordered in white. For a less formal wedding, you can get a plain bridesmaid's gown for just $75 to $150. Beautiful, less-formal gowns (without trains, sequins, pearls, etc.) are available from ready-to-wear clothing designers like Jessica McClintock. Her stunning line of bridal dresses start at just $176. Jazz up a bridesmaids gown in white with a detachable train (one bride told us she had a seamstress make one for $25 plus the cost of fabric) and you have a bridal gown at a fraction of the bridal price.

14 **Check out vintage clothing shops.** A reader in Berkeley, CA shared with us a great bargain shopping tip: vintage clothing stores. In Berkeley, she found a beautiful 1950's wedding gown in excellent condition for just $200 at a local vintage clothing store. Most large cities have such stores; check your local phone book under "Clothes—Vintage."

15 **Shop at bridal outlet stores.** Scattered across the country are outlet stores for bridal designers and retailers that offer substantial savings. See the Best Buy section later in this chapter for more information.

16 **Buy a consignment gown.** These pre-owned gowns are often fantastic bargains. Many apparel consignment shops have popped up in major cities across the nation. Most second-hand gowns sell for at least HALF their original price tags, depending on the condition. How can you find a good consignment bridal shop? One low-tech way is to just look in the phone book under bridal shops or consignment/thrift stores. On the web, we like the Internet Resale Directory (www.secondhand.com). With this site's extensive database you can search by key word, state, zip code and more. For California, the site lists a whopping 6100 second hand stores! Another 'net source for consignment shops is the National Association of Resale and Thrift Stores at www.narts.org. Or bypass the store and look for a second-hand gown in the e-classifieds on Nearly New Bridal (www.nearlynewbridal) or on auction sites like eBay (see review later in this chapter).

One caveat: there is a limit to how many times a gown can be altered without losing its basic design. Consider how much a dress has been previously altered before you buy. The best advice: if you find a second-hand gown you want, place a small deposit ($25) to hold it. Come back to the shop with a seamstress and let her look it over to make sure alterations can be successful and cost effective. If the second-hand shop has a seamstress, get this evaluation in writing—"the gown had the previous alterations, needs the following work and the cost would be $XX." That way if there's a problem, you'll have a paper trail.

17 **Swap the fabric.** Fallen in love with a silk gown but can't afford the silk price? You still might be able to afford that gown—just ask if the manufacturer offers the same style in a less-expensive fabric. Not all designers offer this option, but it might be worth asking. You can save $300 or more with a simple fabric swap.

18 **Check the next state over.** A reader in Los Angeles emailed us this tip. She found the same, brand-new Diamond gown that cost $2200 to special order in LA . . . was just $1300 in a Portland, Oregon shop. Another bonus: Oregon has no sales tax, saving the bride another 7% ($150). Why the major price difference? It's hard to say, but expensive overhead in big cities like LA or NYC sometimes leads to bigger markups. Hence, it may pay to check out prices in a nearby state (call the gown's designer to find the names of other dealers). Remember that if you order a gown in another state and have it shipped home across state lines, you may not have to pay any sales tax. Yes, you have to arrange for alterations on your own, but that typically isn't that much of a challenge.

19 **Make a run for the border.** Both Canada and Mexico offer good bargains on wedding gowns. In the Great White North, a favorable exchange rate makes Canadian-made dresses seem like steals to US brides. An example: a New York bride told us she found a $1250 Paloma Blanca dress for just $1098 Canadian in Toronto. That works out to $735 in US dollars, a 40% savings (given the prevailing exchange rate). And thanks to NAFTA, the bride didn't have to pay any duty or taxes at the border. Check the Canadian bridal site WeddingBells.com for shops that are near the border. Similar deals can be found in Mexico, particularly in border towns like Juarez (near El Paso, Texas). There are 33 bridal shops on several blocks of Avenida Lerdo in Juarez selling bridal gowns for $150 to $180 and maids dresses for $75. One tip: a bride suggested NOT telling the shops if you've traveled a long distance—shops tend to charge higher prices to brides who've made major trips to gown shop, figuring your likely to spend more than brides who live just across the border.

20 **Hire a student.** Got a fashion school nearby? The Academy of Fashion Design in San Francisco (888) 493-3261 refers students and recent graduates who can do custom wedding dresses. One reader told us she got a price quote of $500 (including fabric) for an elaborate gown, which is quite a deal. Check your local phone book for possibilities.

21 **Look for charity sales.** Making Memories, a non-profit foundation based in Portland Oregon that grants final wishes to women with breast cancer, holds "Something Old, Something New" gown sales across the country in 14 major cities. All gowns are donated by brides (who get a tax write-off) and all the proceeds go to the foundation's work. Over 3000 gowns are sold each year at these sales, including 250 gowns that were donated by designer Demetrios. For more information, contact Making Memories at (503) 252-3955 web: www.makingmemories.org.

22 **Rent a gown.** A groom can rent a tux, but a bride can't rent a bridal gown. Or can she? Actually, we found several shops that rent bridal gowns and bridesmaids dresses—and the savings are dramatic. Rental prices for bridal gowns range from $75 for simple dresses to $600 for expensive designer gowns. That's right, you typically can rent one of those exquisite designer gowns dripping with pearls and lace that would retail for $1000 or $2000 for under $600. Most rental shops require a $100 to $200 deposit. The dresses, which are professionally cleaned after each rental, can be altered to fit. The only drawback to renting may be the search required to find a good rental shop—there are typically only one or two in each city (if any at all). For example, while you'd expect to find a rental shop like Just Once in New York City (290 5th Ave., 212-465-0960), what about a smaller town like Kansas City? Even here we found a rental shop: An Alternative (888) 761-8686 or (816) 761-8686. Look in the phone book under "Bridal Shops" for rental stores.

23 **Make your own headpiece.** Sure, sewing a wedding gown from scratch isn't for every bride, but consider the headpiece. The average bridal veil and headpiece is little more than a comb (or headband) with some ribbons, silk flowers and a few fake pearls. Attach a veil and poof! You've got a bridal headpiece. The fact bridal shops sell them for $100, $200 and even $300 should be a federal crime. Our advice: make your own. Go to any craft store like Michaels (800-MICHAELS, www.michaels.com) and pick up the forms and supplies to do it yourself. One reader found rhinestone tiaras at Michaels for $15 to $40 and ribbon edged veils for $15. Another helper: the Miracle Bow. This $5 barrette (made by Offray & Sons, call 301-739-6314 for store near you, web: www.offray.com) comes with four-step instructions for making pretty bridal headpieces. Attach a piece of veiling (three yards of tulle is only $20) with velcro to the Miracle Bow and you've got a complete headpiece and veil look . . . at a fraction of bridal store prices. See the box on the following page for stories from our readers about their do-it-yourself headpieces.

Biggest Myths about Bridal Gowns

MYTH #1 *"Considering how expensive those designer bridal gowns are, I assume they are being hand-crafted by skilled seamstresses."*

Wrong. We spoke to a bridal apparel industry veteran who painted a very unflattering picture of how most bridal gowns are manufactured. Most "designer" gowns advertised in US and Canadian bridal magazines are made overseas in Asian factories (critics call them sweatshops), mass-produced in batches and machine stitched or beaded. Here are the details:

First, the bridal manufacturer waits until they receive a certain number of orders for each size (that's why it takes so long to get a gown). Let's say they wait for ten orders of size 8 gowns in a particular style. When the orders come in, they stack 10 layers of fabric on a conveyer belt, which are then cut by a laser. Later, machines sew the seams together. Even the lace added to the dress may have been machine-beaded at another location. Basically, that's why so many gowns look like disasters, with unfinished seams, no lining and shoddy construction. The assembly process has more to do with factory assembly lines than human beings lovingly hand-sewing the gowns. As a result, gowns are not custom-made to your measurements but rather are rough approximations that often require additional alterations (read: money).

Another factor contributing to the lack of quality: a vast majority of bridal gowns sold in North America are actually sewn in places like China, Vietnam and Taiwan. Manufacturers search the globe for the

REAL WEDDING TIP

Make your own headpieces!

Naomi from New York wrote to us about why brides should consider making their own headpieces:

"I also wanted to relate to you my wedding veil story. You mention in your book that most veils and headpieces cannot possibly, in labor or materials, equal the $150-$300 price tag. I tended to agree when I read this but must admit that I didn't really realize how true this was until I took a visit to a bridal salon. After selecting my gown, I thought it would be a good idea to try on a few headpieces. I did keep an eye on the prices, they ranged from $90 (a comb, a few "silk" flowers, a few ribbon streamers, no veil) to $150 (an elbow tip veil with a slightly embellished comb) to $190 (a "silver" headband wrapped with plastic beads and a few "silk" roses, no veil). How could anyone possibly buy these? Your point, however, was really driven home when I spied a rather simple veil. It was shoulder-length, had no beading, no special finishes, the comb undecorated and as far as I could possibly tell, was made out of plain tulle. You can imagine my reaction when I flipped over the tag. No kidding: $290. I stopped trying on veils at that point.

"A few days later I thought to myself, maybe its *hard* to make veils, maybe that's why they're so pricey. Change of mind came quickly after making a trip to my local fabric and crafts store. I bought two patterns (Butterick #4649 and McCalls #7984), some materials and headed home for an afternoon of crafting. All in all, it was a fun day and at the end I had myself a beautiful, fingertip veil (tulle) attached to a crown of organza roses and silk lilies. Was it hard to make? No. And the cost of my unique and elegant headpiece? No word of a lie, $40."

Another bride from Los Angeles wrote:

"Brides, I am certainly no Seamstress Extraordinaire, but, for gosh sake, MAKE YOUR OWN VEILS!!!! There are all kinds of guides and patterns at craft stores—costume patterns and historical fashion/costumes books also make excellent sources. Unless you want a rhinestone tiara, please skip the (ahem) "professional" bridal veils. For about $12.50 (that's 3 yards of tulle, some fabric glue, thread, trim, and an extra-large comb from the 99¢ store) I will be making a better-quality veil than what I've seen in these so-called "exclusive" salons. . . and it means more to me personally, too. For example, I am also using 24 faux-pearls from an old, broken necklace once belonging to my grandma. The pearls are far-better quality than the plastic monstrosities used today, and have the added bonus of being sentimental."

lowest priced labor. The goal is to produce the dress at the lowest cost, not necessarily the highest quality.

Yes, there are still a handful of bridal gown makers that still hand-sew gowns here in the U.S. or Canada. While the quality of these dresses is better than assembly-line gowns, the downside is the price—most cost $1000, $2000 or more.

MYTH #2 *"I saw a dress in a bridal store that was made of Italian satin. Is that a luxury fabric from Europe?"*

Actually, no. More than likely it's a synthetic fabric made in Asia. Of course, Italian satin sounds more romantic than, say, Filipino Polyester. But that's what it is—and that points up a common marketing trick in the bridal industry. In their effort to make bridal gowns at affordable price points (under $500), manufacturers have to use synthetic fabrics instead of silk. But, most makers know that the words "polyester" or "acetate" don't get brides hearts racing. So, instead they come up with bogus names like Italian satin, Regal satin, or (our favorite) Silky Satin. Are they made of silk? Don't bet on it. If the tag doesn't say 100% silk, it isn't.

MYTH #3 *"Every bride I see pictured in bridal magazines looks like an overstuffed cream puff. Other dresses look like chandeliers on a bad acid trip. Is this all there is?"*

Getting married does not require you to lose all your fashion sense. Too often, the bridal apparel industry stereotypes all brides to fit certain molds. You must look like Cinderella or, if you're daring, perhaps Snow White. Well, we say, no Virginia, you don't have to look like TRADITIONAL BRIDE on your wedding day if that's not your style. Consider some snazzy alternatives. Designers like Maggie Sottero (call 801-255-3870 for a dealer near you) have high-quality fabrics and sophisticated silhouettes with minimal beading or lace. Most of Sottero's dresses are in the $550 to $1100 range. Another designer: bridesmaids maker Watters & Watters has beautiful designs that can often double as informal bridal gowns.

MYTH #4 *"We have a reputable bridal shop in town that has a 'Plan B' purchase option for their gowns. If you pay up front, they will discount the price 20%. The dress is shipped to your home and you arrange all the alterations. I assume this is some kind of scam?"*

Nope, it's legit—more and more bridal retailers are offering "no frills" deals to compete with 'net and mail order discounters. In exchange, you typically have to pay up front (the same way many discounters work) and have the gown shipped to your home. Then you have to find a seamstress. While this is not impossible, it is a bit more work. Hence, no-frills deals are best for gowns that sell for $1000 or more—then the savings may make all the extra hassle worth it.

MYTH #5 *"I am considering ordering my dress from a mail-order discounter or online. Bridal shops warn me if something goes wrong with the dress, the discounters won't fix the problem."*

The Running of the Brides: Snagging a Designer Gown for $249 at Filene's

There is probably no bridal event more famous in the U.S. than Filene's Basement sale. If you happen to be near Boston when the sale is on and think you can survive the scene, this is definitely one event not to miss.

That's because Filene's sale features designer gowns that cost $1000, $2000 and even $3000—all marked down to an amazing $249. Yes, you read right. $249. As you might expect, bargains like this attract a crowd.

After interviewing several brides who braved the sale and got great deals, we'd like to offer our tips for making the most of Filene's Basement Bridal Sale.

1. Plan in advance. Filene's Basement does *not* regularly carry bridal gowns. Each year, they collect discontinued samples (most are size 10's) and other dresses from bankrupt shops and designers. When they've collected enough gowns, they hold the sale at only one location: downtown Boston (617) 542-2011. The sale is usually held four times a year—February, May/June, August and November. (Call the store directly for the latest schedule).

2. Brace for bargains. No matter what the original retail price, all gowns are marked at $249. Filene's spokesperson told us she's even seen one dress originally priced at $7000, although most would retail in the $1000 to $2000 range.

3. Arrive early. While the doors open at 8 am, brides start lining up as early as 5:30 am to 6 am. Several hundred brides will be in line by the time the doors open.

4. Bring an entourage. These gowns are heavy—some brides bring an entourage of friends and family to help them hold dresses. Of course, second opinions are nice too. In addition to bridal gowns, Filene's also sells bridesmaids, mothers-of-the-bride and other formal dresses at the sale.

5. Dress appropriately. Sneakers are a must. Forget your purse or let a friend carry it. While dressing rooms are available, most brides just try

Here's a common scare tactic full-price retailers use to frighten brides: "if you order via the mail or online and a problem happens with your order, you are left high and dry." Nothing could be further from the truth. We found many reputable discounters (whether they operate via mail order or from a web site) that have excellent customer service reputations and stand behind what they sell. For example, Discount Bridal Service has over 300 deals around the country that can help troubleshoot problems (many dealers are themselves seamstresses). And we've

on the dresses right there in the aisles. "Some women wear leotards or bodysuits," says Filene's spokesperson, "but others are in the underwear they plan to actually wear under the wedding gown—they are not shy."

6. Brace yourself. This is not a sale for the meek—brides can get darn aggressive. Waiting brides have broken down the door at the entrance at least five times over the years. When the doors open, everyone rushes to the racks. All the gowns are gone in 32 to 46 seconds (this has been timed by more than a few amazed reporters, says Filene's.) In the feeding frenzy, fist-fights have broken out, although Filene's says security is on-hand to keep the event from becoming a melee. We should note that, fortunately, in recent years the insanity of Filene's sale has toned down a few notches—brides tell us sometimes there are even gowns left on the rack after a few hours!

7. Grab anything. Here's a bummer: gowns are not separated by size. Everything is mixed together. Hence, the best strategy would be to grab just about anything. Then let the bargaining begin.

8. Be prepared to haggle. At many sales, brides will trade with one another to find the style or size they want. That's why you should grab as many gowns as you can—more bargaining power. If you're a size 8 and you've grabbed a size 14, *don't* put it back on the rack. Instead, trade it with another bride for a dress you like. You might have to barter several times before finding "the" dress.

9. Mix and match. Here's a smart strategy: mix and match different gowns. Some brides have had a seamstress combine pieces of two or more gowns they found at Filene's sale. Take the lace from one dress, combine it with the fabric and train from another and voila! A designer look at a fraction of the designer price. Remember the cost of embroidered lace and silk fabric today is far more than the $249 cost of each dress.

10. Cut it down. You may find the perfect gown at Filene's sale—except it's two sizes too big. Yet at these prices, you may be able to easily afford to have a seamstress cut it down to size. One bride had a size 14 re-made into a size 4.

found the best gown web sites will work hard to correct any problem with a dress order. We'll review the best discounters later in this chapter in the "Best Buy" section.

MYTH #6 *"I know brides must always wear white but I've tried on several white gowns and they make me look like death warmed over. My mom says I have no other choice—it's white or nothing."*

Tell your mom you *do* have a choice. Almost all gowns also come in ivory (although this shade varies from designer to designer). But that's not all the color possibilities. Several gowns now are available in subtle blush colors like platinum (grey), rum pink and "café" (a darker ivory).

Helpful Hints

1 **Shopping for a gown is an exhausting process.** Take frequent breaks and don't try to squeeze too many shop visits into one day. Limit yourself to two to three stores, leaving time to think about which gown you like most.

2 **Sometimes the first dress you try on is the one you pick.** We're always surprised by the number of brides we've met who buy the first gown they tried on. Perhaps the first impression you get from that first gown is the one that most sticks in your mind. Warning: bridal retailers are wise to this phenomenon and, hence, bring out their most expensive gown for you to try on first.

3 **Pick your price range carefully.** And insist that the bridal shop stay within it. Beware that some bridal retailers will try to "upsell" you—if you tell them you only want to spend $800 or less, they bring out that "extra special" dress that's $1100 . . . hoping you'll fall in love with it anyway. For that reason, if the shop asks your budget, you might want to low-ball the figure somewhat.

Pitfalls to Avoid

PITFALL #1: THE GREAT DISAPPEARING BRIDAL SHOP!

"I ordered my gown from a reputable shop that had been in business for years. Imagine my surprise when I turn on the local news and find the shop has gone bankrupt! And now, I have no gown."

Yes, this DOES happen. We have documented numerous cases of bridal shops that have gone belly-up, taking deposits from brides and delivering nothing but empty promises. Just as we went to press, another big bridal retailer went bankrupt in Detroit, leaving at least 150

Michigan brides without dresses.

And isn't just big cities—we've received emails from readers who report shops that have closed in towns big AND small, in every corner of the US and Canada. Why does this happen? In recent years, bridal retailers have been beset with new competition, from chains like David's to web sites that discount gowns. This has forced some weak bridal retailers out of business and into bankruptcy court.

Big deal, right? Retailers come and go every day, you say. Yes, they do—but when bridal shops fail, it often leads to near riots. As you know, all bridal retailers take HUGE deposits from consumers for "special order" gowns. If a shop fails, all that money goes POOF! The shop suddenly closes (or, more accurately, their landlord pad-locks its doors), leaving brides without deposits or gowns. Word of this closing usually gets out to local area brides, who storm the store trying to get their merchandise. Police have been called to quell rioting brides in several cities who have actually attacked closed bridal stores (and their employees). It isn't a pretty sight.

So what can you do to protect yourself? Not much, as it turns out. As you can guess, it is hard to predict WHICH bridal retail might fail, since these small mom-and-pop shops are privately run operations. You can't avoid this problem by picking long-time retailers; we've seen shops tank that have been around for 50 years. And don't expect much help from bridal gown manufacturers—most would prefer to NOT talk about this problem.

The best protection: put that deposit for your gown (or any merchandise) on a credit card. As you read earlier, this is your best defense against take your money and run retailers. If you leave plenty of time before your wedding when ordering a gown (at least six months), you might be able to reorder the dress through another shop.

(What if you order from a shop that disappears? Check our web site BridalGown.com for Bridal 911, an article with tips on how to deal with this type of emergency).

PITFALL #2 BAIT AND SWITCH WITH ADVERTISED GOWNS.

"I fell in love with this dress in a bridal magazine. I called the local shop listed in the ad—they told me they didn't have that design, but had others 'just like it.' I was so furious . . . is this a scam or what?"

Well, it certainly isn't ethical. Believe it or not, dress designers do not always require their dealers to carry the advertised gown—even if the store is listed in the ad! While the shop may have other gowns by the same designer, the dress you fell in love with is sometimes nowhere to be found. Usually the shop comes up with some excuse (our favorite is "the designer decided not to cut that sample yet") and then subtly tries to "switch" you to a "similar design we have in stock."

Why do shops do this? More profit. Shops lure brides into their store with advertised gowns and then try to switch them to unadvertised or private label dresses. These gowns are sold at bigger mark-ups.

We urge the industry to stop this practice. Don't patronize shops who pull the "bait and switch" scam. And shame on the bridal magazines for allowing this charade to happen in the first place.

Another twist to this pitfall: stores who lie and say they have the advertised gown in stock. Once you arrive, the sales clerk announces that the sample "was just sold yesterday. Would you like to see other dresses?" The best way to avoid this is to call the store on the day you plan to visit. Confirm the dress is still there and get the name of the person who verified this information over the phone. That way you can hold someone personally responsible if a bait and switch occurs.

Pitfall #3 Inflating the alterations bill.

"I wear a size 6 in street clothes and I was rather surprised when the sales-woman at the bridal shop told me I needed to order a size 10. In fact, the sample gown was a 10 and it really didn't fit. What size should I order?"

First, understand that bridal sizes do not correspond to real-world sizes. Clothes sold in department stores generally conform to an industry-wide sizing chart. Hence, a dress that's a size four in Macy's is roughly the same dimensions as a size four at Bloomingdales. Not so in the bridal world. As amazingly stupid as it sounds, EVERY bridal gown manufacturer uses their own size chart, which can greatly vary from designer to designer. Adding to the confusion: bridal gown sizes run small compared to ready to wear. If you wear a size 8 dress, you might be a 10 or 12 in bridal apparel.

Given the uncertainty surrounding wedding dress sizing, some dishonest bridal shops may recommend sizes that they know are too large for the bride. Then, when it comes in, guess what? It needs expensive alterations! Here are our tips to make sure you get the correct size bridal gown:

♥ **Don't pay attention to the sample gown.** Most sample gowns are tried on so many times that they stretch—what once was a 10 may now be a 12 or even a 14! Bridal gown manufacturers even warn their own dealers not to rely on sample gowns when sizing a bride!

♥ **Instead, get measured with a vinyl tape measure.** Needed measurements include bust, waist, hips, and from the base of the throat to the hemline (called "hollow to hem"). Don't let the bridal shop use a cloth measuring tape, since it can stretch over time and give inaccurate measurements.

♥ **Ask to personally see the manufacturer's sizing chart.** Each manufacturer has his own sizing chart; a copy is sent to each of their retail dealers. Just because you wear a size 8 in "street clothes" does not mean you will wear a size 8 in bridal gowns.

To show you how nutty the sizing process is for bridal gowns, consider a bride with the measurements of 36, 26, 38 (bust, waist, hips). This same woman would wear a size 8 in a Bianchi, size 10 in a Sweetheart and a size 12 in a Demetrios/Ilissa. In fact, we analyzed the size charts of the top 35 bridal manufacturers and found the above bride would be a size 8 in 3% of the designers' gowns, a size 10 in 34%, a size 12 in 45% and even a size 14 in 18% of the designers. Yes, this very same woman could wear a size 8 OR a size 14, depending on the gown's maker.

On our web site BridalGown.com, we print the size charts for the top 40 biggest bridal designers in the U.S. and Canada. That way you don't have to rely on the shop to disclose this information to you. (See the back of this book for more details on that web site).

♥ **Given your measurements, pick a size that closely matches your largest measurement.** Why? That's because it's always easier to make a bridal gown smaller; expanding a bridal gown is much more difficult. Make sure the size you pick is clearly marked on the sales receipt.

♥ **Don't get too caught up in the size number.** Some brides we interviewed get personally insulted when the bridal shop tells them they need X size, which is several numbers larger than their street clothes' size. Our advice: don't fixate on that number. Remember, it's the bridal designers who are insane, not you.

To sum up, in our research we discovered that brides encounter problems in this area when they let the shop pick the size for them. Instead of measuring you, some salespeople just *guess* what your size is. Then the dress comes in and guess what? It needs to be chopped down, say, from a size 14 to a 10. And guess who pays the $200 or $300 alterations bill?

In retailer's defense, however, we should note that some bridal manufacturers are notorious for shipping gowns that are incorrectly sized (that is, too big or small given their own size charts). Mori Lee and Maggie Sottero are two big offenders in this category, but it happens with other designers as well.

So, if your gown doesn't fit, is this intentional fraud to profit on alterations or an "honest" mistake made by unskilled salespeople—or a manufacturer goof? It's hard to say. The bottom line: be careful. If you accept the shop's "advice," write on the receipt that "Shop Recommends Size." If the dress comes in way too big or too small, you have more leverage in negotiating a solution.

PITFALL #4 MANUFACTURER GOOFS ON SIZING.

"I ordered a bridal gown in a size 12. When it came in, it was way too big—even though it had a size 12 tag in it, the dress was no where near those measurements. The shop owner just shrugged her shoulders and told us their seamstress could fix the problem . . . for a hefty charge. What should I do?"

Sizing goofs are a common problem in the bridal biz; we've seen numerous cases of gowns that came in too big or too small. In our opinion, the manufacturer is fully responsible for shipping the correct size. If the order is incorrect, the manufacturer should fix it free of charge. If there is not enough time before the wedding to send the dress back, we believe the manufacturer should pay the shop to alter the gowns to the correct size. The bride is definitely not at fault and should never be charged.

In order to protect yourself from this pitfall, make sure all ordered bridal merchandise is inspected and measured when it comes in BEFORE you make a final payment. Try on the gown or use a tape measure to confirm that a garment's dimensions match what was ordered. We recommend this since many incorrectly-sized gowns are marked with tags that indicate the correct size.

Compounding this rip-off are some shops that refuse to fix defective merchandise. Whether it's the wrong size or botched lace detailing, we've encountered some merchants who refuse to make good. Some claim "there's not enough time before the wedding to send the dress back." We say that's tough—bridal retailers have a clear responsibility to deliver the right merchandise in the correct size within the time frame promised. The best bridal shops will go to bat for their customers, insisting manufacturers "rush cut" a new gown to replace defective merchandise.

How many dresses come in flawed? One major retailer who sells 10,000 bridal gowns a year told us that, shockingly, two out of every three dresses comes in with a flaw. In about half of those cases, the problem is minor and can be easily fixed. However, the other half include such serious problems as the wrong size or poor workmanship. These must be sent back to the manufacturer to correct.

PITFALL #5 THE BIG SWITCHEROO.

"My bridal gown came in yesterday and boy was I surprised! The lace and fabric looked nothing like the sample gown I tried on or even the magazine picture. What recourse do I have?"

"The bridal shop told me my gown would take 14 weeks to get in. However, after just three weeks, the shop calls to say the dress is here! It looks suspiciously like the used sample I tried on. Have I been taken to the cleaners?"

This scam often appears in two flavors: the lace/fabric switcheroo and the "sample gown shell game." First, you must realize that many manufacturers reserve the right to change the lace, fabric and trim on any bridal gown. We've seen several cases where a manufacturer substituted a cheaper lace when they ran out of the more expensive kind. A recent example that crossed our desk involved a designer who omitted the beading on a dress.

If you're unhappy with the substitutions, ask the bridal shop to go to bat for you. Reputable bridal shops may be able to negotiate a solution (free alterations, a partial refund, etc.) with the manufacturer. If time permits, the gown may be sent back to the manufacturer to make it correct. (Note: many manufacturers can ship a correct dress overnight—don't let the shop bully you into thinking you need more time).

We urge all bridal manufacturers to deliver what they promise. If they can't, the bride should be notified and given the opportunity to cancel the order. Substituting lace, fabric or detailing is a deceptive practice and should be stopped.

What about the "sample gown shell game"? This is when a store promises to order a brand new gown, but instead tries to pawn off the used sample dress you originally tried on. The bottom line: you are duped into paying full price for a used gown—clearly an unlawful deceptive trade practice. We've heard reports that this insidious scam is rampant at some shops in Chicago and Detroit, though it can happen anywhere.

Here are some rather ingenious ways to spot this rip-off, as submitted by our readers. First, take a needle and red thread with you to the bridal shop. While you're in the dressing room, sew this thread inside the sample dress in an inconspicuous location. If the shop tries the scam, you can spot the used "sample" by the thread.

Another protection is to take a picture of the gown. But most shops don't allow pictures, you say? Sneak a small camera in your purse and snap a few pictures in the dressing room, after the salesperson leaves. The pictures will help you remember all the details and styling of the sample dress—just in case the shop tries to substitute that used sample or a different gown altogether. One bridal shop employee tipped us off to this scam, saying they often substituted cheaper dresses on brides since they could never remember what they ordered several months ago!

A side bar to this issue: sometimes a dress really does come in early. While you might be suspicious that a shop is trying to pull a "sample shell game" on you, there are cases when special order dresses arrive with lightening quickness. Why? Some bridal manufacturers keep "hanging stock" of popular styles in common sizes. These can be quickly shipped to stores, despite stated 12 week order times. Unfortunately, shops don't know what stock a manufacturer has on hand, so it's a crap shoot when you order a dress as to exactly when it will arrive.

PITFALL #6 WHOOPS! WE FORGOT TO PLACE THE ORDER!

"I ordered a gown from a bridal shop five months ago. Now the dress is overdue. I've been calling the shop for the last several weeks to find out when it will be in. Finally, someone at the shop admitted they forgot to place my order! I couldn't believe it! And now they won't give me a refund, instead suggesting I buy a gown out of their stock. What should I do?"

Contact your attorney. When a shop fails to place an order, they are breaking a valid contract and should give you a refund. A pitch to buy a sample gown is terrible. Unfortunately, we have heard of several cases in which bridal shops just forgot to place the order. They simply shrug their shoulders and say "we're sorry!"

Protect yourself by dealing with a reputable shop (find one using the sources we list earlier in this chapter). When you place an order, get a promised delivery date. A few weeks after the purchase, call the bridal shop to confirm the shipping date (they receive this from the manufacturer). The more communication you have with your shop the more likely you will get your gown.

PITFALL #7 BOTCHED ALTERATIONS.

"My bridal gown came in three weeks ago and it was beautiful! However, when I picked it up after alterations, I couldn't believe my eyes! That same gown was a disaster—the seamstress botched the simple hem and bustle! How could I have prevented this?"

Bridal shops love to pitch their "expert alterations" service to brides as the only alternative for their gowns. In reality, their "expert seamstress" is sometimes a person they hired last week for $5 per hour who has only altered her daughter's prom gown. No wonder this is one of the biggest problem areas consumers have with bridal shops.

To be fair, bridal gowns aren't the easiest garments to alter. The fabric is slippery and intricately-beaded gowns can make even the most simple alterations challenging. Some bridal shops, however, invite consumer complaints by hiring inexperienced seamstresses who then botch the alterations. This is especially problematic around prom season when overwhelmed bridal shops bring in "stringers" to help complete alterations. (One tip: insist the head seamstress do your alterations).

Another troubling trend: bridal retailers that "sub" out alterations to another company and then disavow any responsibility if there is a problem. We estimate one-third to one-half of all bridal retailers sub-contract their alterations. How does this work? When you ask the shop for alterations, they refer you to another company that might be right next door. Or they might have an independent seamstress come visit the shop to do fittings twice a week.

All this works fine when things go right. If a problem exists, however, brides tell us shops suddenly wave open palms and claim they have no control or responsibility for the seamstress—despite the fact they referred her and perhaps even let her use their shop for fittings.

In general, you can prevent this problem by asking to meet the seamstress *before* you do the alterations. (If the shop subs out alterations, ask who is responsible if a problem develops). Ask the seamstress about her experience with bridal gowns. Ask to see the work area. If it looks like a sweatshop or if you sense the seamstress is unqualified, get the gown altered somewhere else. Many communities have "free-lance" seamstresses who do excellent work at much more affordable rates.

PITFALL #8 SAMPLE GOWNS MAY NOT BE BARGAINS.

"I don't have enough time to order a gown before my wedding. I was thinking of buying a sample gown. Are there any things I should watch out for?"

Sample gowns may be a terrific buy or a terrible nightmare. As we explained earlier in this chapter, sample gowns (just like demonstrator models) are cleared out periodically to make room for new styles. Many are marked 20% to 50% (or more) off the retail price. The big pitfall here: most sample gowns are in less than great shape. That's because most have been tried on dozens (if not hundreds) of times by different shoppers. Sample gowns may be dirty, stained (especially from makeup) and beaten up. We've seen several that have beads missing and lace that is falling off. Furthermore, the gowns are stretched out and often in no way resemble their original size.

Of course, the condition of sample gowns varies greatly from store to store—some simply take better care of their merchandise. And the condition of the sample will determine its price. Nearly new sample gowns with little damage may only be discounted by 20% or less.

If you go this route, go over the dress with a fine tooth comb. If the shop agrees to clean the gown, get a written guarantee that the purchase is contingent on your approval of the gown after the cleaning. Cleaning a bridal gown is tricky since some dry-cleaning chemicals can discolor the glue used to affix beads/detailing. An inexperienced cleaner can destroy a bridal gown.

Another tip: don't forget to factor in repairs to your budget. Extensive cleaning and alterations can make a sample gown bargain no deal at all.

PITFALL #9 SALON-STYLE SHOPS.

"I went to a bridal salon where they kept all the gowns in the back. They told me they'd bring out the gowns they thought I would like. Is this kosher?"

We're not big fans of bridal shops that operate "salon-style." In most cases, these shops keep all their gowns out of sight and then ask you for your likes, dislikes, and price ranges. Unless you know exactly what you want, salons can be trying. First of all, the salesperson brings out what *she* thinks you want to see. We've been to several of these salons and they've yet to figure out what I want. Instead, they tend to bring out what they want to sell (i.e., an expensively-priced gown). We suggest you shop at stores that allow you to see the merchandise. While you can't get a complete picture of what a gown looks like hanging on a hanger, you can tell which detailing (necklines, bodices, beading) you like and have a better feel for prices.

PITFALL #10 HOTEL SALES, GOWN COUNTERFEITERS, OBSCURE BRAND NAMES.

"I saw an ad in our paper for a big sale of bridal gowns at a local hotel. They offered large discounts and unbelievable prices. Is this for real?"

Yes, most of these "one day only" sales offer legitimate deals. Where do they get the gowns? Most sales are run by liquidators who are looking to dump merchandise from bankrupt bridal stores. Of course, these deals are "as is" and "cash and carry"—don't expect any special services like cleaning or alterations. There are typically no refunds in case you get the gown home and decide you don't like it.

The only complaint we hear about hotel bridal gown sales are inflated claims of savings. Some liquidators mark these gowns (mostly samples) with ridiculous retail prices—prices that were never charged to begin with. As a result, the huge promised savings is often less than it appears. And, as we mentioned earlier in this chapter, don't forget to factor in repairs, cleaning and alterations into these "deals."

Another issue we hear about: counterfeit gowns. In recent years, a large number of knockoff dresses have flooded the U.S. and Canada. Some bridal retailers market these gowns as "designer originals." Of course, with the tags torn out, who can tell? Prevent being taken in by calling the designer to see if the store is an authorized dealer of the dresses they claim to sell.

In recent years, we've noticed another interesting trend in bridal retail: the rise of obscure brand names. In order to compete with discounters and warehouse chains, some bridal retailers have stocked dresses from little-known, unadvertised designers. While this isn't a rip-off per se, we've noticed some stores have taken HUGE markups on these gowns, figuring if you can't comparison shop the dress, how will you ever know if you're paying three times retail?

On our web site BridalGown.com we give approximate retail prices for over 100 different bridal designers (more than we have room to review in this book). That way, you can tell if you're being taken for a ride. See the back of this book for more details on that free web site. Of course, with new bridal gown brands popping up every day, sometimes even we struggle to keep up with changes in this business. Feel free to email us at authors@BridalBargainsBook.com if you have a question about a bridal designer brand you've never heard of.

PITFALL #11 RIP-OFF CHARGES FOR LARGE SIZES, PETITES AND RUSH ORDERS.

"Okay, I'm not one of those anorexic models you see in the magazines. However, when I visited a bridal shop, all they had were size 10 dresses to try on! Then, they told me they charge extra for 'large sizes!' Is this salt in the wound or what?"

Yes, the bridal industry slaps brides who need a large size with a "penalty fee" that can be as much as $50 to $200 or more. But don't feel too singled out, there are also extra charges for petites. The industry claims the extra costs come from "special cuttings" and "increased fabric costs," but we haven't bought that line. One solution: if you're a petite, order a regular size dress and have it altered. Our sources say it just isn't worth it to shell out the extra charges to get a petite.

What's most frustrating about large and petite extra fees: only bridal stores charge them. Walk into any department store or leaf through a clothing catalog and you won't see ANY charges for dresses in sizes 18 or 20 (or petites for that matter). In the few catalogs that do have up charges for "woman's sizes," the extra cost is maybe $5, not the $200 you see in bridal shops.

Another rip-off: rush charges. Even if your wedding is still three months away, some designers still insist on "rush fees" to get you the dress on time. However, just because the manufacturers can't figure out how to sew a gown in less than three months, doesn't mean you should pay a premium.

A solution to this pitfall: consider the alternatives (second-hand shops, off-the-rack warehouse stores) where you can quickly find a gown, without all the penalty fees. A good example: David's, a national chain of off-the-rack bridal stores, that actually stocks gowns in sizes 4 to 26. Read more about them in our Best Buy section later in this chapter.

Finally, we'd reject any bogus fees like those discussed earlier in this chapter. No bride should have to pay to have her gown shipped to a bridal shop; penalty fees for not paying in full when an item is ordered should also be avoided. Remember that ALL of these fees are negotiable. Feel free to question any charge and tell the retailer if they want your business, they can remove the junk fees.

Along the same lines of rip-off charges for special requests, we've noticed another troubling trend at some bridal retailers—huge mark-ups on some imported brands. Thanks to an industry-wide slump in sales, some retailers are desperate to make profits. In Chicago, one bride discovered a Vow & Vogue dress at a tony bridal shop on Oak Street for $1400. The gown's actual retail: $850. We've heard scattered reports that cheap, imported lines like Mori Lee, Monique and Vow & Vogue are being marked up *way* over the gowns' actual retail prices. The best advice: shop around to get comparison prices.

Pitfall #12 Deceptive discontinuations.

"I saw a great gown in a bridal shop last week. Yesterday, they called me to tell me my dress has been discontinued, BUT if I placed my order by Friday, they could still get my gown. Is this legitimate?"

Probably not. This is a common tactic by some dishonest bridal shops that try to pressure brides into quick decisions. Now while it is true that some gowns are discontinued every season, we're suspicious of shops who use this as a pressure tactic to get you to order the gown TODAY. If you doubt a shop's veracity, call another shop that also carries that same manufacturer to confirm the gown's status.

A similar rip-off to this: shops that pressure brides to put down $100 deposits on gowns to hold "special sale prices." Brides have emailed us stories of sales people who have promised such deposits are fully refundable—only to learn a few days later that isn't true. Remember: no gown deal is so special that you can't sleep on it. And if you want to put a deposit down, get any promises about refunds in writing.

Pitfall #13 Shops that hold back orders.

"I ordered a bridal gown that the shop said would take three months to get in. Four months later, I have no gown and just excuses from the shop. When I ask for a confirmation that they placed the order, I get stonewalled. While my wedding is still two months away, I'm worried."

And you should be! This is another common scam perpetrated by some shops. Instead of immediately placing the order with the manufacturer, they hold on to it. Why? Well, financially-strapped stores may be tempted to use your money to pay other bills—ordering the gown immediately means having to pay the invoice that much faster. How common is this problem? Even Vincent Piccione, president of Alfred Angelo (the second-largest gown maker in the US), recently acknowledged how widespread the tactic is. "A major problem that concerns us is retailers who hold on to orders. This is one practice that should be eliminated, thereby putting an end to the root cause of so many horror stories that plague the industry," Piccione said in an industry trade journal.

A parallel scam is the "involuntary lay-away" rip-off. In this case, the bridal shop claims it will take much longer than reality to get in a special-order dress. Most designers fill orders within three or four months, with six being the maximum. Yet, some of our readers report shops who claim it will take *eight or ten months* to get in their dress. What's happening? Perhaps the shop is using your money to pay their electric bill or other expenses—and plans to order your dress a few months down the line. In a sense, this is like an "involuntary lay-away" plan, where the shop holds your money for several months longer than necessary.

How can you avoid this problem? First, put the deposit on a credit card. Second, stay on top of the situation. If your dress is due in May 1, don't wait for the shop to call you to say the dress is in. Take the initiative and contact the shop to make sure the dress is on time. And don't wait until mid-June to start complaining about a late dress. Yes, it may take many angry phone calls, faxes and letters to get the dress—but don't wait until it's too late.

PITFALL #14 IT AIN'T OVER IF IT'S OVER.

"My fiancé and I fell on hard financial times and had to postpone our wedding. The problem is I had already ordered a gown. When I contacted the shop, they told me I couldn't cancel the order. Help!"

Most (if not all) bridal shops have "no refund, no cancellation" policies on special-order bridal gowns. Wedding called off? Death in the family? It doesn't matter—you're still on the hook to buy the dress. That means the shop can also take you to court to force you to pay the balance due on the dress.

If you're merely postponing your wedding, ask the shop if you can get "store credit." At least you might be able to use this in the future, or sell the credit to a friend.

PITFALL #15 LAYAWAY SCAMS.

"I put a bridal gown on layaway at a bridal shop for a few months. After making payments, the shop called to say my dress was now discontinued! My only choice was to take the sample, which was dirty and damaged!"

Layaway sounds like a good idea—in theory. If you don't have the money to buy an item immediately, you reserve it by making monthly payments. While that might work for some items, bridal isn't one of them. Too many things can go wrong when you try to put a bridal gown on layaway—styles get discontinued, items disappear and worse. This is compounded by some unethical retailers, who may try to force you into a deal you don't want because they now have all your money. Our advice: avoid layaway. If you must put a dress on layaway, only do it for a month or so. Payments for six months or a year can open up a can of worms.

Reviews of Selected Bridal Manufacturers

Here is a look at some of the best manufacturers of bridal gowns. Since there are over 200 manufacturers of bridal apparel, we don't have the space to review every one. Instead, we decided to concentrate on those who are the best and most visible. Our rating system (the key is given below) is based on our extensive research into bridal apparel. Since 1988, we have visited over 500 bridal shops and tried on hundreds of gowns from dozens of manufacturers. We also attend the bridal wholesale market in New York City once a year to view designer's collections and visit one-on-one with the manufacturers. Hence, our ratings reflect our opinion of the manufacturer's offerings, creativity, prices and quality at the time of this writing. *Please note: these manufacturers do not sell gowns directly to consumers. We have included phone numbers to call at the end of each review to help you locate a local store or dealer that carries each designer.*

If you like this section, you'll love our new web site BridalGown.com. This free web site provides a more in-depth look at the bridal designers reviewed here (plus many more we don't have room to review in this book). We provide detailed sizing charts, background info and dress descriptions (with actual style numbers and suggested retail prices). And it's all free, of course.

THE RATINGS

A	EXCELLENT . . . .OUR TOP PICK!
B	GOOD . . . . . . .ABOVE AVERAGE QUALITY, PRICES AND CREATIVITY.
C	FAIR . . . . . . .COULD STAND SOME IMPROVEMENT.
D	POOR . . . . . . .YUCK! COULD STAND MAJOR IMPROVEMENT.

A.B.S. by Allan Schwartz Here's the new wave of bridal manufacturers—designers who sell their gowns in regular stores AND online. ABS is a trailblazer in this category, selling their gowns both from their own web site and in specialty shops and department stores. Designer Allan Schwartz launched this bridal line in 2000 after earning fame (and Oprah guest-shots) for his instant knock-offs of Oscar gowns. Brooklyn-born Schwartz was one of the founders of Esprit and designed sportswear and formalwear before branching out into special occasion wear (and now, bridal). This isn't a big collection (a handful of styles, many of which are designed as social occasion dresses but can easily double as informal bridal gowns), but the prices are reasonable. Most run $200 to $300 and feature "modern" lines, so don't expect any long trains or full skirts. The best part of ABS is their fabric, include peau de soie, crinkled silk, silk chiffon, and satin charmeuse. Sizing is limited (2 to 14), but at least you can order online with just a few clicks. What a concept! (We'll discuss ABS more in the bridesmaids chapter). *For a dealer near you, call (212) 398-0330. Web: www.absstyle.com.* **Rating: B+**

Alfred Angelo Angelo is one of the largest bridal manufacturers in the US and Canada, but in some ways they've been their own worst enemy. A bruising battle in 1997 with an apparel union led to late deliveries, angry brides and bitter feelings among bridal retailers that still haven't healed today. Angelo has downsized over the years and now isn't the fashion or market leader it once was. Still, with dress prices that range from $250 to $800 (most are about $500), Angelo has something for everyone. And the gowns are widely available—besides hundreds of retail dealers, you can find them in the JCPenney catalog and at their company store in Deerfield Beach, Florida (954) 846-9198 (see later in this chapter for details). You get what you pay for with Angelo—those $800 gowns are much better quality than the $400 ones. Yes, the Angelo gowns sold in the Penney's catalog are the same quality as those some in regular bridal shops (just scaled down in terms of ornamentation). Angelo also makes the Givenchy line, an upper-end couture label that runs $2300 to $3800. The biggest disappointment: Angelo is no longer the fashion innovator it once was. While they have obviously been distracted lately, it's latest styles are mostly "me-too" looks. New to Angelo: "company stores" that showcase the designer's entire line (see "Best Buys" later in this chapter for more details). Also new: Angelo recently acquired the upper-end Nancy Issler line. *Sizes 4 to 20, with a limited number of styles available in woman's sizes 16 to 28. Call (800) 531-1125, (800) 528-3589, (561) 241-7755 for a dealer near you. Web: www.alfredangelo.com* **Rating: C+**

Alfred Sung *See the Canada section at the end of this book for a review of this designer.*

Alvina Valenta After a stint at Christos, designer Victoria McMillan decided to strike out on her own. A Philadelphia native, McMillan started this bridal line in the basement of her Long Island, NY apartment. It's come a long way from those humble beginnings. Valenta is now part of the JLM Couture company that is the parent for Lazaro, Jim Hjelm and Occasions bridesmaids. Valenta's fabrics are amazing, including silk satin and jacquard. Of course, all this doesn't come cheap: an Alvina Valenta gown will set you back $1950 to $3450 (most are $2000 to $2500). For that price, however, you get excellent quality construction—even the *inside* skirt hems are lined with lace. *Sizing is limited: 4 to 24, with sizes 18 to 20 an extra $350. For a local dealer, call (212) 354-6798 or (212) 354-8137. Web: www.alvinavalenta.com.* **Rating: A–**

The Top Bridal Designers Compared

Name	Rating	Buzz	Cost	Catalog	DELIVERY Standard
ABS by A. Schwartz	B+	↑	$		8
Alfred Angelo	C+	↓	$		10 to 12
Alvina Valenta	A-	↔	$$$		14
Amsale	B	↔	$$$		13
Bianchi	B+	↓	$$ to $$$	●	8 to 12
Bonny	A-	↔	$	●	10 to 12
Bridal Originals	C+	↓	$		6 to 12
Christos	B-	↔	$$$		10 to 14
Demetrios/Ilissa	C+	↑	$ to $$$	●	12 to 14
Diamond	B+	↑	$$$		12 to 16
Eden	A	↔	$ to $$		10 to 12
Emme	B	↔	$		10 to 12
Eve of Milady	C-	↓	$$ to $$$		16
Forever Yours	C+	↓	$		12 to 14
Galina	A-	↓	$$ to $$$		12
Ian Stuart	B	↓	$ to $$$		10 to 12
Impression	B	↑	$ to $$		11 to 13
Jacquelin	B+	↔	$		10 to 12
Janell Berte	A	↑	$$ to $$$		8 to 10
Jasmine	B+	↓	$ to $$$		12 to 14
Jessica McClintock	A-	↑	$	●	2 to 6
Jim Hjelm	A-	↔	$$ to $$$	●	10 to 12
Lazaro	B	↓	$$$		10 to 16
Maggie Sottero	A-	↑	$ to $$		20
Marisa	A	↑	$$ to $$$		14
Mary's	C	↔	$		10 to 12
Mon Cheri	B+	↓	$		12
Monique	A-	↑	$ to $$	●	10 to 12
Monique L'Huillier	B	↔	$$$		12 to 14
Moonlight	B	↓	$ to $$$	●	12 to 14
Mori Lee	B+	↑	$		10 to 12
Paloma Blanca	B-	↑	$$ to $$$		12
Priscilla	A-	↓	$$$		8 to 12
Private Label by G	B+	↔	$		10 to 12
Pronovias/St. Patrick	A-	↑	$ to $$$		9 to 10
Robert Legere	A	↑	$$$		10 to 12
Scaasi/Forsyth	B+	↔	$$$		12
St. Pucchi	B	↓	$$$		16
Sweetheart	B	↔	$		10
Tomasina	A-	↑	$$$		12 to 16
Venus	B+	↔	$ to $$		12 to 14
Vera Wang	C	↓	$$$		12

Notes: RATING: *Our opinion of the designer's quality, value and fashion.* Buzz: *Is the designer's star rising, falling or static?* Cost: *The range in retail prices: $=under $800, $$=$800 to $1200, $$$=over $1200.* CATALOG: *Does the designer have a consumer catalog?* DELIVERY—STANDARD: *The average number of weeks for delivery* RUSH CUTS: *Some designers offer rush service for an extra fee. Some designers don't offer rush cuts, but have certain in-stock styles for quicker delivery.* SIZING—PETITE: *Designers who offer special petite sizes. Some offer petites for all styles, while others only do petites on a selected number of designs.* LARGE: *Nearly all designers*

Rush Cuts?	SIZING		OPTIONS		Key: ●=YES
	Petite	Large	Extra Length	Custom Changes	Charge for Color
	●	●	●		
●		●	●	●	
●		●	●	●	
●	●	●		●	
●		●		●	
		●			
			●		
●			●	●	
●					●
●	●	●	●	●	●
		●			
●					●
●			●	●	
●		●	●	●	
●		●	●		
●		●	●	●	
●		●	●	●	
●		●	●	●	
		●			
●		●	●	●	
●		●	●	●	
●		●			
●	●	●	●	●	
●		●	●	●	
●				●	
		●	●		●
●		●	●	●	
●	●	●	●	●	
●		●	●	●	
●		●	●		
●		●	●	●	
●			●	●	
●			●	●	
		●	●	●	
●	●	●	●	●	
●				●	

offer gowns in sizes 4-20. We classify any size larger than a 20 as a "large size." Some designers just offer sizes 22 and 24, while others go up to a 44. As with petites, only selected styles may be available in larger sizes. Most designers charge extra for large sizes. EXTRA LENGTH: *Some designers offer extra skirt length for taller brides for extra fee.* OPTIONS—CUSTOM CHANGES: *Some designers let you customize a dress or offer "custom cuts," dresses that are made to your exact measurements.* COLOR CHARGES: *Most designers offer dresses in white or ivory for the same price. The few that charge extra for ivory (or for any other color or color combination) are noted here.*

Amsale Ethiopian-born designer Amsale Aberra was inspired to launch her own bridal line in 1986 after her frustrating search for a wedding dress one year earlier. Aberra was turned off by all the frilly, lace-encrusted gowns of the 80's and wanted something simple, where the fabric was the focus. The resulting plain gowns were a big hit earlier in the 1990's (many other designers copied them), but Amsale never caught on a big way. Why? Prices, for one. The *least* expensive gown is $2500 and the rest range up to $3900. Yes, the construction is excellent (built-in crinolines, double-face silk satin fabric to die for). But, the rest of the market has caught up to Amsale—you can find this look from other designers at prices that are 30% under Amsale. In recent years, Amsale introduced a new "blue label" line called Amsale Aberra with prices that run $4000 to $5250. In addition to retail dealers, Amsale has her own boutique on Madison Avenue in New York. *Sizes 4 to 20, with an extra charge for sizes 16 to 20. For a local dealer, call (800) 765-0170 or (212) 971-0170.* Web: www.amsale.com. **Rating: B**

Also Known As

Here's a pocket translator for all the names you'll encounter in the bridal magazines. If you don't see a name you're looking for here, check out the index at the back of the book.

Name	What it is	Whom to look up
ADA ATHANASSIOU	DESIGNER'S NAME	SEE DIAMOND
AMALIA CARRARA	GOWN COLLECTION	SEE EVE OF MILADY
ANGEL & TRADITION	GOWN COLLECTION	SEE VENUS
AVINE PERRUCI	GOWN COLLECTION	SEE ST. PUCCHI
BOUQUET	GOWN COLLECTION	SEE GALINA
CHRISTINA	GOWN COLLECTION	SEE JACQUELIN
CLASSIQUE	GOWN COLLECTION	SEE MORI LEE
CRYSTAL	AD NAME	SEE IMPRESSION
DIVA	GOWN COLLECTION	SEE PALOMA BLANCA
EMANUELLE	GOWN COLLECTION	SEE EVE OF MILADY
ENCHANTMENT	GOWN COLLECTION	SEE MORI LEE
EVA FORSYTH	DESIGNER'S NAME	SEE SCAASI BRIDE
FANTASY	GOWN COLLECTION	SEE FOREVER YOURS
GINZA COLLECTION	GOWN COLLECTION	SEE PRIVATE LABEL BY G
ILISSA	COMPANY NAME	SEE DEMETRIOS/ILISSA
INNER CIRCLE	GOWN COLLECTION	SEE JIM HJELM
INTRIGUE	GOWN COLLECTION	SEE FOREVER YOURS

Bianchi This venerable bridal manufacturer traces its roots to 1950 and still turns out well-made gowns from their Boston factory. The designer was adrift fashion-wise until it was sold in 1998 to new owners, who promptly tried to modernize Bianchi with new designs and a hip advertising campaign. Bianchi now offers three collections of gowns: Tiamo ($1340 to $2300), Exclusives ($1090 to $1558) and Bianchi II ($978 to $1100). Both Tiamo and Exclusives are confined (that is limited in distribution). So, has Bianchi fixed its problems? The jury is still out on that one—the new fashions haven't exactly set the industry on fire. Yes, the fabric is beautiful and the quality high (all gowns are sewn in their modern Medford, MA plant)—but Bianchi still lacks sizzle in the design department. Whether Bianchi can still be a factor in the bridal market remains to be seen. *Sizes 2 to 24; for sizes 18 to 24 add $80 to $100. Petites are also available. For a dealer, call (800) 669-2346 or (978) 738-9790. Web: www.houseofbianchi.com.* **Rating: B+**

MADELINE GARDNER	DESIGNER'S NAME	SEE MORI LEE
NOW AND FOREVER	GOWN COLLECTION	SEE FOREVER YOURS
PALLAS ATHENA	GOWN COLLECTION	SEE VENUS
PRINCESS COLLECTION	AD NAME	SEE DEMETRIOS/ILISSA
PRIVATE COLLECTION	GOWN COLLECTION	SEE JIM HJELM
PRIVATE COLLECTION	GOWN COLLECTION	SEE JACQUELIN
ST. PATRICK	GOWN COLLECTION	SEE PRONOVIAS
RANDY FENOLI	DESIGNER'S NAME	SEE DIAMOND
RAVISSANT	GOWN COLLECTION	SEE BRIDAL ORIGINALS
RICCIO	GOWN COLLECTION	SEE RICHARD GLASGOW
SAISON BLANCHE	GOWN COLLECTION	SEE EDEN
SIGNATURE DESIGN	GOWN COLLECTION	SEE PRIVATE LABEL BY G
SINCERITY	GOWN COLLECTION	SEE IAN STUART
SL SIGNATURE	AD NAME	SEE VICTORIA'S
SPOSABELLA	AD NAME	SEE DEMETRIOS/ILISSA
TANGO	GOWN COLLECTION	SEE MOONLIGHT
TIAMO	GOWN COLLECTION	SEE BIANCHI
TIFFANY	GOWN COLLECTION	SEE JACQUELIN
VISIONS	GOWN COLLECTION	SEE JIM HJELM
YOUNG SOPHISTICATES	AD NAME	SEE DEMETRIOS/ILISSA

Bonny This is a small, import line with little exposure, yet we've been impressed with their quality. For example, the beads and sequins are sewn on—for gowns that retail for $370 to $870, that's unusual. Most of Bonny's gowns are in the $500 range, making them a good buy for the quality offered. Bonny has one of the best ivory fabrics in the business and features gowns that are ornate but not overdone. If you like lots of lace and beading, this line won't disappoint. *Sizes 4 to 20 and 38 to 40 (for an extra $50). For a local dealer, call (800) 528-0030 or (714) 961-8884. In Canada, call (519) 725-2588. Web: www.bonny.com.* **Rating: A-**

Bridal Originals Despite the name, Bridal Originals' fashion isn't that original. The typical look is a traditional "Cinderella" style dress with beaded bodice and a skirt covered with lace appliqués. Prices are $370 to $850 for formal gowns, although Bridal Originals also makes several informal wedding dresses (no trains) that start at an amazing $158. Popular in the Midwest, Bridal Originals was started in 1950 by a St. Louis family and is still family-owned today. In recent years, the company has tried to update its conservative image. The new "Ravissant" line features "cleaner, upscale" looks with hip fabrics like sheer organzas. At $520 to $850, these dresses are impressive. One plus for Bridal Originals: this designer has extensive large size options. Many gowns are available up to size 30 and Bridal Originals encourages its dealers to stock large size samples. *Sizes 4 to 30 (for sizes 22 to $30, add $50). For a dealer, call (800) 876-GOWN or (618) 345-2345. In Canada, call (416) 593-4295. Web: www.bridaloriginals.com* **Rating: C+**

Christos Where does this guy come up with these dress ideas? Take a recent Christos dress featured in a *Modern Bride* ad —a tip-of-the-shoulder gown featured pearl and sequin edging and a *velvet* bodice. Top that off with a net skirt flocked in a floral velvet pattern. Sure, it's darn pricey at $2250, but you've got to give Christos bonus points for creativity. Yes, Cyprus-born designer Christos Yiannakou's bridal gown house is older than dirt, but he (or, more accurately, his design staff) still churns out gowns that wow brides with delicate lace and luxurious fabrics. Even though dimensional lace is Christos' hallmark, it's used sparingly as bodice decoration or as a slight touch on a hemline or train. The quality is above-average, but you're going to pay for it: Christos' gowns *average* $2500. Unfortunately, this designer is super-secretive. Despite some 40 years in the business, Christos operates like it's a subsidiary of the CIA. In fact, we were shocked when Christos recently debuted a web site that not only includes gown pictures but also sizing and price information (sizes 4 to 20; overall prices $1400 to $5000). *Call (212) 921-0025 to find a local dealer. Web: www.christosbridal.com* **Rating: B-**

Looking for a large size?

A reader in Albuquerque, New Mexico called us with this frustrating story—she fell in love with a gown, only to learn the gown's manufacturer doesn't offer large sizes. In fact, less than half of the bridal designers we researched carry "large" or "women" sizes (that is, sizes larger than 20). Some designers only carry sizes 22 and 24, while others go up to 44. Most charge an extra fee, which ranges from $20 to $200. Here's a list of designers who offer larger sizes: Alfred Angelo, Alfred Sung, Alvina Valenta, Bianchi, Bonny, Bridal Originals, Eden, Forever Yours, Impression, Jasmine, Jessica McClintock, Jim Hjelm, Justine, Lazaro, Manale, Mary's, Mon Cheri, Monique, Moonlight, Mori Lee, Paloma Blanca, Private Label by G/Ginza, Sweetheart, Venus, Vow & Vogue. (For more information, see the designers' individual reviews in this section or our web site at BridalGown.com).

David's *See review later in this chapter.*

Demetrios/Ilissa No designer typified 1980's wedding excesses better than Demetrios. His over-encrusted designs were everywhere, even inspiring the birth of an entire bridal magazine (*For the Bride*). Yet this designer's star has faded somewhat in the last few years. While Demetrios has tried to adjust to the more casual 90's with toned-down dresses, he just hasn't quite come to grips with the "less is more" demanded by today's bride. Demetrios' standard look is still the all-over lace sheath, decked out in enough beads and sequins to light up a small town. In order to make sense of his voluminous line, Demetrios divides his gowns into four basic collections. The "Young Sophisticates" gowns, running $900 to $1150, feature slightly less ornate bodices and princess silhouettes in such fabrics as matte (polyester) satin (in fact, all the fabrics in this line are man-made). On the low end, Demetrios has repositioned the Sposabella line as more of an entry-level price point. You'll find gowns that start at $590 with such styles as a strapless dress with beaded bodice and hem lace. The most expensive Sposabella dress is $900. (And, just to confuse you Canucks, Sposabella is the name Demetrios operates under in Canada.) The best value for the dollar might be the Princess Collection, which runs $790 to $990. Here you can find up-to-date looks (halter necklines, tank tops, empire waistlines) in matte satin, chiffon or organza, all accented with heavy beading. These dresses pack a strong punch. Finally, the 2000 collection is probably the most expensive; these gowns have limited distribution, silk fabrics, cathedral trains and price tags running $1000 to $2000. Quality, workmanship and deliveries are erratic—Demetrios uses several plants across the globe.

Some do better work than others. Another factor dragging down their rating: sizing, which is very limited. *Only sizes 4 to 20 are available (18 to 20 are $100 extra). Call (212) 967-5222 to find a local dealer. In Canada, call (514) 385-5777. Web: www.demetriosbride.com.* **Rating: C+**

Diamond Collection Style-leader Diamond consistently turns out top-quality gowns at prices that are somewhat less than their couture competition. The gown maker actually boasts two major designers: Randy Fenoli and Ada Athanassiou. As you'd expect, each has a slightly different style: Randy is more traditional (ball gown silhouettes, moderate amounts of lace), while Ada leans toward the European contemporary side (sleeker silhouettes that rely less on lace, more on fabric). Prices start at $1900 but can top $3790—most are about $2200 to $2500. Not cheap, but that's still quite a bit cheaper than what Vera Wang charges. For the money, Diamond gives you top-quality silk fabrics and excellent construction (all gowns are made in New York City). *Sizes 4 to 20; sizes 18 and 20 are an extra $100. Call (212) 302-0210 to find a local dealer. Web: www.diamondbridal.com.* **Rating: B+**

Eden This is one of our favorite gown lines for fashion *and* value. Eden has one of the largest selections of gowns in the $300 to $500 range. Among their best deals is the "value collection," a half dozen styles that sell for just $338 to $400. No, that's not a typo—you can buy a full-length gown with train for under $400. Eden's other designs range up to $680. The fashion is right on the mark, stylish but not overdone. Eden's quality is above average. New in recent seasons is Eden's "Saison Blanche," an upscale line with lots of Pronovias knock-offs in mostly silk fabrics for $660 to $1320. *Sizes 4 to 22; petites and large sizes are available in some styles for an extra fee. Call (800) 828-8831 or (626) 358-9281 to find a local dealer. Web: www.edenbridals.com* **Rating: A**

Emanuelle *See Eve of Milady.*

Emme This line shares ties to Impression (the owners are brothers), which is famous for their knock-offs of Eve of Milady gowns. In fact, many of Emme's gowns look like Eve's Emanuelle line. The quality is average; all the gowns are sewn in China. While Emme doesn't have a catalog, they do have a web site with gown pictures, a store locator and more. A little secret about Emme: the designer also makes gowns under the name "Renditions," which knock-off Amsale, Tomasina and other couture looks. Emme's prices make these gowns a good value at $330 to $630. Quality is above average. *Sizes 2 to 30. For a local dealer, call (888) 745-7560 or (281) 634-9225. Web: www.emmebridal.com* **Rating: B**

Alterations: $250 for a 'custom' fit?

One of the best euphemisms in the bridal business is what the shops refer to as "custom fitting." Whatever you call them, alterations are a high expense area.

After shelling out $500 to $1000 (or more) on a gown, many brides are surprised to learn that their gown requires "custom-fitting." That's because few gowns are made to your measurements—most are made on assembly lines to correspond to a standard size. This may be *close* to your measurements. Close, but not close enough.

Remember the survey we quoted earlier in the chapter, when we revealed the same bride would be a different size in different designers' gowns? Well, the other news from that survey is that 60% of the time, the bride will need additional alterations. Er, "custom-fitting."

So, what's a fair price for a little tuck here and there? The average bridal gown racks up $75 to $150 in alterations. A common fix: the hem, which can range $35 to $55. To alter the bodice side seams is $15 to $25. Other common alterations are train bustles, sleeve adjustments and shoulder alterations. Note those are *average* prices—couture gowns (dresses that sell for $1500 or $2000 and more) can rack up much higher alterations bills, sometimes $200 to $400.

One disturbing trend: some bridal shops now charge a "flat fee" to alter the dress, regardless of how simple or complex the alterations are. One bridal shop in Modesto, CA now charges a whopping $250 fixed fee, which includes all alterations, train bustle and a pressing.

Here's the biggest rip-off: shops that raise the price of alterations for more expensive gowns for no reason at all. According to an article in *Vows: The Bridal Business Journal*, "shops that have a higher price point, charge more for alterations. These more expensive dresses are not more difficult to alter, nor do they fit badly. It's a matter of what the market will bear."

Wow! Can you believe it? Just consider it a little gift from the bridal industry—for those of you who purchase expensive (i.e., anything over $800) dresses, you get the privilege of being overcharged on alterations.

To be fair, we should note that some couture gowns rack up higher alteration fees exactly because they are so well made—shops must spend extra time to de-construct these gowns to do a simple hem. And that extra time is reflected in higher costs.

So, how can you avoid these problems? First, realize that some shops offer alterations for free. Of course, you can also take your gown to an independent seamstress (local fabric stores often have recommendations). This avoids the bridal shop altogether and, in some cases, may be the best route.

Enzio This is a private label brand that is only sold at David's Bridal, a national chain of off-the-rack stores. See Spotlight: Best Buy for more info on David's later in this chapter.

Eve of Milady Bridal stalwart Eve of Milady's designs are often copied by lower-price importers. And it's no wonder: Eve's innovative use of lace makes her dresses a favorite of the upscale set. So, why do we give her a low rating? First, consider the prices. The designer's cheapest gown is $1400 and many soar above $3000. Want ivory fabric? Add another $100. A matching headpiece can run $250—and that's *wholesale*. Eve's reputation for customer service and deliveries is merely average (and that's putting it charitably). We also take exception to their marketing policies: Eve advertises her gowns under pseudonyms, including Amalia Carrera, while conveniently leaving out any mention of the parent com-

---

Headpieces and Veils

If you think bridal gowns are overpriced, you haven't seen anything yet! Wait until you see the price tags on headpieces and veils! You may have to be revived with smelling salts. That's because hefty markups on these items regularly push the prices of headpieces/veils over $150 and even $300.

Now let's look at what you are actually buying here. Let's see, we have a headpiece frame which costs about $5 in fabric stores. Then you add some basic lace, fake pearls and plastic beads. Top it off with veiling which costs $2 to $5 per yard at most fabric stores. Sure, the labor involved to assemble these things isn't cheap, but we still don't comprehend how this all adds up to $200.

Our best advice on headpieces and veils is to consider going the do-it-yourself route here. If you have a relative who can sew, here is where they can help you. A great book on the subject is *I Do Veils, So Can You: A Step by Step Guide to Making Bridal Headpieces, Hats and Veils with Professional Results* by Claudia Lynch (Harpagon Productions, $19.95). Call (800) 295-0586 or (440) 333-3143 to order.

Another option is resale/consignment shops that sell headpieces and veils for about $100 or less. Don't forget that you can rent a headpiece and veil at rental shops for a fraction of retail prices. One rental shop we visited had over 20 styles that rented for $25 to $30 each.

Another tip: when you have your dress altered, ask the seamstress to save any scraps of fabric and lace. You can then use these on your headpiece. A good source for do-it-yourself supplies to make headpieces is Michaels Arts & Crafts (800-MICHAELS, michaels.com), a nationwide craft chain.

pany. New in recent years is the "Emanuelle" line, a series of scaled-down Eve dresses ($800 to $1000). While that sounds great, we still don't recommend Eve or Emanuelle. *Sizes 4 to 20, with an extra $100 for sizes 18 and 20. Call (212) 302-0050 or (201) 804-8887 to find a local dealer.* **Rating: C-**

Forever Yours New York gown importer Forever Yours' main calling card is price: their informal (no train) gowns start at a mere $240. Formal dresses with trains are $400 to $850. While that's great, the quality of the gowns didn't really impress us (although some styles have built-in crinolines). The fashion was also "me-too," with a heavy emphasis on traditional styles dripping with lace and beads. On the up side, sizing is generous (petites and large sizes) without any extra charge. *Sizes 1 to 30. Call (800) USA-Bride for a local dealer; in Canada, call (800) 801-7202. Web: www.foreverbridals.com.* **Rating: C+**

Galina One of our picks for best bridal designers, Galina pioneered many of the hot bridal looks of the past decade. The company has been around since 1959 and is one of the best quality domestic-made lines in North America. Fine fabrics are the trademark of Galina, whose dresses tend to be elegantly detailed with simple trains and hemlines. A pleasant surprise is Galina's budget-priced line, called "Galina Bouquet." These gowns range from $800 to $930, while the regular Galina gowns retail for $1300 to $2200. Another plus: Galina doesn't shy away from color, making some of the most beautiful pale pink gowns available on the market. *Sizes 4 to 20, with an extra $200 charge for sizes 16 to 20. Call (212) 564-1020 to find a local dealer. Web: www.galinabridal.com* **Rating: A-**

Group USA Group USA is sort of a David's wannabe—they sell gowns off the rack at decent prices (most are under $800). Unlike David's strip mall locations, however, Group USA favors outlet malls. The company has about 25 stores, but not all have bridal salons (Group USA also sells career wear and special occasion dresses). Check their web site for the latest locations. Group USA is so new to bridal, we don't have much feedback from brides on them yet. But they might be one to watch. *Web: www.groupusaonline.com*

Gloria Vanderbilt This is a private label brand that is only sold at David's Bridal, a national chain of off-the-rack stores. See Spotlight: Best Buy for more info on David's later in this chapter.

Ian Stuart This designer was probably the most talked about newcomer to the bridal market in recent years. Launched in 1998, both the designer and owners of Ian Stuart are veterans of Sweetheart, the middle of the road bridal designer reviewed later in this chapter. Like Sweetheart, Stuart aims to produce gowns for the middle of the bridal market. "Glamorous couture styling at affordable price points," was how Ian put it to us in a recent interview. So, did he succeed? Well, yes and no. We saw their recent collection and thought it was hit or miss, without a clear direction. At least the prices were moderate (most average about $1000, although the range is $680 to $2300) and custom changes (sleeve length, trim) are available. Nearly all the gowns are made of man-made fabrics (matte polyester satin, Japanese organza) and manufactured in Asia. Stuart also has a separate line called "Sincerity," with toned-down styling and prices ($420 to $700). So, what's the verdict on the line? It's mixed, say retailers who occasionally gripe about Stuart's customer service and quality. And Stuart's fashion in the past year took a bizarre turn, with a new concept they call "detachable metal work" for each gown. "Available in gold or silver, we have created bodice pieces, muscle bracelets and shoulder straps," says the designer. No word on whether they'll have matching chain mail or breastplates. Besides the Joan of Arc accessories, on a more serous note, we should point out we've been turned off by the company's attempt to push aggressive mark-ups—-hard to believe, but the designer specifically suggests retailers mark-up gowns two or three times the industry norm. Hence, for a $315 wholesale dress, the designer suggests stores sell this for $895 (instead of the regular keystone of $630). While it is a free market (and we like the fact that some gowns include matching gloves or handbags), we feel consumers should be forewarned of this practice—-and if you want an Ian Stuart gown, check with discounters to make sure you are not over-paying. *Sizes 4 to 20; plus sizes 24 and 26. For a dealer near you, call (914) 369-6631. Web: www.ianstuart.com.* **Rating: B**

Impression Impression's legal battles with Eve of Milady have hurt the company. In 1997, this copycat designer got slapped with a preliminary injunction for using Eve of Milady's copyrighted lace patterns on their dresses. The company tried to bounce back in 1998 by hiring Zurc, a bridal designer who used to work with the now defunct Joelle. The results were promising: we previewed their recent collection and thought Zurc did a good job of updating the line. Zurc continued that winning streak in recent seasons with a stunning new fabric color (platinum) as well as impressive embroidery work that echoes Scaasi's designs. Impression's dresses ($590 to $1250) feature clean silhouettes with touches of embroidery or lace. All the dresses are made in Taiwan and China. While we liked Impression, there is still a cloud over this designer. Whether Zurc can pull them out of this funk remains to be seen. *Sizes 2 to 30 are available. Call (800) BRIDAL-1 or (281) 634-9200 to find a local dealer. Web: www.impressionbridal.com.* **Rating: B**

Designer R.I.P.

If you have a long engagement, you might be tempted to whip out an old magazine to see if you can find a bridal gown. Be careful—bridal designers come and go like Top 40 boy bands. And most styles are only in production for a short time; some gowns are discontinued just a few months after they debut. Hence, don't go looking for a dream dress from a 1995 bridal magazine. Odds are, it is long gone. Here is a list of designers that have bit the dust in recent years: Carmi Couture, Fink, Lili, Joelle, Country Elegance by Susan Lane and San Martin.

Jacquelin Bridals Jacqueline Bridals (also known as Tiffany, Private Collection and Christina) features more contemporary fashion than other mid-priced designers who import gowns from overseas. A typical offering from Jacquelin is a matte satin, sleeveless A-line dress with chapel train. Not bad for $360. In fact, the entire line is quite affordable, ranging from $250 to $560. You will find a little of everything in their collection, from fashion-forward looks to dresses that are covered in ruffles (a la the 1980's). Most of the fabrics are man-made, with a smattering of matte satin, chiffon and crepe. Our reports from brides say the quality is above average and the sizing is generous (sizes 4 to 42). Jacqueline has a sister line called the "Christina Collection," a dozen dresses that sell for $600 to $800. This all-polyester satin line features upgraded laces and styling. The company even offers custom cuts (made to your measurements), style changes and fabric swaps. One frustrating note to this designer: Jacqueline Bridals lives a stealth-like existence—Jacqueline has no catalog and rarely advertises (but they do have a web site at www.jacquelinbridals.com with gown pictures and style numbers). Another caveat: Jacquelin has had some production problems with their "Private Collection" line, causing delays in deliveries during the busy summer wedding season. *Sizes 4 to 42. For a dealer near you, call (941) 277-7099. Web: www.jacquelinbridals.com* **Rating: B+**

Janell Berté Unusual fabrics are the hallmark of Pennsylvania-based designer Janell Berté, whose pricey creations are sold in 75 bridal shops nationwide and a half dozen Berté boutiques. How pricey? Berté's regular gowns run $1910 to $3750, although the less expensive "Collection" dresses run $1000 to $2000. But check out the fabrics: textured silk organza with metallic threads, a silk jacquard chiffon or even a velvet burn-out. Berté recently rolled out a line of imported hand-embroidered veils. These limited production pieces in three different lengths will retail for $250 to $300. Quality is excellent; all the gowns are made in Pennsylvania. Finally, we have to give Berté an award for her ultra-cool web site. *Sizes 2 to 20; sizes 18 and 20, add 10% to the gown price. For a dealer near you, call (717) 291-9894. Web: www.berte.com* **Rating: A**

Jasmine This Illinois-based importer (the gowns are made in China) divides their line into two parts: the main Collection gowns for $500 to $790, while the Haute Couture line is $870 to $1700. The best part to

Big Mark-Ups Ahead: Accessories and Extras

Here's a quick quiz: where do bridal shops make the most profit? If you answered "dresses," think again. Actually, it's those "bridal accessories" that truly keep the cash register humming. Items like crinolines, lingerie, shoes, garters, gloves, stockings and jewelry are a major profit center for bridal retailers.

And, amazingly, the industry makes no bones about the fat profits it fleeces from brides and grooms on these items. According to *Vows* (an industry trade journal), "Accessories are an important, lucrative part of the bridal business." One executive of a hosiery company advises shops to "go ahead and get the garters, the gloves and stockings for the entire bridal party—they're easy add-on sales. The mark-up on them is usually 100 percent and that's quite easy to achieve."

And some shops don't stop at 100%. *Glamour Magazine* interviewed one furious bride who was suckered into buying a $28 bra at a bridal shop. The boutique owner told her she *must* wear that bra. When she got home, she discovered that the manufacturer's price tag said $22. Hence the bridal shop had taken an $11 bra (at wholesale) and marked it up to $28—a tidy 155% mark-up. Along the same lines, one bridal shop owner in Lincoln, Nebraska confesses: "I buy bridal garters for 85¢, put a bow on them and then sell them for $24.95! It's amazing what a fancy little bow will do." At a 2800% mark-up, that IS quite an amazing bow.

According to another recent article in *Vows*, "a three-time mark-up (by bridal retailers) is not unusual" on bras, said a lingerie wholesaler. "I know stores that are getting four times cost," bragged another bra maker. How can they take such huge mark-ups? That's because bras sold to brides have low wholesale prices (thanks to a lack of fancy lace trim). Hence, a bra that sells for $10 to $15 wholesale can be marked up to $30 to $45 retail at a bridal shop, a major rip-off in our opinion.

Of course, the accessories don't stop at the bride. Ring pillows, cake tops, guest books and attendants gifts are items you *must* have, says the bridal shop. Just listen to what wedding guru Beverly Clark (who, by the way, has her own collection of bridal accessories that she hawks) advises to bridal retailers in *Vows*: "Each time the wedding entourage enters your store, you have an opportunity to increase your overall dollar volume, in excess of $300 per party." And here's the kicker: "In this econo-

Jasmine is all the options they offer: you can swap the fabric, request a longer train, make sleeves shorter and so on. All that customization at this price point is unique. Quality is good, but styling has fallen behind such industry stars as Pronovias and Mori Lee in recent seasons. *Sizes 4-28. Call (800) 634-0224 or (630) 295-5880 to find a local dealer. Web: www.jasminebridal.com.* **Rating: B+**

my," Clark said, "you [the bridal retailer] have to get every dollar out of the bride." Isn't that nice? And people wonder why the bridal industry gets such a bad rap.

Avoiding the big rip-offs in this category is tricky. Nearly a third of all brides fall victim to sales hype and buy accessories at bridal shops. While brides try on gowns, owners of bridal shops often sneak out those bras, jewelry, hosiery and other do-dads. There may be subtle and not-so-subtle pressure to buy the "whole outfit." We say resist the pressure and shop around. For example, those $70 shoes at bridal shops (which *Glamour Magazine* says are "usually made of poor-quality, dyed-to-match satin") may be much cheaper at chain shoe stores. Those stores also offer a wider selection. One bride told us she found white leather pumps for just $22 at a department store end-of-summer sale. She added some beaded clip-ons ($4 to $10 each) from a shoe store and had a great look for less than *half* the bridal shop price.

For the good deals on shoes, check the web. Shoebuy.com has 40 options for brides and bridesmaids, from basic dyeables for just $37.95 to designer options like Nicole Miller. Payless.com has dyeables in a variety of heel heights for $30 to $35. DiscountDyeables.com also has good deals—$39 for a satin pump.

Forget the jewelry at bridal shops. Much of it is fake and grossly over-priced—sometimes two to three times the retail prices of other stores. Other, non-bridal stores are likely to have better prices. The same goes for gloves, lingerie, guest books and more. The best shops will rent slips and petticoats for a fraction of retail prices.

And don't think the bridal industry has forgotten about the groom either. One of the biggest profit areas in formal-wear rental has nothing to do with the tuxedo—it's the shoes that are the money-makers. Yes, we're talking about those cheesey, plastic black shoes that bridal shops and tux places buy for $14 each. Shops turn around and rent them for $10 a pop—since the shoes can be rented out 20 times or more, each pair can reap revenues of $200! According to *Vows*, the magazine conservatively estimated the profit from shoe rental at a fat 55%. "That is over three times the profit that most operators enjoy on a tuxedo rental." And the key word in that sentence is *enjoy*. Our advice: skip the shoes and buy a nice pair of black shoes. Since you'll wear them again and again, in the long run, you'll probably come out ahead.

Jessica McClintock This ready-to-wear designer has won a lot of fans with her well-designed, yet affordable bridal apparel. Based in San Francisco, McClintock's designs are fresh and innovative, described as "very feminine." Unlike other designers that limit distribution, McClintock seems to have a "more is better" philosophy—you'll not only find these gowns in regular bridal shops, but McClintock also has her own stores (which carry an edited version of the line) and an outlet store in San Francisco (more on that later in this chapter). No matter where you find them, you'll notice the great value: gowns run $176 to $540, with most in the $350 to $400 range. Sure, the fabrics are synthetic and the quality is only average, but hey, it's still a great deal for the dollar. And delivery is much faster than other bridal makers (just two to six weeks). *Sizes 4-16; 18W to 28W. Call (800) 333-5301 or (415) 495-3030 to find a local dealer. Web: www.jessicamcclintock.com.* **Rating: A-**

Jim Hjelm Hjelm divides its gowns into two main collections: Visions and Couture. The lower-priced Visions ($770 to $1030) features mostly plain gowns that are good buys, although most are made of polyester (satin, chiffon, etc.). Want silk? Step up into the "Couture" line ($1690 to $2750), where you'll find silk duchess satin among other fabrics. Finally, there is the Private Collection, a handful of pricey creations with limited distribution that run around $2000. The styling on this line has waned in recent years; Hjelm lost their lead designer in 1999 and the new design staff hasn't quite hit any homeruns since then. We've sensed this company has focused more on their hot "Occasions" bridesmaid line in recent seasons than the bridal gowns. Nevertheless, quality is good (all gowns are made in New York City). *Sizes 2 to 24; Extra charges for sizes 18 to 24 are $150 to $200. Call (800) 924-6475 or (212) 764-6960 to find a local dealer. Web: www.jlmcouture.com* **Rating: A-**

Lady Eleanor This is a private label brand sold at David's Bridal, a national chain of off-the-rack stores. See Spotlight: Best Buy for more info on David's later in this chapter.

Lazaro This line was launched in 1994 by Jim Hjelm to give the company a young, hip look. It worked. Designer Lazaro Perez's fresh designs make him one of the industry's fastest rising stars. Sure, the price aren't cheap ($1500 to $3700, but most are $2600), but where else can you find these looks? Lazaro combines luxurious silk fabrics and subtle splashes of color to make one-of-a-kind looks. Unfortunately, Lazaro's quality is inconsistent—we've received complaints about flawed dresses delivered to retailers. The result: brides have had to wait to get corrected dresses as their retailers ran the gauntlet of Lazaro's flawed cus-

tomer service system. As a result, we have lowered Lazaro's rating this time out. *Sizes 2 to 24, with an extra $150 to $200 for sizes 18 to 24). For a dealer near you, call (212) 764-5781. Web:www.lazarobridal.com*
Rating: B

The Catalog Chase

As you might guess, major gown designers have catalogs that picture their dresses. So you can just call them up and get a copy, right? Wrong. Most bridal dress designers do not send out catalogs to *consumers*—and some can be downright hostile on the phone when you ask. Instead, designers dole out glossy full-color catalogs to bridal shops, hoping they'll use them as sales tools.

Fat chance. Most shops horde the catalogs and reprints of ads from bridal magazines, afraid that if they pass them out, their customers will use them to comparison shop competitors. Interestingly enough, several shops debated this topic in a recent issue of a trade magazine for bridal retailers. "(Catalogs are) just putting a tool in (the bride's) hands to price shop you to death," an Ohio bridal shop owner said. "I think catalogs are wonderful," added a Wisconsin dress shop manager, who uses them as a resource—not for brides, mind you, but for her *salespeople*. She added: "I don't think they should be finding their way into the hands of consumers."

Some bridal retailers cut up the manufacturers catalogs and put them into binders. That's what we discovered on a recent visit to several bridal shops in Florida—shops asked brides to first flip through the binders to decide on various styles before they hit the racks. Of course, these dress pictures were carefully edited to remove any mention of the gown's manufacturer/designer or style number.

Of course, not everyone has such an anti-consumer attitude. "I don't worry that the bride is going to shop around," said another shop owner who does hand out the catalogs. "We know they are going to shop around. I feel that if they have something with our name on it, they are going to remember us." And even shops who refuse to give out catalogs will relent and give them to customers— that is, *after* a deposit is placed. Another exception to the catalog chase: bridesmaid dress catalogs. Most shops will hand these out so you can show an out-of-town bridesmaid a picture of the dress.

What about designers' web sites? Can you surf your way around the catalog chase? Yes, most designers have put up web sites in the last couple of years. But don't expect many dress details. Most feature gown pictures, but precious little other information (prices, style numbers, sizes and other details are intentionally omitted).

Maggie Sottero Which bridal gowns are designed in Australia, made in China and distributed to the U.S. from Utah? The answer would be Maggie Sottero, which is probably the best example of the globalization of the bridal market. Sottero is Australia's biggest retailer and manufacturer of bridal apparel and they apparently did their homework before coming to the U.S. Their dresses are simply stunning . . . and the prices are amazingly low. Sottero's specialty is corset-style bodices, which can be worn without a bra and make a bride's waist look two sizes smaller (well, that's what they claim). The prices certainly won't make your wallet look smaller, though—-the gowns average just $550 to $1100. That same look from a couture designer could run you $2000 or more. In the past year, Sottero rolled out gowns with Swarovski crystal accents, with prices approaching $1100. Yea, all the fabrics are man-made (no silks), but the quality construction and detailing (including new colored embroidery) make up for this. Sizing is 4 to 28. One major caveat to Sottero: perhaps their gowns have become TOO popular. Sottero has struggled to keep up with demand in the last couple of years. The result: late orders and long waits (as much as 20 weeks) for gowns in the busy summer wedding season. Retailers gripe about Sottero's slow deliveries; the company claims it is working hard to increase production. The bottom line: if you want a Sottero gown, leave PLENTY of time before your wedding. *For a dealer you, call (801) 255-3870, web: www.maggiesotterobridal.com.* **Rating: A–**

Marisa Marisa is our pick as one of the best bridal manufacturers in the market today. "Romantic" is the best word to describe designer Tamara Kristen's original designs. While the skirts are often left unadorned, the bodices of these gowns feature subtle detailing and, occasionally, delicate appliqués. While this is a small line (only a dozen new styles debut per season) and the prices are not cheap (most gowns run $1190 to $2190), you do get value for the dollar. All the gowns have a built-in petticoat and feature excellent craftsmanship. The fabrics (silk shantung, silk-faced satin, organza) are top-notch. *Sizes 4 to 20; some styles are available in sizes 22 to 26 for $300 extra. Call (212) 944-0022 to find a local dealer. Web: www.marisabridals.com.* **Rating: A**

Finding a small designer's web page

Looking for a web page for a small or obscure bridal designer? About.com has a web page with links to dozens of smaller bridal designers. Access it at: http://weddings.about.com/style/weddings/ msubmenu06.htm. Also: our free gown page, BridalGown.com includes "mini-reviews" of the bridal industry's smaller gown makers, complete with web links.

Mary's Mary's (also known as P.C. Mary's) is a Texas-based importer that offers basic styles with middle-of-the-road quality and price. Most gowns are $478 to $600, while informal dresses (without trains) are $300 to $440. The fabrics aren't that impressive— almost all the gowns are made of polyester satin. Sure, the designer has tried to update their look with some matte satin options, but most of the gowns are very traditional in style (ball gowns with basque waists, Queen Anne necklines, etc.). A good sign, however: Mary's new "Moda Bella" is a fashion upgrade, with more contemporary silhouettes. The quality of Mary's gowns overall is only average. *Sizes 4 to 30; sizes 18 to 30 are $30 to $50 extra. Call (281) 933-9678 to find a local dealer. Web: www.marysbridal.com.* **Rating: C**

Michaelangelo This is a private label brand that is only sold at David's Bridal, a national chain of off-the-rack stores. See Spotlight: Best Buy for more info on David's later in this chapter.

Mon Cheri New Jersey based designer Mon Cheri tries to do something that's hard to find in the world of bridal: a dress that's high quality, but still affordable. Instead of flimsy polyester fabrics, Mon Cheri uses silk and higher thread-count poly satins. Each dress is fully lined, so you won't see any loose seams or cheap finish work. Heck, they've designed a two-inch seam allowance into each dress. Best of all, the prices are down to earth— most gowns are $400 to $850. A best buy are the "Traditional Value" gowns ($600 to $820), with built-in crinolines, cathedral trains and more. While we like the value, we've lowered the rating for Mon Cheri since our last edition. Why? Mon Cheri has let its fashion go stale in recent seasons; instead of being an innovator, it's churned out more of the same. *Sizes 4 to 44; petites 3 to 11, womens sizes 16w to 28w. Sizes 18 to 44 and womens sizes an extra $20 to $40. Call (609) 530-1900 to find a local dealer. Web: www.mcbridals.com* **Rating: B+**

Monique Yes, there are TWO Moniques in the bridal market today— Monique L'huillier (who's pricey dresses are reviewed below) and Monique Luo, whose affordable dresses are reviewed on this page and are known as just plain "Monique" and "Monique Luo Couture." Monique (Luo) has been creating gowns since 1993 but now just seems to be hitting her stride. Her innovative use of colored embroidery in past seasons was such a hit that many other designers have copied the look. In the past year, Monique has rolled out more gowns with embroidery and continues to lead the market in that area. Yes, all the gowns are made in China, but the quality and construction is above average. Best of all, the fashion and styling is very current. Unlike other low-price manufacturers, Monique's sense of style is a breath of fresh air. Monique's prices are $600 to $1200 (most dresses are about $800). Fabrics are mostly "silky satin" and "silky organza" (that is, polyester satin and organza), but the quality of embellishments is top-notch. Sizing is generous, with sizes up to 28 available. New in recent years is the Monique Luo Couture line, which is limited to just a handful of stores (half a dozen at last count). We saw some of these gowns pictured on their web site and had to scratch our heads. While some of the looks were innovative with their use of lace and detail, others were way out there (a black wedding dress?). Prices for the couture line are $2000 and up. *Sizes 2 to 28, except the couture line which only goes to a 16. Sizes 18 to 28 add $80 to $160 to the gown prices. For dealer near you, call (626) 401-9910. Web: www.moniquebridal.com.* **Rating: A–**

Monique L'huillier Philippine-born designer Monique L'huillier got her start in fashion working in her mother's dress shop as a child. After attending fashion school in Los Angeles (and studying abroad in Switzerland), she launched her own bridal line in 1996 at the age of 25. L'huillier's trademark look: a plain gown of silk satin with a small touch of embroidery or beading. While we liked the style of the dresses, we found the prices ($1800 to $4500) a bit hard to swallow. In recent years, L'huillier continued to add some glitz to her line; one recent design featured cascading maple leafs in satin and velvet (perfect for that Canadian bride!). Many of the gowns feature delicate crystal beading. *Sizing runs 2 to 18 and delivery takes 12 to 14 weeks (although rush and custom cuts are available). Many custom changes are available at an additional charge. For a dealer you, call (310) 659-9888; web: www.moniquelhuillier.com.* **Rating: B**

Moonlight Designer Carole Hai cites fairy tales as the inspiration for her dress designs. And it doesn't take too much imagination to envision Cinderella or Sleeping Beauty decked out in a Moonlight gown—most of Carole's designs feature big ball gown silhouettes and big tulle skirts that echo animated Disney fashion. Moonlight's gowns are somewhat pricey, considering the fabrics are typically polyester satins (not silks). The Moonlight Collection weights in at $550 to $790. At the upper-end, the Moonlight Couture line ($900 to $1200) features lots of alençon lace but, once again, little silk fabric. Instead, you'll find detailing such as silver bugle beads or lycra fitted sleeves (a la Vera Wang). Moonlight redeems itself on the fabric side with the "Moonlight Silk Rose" collection. These silk shantung gowns range from $1190 to $1300. Another best buy: Moonlight's informal "Tango" line (dresses without trains). Oddly enough, the fashion on these train-less dresses is 180 degrees the opposite of the rest of Moonlight's line. Here you'll find very simple dresses with little lace or beading. Instead, Carole Hai lets the fabric (ribbon organza, satin with dot tulle) take center stage. The prices are excellent—$300 to $500. Overall, quality is above average. *Sizes 2 to 28, with sizes 22 and up running an extra $80 to $120. Call (800) 447-0405 or (847) 884-7199 to find a local dealer. Web: www.moonlightbridal.com.* **Rating: B**

Mori Lee/Regency Why is Mori Lee arguably the country's hottest bridal designer? Three reasons: price, price, price. Combine designer Madeline Gardner's current fashion looks with rock-bottom pricing and you'll quickly realize why these gowns are selling like hot cakes. With over 100 styles, you can find both traditional and contemporary looks here. Prices range from $350 to $690, making Mori Lee a very good buy indeed (even though most dresses are polyester satin). In previous years, Mori Lee marketed a separate line called Regency by Madeline Gardner. That line is gone now, replaced by two new collections: Classique and Enchantment. These gowns will sell for $400 to $500 (Classique) or $490 to $620 (Enchantment). We couldn't tell any real difference between these dresses and regular Mori Lee gowns, except for the fact the Classique gowns seems to have more detailing (crystals, bugle beads, etc). Enchantment gowns featured touches of silver and gold embroidery, swarovski crystals and seed pearls. The only downside to Mori Lee bridal gowns? Quality—frankly, it could be better. The construction and finish of Mori Lee's cheapest dresses often leave something to be desired. The company's delivery and customer service could also be improved. Another bummer: sizing is very limited. Only a few styles are available in a large size (42). And we hear constant gripes about Mori Lee's sizing—gowns often come in too big or too small. So, it's a mixed review for Mori Lee: the prices are fantastic, but the below-average quality tempers our enthusiasm. *Sizes 4 to 24, although only a few selected styles are available in sizes 22 and 24. Add $20 to $80 for sizes 18 to 24, depending on the style. Call (212) 840-5070 to find a local dealer. Web: www.morileeinc.com.* **Rating: B+**

Nina Baldwin This is a private label brand that is only sold at David's Bridal, a national chain of off-the-rack stores. See Spotlight: Best Buy for more info on David's later in this chapter.

Oleg Cassini This is a private label brand that is only sold at David's Bridal, a national chain of off-the-rack stores. See Spotlight: Best Buy for more info on David's later in this chapter.

Paloma Blanca Paloma Blanca's manufacturer (Bluebird) has been turning out bridal gowns in Canada for 60 years. The looks are stylish ("clean and understated" was how they put it) without the big-style price tag—most dresses retail for $1100 to $1350. We saw the gowns at a recent trade show and were impressed. All dresses are completely lined and feature elegant detailing. The only bummer: most of the fabrics are polyester satin. Yea, Paloma uses heavier-weight polyester satin than what the cheap Asia importers use, but we still find this a turn-off. $1350 for a polyester gown? That will buy you a silk dress from other designers. On the plus side, new this year is the "Diva" collection of "full-figured" gowns ($1200 to $1300) in sizes 14 to 26. Paloma's regular gowns are available in sizes 4 to 16. Custom changes are available, *Sizes 4 to 16, with some size 20's. Call (416) 235-0585 to find a dealer near you. Web: www.palomablanca.com.* **Rating: B–**

Priscilla of Boston With 50 years under its belt, Priscilla's trademark is their beautiful fabrics. Where else can you find bridal gowns made of Irish linen or Swiss silk? Of course, you can find plenty of satin and silk in the Priscilla line, but it is these special touches that set the Boston designer apart. Lace is used sparingly on these gowns—don't expect dangling beads or flashy sequins. In recent years, Priscilla has added some splashes of color to its line, with metallic threads or blush color bustles. Prices range from $1580 to $3600; most are about $2000. So, are the gowns worth it? Well, the quality is impeccable. All the gowns are hand-stitched in Charlestown, Mass.; Priscilla doesn't use any "piece-work," separately assembled gown parts favored by lower-price manu-facturers for their cost savings. Priscilla's new ownership has tried to reinvigorate the line, with mixed results. The venerable Boston designer has been eclipsed in recent years by rising stars such as Pronovias on the fashion end and Vera Wang in the celebrity market. One unusual note: Priscilla operates nine "company stores" nationwide, in addition to hav-ing regular retail dealers. *Sizes 2 to 20 and petites. Call (617) 242-2677 to find a local dealer. Web: www.priscillaofboston.com.* **Rating: A–**

Private Label by G/Ginza Collection Want a dress with a heavily-beaded bodice, paired with a skirt loaded with lace appliqués? Don't want to spend more than $600 or $700? Then this is the designer for you: Private Label by G is a Taiwanese-made gown importer that arrived in the U.S. in the mid 1980's. Their strategy is simple: produce a high quality gown at a low price. And the prices are great: $590 to $850 for the Private Label line; $550 to $800 for the "Signature" or Ginza collec-tions. There is even an "informal" line of gowns without trains for $310 to $450 (a great buy). Sure, the "fashion" in this line hasn't changed much in recent years, although we've noticed a few new designs with less lace and detailing. And Private Label specializes mostly in knock-offs of expensive designers like Eve of Milady. But who cares? It's hard to find this much dress with sewn-on (instead of glued) detailing in this price range. Another bonus: large sizes are available. Perhaps the best buy is the Signature collection, with its use of Japanese matte satin, rhinestones and Venise lace—all for under $800. *Sizes up to 42, but no petites. Large sizes (38 to 42) are an extra $100. Call (800) 858-3338 or (562) 531-1116 to find a local dealer. Web: www.ginza.com or www.privatela-belbyg.com.* **Rating: B+**

Pronovias Spanish bridal behemoth Pronovias recently invaded the U.S. and Canadian bridal markets and the verdict is in: it's a smash hit. In business since 1964, Barcelona-based Pronovias is essentially the Alfred Angelo of Europe—they sell $55 million worth of bridal gowns in Europe each year from a base of 100 company-owned stores and 600 independent dealers. Why? The dresses are spectacular—lush fabrics are the calling card of Pronovias. Sure, the Euro fashion is a bit cutting-edge (a bridal pantsuit?), but the prices are surprisingly within reach. The average dress: $1200; some start at $800. Even better: check out Pronovias's lower-price line called St. Patrick, with gowns averaging $700 (with a range from $480 to $1580). One caution: be careful about sizing. Pronovias uses European sizing specs, which are different than those used in the U.S. or Canada. Quality is above average, although we've noticed Pronovias is moving some of their bridal production from Europe to China so that will have to be watched. *Sizes 4 to 24, although all gowns are not available in all sizes; there is an up charge for sizes 18 to 24. Call 516-371-0877 for a dealer near you. Web: www.pronovias.com or www.sanpatrick.com.* **Rating: A-**

Robert Legere If the name Robert Legere sounds familiar, you were probably looking at bridal magazines in the late 1980's and early 1990's. Legere's name was splashed across hundreds of ads for gowns he designed for Diamond. After 13 years with that manufacturer, he departed to do an evening wear line . . . but he just couldn't get bridal off the brain. So, in 1996, he launched his own bridal line. And it appears he still has the old magic with his trademark "dash of color" looks and yummy fabrics like soft-stretch silk Charmeuse and textured embroidered organzas. Prices range from $1700 to $3580, although most are $2500. Yes, that ain't cheap, but you get your money's worth here. And the possible fabric swaps can cut a few hundred dollars off a dress price if need be. Even more unusual for this price range: Legere offers sizes up to 44, with a myriad of custom changes available. The quality is impeccable (all gowns are made in New York City; Legere's retail studio on 37th Street is open to the public). Delivery takes 10 to 12 weeks. There are many designers who sell $2000 dresses, but there are few who offer brides as much pizzazz as Legere. *Sizing 2 to 20 and 38 to 44. For a dealer near you, call (212) 631-0606.* **Rating: A**

Scaasi/Forsyth Just hit the lottery? Here's a designer that might be worth a look. Eva Forsyth designs gowns that have enough gold embroidery to stock a mini Ft. Knox. If that doesn't excite you, check out their Scaasi line, whose plunging neckline gowns might make Madonna blush. If you've got the bod, they've got the dress. Prices are $1600 to $3600. Quality is excellent (you can debate amongst yourselves whether they are worth the high price tags), as is Scaasi's reliability. *Sizes 4 to 18; for size 18, add 15% to the gown price. Call (804) 971-3853 to find a local dealer.* **Rating: B+**

St. Patrick This is the low-price line of Spanish designer Pronovias, reviewed earlier in this section.

St. Pucchi We've always had a soft spot for the impossibly over-the-top bridal gowns from St. Pucchi. Perhaps this is because one of this book's authors grew up in Dallas, Texas, which is also St. Pucchi's home base. For those of you who've never been to Dallas, it is a city that doesn't like to do anything in a small way. Folks down there got big hair, big cars . . . and big dresses. Which brings us to St. Pucchi. "Volume" is an understatement for these gowns, which have been known to swallow small children on occasion. The scaled-back gown fashions of recent years must have come as somewhat of a letdown for St. Pucchi's designer, Rani (the Indian-born designer who started the company in 1985). To her credit, she's tried to tone-down some of her designs (no more gowns with jewels scattered across the bodice. Darn.) We see less lace on her most recent creations and the cut-work on the trains has been reduced. Some of Pucchi's current designs even feature plain skirts. What is the world coming to? Prices range from $1450 to $1800 for the lower-priced Avine Perucci line to $2000 to $6800 for the regular St. Pucchi. The quality of these gowns is above average (all are made in Thailand and Pucchi uses Thai silk), although deliveries are painfully slow (you'll have to cool your heels for four months before your dress arrives). *Sizes 4 to 20; sizes 16 and up have an extra charge. Call (214) 631-4039 to find a local dealer. Web: www.stpucchi.com* **Rating: B**

Sincerity *This is a sub-line of Ian Stuart, reviewed earlier in this chapter.*

Sweetheart Sweetheart is a quintessential "middle of the road" bridal gown designer—they're neither a leader in price nor fashion. Sure, the prices are attractive ($400 to $600), but nearly all the gowns are made of polyester satin. The fashion is OK; Sweetheart has tried to update the look of its gowns in the past year and the results are impressive. Yet there are still 80's throwbacks in this line (with tons of beading and lace) as well as knock-offs of better designers. As for delivery, Sweetheart keeps in stock most styles (and some designs are available in plus sizes up to a 44). As a result, you may be able to get very quick delivery (8 weeks or less). On the other hand, any gown order with a custom change (shorter sleeves or extra train length) takes a whopping 22 weeks (yes, that's nearly six months). Sweetheart blames its overseas production for slow delivery on such orders, but we think they could do better. New for Sweetheart: the company is selling a few "exclusive" designs through JCPenney that offer quick delivery and even some petite sizes. The quality of the gowns is about average. *Sizes 4 to 44; sizes 18 to 44 are an extra $40 to $50. Call (800) 223-6061 or (212) 947-7171 to find a local dealer. Web: www.gowns.com.* **Rating: B**

Tomasina Sometimes you find an amazing bridal designer in a place you wouldn't expect. Like Pittsburgh, PA. While this town isn't home to many bridal designers, we were pleasantly surprised to find Tomasina here, creating some of the most interesting bridal gowns in America. What makes Tomasina special? Check out the embroidery on these gowns. There are styles with delicate lemon blossoms or flocked embroidery swans, and others with intricate woven ribbons. Okay, that sounds cheesy, but trust us, it isn't. While the prices aren't inexpensive ($2000 to $7000, with an average of $2400), you'd be hard pressed to find these looks anywhere else. And the quality is excellent; all gowns are sewn in the US. This is a small line (about 10 new dresses per season) and the sizing is limited (4-22). Delivery takes 12 to 16 weeks and some gowns have matching headpieces, shrugs, jackets, etc. *For a dealer near you, call (412) 563-7788. Web: www.tomasinabridal.com* **Rating: A-**

Venus With 150+ styles, Venus is probably one of the largest import bridal manufacturers in the country. With dealers in both the U.S. and Canada, Venus splits its voluminous line into four groups: regular Venus, informals, "Angel & Tradition" (a new lower price line with some unique beading) and a separate collection called Pallas Athena. Overall, Venus' formal gowns range from $400 to $900, while informal styles (without trains) are $200 to $360. Matte satin is a common fabric, but there are a few styles in chiffon and shiny polyester satin. In the past, the separate Pallas Athena was slightly lower price and less ornate than the regular Venus gowns, but we don't see much difference today. As for a fashion direction, Venus is all over the board—you'll still find traditional looks of shiny satin gowns encrusted in beads and lace . . . but the line also includes more contemporary silhouettes and fabrics. Perhaps Venus' best deals are in their informal line. And the word "informal" is really a misnomer. These are really formal bridal gowns—the only thing missing is the train. In business since 1985, Venus gets better marks for quality than other similar importers. We also like that the manufacturer offers all gowns in petite sizes, a rarity these days. If the company beefed up its value with more silk gowns in lower price points (under $800), they'd definitely earn a higher rating. *Sizes 4 to 30 and petites 3-15. Extra charges for sizes 18 to 26 are $40 to $240; petites $40. Call (800) OH-VENUS or (626) 285-5796 to find a local dealer. Web: Venus doesn't have its own web site, but does have some of its dresses on the WeddingChannel.com.* **Rating: B+**

Vera Wang In the bridal market there are pricey gowns that are worth it. And then there are those that are made by Vera Wang—exorbitantly priced gowns that are definitely *not* worth your hard earned money. For those of you who didn't watch the Winter Olympics of 1994, Wang came to prominence in the fashion market after she designed a white outfit for Nancy Kerrigan. After conquering the skating fashion world, Wang rolled out bridal gowns and, shortly thereafter, bridesmaids. After looking at these dresses, we wondered, what's the big deal? At prices that approach a down payment for a nice house (a $6000 bridal dress, anyone?), you'd expect the gowns to be made from some precious metals and trimmed with pure platinum beading. No such luck. The fabrics are merely average and, worst of all, the fashion is "been there, done that," despite some recent efforts to jazz up the line with a bridal separates line called "Pieces." And why spend a fortune on a Wang dress when you can get it at a discount? That's right—Wang quietly does "trunk show" sales in New York (call the number below for the latest schedule). According to an article in the *Los Angeles Times*, one bride picked up a $3000 gown for just $400 at this sale. "The only downside," the bride told the reporter, "was I had to stand in line for two hours with 1500 other bitchy brides." Now, $400 is a more realistic price for a Wang bridal gown. If you don't live near New York City and can't get to this sale, we suggest forgetting about this designer . . . and buying that home instead. *For a dealer near you, call (800) VEW-VERA or (212) 575-6400. Web: www.verawang.com* **Rating: C**

Other designers. Since space is limited in this book, we have reviews of many other bridal designers on our free web site BridalGown.com (see the back of the book for details). Here is a partial list of the 46 other designers reviewed online: Aleya, Amadine, Amici, Amy Lee, Amy Michelson, Ana Hernandez, Angel Sanchez, Ann Barge, Ana Christina, Antonio Fermin, Anu Pam, Avica, Barbra Allin, Birnbaum & Bullock, Badgley Mischka, Bayje, Bolo Vasquez, Carmela Sutera, Carolina Herrera, Casablanca, Catherine Regehr, Chris Kole, Christina Arzuga, Cupid, Cynthia C & Company, Elizabeth Fillmore, Edguardo Bonilla, Eugenia, Givenchy, Guzzo, Helen Morley, Judd Waddell, Justine (Bridals By), Lila Broude, L'Amour, L'ezu Atelier, Manale, Melissa Sweet, Mika Inatome,

Montique, Nancy Issler, Paula Varsalona, Reem Acra, Rena Koh, Richard Glasgow, Rivini, Roberta, Romona Keveza, Tatiana of Boston, Ulla Maija, Victoria's, Wearkstatt, Yolanda, Youlin, Yumi Katsura.

Canada designers. The following Canadian bridal makers are reviewed in our special Canada section in the back of this book: Amici, Barbara Allin/Allin Rae, Catherine Regher, Gordon, Guzzo, Ines Di Santo, Justina McCaffrey, Madison Collection, and Rivini.

Can't find a designer you are looking for? Remember to check the index of this book; some designer names are part of a major bridal line (such as Private Label by G and Ginza). See the "Also Known As" box earlier in this chapter for designer aliases.

SPOTLIGHT: BEST BUY #1

DISCOUNT BRIDAL SERVICE
(Over 300 representatives nationwide)
(800) 874-8794
www.discountbridalservice.com

Discount Bridal Service (DBS) is a mail-order company that offers 20% to 30% discounts on almost all nationally-advertised bridal apparel. Hold it! How can that be, you ask?

Well, DBS has found an interesting way to get you those same fancy designer gowns without the fancy designer price tag. Here's how they do it: DBS has a central headquarters in Baltimore, Maryland and a network of over 300 representatives in major cities. The reps don't have typical bridal shops with all the high overhead and bloated inventory expense. By cutting out expensive overhead, DBS passes the savings along to brides in the form of sizable discounts.

For example, we priced one fancy designer gown dripping with lace and pearls at a retail price of $2390. Then we called the local DBS rep in our city and found that she could order the very same dress for just $1700! Wow! That's a savings of $690 or nearly 30%! Other bridal gowns we priced were available at 20% to 25% discounts, with great deals on bridesmaids, headpieces/veils, flower girl and mother of the bride dresses as well.

The best part of DBS: you work one-on-one with a rep in your city. Unlike discount web sites that work via email or long-distance phone calls, DBS offers face-to-face consultations with local reps who provide advice on sizing, accessories or other aspects of your wedding.

So what's the catch, you say? Well, DBS' prices aren't as low as their dot-com competitors, although the difference is typically small. And you have to pay for shipping, freight and insurance on all orders...but that came to just $30 extra on the gown we priced. Another disadvantage: DBS requires all orders to be paid in full in advance. Also, some dresses take more time than normal to order—up to six months in some cases.

When you order a gown from DBS, the merchandise is directly shipped to your home address after being inspected at their headquarters. If the gown needs alterations, DBS reps can usually refer you to one of several local seamstresses (some DBS reps actually are seamstresses themselves). Another big plus for DBS: while most bridal shops carry just 10 to 12 bridal apparel lines, DBS can order from over 100 different manufacturers.

So what do regular bridal shops think of DBS? Well, most of their comments are unprintable here. Basically, many bridal shops are mad as all heck that brides can get gowns at such big discounts. Bridal shops are also angry that consumers come into their shop to try on their gowns and then go to DBS to buy. Of course, all this is just sour grapes—if shops provided good service and lower prices, there would be no reason to order from DBS.

Other bridal shops question the authenticity of the company, wondering how they can order those same designer gowns. Surprisingly, this is a good example of the behind-the-scenes struggle between retailers and manufacturers over discounting. While everyone (except brides) complains about discounting, many of the manufacturers are quietly selling to discounters like DBS.

Perhaps the biggest challenge to ordering a gown from the company is identifying the exact dress. With many shops coding and concealing the identity of the gowns, the best solution may be to find a picture of the same gown in a bridal magazine or on the web. Since many gowns are advertised at one point in their life, DBS can nail down the exact manufacturer and style by just knowing the magazine issue and page number (or web site page).

Here are a few other "frequently asked questions" about this mail-order service we hear from brides:

♥ **DOES DBS TAKE CREDIT CARDS?** When DBS first started, it was cash or check only. Fortunately, that's changed. Now, 60% of DBS dealers take credit cards. And if your local dealer doesn't accept plastic, you can request the order be processed through the main office (which has credit card capability).

♥ **I CALLED THE DESIGNER AND THEY SAID THEY DON'T SELL TO DBS. WHAT GIVES?** Some designers are telling the truth—and others aren't. It's true that DBS buys some of its gowns through "third-party sources" (such as another bridal shop who carries the line). In other cases, designers sell directly to DBS, but deny it in public. Why? They don't want to offend their full-price dealers. Yet, the bridal industry is a very small cottage business—everyone knows what everyone else is doing. So, the designers' denials ring false to us. Anyway, it doesn't matter to you—DBS sells first-quality, name-brand gowns, not copies or clones. We wouldn't recommend any company in this book that sells counterfeit merchandise.

♥ DOES IT TAKE LONGER TO ORDER A GOWN FROM DBS? Yes, sometimes. However, this varies from designer to designer, even gown to gown. The best bet is to call and ask. What causes this delay? One reason is DBS' quality assurance program; all gowns are first shipped from the manufacturer to their Baltimore, Maryland headquarters for inspection. After it passes, it's shipped on to you—this extra step can add time. Even if you have to pay a rush charge from DBS, it still may be less than the price at a local shop. Compare prices to make sure you're getting the best deal from any source.

As a side note, DBS representatives often offer discounts on wedding invitations and other accessories. Even if you decide not to order a gown from DBS, they may be able to save you money on another aspect of your wedding. The bottom line: we highly recommend Discount Bridal Service. Of all the discounters we found, this company is the most reputable and has the best customer service.

Be discreet with a discount gown purchase

If you decide to order a gown from a discounter (be it Discount Bridal Service or a web site), be smart. Remember that these guys are very controversial among manufacturers and retailers. Don't do what one bride did when her dress (ordered from a discounter) was two days late—she called the dress' manufacturer and grilled them about why it was late. And she mentioned what a big discount she was getting. While she got her dress, she also got an obscenity-laden lecture from the designer about supporting those evil discounters. And by loudly announcing the discount, the bride jeopardized the discounter's supply lines. The bottom line: the price you paid for their dress is no business of the designer/manufacturer.

Another tip: be savvy about alterations. If you take your dress to a full-price shop for alterations, by all means, DO NOT tell them you got it a web discounter. Some bridal shops will sock such brides with HUGE alteration and pressing charges, just to punish them. One bride found this out when she brought her gown to a shop in the discounter's mailing box (not smart). The bridal retailer refused to do the alterations and kicked her out of the shop.

SPOTLIGHT: BEST BUY #2

DISCOUNT GOWN WEB SITES

Just about any product is now available for sale on the web—and more often than not, it's being sold at a discount. So why not bridal apparel?

Yes, you can save big bucks on bridal gowns and bridesmaids dresses on the net. In this section, we'll review our picks of the top eight places on the web to buy gowns. How much can you save? About 20% to 40% off retail. But before you fire up the browser and surf for dress deals, consider these facts:

1. Like many things on the web, selling bridal gowns in cyberspace is still in an embryonic stage. Sites range from those with indepth pricing information to others that are merely one-page ads with little detail. If you're looking for hi-tech web sites with on-line pricing guides, you'll be sorely disappointed. Price quotes are given out via the phone or email. And forget about online ordering. When you want to actually buy, most sites direct you to email or call a phone number (sometimes toll-free, sometimes not) to place the order.

2. When shopping a discounter, do your homework first. Gather information on colors and options. After narrowing down your choices to just your top picks, *then* contact a discounter for a price quote. This is only fair, since hogging a discounter's time, be it DBS or a web site, only reduces the response rate for everyone. We know some brides that have carpet-bombed discounters with email requests for 16 dress quotes . . . or with color questions that could be easily answered at the designer's web site.

3. Our biggest beef with these web sites is that (at this point) they are all run by *local* bridal shops—there is no Amazon.com of bridal. And it is hard to tell long distance whether the shop is reputable just by the look of their Web graphics. Mail-order (which is essentially what bridal shops are doing over the web) is a totally different business than retail—you have to deal with shipping logistics, long-distance customer service and all sorts of other complications. We'd like to see someone have at least three years experience doing this operation (selling dresses over the Web) before we'd give our hard-earned cash as a deposit. And, as of this writing, few pass this test (we review some of the better known sites below).

4. Remember that discount deals are typically for mail-order customers only. Most bridal web sites that sell gowns also operate physical stores. So does that mean you can get a discount deal via email and then go to the store and get the same price? No, special web prices are almost always for folks who don't come into the store, try on gowns and use the store's alterations service. While most web sites don't explicitly say this, several brides have confirmed these practices to us.

5. Another caveat: many gown designers and manufacturers are livid about web sites that discount their dresses. Some have threatened to cut off accounts who sell through an "unauthorized 800-number or web site." While most of the designer's protests are mere saber-rattling (few have actually cut off 'net sellers), there is a risk—albeit it small—that your gown order could be caught in the cross-fire. Unlike Discount Bridal Service (which has a solid network of dealers and a decade-long track record of filling orders), many of these web sites are on shakier ground. Since the entire world of bridal on the web is changing rapidly, we'll post the latest updates on this subject on our web site at BridalGown.com.

So, here's our advice: be careful out there. Confirm the web site is an authorized dealer for the brand you want. Only a handful of web sites are actually authorized dealers of the manufacturers they claim to sell. A wise move: call the designer or manufacturer first before you order. (Remember that some web sites may be authorized under their parent retail shop's name, not their on-line address—ask the site how they would be listed in a designer's records). Finally, use a credit card for all deposits and final payments.

Our round-up of discount gown web sites, in alphabetical order:

♥ BRIDAL MARKETPLACE. *www.bridalmarketplace.com* Michigan-based Bridal Marketplace offers discounts up to 40% on such brands as Jim Hjelm, Demetrios, Mori Lee, Mary's, Victoria's Alfred Angelo and Sweetheart. Their simple web site does include a toll free number (800) 968-0338 and a good FAQ with their order policies. While we found the info helpful, we thought Bridal Marketplace's web site was rather chaotic—click on the gown catalog and you are linked to a Yahoo storefront for the "Designer Discount Bridal Salon," which is apparently another alias the company uses. The same thing happens when you click on the invitations link, which shunts you to a different web store. While we realize these free store fronts let retailers get on the web cheaply, it is rather confusing to have a site with so many faces. Another bummer: our email request to the site for more information on their background went unanswered. **Rating: B-**

♥ BRIDESAVE.COM *www.bridesave.com.* BrideSave.com (see Figure 4 on the next page) has one of the 'net's more voluminous bridal sites: you can view/buy gowns, veils, shoes, bridesmaids, accessories and invitations. There are also planning tools, budget worksheets, and even a "hold rack"

Figure 4: BrideSave.com's well-organized web site lets you search for gowns, bridesmaids, accessories and more.

for gowns that interest you. We also liked the detailed ordering, sizing and guarantee policies—a refreshing change from other gown sites that are sketchy at best on these topics. As for the gowns, expect to find middle-of-the-road designers like Alfred Angelo, Venus, and Bianchi. You can also find such hot lines as Maggie Sottero and Diamond here. Best of all are the discounts: about 20% to 30% off retail (gowns range from $178 to $4300). And we loved the gown search option, which lets you browse gowns by designer, fabric, price or a half dozen other attributes. Also great: BrideSave works hard to make sure all the gowns pictured online are currently in production; discontinued gowns are quickly removed from their web site. With 2000 gowns, 1000 bridesmaids, 700 headpieces/veils, and 700 shoe offerings, you'll be hard pressed to find a better selection online. Even though BrideSave.com is relatively new (in business since 1999), their track record at customer service is solid. Another bonus: BrideSave only sells gowns for which they are an authorized dealer. **Rating: A**

♥ **GOWNS ONLINE** *www.gownsonline.com; (408) 985-5594.* This web site has a cool magazine search feature that lets track down a dress from a bridal magazine picture. Even if Gowns Online doesn't carry the brand, you can find the style number and retail price for just about any ad. Overall, we thought this site was impressive—they are owned by New Things West, a 10-year old bridal shop near San Jose, CA. The brands they offer on-line include Diamond, Jim Hjelm and Maggie Sottero. And the discounts? Up to 40% for bridal gowns, about 25% for bridesmaid dresses. Shipping is included in their price quotes for bridal gowns and bridesmaids dresses shipped to one address. Maids' gowns shipped to multiple addresses incur a $12 per dress charge. **Rating: B**

♥ NETBRIDE *www.netbride.com* This site won't win any design awards, but there is plenty of information here on how to order a gown, from shipping times to sizing advice. What the site doesn't say is NetBride are owned by Rush's, a Minneapolis bridal shop. On the upside, NetBride carries a wide variety of brands, from Bonny to Bianchi and even some couture names like Scaasi and St. Pucchi. The only problem: NetBride sometimes quotes prices on gowns they are not authorized to sell. While the feedback on this site has been positive, we always urge caution about ordering from a site that is not an authorized dealer for the gown you want. Check with the manufacturer to confirm this detail. **Rating: B**

♥ PEARL'S PLACE *www.pearlsplace.com; (504) 885-9213.* Pearl's Place was one of the first bridal shops to open a cyberspace outpost. The Metairie, Louisiana shop specializes in the "better" couture labels, the ones that are hard to find at a discount anywhere else online. Pearl's has been in business since 1971 and online since 1998. Don't expect much from their web site—it's a one-page affair with lots of text about the lines the store carries, ordering info, etc.

What do readers think of Pearl's? Well, Pearl's seems to be a graduate of the Jeckel & Hyde School of Customer Service. Owner Fred Schulman (who seems to be perpetually chained to his computer) gets high marks from our readers for prompt quotes and answers to email queries. Unfortunately, brides are then directed to contact the actual store to order—and that's were the Mr. Hyde part comes in. We have dozens of angry emails from brides who say they were put on never-ending hold (Pearl's has no toll-free number) and treated rudely by the store's staff. Strangely enough, there seems to be no rhyme or reason to when and why this happens—some brides praise their Pearl's experiences; others want to take a rocket launcher to the place. (You can read all the comments on Pearl's and other discounters on BridalGown.com).

We can only surmise that Pearl's first priority is their in-store customers. Unfortunately, the company has no specific personnel dedicated to take and service web orders. And the company lacks a written agreement for their web orders, which has led to disputes over promised shipping dates. So, it's a mixed review for Pearl's. The discounts (20% to 30%) are great, as is the availability of couture labels. Yet the spotty customer service leads us to take this company down a notch or two from our last review. **Rating: B–**

♥ **PRICELESS BRIDALS** *www.bargainweddinggowns.com; (818) 340-6514.* The online off-shoot of a Southern California bridal shop by the same name, Priceless offers to beat any written price quote by their competitors. The web site lists several designers that are available, including Alfred Angelo, Galina, Mori Lee and even upper-end lines like Diamond and Scaasi. A reader who ordered her gown from Priceless said she was happy, even though the gown was a little late (Priceless waived the shipping fee, however). "Priceless is a little harder to get in touch with than Pearl's—that is they don't answer their email as quickly and you have to nag them a bit," said the bride. "But the dress I received was very pretty and for $350, it can't be beat." Shipping is $10 within the state of California; $15 to other states. Another interesting note: Priceless is one of the few web discounters that also occasionally hosts eBay auctions. Go to eBay.com and search for bridal gowns or wedding dresses.

♥ **RK BRIDAL** *www.rkbridal.com; (800) 929-9512.* This New York City-based retail shop has one of the better-known web sites that sells gowns at a discount. On a recent visit to the site, we noticed several "Gown Specials of the Week," which included prices, style numbers and a link to a picture of the dress. Of course, you can also get a price quote for dresses from 30 manufacturers. Many of the lines are upper-end, couture dresses that are hard to find at a discount. Delivery takes 12 to 16 weeks for bridal gowns, 8 to 9 weeks for bridesmaids and RK does take credit cards. One plus: RK's price quotes include shipping and delivery charges. RK Bridal has a shop in New York's garment district at 318 West 39th Street (between 8th & 9th Ave.), although most of the prices there are not discounted like they are on the web. Our readers generally report positive experiences in dealing with RK, which has been in the bridal retail business since 1985. The company responds quickly to email requests and has been reliable with deliveries. **Rating: A**

♥ **WEDDING EXPRESSIONS.** *www.weddingexpressions.com; (319) 753-5217* Burlington, Iowa isn't exactly the place you'd expect to find a major player in the internet gown chase, but hey, this is the web. You CAN be located virtually anywhere. And ironically, Wedding Expressions has a site that out-does many of their big-city competitors. There's much to browse here, from bridal accessories (favors, gifts, books) to invitations, candles and more. And, yes, they sell gowns. See a gown you like in a magazine? Just pick the magazine and page number and the site will give you a discounted instant quote. Or you can send the site an email request for a dress quote. Prices are about 20% to 35% off retail, depending on the brand. And if you want a bigger discount, check out their "Stock Gowns" area with samples, overruns and other dresses, all marked 50% or more off retail. Wedding Expressions mostly carries

middle-of-road designers like Venus and Bonny.

All in all, this site is quite impressive. They even offer secure, online ordering (you can pay by credit card or check). Best of all, the company has established a good track record in filling orders and customer service, according to our research. Wedding Expressions' site should be required viewing for all 'net gown sellers. **Rating: A**

What about other sites on the web that sell gowns? Yes, we realize there are at least a dozen more sites out there, but we didn't review them here. Why? The sites above had the best feedback from our readers and the longest track records. If you have a question about brides' experiences with another site, you can always check the message boards on our site www. BridalBargainsBook.com. Or email us at authors@BridalBargainsBook. com with your stories, questions and comments.

PROS AND CONS

Should you buy a dress from local retailer or an online discounter? Here is a summary of the pros and cons of each option.

OPTION	PROS	CONS
DISCOUNT	GREAT PRICE: 20-40% OFF RETAIL	SOME REQUIRE UPFRONT PAYMENT WHEN ORDERING
	NO SALES TAX; NO PUSHY SALESPEOPLE	MUST KNOW EXACT DRESS YOU WANT
	INDIE SEAMSTRESS CAN BE MONEY-SAVER	MUST COORDINATE ALTERATIONS YOURSELF (HASSLE)
	NO MESSY BRIDAL SHOPS	LONG-DISTANCE RELATIONSHIP VIA PHONE OR EMAIL
	GET DRESS SHIPPED DIRECTLY TO YOU	MUST STORE YOURSELF
RETAIL	FULL SERVICE OFTEN INCLUDES ALTERATIONS	FULL RETAIL PRICE . . . AND SOMETIMES MORE
	CAN TRY ON DRESSES	LIMITED SELECTION
	PAY HALF DOWN; HALF WHEN DRESS COMES IN	SERVICE SOMETIMES SLIPS AFTER THEY HAVE YOUR MONEY
	EXTRAS LIKE PRESSING, GOWN STORAGE AND PAYMENT PLANS	DID WE MENTION YOU PAY FULL RETAIL PRICE?

SPOTLIGHT: BEST BUY #3

DAVID'S
Call (800) 399-2743 for a store near you
www.davidsbridal.com

What a long strange trip it's been.

David's, the country's largest chain of bridal shops (110 and counting, see Figure 5), has changed dramatically from their humble beginnings in South Florida in 1990. When we first visited David's in Tampa in 1993, they were known as "David's Bridal Warehouse." And a warehouse was what it was—rack after rack of gowns sold "as is" at deep discount prices. The crammed-together inventory, lack of dressing rooms and harsh fluorescent lighting gave David's all the ambiance of a K-Mart.

How times have changed. We recently visited a brand new David's in Colorado and boy, things *are* different. The airy, 25,000 square foot store featured high ceilings, tapestry carpet, subtle lighting and a HUGE dressing area, all walled in mirrors. It's no wonder David's has dropped the "warehouse" from their name—it looks like a regular (albeit big) bridal salon.

What hasn't changed are the gowns—David's still sells everything off the rack. Unlike traditional stores that stock only sample gowns and force you to wait months for a "special order," David's is cash and carry. You see a gown, find your size (they stock sizes 2 to 24), pay for it and then walk out the door. What a concept.

But what exactly is David's selling? Well, these are not designer-brand dresses. In fact, ALL the gowns in David's are their own "private label" or in-house names. David's has plants in Asia that churn out copies of all the hip styles sold in regular stores. And the prices are attractive: most synthetic fabric styles are $165 to $1050; most average $450.

So, how's the quality? We tried on a satin tank top style with tulle skirt. The plain bodice was pleasing, but we couldn't help but notice the flimsy fabric and poor workmanship (for example, unfinished seams inside the dress). The price, $350, made it a decent buy—but no tremendous bargain. In fact, we thought most of dresses at David's were comparable in price and quality to other low-end bridal designers (Mori Lee, Alfred Angelo, Sweetheart, etc.).

And we have more than a few gripes with the way David's does business. First, consider the bogus brand names. Instead of being honest with consumers about the dresses they sell, David's tries to trick brides into thinking they are getting a designer gown. The racks are full of dresses with labels that say Lady Eleanor, Gloria Vanderbilt, Oleg Cassini, Enzio, etc. Don't be fooled—these dresses are all made in the same Asian factory, exclusively for David's. You won't find them anywhere else. David's merely licenses the famous-sounding monikers to give their dresses some cachet.

Gripe number two: fake savings. Some of David's dresses sport tags that say "Original price: $1000. Our price: $599." Sounds like you are getting a deal? Don't bet on it. These dresses were never offered for sale at the original or "compare at" price. David's should discontinue this blatantly deceptive practice. Of course, the company does have sales, but this practice involves dresses sold all the time (not just during a promotion.)

And what about those sales? David's is famous for running $99 dress sale ads in local papers. Brides complain to us that when they arrive at these "sales," all they find is a few trashed sample gowns at $99. All the good merchandise is at regular price. (An insider note on the $99 sale: apparently, David's sends advance notice of the sale to "registered" brides, who get first crack at the sale before the public.)

Another major complaint area: bridesmaids dresses. While bridal gowns are sold off the rack, David's offers a private collection of bridesmaids gowns ($99 to $180) that are sold by special order. The good news is the fashion for David's maids' dresses, which has improved markedly over the last few years. David's even offers mix-and-match separates with tops at $29 to $49, skirts $59 to $79 and wraps for $20.

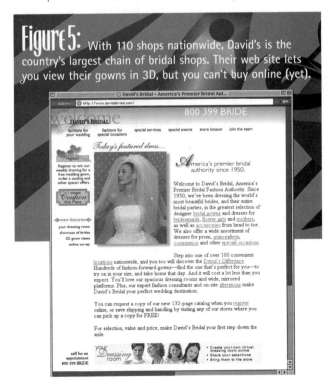

Figure 5: With 110 shops nationwide, David's is the country's largest chain of bridal shops. Their web site lets you view their gowns in 3D, but you can't buy online (yet).

The bad news: we still get numerous complaints about David's "special order" process, from orders arriving late, wrong, damaged or worse. And this goes for more than just maids' gowns, the same goes for bridal gowns, purses, and accessories that need to be special ordered. Our general advice for David's: unless the item is actually in stock at the store, don't buy it.

So, we have to give a mixed review to David's. Some of our readers tell us they love David's—especially since you can try on a variety of styles in your actual size. This is especially a plus for those who need a large size. For those in a hurry, the ability to buy a dress off the rack that same day is a unique advantage to David's.

But . . . many brides criticize the store for "cheap-looking" gowns that aren't any special deal. And the service? In Philadelphia, a bride told us she encountered a David's salesperson "trained in the Gestapo school of human relations." The zoo-like atmosphere (forget going on a Saturday) turns off other brides, as do the dresses, which can have makeup stains and other signs of wear and tear.

Some late breaking news on David's as we went to press: In July 2000, David's was bought by the giant May Co., which operates 422 department stores in 35 states under the names Hecht's, Foley's, Filene's and Robinsons-May. We expect May's deep pockets to help finance David's continued expansion. We also hope May can bring some polish to David's customer service. At this point, however, it is too early to tell what exactly May has planned for David's.

SPOTLIGHT: BEST BUY #4

BRIDAL OUTLETS

With an outlet mall in just about every corner of North America, it seems you can find any product at less than retail—sweaters, cookware, stereos, you name it. But what about a bridal gown?

Surprisingly, there ARE bridal outlets out there . . . they just take some effort to find. Most are NOT in those fancy outlet malls on the interstate. Instead, bridal outlets are located in off-the-beaten path locales. Here's our look at the best bets:

♥ **"1385 BROADWAY"** is probably the worst kept secret in the bridal business. That's the address in New York City for the "Bridal Building," the place where many bridal designers and gown makers have their showrooms and sales offices. During the week, the public is not allowed in these wholesale-only offices. But . . . with little fanfare, those same showrooms are open to the public on Saturdays.

When you visit the building, you can literally taste the irony. Yes, the same bridal designers who rail against discounting as the evil scourge are themselves quietly cutting deals at 1385 Broadway (and its sister building at 1375 Broadway).

Here's how it works: when you walk in the building, a sign lists which floors are open that Saturday. The showrooms are scattered on different floors—and you don't really know who is open until you get there. In some cases, we found designers' offices offering 50% off samples or brand-new gowns that can be special-ordered for 25% off. Sometimes the designers themselves are available in person to show their lines.

Now the downside: you never know WHICH showrooms will be open on any given Saturday. And forget about calling the designers in advance to ask—many simply deny they are ever open on Saturday. Hours can vary; some are open all day. Others just from 9 am to 1 pm. And watch out for alterations charges—some designers charge exorbitant fitting fees, such as a flat $200 no matter what work needs to be done.

In the past few years, the scene has changed a bit at the Bridal Building. First, many major gown manufacturers have abandoned the building (and New York's high rents) by moving their showrooms out of the city. In their place, we've seen several smaller designers and seam-stresses move into the Bridal Building. In some cases, these smaller salons are selling overstock samples from major gown makers; other times, they are selling their own creations.

So, is it still worth it to trek to the Bridal Building? Well, if you live in or near (or plan to visit) New York City, you might as well go look. It can't hurt. We found some of the deals to be great—one designer bridal gown in excellent condition was originally $1300, marked to $600. Our read-ers report one major bridesmaid designer sells their $160 gowns for just $95 on Saturdays.

But . . . you might find similar deals from the other discount sources we list in this chapter (like RK Bridal, the web site and store in the Garment District reviewed earlier). So, educate yourself on the design-ers, prices and selection before you go to the bridal building. And don't forget to factor in the price of parking and tolls for not only the initial visit but also any follow-up fittings.

The Bridal Building isn't the only place to get bridal gown bargains in New York City. Among the best new gown outlets is THE GOWN COMPANY (328 E. Ninth Street, 212-979-9000; web: www.thegowncompany.com). Their small shop in the East Village is a little known, semi-secret outlet for fancy couture designers like by Badgley Mischka, Helen Morley, Oscar de la Renta, Peter Langner, Robert Legere, and Vera Wang. The prices are fantastic—at least 50% and up to 75% off retail. And watch out for their sale events on Badgely Mischka gowns, held four to five times a year at the Lombardy Hotel. Best of all, the gowns come directly from designers (they are showroom samples), so they are in good condition. The only bummer: size selection is limited, mostly 4 to 10 (although a few 2's and 12's occasionally pass through the doors).

While in New York City, be sure to stop by **JUST ONCE**, at 290 5th Ave. (212) 465-0960. While it isn't an outlet, Just Once is probably the city's most famous dress rental shop—that's right, you can RENT some of those pricey couture gowns you see in fancy stores at a fraction of retail. Just Once is a small shop but worth the visit—most gowns rent for $500 to $1000, or 50% to 75% less than retail. The shop helps with alterations and fittings as well as accessories and other details.

Also in New York (Brooklyn, that is): **KLEINFIELDS**, the massive bridal store with more than 50 years in the business. Yes, Kleinfelds carries nearly every gown on Earth but we've been turned off by their policies (they rip tags from their sample gowns) and financial troubles. Kleinfelds was in a death spiral a few years ago and has gone through several owners. The latest (and we're not making this up): actor Wayne Rogers, better known as M*A*S*H's Trapper John MD. Whether Trapper can restore Kleinfelds luster remains to be seen. For now, we recommend skipping this store.

♥ **JESSICA MCCLINTOCK** has not one but FOUR outlets for her popular line of bridal apparel. Unfortunately, the flagship outlet store (dubbed Gunne Sax) in downtown San Francisco closed in 1999 but you can still find McClintock outlets in South San Francisco (415) 553-8390, Mont Clair (909) 982-1866 and Huntington Beach (714) 841-7124. There is also an outlet store in El Paso, Texas (915) 771-9550. All outlets carry past-season styles of bridal gowns, bridesmaids dresses and all kinds of accessories.

We recently visited the San Francisco outlet and were impressed. We saw dozens of bridal gowns (priced from $225 to $500), plus bridesmaids dresses, flower girls, party dresses and more. Most of the bridal gowns were discounted 10% to 25%, but we understand periodic sales offer even better deals. We've heard of brides who found $5 formal bridal gowns (no, that's not a typo). While the deals weren't that fantastic when we were there, we did notice a large rack of informal gowns on sale for just $80. You can then buy a separate train ($20 each). Top off your bargain ensemble with a pair of white shoes with lace trim, on clearance while we visited for just $5 a pair. Wow.

Most gowns we saw at the McClintock outlet were sizes 8-14, although a few 4-6's and 16-20's were floating around. Surprisingly, the dresses were in pretty good shape—most were in protective bags and had very little damage or wear. Watch for those end-of season clearances for the best deals (you can put your name on their mailing list to get notices).

Also in the San Francisco Bay Area is the **PROTEUS' DISCOUNT BRIDAL STORE** at 300 Brannan St, (415) 495-7922. (Proteus is not related to Discount Bridal Service, by the way). Owners Harlan and Yvonne Russell

"Factory stores" trend puts new twist on outlets

Beset by competition and faltering retail dealers, bridal gown manufacturers have rolled out a new weapon to fight chains like David's: the factory store. Demetrios kicked off this trend in 1999 with the launch of "Brides by Demetrios" in San Diego. Subsequent Demetrios stores have been opened in Las Vegas, Seattle, Orlando and Albuquerque. According to the company, future outlets are planned for Scottsdale, and Portland, Oregon (and perhaps another two dozen cities). Call Demetrios at (212-961-5222 or web: www.demetriosbride.com) for the latest locations.

So what are these factory stores? In a way, these stores are a hybrid between discount outlets and pure retail locations. The best advantage for consumers is selection. Demetrios loads his stores with his ENTIRE collection (about 800 styles), in sizes 4 to 26. Unlike regular bridal shops that may just carry a few styles in a line, factory stores let a manufacturer showcase their entire line. Of course, if you don't like the Demetrios look, this isn't the place to shop. Brides by Demetrios stores only stock Demetrios bridal gowns (along with bridesmaids gowns, accessories and all the other usual stuff).

Unfortunately, prices are typically at full retail. But we have heard from readers that the Demetrios stores will match quotes brides have received from online discounters, so it may not hurt to ask. Of course, while you might pay full price, you also get full service (on-site alterations are available at most stores). Another tip: look for sale racks at factory stores. Demetrios stores have a large selection of discontinued dresses that are $299 to $699, about 30% to 50% off retail.

We should also note that Demetrios quietly operates an outlet store under the name "Bridal World" near San Diego in Chula Vista (250 Third Avenue, Chula Vista, 619-426-2100). A sharp-eyed reader discovered this bargain find, noting that all the gowns were in great shape and priced at $499, regardless of their original retail! We called the outlet to confirm the prices and found they often run sales with some dresses reduced to $99. A wide variety of sizes (4 to 24) are available.

Of course, Demetrios isn't the only designer going the "factory store" route. Jessica McClintock (see previous page) has for years operated her own stores. Newcomer A. B. S. by Allen Schwartz (212-398-0330, web: www.absstyle.com) is hawking their bridesmaids gowns in both factory stores and online. And even industry stalwart Alfred Angelo has opened a "company store" (1700 Powerline Road, Deerfield, FL, 954-846-9198) that carries their current styles, along with a small clearance rack.

All of this is good for consumers, in our view. Factory stores give brides another option for gown shopping and piece of mind in knowing the store is manufacturer-owned. Whether these stores will be aggressive with pricing and special sales remains to be seen, but expect to see more in the coming years.

have been in the business since 1986. On a recent visit, we saw several large racks of name-brand designer bridal gowns from $200 to $1500 (most average $300 to $600). You can buy off-the-rack and save 40% or more—or special order a gown at a 25% discount. We also saw discounted headpieces for just $25 to $90. Yes, some readers have been put off by Proteus' discount digs (they are located in a somewhat grimy neighborhood near downtown San Francisco), but we found the deals to be worth the effort and the staff to be quite friendly. Parking can be difficult.

Looking for a Vera Wang bridal gown? How about one for $47? Yep that's the incredible steal one of our readers snagged at another San Francisco discounter, JEREMYS (Two South Park, corner of Brannan and 2nd Street, 415-882-4929). Jeremys sells discontinued designer samples from tony department stores. One caveat: Jeremys doesn't ALWAYS have bridal gown samples in stock. Call before you go.

♥ JCPENNEY (800) 222-6161 has 12 "catalog outlets stores" that carry bridal in a few states (most of which are in the Midwest). Our readers have praised the selection and prices for both bridal gowns and bridesmaids dresses. One reader found a bridal gown for just $305 at a Penney's outlet that was very similar to a gown at David's that was "reduced" to $500 on sale. Call your local JCPenney store for outlet locations near you.

♥ Arizona brides can find deals on bridal gowns at AFFORDABLE BRIDAL WAREHOUSE in Phoenix (5533 N. 7th Street, 602-279-4933). This shop sells first-quality over-runs from several famous designers from 30%

REAL WEDDING TIP

Penney's outlet bargains

Barbara C. of Ontario, CA saved nearly 50% on an Alfred Angelo bridal gown by visiting a Penney's outlet store that carries bridal:

"The JCPenney outlet store in the Ontario Mills Outlet Center has a good selection of dresses, both bridal and bridesmaids. Low and behold, in just 20 minutes, I walked out with the dress of my dreams: an Alfred Angelo originally priced for $525, but at the outlet, it was $299. Plus, I opened a credit card account there and saved another $50 because of a 15% discount. Tax included, I paid $275.00! It is gorgeous! I recommend all brides in the area to check this out—it might be worth your while. Ontario Mills outlet is at the intersection of the 10 and 15 freeways in Ontario, CA."

to 70% off. Prices range from $99 to $799 (the average is $400). Most gowns are sold off-the-rack (sizes 4 to 44), but special orders are also discounted about 10% to 20% off retail. Affordable Bridal Wearhouse also sells bridesmaids gowns (by special order), flower girl dresses (starting at $39), shoes, bras, veils, headpieces, and other accessories.

Gown Preservation: The Dirty Little Secret of the Bridal Industry?

Bridal gowns in dress shops take an incredible amount of abuse. Make-up stains, filthy hemlines, lace that gets dirty—repeated try-ons can turn the most beautiful white gown into a mess.

So, if a bridal gown gets stained, do dress shops send it out to one of those expensive, national gown cleaners? Or even a local dry cleaner? Nope, here's the surprising secret: most bridal shops just pop that dirty gown into a washing machine in the back of the store.

You read right—many dress shops simply wash bridal gowns in a regular washing machine to remove dirt, make-up stains and other signs of wear and tear. Now, we find this highly ironic since many of these same shops pitch their customers to use very expensive, nationwide "gown preservation" companies that charge $150, $250 or more to "preserve" the gown after the wedding. In a business where "custom-ordered" gowns require $150 in alterations and accessories like veils are grossly overpriced, this is probably the final insult to brides who have traversed the wedding industry—the gown preservation scam.

Just what do these gown preservation companies do for all this money? Well, just ask recent bride Shelley Brown-Parish of Hampton Falls, NH. On the advice of the bridal shop where she bought the gown, she paid $250 to Nationwide Gown Cleaning Service of Flushing, NY to clean and preserve her $3800 Scaasi wedding gown using their Zurcion method. The allegedly clean gown was returned to her in a sealed box, along with a notice saying if the box was opened, the company would not guarantee the dress.

Four years later, Brown decided to sell the gown and took it to a local consignment shop. When the box was opened, she was horrified. "The entire gown had changed color from white to ivory," she said, noting it had "large yellow stains all over the dress, blue ball-point pen marks on the front and on the train, and also had blood stains where the gown had been fastened to the tissue in the preservation box." Nationwide Gown Cleaning (which also goes under the names Continental Gown Cleaning and Prestige Gown Cleaning) said they'd re-clean the gown and have it back to her in two weeks.

One year later, Brown still didn't have her dress.

After complaining to the Better Business Bureau and bringing her story to the *Boston Globe*, the company still refused to return her dress. So, she sued them. After a local TV station picked up the chase, she finally got the gown back, which was *still* dirty and now smelled of cigarette smoke! The dress is now so famous it was featured on a recent NBC's "Leeza" show on wedding scams as an example of what can go wrong with these gown preservation companies.

Thankfully, the Federal Trade Commission is also on the case. In May 1998, the FTC sued Nationwide (Prestige) Gown Cleaning, charging them with false advertising and deceptive trade practices. Specifically, the FTC charged that Nationwide/Prestige broke the law by claiming its Zurcion method was the only method by which dresses could be cleaned—and for failing to disclose to consumers the conditions of its warranty (which forbids brides from opening their gown boxes). At press time, Nationwide is contesting the charges and the suit is unresolved.

So what lessons does this have for other brides?

First, we think this whole "gown preservation box" scheme is a rip-off. According to the National Association of Resale and Thrift Shops, over 80% of bridal gowns brought into re-sale shops to be consigned in their original, unopened, sealed boxes are found to be dirty. These national gown preservation companies are duping brides into thinking their gowns are being preserved when evidence shows they're not even being *cleaned*. Here's our advice for brides who want to preserve their gowns:

1. Don't. If you're saving the dress for your daughter, you're assuming the dress will fit her, not have yellowed or gone out of style. That's a slim shot at best. A better idea: donate your gown to the charity gown sale run by the Making Memories foundation. Donating your gown not only gives you a tax deduction, but also affords another bride a good deal—and all the proceeds go to breast cancer patients. Check their web site at www.makingmemories.org for details.

2. We recommend consigning your dress at a local re-sale shop as soon as possible after the wedding. Or try selling your gown on eBay.com. Why? Styles change and dresses start to age quickly. Take the money and put it towards a savings account for your first child.

3. Clean and preserve it yourself. Most bridal gowns are made of synthetic fabrics (satin, taffeta, organza and tulle) that can be cleaned in a washing machine. Cold water, a gentle cycle and a pure detergent (no fabric softeners or bleach) is best. Some bridal shop owners first spray the inside and outside of the dress with Shout or Spray 'N Wash. Hang dry on a plastic hanger. Note: before washing, you should test the beading or pearls. Place one bead/pearl in cold water for ten minutes and see if it disintegrates (some designers use very cheap pearls). If it passes the test, you can clean the gown at home.

4. After the dress is clean, wrap it in a clean, dry, white cotton sheet. If you want to stuff it with tissue paper, make sure it's acid free paper (available from local arts supplies or craft stores or call the Container Store at 800-733-3532). Put it in an acid-free box (also available from the sources above) and store it in a cool dry place—no attics or basements.

5. If this sounds too daunting, take/send it to a reputable cleaner. Nope, we don't have any specific recommendations for gown preservation companies, but whatever source you use (local or national), be sure to check references and the Better Business Bureau to see if the cleaner has a good record. Another tip: if the gown is expensive (over $500), insist that the shop only release the gown when you show a photo ID.

One final caveat—even if you do all the above steps and use that acid-free box, there is no guarantee that the dress won't yellow. Whether you pop that dress in the Maytag or send it to an expensive gown preservation company, there is still a good chance it will discolor.

Bridal Magazines: Friend or Foe?

One of the first things you probably did after you got engaged was trot down to your local newsstand and pick up a copy of a bridal magazine. Hoping to find answers to wedding questions, you thumbed through all the glossy advertisements.

But what kind of advice are these magazines giving consumers? And who's side are they on anyway? The short answer is: not yours. And the advice is silly at best. For example, in a special section titled "A Lavish Wedding For Less," *Bride's* magazine reveals that "the fewer prints you choose for your photo album, the less you'll pay." No kidding.

One glaring example of dumb bridal magazine advice was a whopper in *Bride's* June/July 1997 issue. In an article on how to avoid costly alterations when buying a bridal gown, the editors advise brides to "order the gown in a length you need so the hem won't have to be altered. A customized hem may cost 10% to 15% more." The problem: while many designers offer extra length, the vast majority of bridal gown makers will NOT allow you to specify the *exact* length needed. Most just sell you an extra six inches—then you'll probably have to shorten the dress, incurring those alterations costs you were trying to avoid.

Of course, *Modern Bride* magazine is just as absurd. In an article titled, "50 ways to Stretch Your Wedding Dollars," the rocket scientists at *Modern Bride* suggest "hiring a professional wedding planner." Later, they advise "stick to your budget. If you want a more expensive dress, cut back in another area." Sure.

Even that arbiter of New England taste and blue light specials, Martha Stewart, isn't immune to passing out misleading information to engaged couples. In a recent wedding issue of her namesake magazine, she claims that "samples allow a bride to select a style; (then) each dress is custom-made to fit the bride." Be sure to send Martha your alterations bill when that custom-made dress needs some nips and tucks.

Of course, suspiciously missing in all these articles are any real tips on saving money on such items as the bridal gown. Why, you might ask? Just take a look at these magazines—the majority of their advertising comes from bridal designers. And those designers would prefer you buy a dress at full retail. Forget about renting or discount sources.

In a 1992 article in the *Wall Street Journal*, *Bride's* magazine admitted to blocking ads from companies that discount or rent dresses. Rather sexist from a magazine that takes plenty of ads for guys tux rentals, eh? And it's ironic that Bride's and the other bridal magazines have plenty of ads for discounted, mail-order *invitations*. Somehow getting a good deal on invites is fine, but a discount on dresses is wrong?

"*Bride's* has NEVER accepted these ads," the publisher said in a letter to full-price retailers, reprinted in the *Journal*. "[We] believe that these can only hurt your business." And the magazine's.

WEDDING PARTY APPAREL

Pop quiz: can you name 12 ways to find a bridesmaids dress that won't break the bank? And doesn't look hideous? We reveal the answers, plus review the hottest maids' designers and the best mail order catalogs. Finally, let's not forget the groom—we'll take a look at tuxedos and several ways to cut that expense.

Bridesmaids' Gowns

What Are You Buying?

Perhaps nothing symbolizes what's wrong with the "wedding industry" more than the bridesmaid's gown. Have you seen any of these abominations to fashion? Cheap polyester fabric, ugly colors, absurd detailing—it seems like a bridesmaid's gown can transform any woman into a shiny satin nightmare. What's most appalling about bridesmaids' gowns is that they are actually designed that way! It's a crime against nature.

We're not sure why bridesmaids' gowns are designed as "disposable" dresses, meant to be worn for only one day and then thrown away. The most popular price range for bridesmaids dress is $130 to $160, although you can find maids gowns for as little as $79 in catalogs. On the upper end, the "couture" bridesmaids designers expect you to shell out $200 to $300 for their creations. And, of course, those figures don't include expensive alterations—er, "custom fitting."

The most hilarious part of this travesty is the suggestion by bridal shops that (are you ready for this?) most of their bridesmaids' gowns can be worn again! Yea, right. How many New Year's Eve parties have you been to where women wore bridesmaids' gowns? Please, we wish these bridal shop owners would stop saying such drivel. Ninety-nine percent of all bridesmaids' gowns are banished to the back of the closet within hours of the wedding.

Anyway, your bridesmaids have to wear something to your wedding. So here are our suggestions.

Our Recommendations for Bridesmaids' Gowns

♥ BUY THE CHEAPEST BRIDESMAIDS' GOWNS YOU CAN STOMACH. Some of the basic styles sell for about $100. For example: Penney's bridal catalog shows bridesmaids gowns starting at $89. And Mori Lee's bridesmaids may not be the best quality (see review later in this chapter), but hey, you can't beat the prices ($100 to $135). The nicest thing you can do for your bridesmaids who are on a tight budget is not burden them with paying for a $300 gown that they can only wear once.

♥ CONSIDER AN ALTERNATIVE TO TYPICAL BRIDESMAIDS' GOWNS. Yes, there *are* beautiful gowns your bridesmaids could actually wear again. As you might expect, these gowns are designed not by bridal designers, but by "ready-to-wear" manufacturers. Check out a department store or mail-order catalog for possibilities. One bride told us she found beautiful *silk* dresses at Talbot's (call 800-225-8204 for a catalog or store near you) for just $90 to $168. See later in this chapter for more info on Talbot's and other mail order catalogs.

Brides in Cyberspace: What's on the Web?
Chadwicks
Web: www.chadwicks.com, see Figure 1.

What it is: The online outpost for affordable maids gowns.

What's cool: Chadwick's is perhaps the best alternative to shelling out $200 on a maids' gown at specialty stores. This crisply designed web site features a dozen gowns in their "social dresses" category that could easily double as bridesmaids dresses. And the prices! An amazing $59 to $139, with some stunning choices UNDER $100. Chadwicks boasts a nice variety of silhouettes and current looks, from strapless dresses to ballgowns.

Figure 1: Whoa! A stylish bridesmaids gown for just $89? Chadwicks makes it possible.

Needs work. Well, sizing is rather limited (just 4 to 16), although some styles are available in petites and woman's sizes. And the site suggests you call their toll-free number to order if this is for a bridal party, instead of ordering online. Also: Chadwicks doesn't always show all the available colors of a gown online; swatches would be helpful in those cases.

So, can you buy a bridesmaids dress online, direct from a designer at a low price? Well, not yet. Some designers are experimenting with the 'net—Alfred Sung quietly hawks their bridesmaids dresses from a separate site (www.BestBridesmaid.com), but the prices are no steal (about $30 OVER retail). And newcomer A.B.S. by Allan Schwartz is selling online (see review later in this chapter). However, most big bridesmaids designers (After Six, Bill Levkoff, Watters & Watters) use the web just as a virtual catalog and direct brides to retailers to place orders. But the day for online bridesmaids dress sales may be just around the corner. Stay tuned.

Getting Started: How Far In Advance?

Most bridesmaids' gowns take two to four months to special order from bridal shops. If you are getting married in popular summer months, give yourself a little more time. In general, once you have selected the bridal gown, begin the search for bridesmaids' apparel. What if you don't have four months? Most of the major bridesmaids makers offer "rush service"—a limited selection of styles available in about six to eight weeks. Mail-order catalogs take only a week or two to ship most in-stock gowns. And don't forget David's (reviewed in the last chapter). This off-the-rack chain does carry some in-stock maids' gowns in a variety of sizes.

Step-by-step Shopping Strategies

♥ **Step 1:** After buying your bridal gown (and hence deciding on the setting and formality of your wedding), start the search for bridesmaids' gowns. Shopping for brides-maids' dresses before you find your gown will only distract you.

♥ **Step 2:** Take into account your bridesmaids' ability to pay for the dress. (Traditionally, the bridesmaid pays for her gown plus alterations.) Are your bridesmaids starving college students or dot-com entrepreneurs earning six figures a year? Obviously, this is a big factor in your decision.

♥ **Step 3:** Given the financial condition of your attendants, start the shopping process. Follow much the same steps as for finding a bridal gown. Look at fabrics, finishes, and styles.

♥ **Step 4:** When you decide on a gown, announce your decision to the bridesmaids. Make sure each bridesmaid is individually measured and receives a written receipt that specifies the manufacturer, style number, size and delivery date.

♥ **Step 5:** Be sure to leave two weeks or more for alterations—even longer if the dresses have to be shipped to out-of-town bridesmaids. Get written cost estimates on any alterations before the order is placed.

Top Money-saving Secrets

1 **Package Discounts.** If you order your gown from a bridal shop, they may offer a discount if you order all the bridesmaids' dresses there as well. This discount can range from 10% to 20%. Sometimes this is negotiable, so ask. (Be aware that some bridal shops mark up maids' gowns before they offer you a "discount." See the pitfalls section later in this chapter for more on this. Always check prices with a couple of sources to make sure you are getting a true discount).

2 **Rent or buy second hand.** Resale/consignment shops often carry matching bridesmaids' gowns at attractive prices in a range

of sizes. Rental stores rent bridesmaids' gowns at a fraction of retail prices. Some stores that rent gowns: Formals Etc. has six stores in Louisiana and three in Houston that rent bridal gowns (for $200 to $300) and bridesmaids dresses ($75). Call (318) 640-3766 (web: www.formalsetc.com) to find a location near you. Formals Etc. even offers "combo" packages with a bridal gown, headpiece, slip and shoes for $325. Another rental store: if you live in Kansas City, check out An Alternative (888) 761-8686 or (816) 761-8686.

3 **Check out the discounters.** Two possibilities: Discount Bridal Service and the discount gown web sites reviewed in the last chapter. Typical savings run 20% to 40%, depending on the brand.

4 **Sew your own.** What's a bridesmaid-style dress, anyway? A basic dress pattern with little detailing or fuss. And can't you just buy typical bridesmaid fabrics like taffeta or crepe at a fabric store? We've heard from several brides who had their favorite aunt sew their bridesmaids dresses. While not a solution for everyone, this concept has its merits.

5 **Pick a color, any color.** Instead of forcing all the bridesmaids to wear the same dress, just give them a color (a swatch is best) and then have them buy separate dresses. Sure, they won't exactly match in style, but who cares? Let the bridesmaids shop their favorite dress shop and find a style that they can wear again. (One tip: suggest to the brides a basic style or skirt length). Obviously, you can't be a control freak to follow this tip, but it might be worth a shot.

6 **Hit the department stores.** Thanks to a change in fashion trends, hip bridesmaids dresses now look much like the same offerings found in department stores. And there's good news: those department stores offer much lower prices (and higher quality) than bridal shops. One reader emailed us to point out that Bloomingdales has many bridesmaid-looking dresses that are available off-the-rack or orderable in different colors, sizes, lengths, etc. She hit a sale and got her dresses for just $60. Even if you pay full price (about $100 to $200 at most stores), you can at least try on several styles, colors and sizes right in the store. Plus you don't have to wait for an eternity for a "special" order to arrive—most department stores will track down different colors/sizes at nearby locations. Another option: mix and match separates. Dillard's department stores (web: www.dillards.com) launched a line of Alex Evenings satin separates in sizes 4-18 in four colors. Match a top (four choices from $59 to $69) and a skirt (another four options ($69 to $89) and you've got a stylish look at 30% less than what bridal specialty stores charge. (The only bummer: it takes 10 to 12 weeks to order; contact their Tonight's Occasion department for more details).

7 **Buy the gloves at a discount.** Don't pay high retail prices for bridesmaids gloves—we found a mail order outfit, Discount Gloves (800-479-4696; www.bridalgloves.com), that offers a 20% to 30% discount off nationally-advertised gloves. It works like Discount Bridal Service: to identify the gloves, give them the page number of a magazine ad or the bridesmaid dress info (style, color, etc.)—they do the rest. Most full-length gloves (made by the same companies advertised in bridal magazines) are only $20 a pair. And there is no charge for shipping or sales tax (if you're outside New York state). The same company also discounts matching handbags and other maids' accessories.

8 **Do it by mail.** Who says you have to order a bridesmaids dress from a bridal shop? The best bargains are often from mail order catalogs like Talbot's (which has retail stores and a web site as well, see below), Bloomingdales by Mail (800) 777-0000, Spiegel (800) 345-4500 and Chadwick's of Boston. Heck, even Penney's (800) 527-8345 (web: www.jcpenney.com) has a web site and catalog that sell bridesmaids gowns for as little as $89. Another key advantage to mail order: returns. Get in a size that doesn't fit? A flaw in the dress? Most catalogs have a "no hassle" return policy that makes exchanges a snap. Contrast that with some bridal retailers whose attitude when something goes wrong is: "Tough! Even if all the sizes are wrong, you ordered those hot fuchsia dresses with butt bows on a NON-RETURNABLE basis, honey!"

Both Talbot's and Chadwicks have been singled out by our readers for great deals. Here are some details:

♥ **TALBOT'S.** (800) 882-5268; web: www.talbots.com A nice selection of dresses retails for about $150, but we've seen sales with prices about $100 to $125 (some designs are silk). Talbot's winter sale is a must-see event, with prices as much as 75% off. If you live in Massachusetts, check out the Talbot's outlet in Hingham. One reader said she found beautiful navy blue dresses for just $11.60 each!

♥ **CHADWICK'S OF BOSTON.** (800) 525-6650; web: www.chadwicks.com. Yes, we've already reviewed Chadwicks earlier in our CyberBride section, but don't forget about their catalog as well. You can find an amazing selection of bridesmaids gowns for just $59 to $139. A reader in Chicago had great success with a Chadwicks dress for her bridesmaids: "Sure, it's a cheesy little catalog full of cheaply made, frilly looking clothes. But who cares? The girls will never wear their dresses again, but they were perfect for my garden wedding." Even when you add in matching shoes (which Chadwicks also sells) and shipping, your bridesmaids can escape for $125 or less for a total outfit. One tip: order early, since popular items tend to get back-ordered.

As a side note, you can also go mail order to save money on other parts of the bridesmaids ensemble like hosiery. One Hanes Place catalog and web site (800) 300-2600 (web: www.onehanesplace.com) sells "slightly imperfect" hosiery for 40% off retail. If you want your bridesmaids to wear matching hosiery, check out their Silk Reflections line in eight colors for just $9.32 for 4 pairs. The catalog we saw also featured a 50% off close-out on a textured pair of hose for just $3.75 per pair, in eight different colors. The more you buy, the bigger the discount. We've seen similar pantyhose in bridal retail shops for three or four times the prices in this catalog.

9 **Avoid rush cuts.** Bridesmaids dresses are expensive enough when ordered at full retail. Add in that extra "rush" fee (incurred when you order a dress with less than two to three months before your wedding) and you'll see the price rise another 20%. Don't delay making this decision as you plan the rest of your wedding.

10 **For shoes, go surfing.** Avoid retail stores and their $70 price tags. The web has many discount sources for dye-to-match satin shoes. In addition to those sources mentioned in Chapter 2 (see the Accessories box), Discount Dyeables (www.discountdyeables.com, see Figure 2) has shoes that start at an amazing $28. The site even carries dyed-to-match handbags. And, no, you don't have to go to a fancy retail

Figure 2: Why have your maids shell out $70 for dyeable satin shoes when you can find them online for $28?

shop and pay through the nose for dyeing (most web sites don't offer dyeing services). Our advice: go to a shoe repair shop. They charge $5 to $15 a pair for dyeing—and don't forget to negotiate a discount if you have more than four pairs.

A few notes about dyed-to-match shoes: the dye is NOT water proof. If you are planning an outdoor wedding, remember wet grass can cause the dye to run and stain. It is also difficult to get every last shoe to match; and the color may look different in outdoor light compared to indoors.

11 **Hit the outlet stores.** Many of the stores we mention in this chapter have outlet stores. Check the web site Outlet Bound (web: www.outletbound.com) to see if one is near you. Examples: Talbot's has ten outlets around the U.S.; Spiegel has 17 outlets. While

BRIDESMAID OPTIONS

Why spend $200+ on a bridesmaids gown from a bridal shop when you can get a similar gown from a department store or catalog at HALF the price? Here's how several options compare to the standard issue bridesmaids dress found in bridal stores (we used a Levkoff gown for comparison):

WHERE	WHAT	PRICE	FABRIC
LEVKOFF (AT A BRIDAL SHOP)	STRAPLESS 2-PIECE SLIP DRESS	$158; OTHERS $120-$250	POLY TAFFETA
SPIEGEL SPIEGEL.COM	STRAPLESS SLIP DRESS	$79; OTHERS $90-$124	POLY VELVET
CHADWICKS CHADWICKS.COM	SLEEVELESS DRESS WITH ROSETTE TRIMMED SHIRRED, EMPIRE BODICE.	$99; OTHERS $79-$139	POLY CHIFFON FULLY LINED
BLOOMINGDALES BLOOMINGDALES.COM	SLEEVELESS STRETCH LACE BODICE, GATHERED AT WAIST	$99; OTHERS $79-$110	NYLON, ACETATE

Notes: As you can see, the biggest advantage to ordering a standard "bridesmaids dress" like a Bill Levkoff design from a bridal shop is the wide availability of sizes and colors. Few mail order sources sell large sizes (above a 16 or 18) and extra length is rarely available. Colors are also limited—if your heart is set on a particular odd color, a standard bridesmaids dress might be the only solution. Another advantage to this tip is more hit or miss depending on when you go, it might be worth a trip if you have an outlet within close driving distance.

12 **Skip the accessories.** Bridesmaids designers have been turning out all manner of matching accessories like shawls, purses and shoes in recent seasons. The prices, however, are outrageous. Watters & Watters now pitches matching purses for $44 and satin dyeable shoes for $90 to $144! Shawls and wraps add another $30 to $60 to After Six's dresses. Remember you can buy some items like dyeable satin pumps online for just $30 or so. And try to avoid needing a shawl or wrap by selecting a bridesmaids style that isn't so bare to begin with. Finally, just skip some superfluous items altogether. Do your bridesmaids really need a $44 handbag died to match their chartreuse gowns?

COMPARED

SIZES	COMMENTS	RETURNABLE?
SIZES 4-22 SOME STYLES IN 38-42	AVAILABLE IN 18 COLORS DELIVERY: 12-14 WKS. SHIPPING INCLUDED	ARE YOU KIDDING?
MISSES (4 TO 16) DELIVERY 3-6 DAYS	TWO COLORS; SHIPPING $12	YES, EXCHANGE OR FULL REFUND
MISSES (4-18)	THREE COLORS; DELIVERY 6-9 DAYS SHIPPING $8-$12	YES, EXCHANGE OR FULL REFUND
MISSES (4-12)	TWO COLORS; DELIVERY 3-9 DAYS SHIPPING: $10.95-$12.95	YES, EXCHANGE OR FULL REFUND

standard bridesmaid gowns: they guarantee the dye lots will match if you order several gowns. Of course, you pay for that, almost TWICE the price of mail order options. Plus delivery is much quicker using mail-order and department stores, a matter of days versus 12-14 WEEKS for a standard issue bridesmaid gown.

Helpful Hints

1 **Don't go shopping with more than one brides-maid.** If you want to make the process of shopping for bridesmaids' gowns go as smoothly as possible, just take along ONE friend or relative. Too many bridesmaids (each with their own opinions and tastes) will only complicate the decision. Make the decision and announce it to the other bridesmaids. Don't expect everyone to love your decision (and, unfortunately, some bridesmaids may be tacky enough to tell you about it to your face).

2 **You may be on the hook for deadbeat bridesmaids or groomsmen.** Here's an ominous trend: some bridal retailers are forcing brides and grooms to sign contracts that say they are responsible for payment on ANY dress purchase or tux rental by their wedding party. Yes, when your flaky maid of honor passes a hot check to the bridal shop for the balance on her bridesmaid gown, YOU could be on the hook. While we sympathize with any retailer when it comes to dealing with deadbeats, forcing couples to cough up money is a bit much. We would urge couples to refuse to sign such deals.

Pitfalls to Avoid

PITFALL #1 SQUARE PEG, ROUND HOLE.

"Help! I want my bridesmaids to wear this slinky dress I saw in the magazines, but when we went to order, none of the girls fit the size chart! The bridal shop recommended a size 14 for a girl who normally wears a size 6. When the dress comes in, won't she be socked with expensive alterations?"

Do you have the body of a supermodel? Well, we sure don't. But, unfortunately, most bridesmaids dress manufacturers have size charts that are designed for bizarre, alien woman with exaggerated Barbie Doll figures. Giraffes with breasts.

Take, for example, that above story. The bridesmaid in question had measurements of 36" bust, 29" waist, 37" hips. Now, look at the size chart for Jordan, one of the U.S. and Canada's biggest bridesmaids designers.

	SIZE								
	4	6	8	10	12	14	16	18	20
Bust	33	34	35	36	37	38.5	40	41.5	43.5
Waist	24	25	26	27	28	29.5	31	32.5	34.5
Hips	36	37	38	39	40	41.5	43	44.5	46.5

So, what size would YOU order? Let's see, the bridesmaids bust (measured at the fullest part of the chest; this is NOT her bra size) would fit into a size 10. BUT, look at that waist—it needs a size 14. And the hips? Try a size 6.

Because it is always easiest to alter IN a dress (instead of letting it out), we recommend ordering the size that corresponds to the bridesmaids LARGEST measurement. That would be a size 14. As you'll note, however, this will require significant alterations, as the dress will have to be taken in a couple inches at the bust and hips.

This problem has been exasperated in recent years by all the new, body-hugging styles churned out by bridesmaids designers. Those slinky dresses are definitely a step forward fashion-wise, but all this haute couture has run head long into the reality of women's bodies. The fact is, many bridesmaids just don't fit the bizarro size charts. As a result, some are being socked with HUGE alteration bills to remake (or drastically cut down) these gowns.

What makes this problem even more complex is the fact that each bridesmaids designer has just ONE size chart. This chart covers a wide range of dress styles, from a loosely fitting empire waisted gown to a body-hugging sheath. If you go for an empire-style dress (which is tightly fitted in the bust), the measurement that counts the most is, of course, the bust. But if you plan to have your bridesmaid don a slip dress, watch out—those waist and hip measurements will be critical.

One thing you can be sure of: almost all bridesmaids dresses require alterations. Even if a bridesmaid exactly matches the size chart, she'll still probably need some minor alterations (a skirt hem, a bodice tuck here and there). That's because these dresses are not custom-made to your measurements—heck, sometimes they don't even correspond closely to the size chart itself.

What if your bridesmaids are "off the chart," that is they don't closely correspond to the size charts? Do yourself and them a favor: DON'T order bridesmaids from a bridal shop. Instead, consider some of our alternative dress sources. Catalogs like Talbot's carry a wide range of sizes and (here's a shocker) actually let you return a dress that doesn't fit.

PITFALL #2 DISINTEGRATING BRIDESMAIDS DRESSES.

"I ordered five bridesmaids dresses from a major manufacturer. When they came in, I was shocked! Every single dress was defective. All of the dresses came out of the boxes with threads hanging from every seam and the seams all pulled and puckered. The buttons and loops on the backs of the dresses fell apart when the girls tried to button them. These had to be sewn on four of the five dresses one half hour before I was to be married! The most appalling defect of all was the lace on the front of one of the dresses. It was sewn on crooked and had to be taken off and reattached

*by a professional dressmaker. While my maid of honor was up at the altar
next to me, we could actually hear her dress popping apart."*

Yes, it's no wonder the bridesmaids dress is the biggest joke in the
fashion business. What's most frustrating about this purchase is the
"bait and switch" tactics of the largest bridesmaid manufacturers. Here's
how it works: the bridesmaid *samples* you first try on at the bridal shop
are always pristine and perfect. But what about your special order?
Somehow, the quality slips—and drops through the floor. Consumers we
interviewed describe the workmanship on many of these dresses in one
word: abysmal. And it's not just on the cheap dresses; the ones described
above cost $170 each, according to the bride.

An example of the quality problem with bridesmaids gowns are "invis-
ible zippers." Yes, these disappearing zippers (seen on such hip lines as
After Six and Dessy) are supposed to make gowns look more fashionable.
The only problem: they break, don't work well and cause general havoc.
Some shops have been so frustrated with invisible zippers (they call them
"miserable zippers") that they are replacing them during alterations.

Overall, the best advice we can give is to order early. Leaving enough
time will enable the shop to fix the problems. Another idea is to by-pass
the standard bridesmaid dress entirely. Select dresses at a department
store or from a catalog and have the last laugh.

Pitfall #3 Sizing problems

*"Our $200 bridesmaids gowns arrived yesterday and NONE of them fit
the girls! Some were too big; others too small. What happened?"*

Yes, you carefully shopped for bridesmaids gowns and made sure you
ordered the correct sizes for all the girls after comparing their measurements to the designer's size charts. But then the gowns come and
whamo! Nothing fits.

Yes, here's a dirty little secret of the bridesmaids dress biz: sometimes,
your "special order" gowns won't fit. That's because the bridesmaid
manufacturers goof with the sizing. Among the worst offenders: After
Six/Dessy, Mori Lee and Bari Jay.

What makes this more frustrating is there is little rhyme or reason to
the mis-sizing—some gowns come in too big; others are too small. Then,
adding insult to injury, some dress designers (notably Mori Lee and Bari
Jay) take a "its YOUR problem" attitude toward sizing goofs. Hard to
believe, but these manufactures think you getting such a deal on their
gowns that they refuse to fix any problems, leaving shops and brides
scrambling to alter mis-sized gowns. (On a positive note, even though
After Six/Dessy are guilty of mis-sizing, the designer is at least willing to
fix problems).

REAL WEDDING TIP

Delivery, sizing problems plague maids' order

This California bride wasn't happy with how her bridesmaids dress order from a local bridal shop turned out.

"I can't begin to tell you how disappointed and sorry we are to order maids gowns from a local shop. We were promised the gowns would takes eight weeks to order. At the end of the 15th week, I called them to see how much longer they would be. The owner said that nobody could have quoted me 8 weeks, they always quote between 10 and 12 weeks for bridesmaid dresses. She had no answer when I told her it was nearing 16 weeks! When the dresses arrived, each dress was almost two to three sizes too big. My smallest bridesmaid who wears a size 1 was ordered a size 4 dress. My sister who wears a size 4, was ordered a size 8 dress. What was the purpose of the 40 minute fitting, if they were all going to be issued dresses that were not ordered to fit them? Oh, I guess it was so that the girls could be charged an additional $100+ dollars for alterations on top of the $300 price tag for the dress. It just makes me sick!"

PITFALL #4 CLASHING COLOR MOTIFS.

"I was a bridesmaid in a wedding recently. The bride picked out lovely peach bridesmaids' gowns. Unfortunately, the church was all decorated in bright red—all her pictures looked like 'Night of the Clashing Circus Clowns!' It wasn't pretty."

Be careful when you select the bridesmaids' gowns to take into account the decor of your ceremony and reception site. Many of your wedding pictures will have the sites as a backdrop. Try to pick a color that not only pleases you but also doesn't clash with the decor.

PITFALL #5 DUPED BY DUPIONI.

"My bridesmaids ordered five dresses made of Dupioni silk. What a disaster! The dresses looked like the girls had slept in them and we couldn't iron those wrinkles out!"

Dupioni silk is one of those hip fabrics for bridesmaids dresses that doesn't actually live up to its billing. While the sample dress you first try on may look fine, the actual dresses may have flaws like slubs, dark threads, wrinkles and more. Designers say these "flaws add to the character of the fabric and are part of its natural beauty." Nice try. We think the designers are trying to pass off low-quality silks on an unsuspecting public. You don't pay that much money for dresses that look like they've been slept in. Our best advice is to ask the shop to see a recently arrived order of dresses from that manufacturer—that way you can see what you'll be getting. Or just avoid Dupioni silk dresses altogether.

Pitfall #6 Dye lots may vary.

"I would like to order bridesmaids gowns from two different stores (in different towns). The shop owners all have told me that they won't guarantee that the colors will match, since the fabric will be from different dye lots. Is that true? Could you really tell the difference?"

If you've got bridesmaids scattered across the country, it may be tempting to have them go to a local bridal shop to order the same dress. Our advice: don't. It is true that dye lots can (and do) vary from one batch of dresses to another. The only way to insure they will all match is to order them from the same source at the same time (shipping the ones to out-of-town bridesmaids; they'll have to get their fittings done locally).

Would you really be able to tell a difference in the dye lots? It's hard to say. That depends on the color and fabric—some styles might show more of a color variation than others. It's not worth the risk.

Pitfall #7 Sight unseen colors.

"I ordered $300 bridesmaids dresses in 'blue onyx' from a local bridal shop. The only problem? I didn't see the color chart or a swatch before ordering. The shop had samples in green and burgundy, but only a catalog picture of the blue. When the dresses came in, I was shocked. The color looked nothing like the picture and was terrible!"

Since bridal shops carry a limited amount of inventory, you may be tempted to order a bridesmaids dress in a color you can't see. You may want a velvet dress in "cranberry," but the shop only carries the same style in a "hunter green" taffeta. And even the same color can look different in certain fabrics (velvets versus chiffons, etc.).

The best protection is to insist on seeing a color swatch or color chart to make sure it is what you want. Catalog pictures can be notoriously unreliable—funky lighting in the photo or simple variations in printing can make a "deep plum" dress seem more like bright purple.

Another related problem: designers who use combo fabrics. To spice up their collections, some designers will combine a velvet bodice with organza sleeves. The only problem? The colors in different fabrics might not match as you think they should.

The quote above is an actual email we received from a New Jersey bride. Unfortunately, she was stuck with dresses she described as "god-awful ugly." (Actually, she used more colorful language than that, but you get the idea.) The bridal shop asked the manufacturer to fix the problem and guess what? The manufacturer refused, saying "that's what 'blue onyx' is supposed to look like."

We expect to see more complaints like this in the future. Bridesmaids' dress designers are rolling out more "sophisticated" gowns, with fancy fabrics, two-tone colors and other doo-dads. The sheer variety of choices is overwhelming some retail stores, who don't have samples or swatches that show the myriad of options. As a result, brides are gambling on a color or fabric choice, sometimes with less-than-great results. (Another frustration: some designers even charge for small swatches).

The bottom line: make sure you see the color(s) in the fabric(s) you want before committing to a special-order bridesmaids dress.

PITFALL #8 MARK IT UP TO MARK IT DOWN.

"The bridal shop where I bought my gown offered a 10% discount on maids gowns. That sounded great until I did some price shopping. I found the shop was marking up the gowns over retail before they gave me a 'discount.'"

Fake discounts are a problem in the bridal industry. We've seen retailers confess to the "mark it up before you mark it down" scam—shops will price dresses OVER retail before they give you a so-called "discount." A word to the wise: do some price shopping before you commit to any package deal.

Another trend: no-name bridesmaids dresses. More and more retailers are now carrying "stealth" bridesmaids gowns by no-name manufacturers like Le Stella (888) 626-7888; web: www.lestella.com) and Alexia (800) 235-0681. Don't look for those gowns advertised in bridal magazines or on the web—these makers keep a very low profile. The gowns are typically knock-offs of designer gowns, sewn overseas and sold to retailers at low wholesale prices. Retailers then can feel free to mark-up no-name gowns whatever they want, since it is so hard to price-shop these dresses.

What's worse: some shops do a bait and switch with no-name dresses. We've seen several reports of bridesmaids who ordered a name brand gown and then got a no-name knock-off. One bride ordered a Levkoff dress and got a Alexia copy. How can you prevent this? Be sure you get a written order ticket that indicates the manufacturer's name. Some shops only put their bogus in-house codes on order forms, making it hard to prove what was promised. Then when the bridesmaids dresses come in, check for the designer's label. A telltale sign of the knock-off scam are maids dresses that come in missing designer labels (legit designers like Levkoff almost always put tags in).

Reviews of Selected Bridesmaids Designers

With over $500 million worth of bridesmaids dresses sold each year, there are certainly no shortage of options to consider. Besides manufacturers that just make bridesmaids dresses (Levkoff, Jordan), there are many bridal gown designers that make maids' dresses too. But who has the best quality? The best value for the dollar?

To answer those questions, we intensively research all the different brands, designers and manufacturers. We attend industry wholesale markets to view runway shows and inspect garments. We also talk with retailers about which dresses are best . . . and worst. Finally, we hear from you, the reader. Our email box is flooded each month with questions and comments about bridesmaids gowns.

Please note: these manufacturers do not sell gowns directly to consumers. Call the phone numbers to locate a local store or dealer that carries each designer. Here's a round-up of what's out there:

THE RATINGS

A	EXCELLENT . . . .OUR TOP PICK!	
B	GOOD . . . . . . .ABOVE AVERAGE QUALITY, PRICES AND CREATIVITY.	
C	FAIR . . . . . .COULD STAND SOME IMPROVEMENT.	
D	POOR . . . . . . .YUCK! COULD STAND MAJOR IMPROVEMENT.	

A.B.S. by Allan Schwartz Designer Allan Schwartz's claim to fame is his instant knock-offs of Oscar gowns. His new bridesmaid line made a splashy debut at the recent bridal market, with bright colors (watermelon, fuchsia, chartreuse) and a mix of both two-piece ensembles and assembled gowns. Tops include strapless, thin-strapped and halter styles, while skirts range from mid-calf to floor-length. As we mentioned in the bridal gown chapter, this designer is part of a new breed of gown maker—ABS sells gowns online on their own web site and in stores, both specialty bridal shops and department stores like Saks and Bloomingdales. On the down side, the prices are a bit too high ($200 to $300) and sizing is very limited (2 to 14). Perhaps the best bargain is to get an ABS bridesmaid in white as a bridal gown—now, *that* is a deal. ABS is too new for us to get a read on their quality and reliability, but given their track record in department stores, we expect it to be above average. *Sizes 2 to 14. For a dealer near you, call (212) 398-0330. Web: www. absstyle.com.* **Rating: B+**

After Six After Six isn't just the hottest new bridesmaids designer out on the market today; the company is a bona-fide *phenomenon*. This line was launched by veteran maids' maker Dessy in 1999 and quickly shot to the top of the retail sales charts. Why? Check out the styling—After Six hit the "two-piece" trend right as it took off, with stylish mix-and-match ensembles in a variety of hip hues. And the prices are fantastic: dresses sell for $132 to $178 (shawls and wraps run $28 to $50 extra), much less than similar looks by competitors like Levkoff or Watters and Watters. And After Six has another ace up its sleeve: it provides FREE samples of gowns to retailers, virtually guaranteeing shops will push the dresses to brides (all other bridesmaids makers charge shops for samples). So how is the quality? We'd say it is average, given the price point. Yes, After Six has had a few bumps (their invisible zippers were cursed by retailers for their tendency to easily break), but overall we've been impressed. *Sizes 4 to 24 with an extra charge of $30 to $50 for sizes 18 to 24. For a dealer near you, call (800) 444-8304 or (212) 354-5808. Web: www.aftersix.com.* **Rating: A**

Alfred Angelo Like their bridal gowns, Alfred Angelo's bridesmaids dresses have never been on the cutting-edge of fashion. Yet, we have to give them bonus points for trying—many of the new fashions reflect an updated look with empire waists and A-line silhouettes. The value of the dresses, on the other hand, could use some work. Prices start at $118, but most gowns average $150 to $200. That's rather pricey for dresses made of polyester satin or crepe. And what about the quality? Well, when industry wags refer to bridesmaids gowns as "disposable dresses," guess who they are talking about? Angelo added to its own woes with several mis-steps, including a bruising union fight in the mid 1990's that still leaves a bad taste in the mouth of retailers who remember the delays, missed shipments and worse. *Sizes 4 to 44, but only selected styles are available in large sizes. For sizes 18 and 20, add $10. For sizes 38 to 44, add $30. Call (800) 531-1125, (800) 528-3589, (561) 241-7755 for a dealer near you. Web: www.alfredangelo.com.* **Rating: D-**

Alteration-friendly bridesmaid gowns

Not all bridesmaids gowns are made equal—and some are easier to alter than others. Bridal retailers tell us the GOOD bridesmaids dresses (that is, easy to alter) are made by Alfred Angelo, Bridal Originals and After Six. The worst? Mori Lee, Levkoff (Champagne, New Image), McClintock and Bari Jay are the most difficult, thanks to a lack of seam allowance and other construction shortcuts.

Alyce Designs Alyce offers your basic, bread-and-butter bridesmaids look. As is the trend these days, Alyce is showing a variety of mix and match separates (seven skirts that can be paired with any of seven tops). The fabrics are mostly synthetic. While the quality of the gowns is average, Alyce gets better marks for its deliveries and reliability. The customer service is also very good. What's Alyce's biggest downside? The prices are no bargain. Gowns start at $158 and soar over $300. The average is about $200, too pricey for the quality of construction, in our opinion. Warning: Alyce has many of those combo fabric styles (chiffon sleeves with a crepe bodice, for example). The problem? Sometimes the different shades don't match. Make sure you see the dress you want in the desired color before ordering. *Most of Alyce's dresses are available in sizes 2 to 24 . . . but this designer has some bizarre exceptions. Quite a few styles are only made in more limited sizes (such as 4 to 16). Call (847) 966-9200 for a local dealer.* Web: www.alycedesigns.com **Rating: B**

B2. This is a subsidiary of Belsoie, reviewed below.

Bari Jay Lackluster designer Bari Jay is a good example of what's wrong with the bridesmaids market today—average dresses, average fashion . . . all at *above* average prices. We should note that this designer is trying harder in the fashion department—many of their recent gowns featured updated fabrics (like glimmer knit) and touches of embroidery. All this is similar to other designers; the only difference is Bari Jay's skirts, which are somewhat fuller than other designers. Like Alyce, the company also makes quite a few combo-fabric looks (combining satin and crepe) and several of those hip corsetted bodices. The prices? Are you sitting down? Bari Jay's dresses range from $170 to $232; most gowns are about $200. And the quality? Bari Jay only gets fair ratings from bridal retailers on this score. Customer service and reliability is average to below average. A big gripe about Bari Jay: their dresses often come in way too big, compared to their size chart. *Sizes 4 to 42 are available . . . but only a selected number of styles are available in large sizes 38 to 42. Another note: there are no seam allowances in many of Bari Jay's dresses, which means you should choose the size very carefully. For a dealer near you, call (212) 391-1555 or (212) 921-1551.* **Rating: C**

Belsoie Belsoie is the bridesmaids line of Jasmine that was launched amid big hoopla a few years ago. And the reaction from brides: a big yawn. We're not sure if the line's slow start was due to the dresses themselves or that brides seem to be rejecting all "bridesmaids" dresses in favor of gowns at department stores, catalogs and the like. Certainly, Belsoie's boring ads didn't help. Even though this line features innovative use of fabric, Belsoie's magazine ads failed to create much interest.

And that's a shame, in our opinion. For the money, this is a good dress (fabric, construction). Prices range from $190 to $254—that's not bad for a mostly all-silk line (there are a few styles with poly-chiffon). The looks are similar to Watters and Watters but at a price that's 20% to 40% less. If you want to spend even less, check out Belsoie's "B2" line for $150 to $180. The major difference here is the fabric, instead of silks, you'll find poly-satin, poly-crepe and so on. Kudos to Belsoie for their excellent web site, which lets you view their catalog complete with size and color information for each style. *For a dealer near you, call (800) 634-0224 or (630) 295-5880. Sizes 4 to 28 (with an extra charge for sizes 22 to 28). Web:www.belsoie.com.* **Rating: A–**

Bianchi Finally, a designer who makes stylish bridesmaids gowns that don't cost $300. Boston-based Bianchi is a small player in the bridesmaid market, but sets the style for other designers with their fitted silhouettes, A-lines and other current fashions. We loved the pearl button accents, two-tone designs, and delicate fabric roses. Bianchi divides its large bridesmaid line into three collections (similar to their bridal gowns). The regular maids (available in more stores) run $178 to $250. The Exclusives collection is $200 to $230; Tiamo bridesmaids run $200 to $260 (both Exclusives and Tiamo are available in fewer stores). Okay, that isn't cheap, but the quality of these gowns is excellent, as is Bianchi's delivery and reliability. *Sizes 2 to 24 are available, as well as petite sizes (1 to 13). Call (800) 669-2346 for a local dealer.* **Rating: B+**

Bill Levkoff Bill Levkoff is the 800 pound gorilla of bridesmaids manufacturers. Besides offering his own voluminous line, Levkoff owns (or has a significant ownership interest in) three other bridesmaids designers—Champagne, New Image, and Watters & Watters. (Since each of these other lines operates more or less independently, we'll review each separately.) Levkoff is the market's style leader, splashing his gowns over numerous pages of ads in most major bridal magazines. With over 100 styles, you'll see just about everything fabric and style-wise. Prices, however, are Levkoff's biggest drawback considering most of the fabrics are synthetic: gowns run $170 to $290. Even the separates collection is pricey ($100 to $120 for the tops; $110 to $120 for skirts). While the styles are innovative, the quality of the dresses is another story. On this subject, Levkoff dresses garner merely fair ratings. While Levkoff's *samples* are beautifully tailored, the actual dresses shipped to bridesmaids can be all over the board. We've even heard of problems that occurred within an individual order, where one dress is fine, a second has unfinished seams and a third has a mismatched zipper. To be fair, such consistency problems plague many bridesmaids makers, but we expect more from a market leader like Levkoff. If you plan to order Levkoff gowns, make sure you leave plenty of time to deal with any "surprises." *Sizing up to 42 on some styles, but no petites. Call (800) LEV-KOFF to find a local dealer. Web: www.billlevkoff.com* **Rating: C+**

Champagne Formals   Champagne is sort of like "Levkoff-lite:" same designs, less aftertaste. This division of Bill Levkoff offers many similar styles as their parent company, but at lower prices. A Champagne brides-maids gown is likely to cost $138 to $178. While Levkoff is a style leader, Champagne's fashion is all over the board. Basically, the trade-off is fewer details (no embroidery or beading) and less interesting fabric. The quality of Champagne's gowns is slightly better than its parent, Levkoff, although that isn't saying much. *Sizes 4 to 42, but no petites. Call (212) 302-9162 for a local dealer. Web: www.champagneformals.com.* **Rating: B-**

David's   We review this chain of off-the-rack stores in Chapter 2 under Best Buys. David's bridesmaids (sold under the names Michaelangelo and Oleg Cassini among others) have improved markedly over the last few years. But we still get complaints about the special order process at David's; a safer bet is to just buy off the rack if you can (see Chapter 2 for more details). **Rating: B**

Dessy Creations   You don't often hear the word "stylish" in the same sentence as "bridesmaid's designer," but this company is definitely the exception. Dessy has borrowed from hip, "ready-to-wear" looks to cre-ate some of the best styled bridesmaid's gowns on the market today. "Glamorous" is how we'd describe many of these dresses; you'll see looks reminiscent of Audrey Hepburn and others straight from the Oscars. Over 150 styles are available and Dessy's smart tailoring makes nearly every dress a winner. Unfortunately, all this glamour doesn't come cheap. Dessy gowns start at $178 and can soar to $238. Most are about $200, a big chunk of change to ask any bridesmaid to spend. And what about the quality? Well, while Dessy is well above average, it is

Are gown knock-offs legal?

It's a time-honored tradition in fashion: ripping-off your competi-tor's hot selling design. While you see design-stealing in bridal gowns, it's a virtual epidemic in the world of bridesmaids designs, where one "hot" style quickly appears in several different versions from different makers. And guess what? It's completely legal. Copyright laws do NOT cover apparel (except for logos and certain patterns of lace). Hence it is completely legal to buy a knock-off gown; or to have your aunt (or any seamstress) sew a copy of a hot style.

still a notch or two below industry leaders Bianchi and Watters & Watters. Hence, you're paying big bucks for a good (but not great) gown. On the upside, we like the fact that Dessy has a few "maternity styles" for pregnant bridesmaids, a first in the industry. Unfortunately, sizes are limited for everyone else (only 4 to 20, with no large sizes). Dessy's hot "After Six" division is reviewed earlier in this section. *Call (800) 52-DESSY or (212) 354-5808 to find a dealer near you. Web: www.dessy.com is among the best gown web sites we've seen, complete with on-line catalog (with color, size and price info!) and a store locator.* **Rating: B+**

Galina This designer has recently re-introduced its bridesmaids line after a several year hiatus. The very limited collection (about two dozen choices) ranges from $170 to $280. The styling is definitely current, with a mix of sleeveless sheaths and empire waist silhouettes. Among the unique aspects of this bridesmaid line is Galina's back treatments, with lots of low cut designs with accent bows or buttons. What about the quality? Galina gets good marks on quality, customer service and reliability. One negative: delivery is a little slow, taking 12 weeks on average. Rush cuts are offered "upon availability" for $50 extra. *Sizes 2 to 24. For a dealer near you, call (212) 564-1020. Web: www.galinabridals.com* **Rating: B+**

Jessica McClintock Yes, McClintock's bridesmaids dresses are traditional, but at least they aren't as cheesy-looking as others on the market today. San Francisco-based McClintock produces more tea length dresses than many other designers, although you'll see plenty of floor-length ball gowns and sheaths too. The prices ($96 to $188, with an average of $150) are fantastic when compared to the competition, plus the delivery is quick. Jessica McClintock's bridesmaids have above-average quality, although the company's customer service could stand some improvement. "It sucks," commented one retailer of McClintock's "service," while a bride complained to us that her botched bridesmaids dress order took far too long to remedy. So, it's a mixed review for McClintock—nice styling, decent prices, above-average quality but not-so-great customer service. *Sizes 4-16, 14w-24w. Call (800) 333-5301 or (415) 495-3030. Web: www.jessicamcclintock.com* **Rating: B-**

Jim Hjelm Occasions "Occasions" is the name for Jim Hjelm's bridesmaids line. Style-wise, it is a definite winner. Hjelm says Occasions is a "young, more figure-conscious look, featuring slender silhouettes." Translation: lots of "au courant" looks for skinny bridesmaids. Prices for Occasions, however, are in the stratosphere: $220 to $260. Quality is above average, but not as good as industry leaders Watters & Watters. Whether you think these gowns are worth the hefty price tags is a personal call; Occasions is the only bright spot in Hjelm's lackluster sales of late, so some folks must think so. We remain unconvinced. *Sizes 2-24. For a dealer near you, (212) 764-6960. Web: www.jimhjelmoccasions.com.* **Rating: B+**

How the bridal designers block rental of bridesmaids dresses

In the last chapter, we talked about how bridal magazines block ads from companies that want to rent bridal and bridesmaids dresses to women. By locking these rental firms out of the only national advertising vehicle that reaches brides, the magazines have worked to shut the door on dress rentals.

But that's not the whole story. Several bridal manufacturers have also taken public and not-so-public steps to stop dress rentals. Our investigation into the tactics of Alfred Angelo, one of the largest bridal designers, revealed some surprising information. As one of the top three bridal dressmakers, Angelo's designs are available in hundreds of shops. Angelo recently sent a "marketing statement" to each of its dealers, requiring them to agree in writing that they will "not rent Alfred Angelo Dream Maker dresses to consumers." Stores that rent their dresses face "immediate termination" their account with Angelo.

We asked the company about this practice. Bernard Toll, Angelo's public relations liaison, told us that "we do this for obvious reasons. Alfred Angelo dresses are not designed to withstand multiple wearings, countless alterations which leave telltale needle marks and legally required cleanings. Each Alfred Angelo dress is produced to make just one bride's dreams become a lovely reality on her wedding day."

Now, this is a curious argument. Angelo is essentially arguing that their dresses are of such poor quality that they won't "withstand repeated wearings." Considering the average bridesmaids dress costs $150 to $225, we find this to be appalling. Angelo's arguments seem to give credence to the perception that the industry designs "disposable dresses" of such inferior craftsmanship you can't be expected to wear them more than one day.

The bridal industry says that women "don't want to rent dresses. They'd rather buy." However the actions of the magazines and dress designers indicate quite the opposite—they're trying to stifle the consumer demand for a needed service for purely selfish reasons: women buy $500 million worth of bridesmaids dresses each year. Rental of these dresses would cut that business in half—and force the designers to make dresses that don't disintegrate after one wearing. By renting bridesmaids dresses alone, women could save $250 million each year.

Jordan Jordan's big coup in recent years was the hiring of designer Bill Pesche, the talent behind Hjlem's hot-selling Occasions line. Pesche gave Jordan a much-needed fashion boost, although the reaction among brides has been mixed. Jordan's line is now divided into three collections based on price. The entry-level "Joanie G" line is just $122 to $144. Jordan calls Joanie G "simply elegant," but we'd just call them simple with weak color choices. Regular Jordan gowns feature more detailing and higher prices ($158-$208). On the upper end is the new "Couture" collection with fancier fabrics and "body-conscious" silhouettes for $200 to $264. Overall, the quality of Jordan's dresses is in the middle of the pack—not as bad as some of the industry's laggards, but Jordan's dresses can't compare with the gowns from the market's top designers. Their flimsy "Tina" satin is a good example of the marginal quality. But, then again, Jordan isn't charging top-dollar prices either. And at least Jordan's customer service and deliveries get above-average marks from bridal retailers. The company offers "jet service" (quick delivery) on a half dozen styles for an extra charge. *Sizes up to 42. Call (212) 921-5560 for a local dealer. Web: www.jordanfashions.com* **Rating: B**

Lazaro This hipper division of Jim Hjelm recently debuted a bridesmaids line which is sort of a jazzed up version of "Occasions" (Hjelm's main bridesmaid line). As is the hip trend at the moment, Lazaro is showing lots of two-piece options with such fabrics as Parisian crepe and iridescent taffeta. As you might expect, the separates are priced separately— $120 to $140 for tops, $150 to $230 for skirts. The bottom line: total outfit would run $270 to $370, way too expensive in our evaluation for a dress that is only average in quality. When you compare these gowns to the very similar offerings from After Six (whose total outfit prices are about $160), it makes you wonder. For a dealer near you, call (212) 764-5781 or web: www.lazarobridal.com **Rating: B-**

Marlene's One of our favorite moments in the bridal business is when a manufacturer from Nowhere, USA shows up the big boys in New York City. Such is the case with Marlene's, a bridesmaids gown maker based in the tiny burg of Charlotte, Michigan. Why is Marlene's, in business since 1991, so successful? Well, first, check out the prices. Most dresses are $120 to $220. That's not bad, especially when you consider that Marlene offers impressive customization options. You can swap fabrics (12 choices), choose from different trims (bows, roses, rhinestones or nothing) and then select from various bodices and skirt styles. The result: a custom look at a price that won't break the bank. And how long does this take? Would you believe just two to four weeks? No kidding—Marlene's does all this custom work in half the time that those New York designers take to turn out one of those taffeta nightmares that isn't customized. The quality is also high, according to a survey of bridal shops. The only downside is fashion—it's certainly not as hip as what you see from other dress makers. But if a plain dress will do, then Marlene's will fill the bill. Also: Marlene's web site is a major embarrassment, with dress pictures that look mug shots. And Marlene's distribution is somewhat limited to shops in the Midwest and mid-Atlantic part of the U.S. If you can find them, we'd recommend giving Marlene a try. *Sizes 2 to 32. For a dealer near you, call (800) 826-2563 or (412) 243-7560. Web: www.marlenesbridal.com* **Rating: A**

Mori Lee Here's Mori Lee's bridesmaid philosophy: copy whatever are the top-selling styles from your competitors and sell them at rock-bottom prices. This strategy has served Mori Lee well, as they are now among the top-sellers of bridesmaids gowns in the country. Prices are incredible: $116 to $148. A new line of separates (eight styles) in four colors sells for $124 for a complete gown. The downside? These are the cheapest of the cheap bridesmaids gowns when it comes to quality (all gowns are sewn off-shore). Sizing is very limited (no small or large sizes) and deliveries can be painfully slow. If a problem develops with an order, retailers tell us Mori Lee's attitude is "The dress is so cheap, it's your problem to fix." Hence, retailers have a love-hate relationship with Mori Lee. The gowns are best-sellers but the quality and service has many retailers cursing the company under their breath. *Sizes 6 to 24. Add $10 to $24 for sizes 18 to 24, depending on the style. Call (212) 840-5070 to find a local dealer. Web: www.morileeinc.com.* **Rating: B+**

New Image New Image is another one of those Bill Levkoff-owned bridesmaids lines that offers ho-hum dress designs at prices that aren't much of a bargain. We saw many styles in this catalog that were similar to Levkoff's offerings: a-lines and empire waists, many with simple accents like bows or a touch of embroidery. In a way, New Image is an edited version of Levkoff's line, with about 50 styles to choose from. If the fashion and fabrics are similar to Levkoff, what makes New Image different? Quality, for one. For some reason, the construction and finish of these dresses is a couple of notches above Levkoff (perhaps they have different contractors). And it is a good thing the quality is better, because (like Levkoff) a gown from New Image isn't cheap. Prices for New Image dresses range from $178 to $238, still quite pricey in our opinion. *Sizes up to a 44. Call (800) 421-IMAGE for a local dealer. Web: www.newimagebridesmaids.com* **Rating: B-**

Watters and Watters It took two sisters from Thailand, Archariya and Batana Watters to turn the bridesmaids market on its ear in the 1980's. This Dallas-based duo had a radical concept back in 1986—hey, why not make a bridesmaids dress that looks like a *real* gown? Their company,

Watters & Watters (WW), chucked the giant puff sleeves and shiny taffeta so prevalent in the bridesmaids market for elegant designs in luxurious fabrics.

The results were a smash hit and soon WW became one of the hottest-selling bridesmaids designers. Their success attracted copy-cats (many other designers knocked off their look) and an equity investment from rival, Bill Levkoff. Although Levkoff is part-owner of WW, the company is still run as a semi-autonomous division in Texas.

While the rest of the bridesmaids market has slowly caught up to them in terms of fashion, WW is still a style leader. The company's innovative use of color and fabrics sets the tone for other designers in this category. Silk is a common fabric and you'll find it in several finishes, including dupioni, chiffon and more. WW also has iridescent organzas, velvets and satins.

What's the catch, you say? Well, unfortunately, all this high-style and quality fabrics comes at a high price. WW's dresses *start* at $214 and most average about $250. One even tops $500! On the other hand, you are actually getting a high-quality garment for your money. A dress from WW is a real gown, not some flimsy costume.

Recognizing that those prices are beyond the means of many bridesmaids, WW recently debuted a new lower-priced line: "W Too" features scaled-down versions of WW's regular dresses for $180 to $218. Designer Batana Watters told us W Too features more "edgy, younger styling," albeit with less fancy fabrics (poly chiffon, poly crepe) and fewer details.

New in recent seasons is a collection of accessories, including matching hand bags and shoes. WW has even moved into the separates craze recently, with a few options that run $134 to $238 per piece.

One drawback with both WW and W Too: sizing. The designers only offers sizes up to 24. And in the past we've griped about Watters & Watters's spotty customer service record and slow deliveries... but we're happy to report they've behaved better in recent years. Deliveries can still run behind in busy summer seasons, but Watters seems to have a better handle on production lately. *Sizes 2 to 24 are available. Call (972) 960-9884 for a local dealer. Web: www.watters.com for the Watters line; www.wtoo.com for WToo.* **Rating: A-**

Wtoo. See Watters and Watters review above.

Vera Wang Who takes the award for the most overpriced bridesmaids dresses available today? Why it is Vera Wang, the ice skating-outfit-designer-turned-bridal-mogul. Her bridesmaids look similar to those offered from other designers, but wait! Check out those price tags—a Wang bridesmaid will cost you $260 to $400! Boy, won't your bridesmaid be happy to know you've picked out a gown that costs three times more than it should? And what do you get for those big bucks? Satin, tulle, crepe—just like every other dress on the market. The styles are nothing special either: some are big skirts and satin tank tops, while others are slim, fitted silhouettes. And we hope your bridesmaids don't wear any size larger than a 14—Wang piles on an extra charge of $40 to $80 for sizes 16 to 20. Please. *Sizes 4-20. For a dealer near you, call 800-VEW-VERA. Web: www.verawang.com* **Rating: C-**

Other designers to consider. On our web site BridalGown.com we have a free special report on how to buy (and save on) bridesmaids dresses. We'll give you additional buying tips, discount ideas and sizing advice in this report (which we don't have room for in this section). The report covers additional scams with bridesmaids gowns and also provides advice on flower girl dresses.

Tuxedos

Nowhere are the wedding etiquette rules sillier than for men's formal wear. For example, they say you MUST wear a black tux with tails for a formal wedding after six in the evening. If you don't, the vengeful WEDDING GODS will strike you down, ostracize your family and charge obscene amounts of money to your credit cards.

Now if your wedding is before six you can wear a gray or white short coat . . . but not if the moon is full. And, of course, you must follow the omnipotent "formality" rules that dictate proper dress for weddings that are very formal, just plain formal, semi-formal, pseudo-formal and the dreaded para-formal.

Just kidding.

We believe all this is nonsense. Grooms and groomsmen should wear whatever they believe is appropriate. Who cares what time of day the wedding is? If your wedding is an informal ceremony in a local civic rose garden, you don't have to wear a tuxedo. We know we might incur the wrath of Emily Post for saying this, but hey, do what you want to do. If you look good in a double-breasted tux, wear that. If you don't, look for another style. You get the idea.

What Are You Buying?

Actually, most grooms and groomsmen *rent* formal wear for weddings. Imagine what would happen if men had to shell out the same kind of money that bridesmaids spend on those horrendously ugly bridesmaids' gowns. There would be mass revolts and street rioting. Fortunately, for national security's sake, most men's formal wear is rented. Typically, the groomsmen are financially responsible for their tuxedo rentals, so basically you and your fiancé's only expense is the groom's tux. Here are the three basic options for men's formalwear:

1 Rent. When you rent a tux, you get just about everything: jacket, pants, cummerbund, shirt, tie, cuff links, and, of course, shirt studs (little jewelry that covers your buttons). Notice what's missing? If you answered "shoes" give yourself extra points. While most tuxes rent for $50 to $130 (an average is $90), the shoes are often $10 to $20 extra. Of course, it's more expensive in major metropolitan areas (like New York City, where tux rentals can top $150 and shoes go for $25). A small deposit/damage waiver ($10 to $20) is required to reserve a tux. There are three types of places to rent formal wear:

♥ **CHAIN STORES.** Large formalwear franchised chains (such as Gingiss) are located across the U.S. They basically offer the same styles and brand names. Service can range from helpful to dreadful. Most of these chains don't carry any stock at their stores—a central warehouse is used to dispense the tuxedos. Hence, it's difficult to decide which style is best for you by just looking at the mannequins. To try on a particular style, you must ask the shop for a "trial fitting." For no charge, most shops will bring in a style in your size. The only disadvantage is that this requires a second visit to the shop, rather inconvenient for those of you who lead busy lives.

♥ **BRIDAL SHOPS.** More and more bridal shops are now getting into the business of renting tuxes. However, instead of stocking tuxes at their store, they use a service which supplies them with rentals. Hence, the way you pick a tuxedo is to look through a book with pictures of tuxedo-clad soap stars awash in testosterone. Thrilling. Personally, we'd rather look at the mannequins. Anyway, on the up side, the bridal shops may cut you a deal if you buy the bridal and bridesmaids' gowns from them. On the down side, while bridal shop employees may know a lot about bridal gowns, they may know diddly-squat about men's formal wear.

♥ **INDEPENDENT SHOPS.** Occasionally, we find an independent tuxedo rental shop, one that is not affiliated with a national chain. We often are impressed by the quality of service at these outlets. Furthermore, independent shops may carry a wider selection of styles and designers. You can also find some great deals. For example, Tux Express in Scottsdale, Arizona (480) 991-6655 rents designer-brand tuxes for $38 to $59, far below the prices of the chains.

2 Buy. If you expect to need a tuxedo again for a fancy party or corporate banquet, it may pay to buy. That's because most tuxedos cost $300 to $500 to purchase (although you can find several at discounters for $200 or less). Considering rental fees of $100 a pop, this might be a good investment. See the money-saving tips in this chapter for places on the web to buy a tux or accessories.

3 **Go with your own suit.** Especially for less formal weddings, it is perfectly acceptable for the groom and groomsmen to wear dark suits.

Grooms in Cyberspace: What's on the Web?

Just like in the magazine world, groom's issues often get short-shrift on the 'net. Here are some good links to help:

♥ **GINGISS.COM.** If you just want to look at current styles, check out Gingiss (www.gingiss.com). Their tux gallery has a couple dozen tux pictures and a detailed question and answer section.

♥ **MARRYINGMAN.COM** (www.ungroomed.com or www.marryingman.com) bills itself as the "men's perspective on engagement, weddings and what follows." Updated weekly, this site features a nice selection of short articles and tips. In their "formalwear" section, you can search a national formalwear store directory, download a fitting reminder and measurement form or do the math with a buying versus renting calculator. MarryingMan.com is the best site on the web for grooms, hands down.

♥ **WEDDINGCHANNEL.COM.** Click on "Fashion" and then "Grooms" to view styles from five major designers. Best of all, you can do a search for just the tux you want to see—three button jackets? Only cutaways? You can look just at these our other choices with just a few mouse clicks. Also cool: don't know a mandarin from a tailcoat? Roll your cursor over these terms and the site will show you a small sketch of what each looks like.

Getting Started: How Far in Advance?

Boy, this varies greatly from area to area. In small towns, or for less popular months, you can shop one to two months before the wedding. However, you may need to reserve your tuxedos three to four months before the wedding in larger cities or for popular summer wedding months. If you have out-of-town groomsmen, you may want to leave extra time to get their measurements in.

Money-saving Secrets for Tuxedos

1 **Package discounts.** Almost all tuxedo shops offer a free tux rental with the rental of four, five or six tuxedos. In some cases, tux shops distribute coupons good for $10 or more off each rental. Our advice: *always* ask about group discounts.

2 **Skip the rental shoes.** Why? Those cheap rental shoes can be awfully uncomfortable. Instead, wear your own black dress shoes if you have them and save $10.

3 **Surf for discounts.** ETuxedo (www.etuxedo.com; 888-879-7848) is a large discount seller of tuxes, with prices starting at $169 for a wool tux. Or try their tux separates, with jackets at $149 and pants at $55. Even if you don't want to buy a tux online, you can use this site to compare accessory prices like tie & cummerbund sets, cuff links, or shirts. Another site for tux shoppers is 4Tuxedos (www.4Tuxedos.com) with numerous links to companies that both sell and rent tuxes, plus a good Q&A.

4 **Consider new tux alternatives**. In years past, if you wanted to buy or rent a tux you had limited choices—typically just a handful

Tux Shopping Tips

In the old days, tux shopping was rather simple: if you were planning a formal evening wedding, you wore a single-breasted tux. Daytime or less formal affairs called for cutaways, strollers or morning coats. Now, that's all been thrown out the window—guys are wearing all sorts of tuxes during all times of the day. So, perhaps the best advice is to get a tux that best matches your body. Here are some ideas, given different body types:

♥ **Short, stocky guys.** Jackets with slim shawl collars are a good bet. You don't need any of those broad-shoulder Euro style tuxes; that would be overkill. Instead jackets with natural shoulder lines are best. For pants, avoid styles that have too much break on the foot (which creates a sloppy look); instead, try reverse double-pleated trousers.

♥ **Short, slender guys.** Skip the double-breasted styles and look at single-breast jackets with a low button and wide lapels.

♥ **Tall, slender guys**. These folks have it easy—just about everything works. Double-breasted tuxes with those Euro-style broad shoulders are fine, as are those hip three-button styles that close high on the chest. Trousers can have more break at the foot.

♥ **Tall, stocky guys.** Jacket length is a tough one here; try styles with shawl collars. Consider a jacket with a bit of room to allow for movement.

♥ **Other tips.** Vests are a popular alternative to cummerbunds these days. Be sure to ask whether the vest is a full back or half-back (full looks better if you take off your jacket during the reception). Fit is important— look for a tux rental shop that knows how to measure properly (it's more than just jacket size; shops should also take your inseam and waist measurements). And insist on a fitting BEFORE the wedding to avoid any day-of surprises. Finally, pay attention to the fabric. 100% wool tuxes are best, but there are differences among wools. Have a tux retailer show you the difference between a tropical wool fabric and other options.

of formalwear stores or bridal shops rented tuxes. Now, there is some new competition. Chains like Men's Wearhouse (web: www.menswear-house.com) are rolling out tux rentals to 140 of their 600 stores nationwide. Most of the stores that will rent tuxes will be in the West and Southwest and the prices are great—rentals start at just $50 a tux. Or you can buy a tux at any of the Men's Wearhouses for just $199 for a 100% wool single-breasted style. Since it often costs $100 or more to rent a tux in big cities today, it might be worth buying a tux if you think you'll need one more than just once over the next few years.

Helpful Hints

1 **Fib.** A groom emailed us this tip. Frustrated by his procrastinating groomsmen (who were late for fittings), he suggested other grooms lie about when the measurements have to be in. For example, tell them they must get measured six weeks before the wedding even though the real deadline is just four weeks.

2 **Ignore the "black tie invited" pressure.** Some bridal magazines and retailers are suggesting you put "black tie invited" on your invitations. Is this to encourage your guests to dress up? Or to merely line the pockets of tuxedo rental places? Whatever the motivation, we should note that Crane's Wedding Blue Book (the bible of invitation etiquette) notes that it is NOT proper to specify the type of dress on an invitation. "The formality of dress is indicated by the time of day (of the wedding). After six o'clock is considered formal." Putting "Black Tie Invited" or "Black Tie Optional" is confusing and not necessary.

3 **Consider renting an extra shirt for summer outdoor weddings.** A bride called in this excellent tip—if you plan a summer outdoor wedding, consider having the groom and groomsmen rent an extra tuxedo shirt. That way they can change after the wedding into a fresh shirt for the reception.

Are guys easy marks?

Bridal retailers just love the guys. And it's no wonder. Listen to what one bridal retailer in Colorado said in a private online message board about the tux business: "I love tux traffic! Men will drop a wad of cash without thinking twice about it. I also do a significant amount of mens retail....which I can hardly keep up with right now. We have been selling cotton shirts and vest sets like nobody's business. I also love the markup on mens retail: 135%-150%." A word to the wise: shop around (and online) for tux shirts and accessories (see earlier in this chapter for ideas) before shelling out big bucks at bridal stores.

Did you realize how much rental fees vary from site to site? In this chapter, we'll discuss a group of often-overlooked wedding ceremony sites that are extremely affordable—plus we'll give you six important questions to ask your site coordinator.

Selecting a site for your ceremony first requires a decision on the type of ceremony you want. Wedding ceremonies are divided into two categories: religious and civil.

1 Religious ceremonies. Religious ceremonies (75% of all weddings), of course, are most likely held in a house of worship. Requirements for religious ceremonies vary greatly from one denomination to another. Pre-marital counseling is required by some religions; others forbid interfaith marriages. Often the rules are established by the church or temple's local priest, minister, pastor or rabbi. Call your local house of worship for guidelines and requirements.

2 Civil ceremonies. About one-fourth of all weddings are civil ceremonies. Legal requirements vary from state to state, but usually a judge or other officiant presides over the ceremony. Customs and traditions vary greatly from region to region of the country. For example, we spoke to one hotel catering manager who worked in both Boston, Massachusetts and Austin, Texas. In Boston, she told us nearly 75% of couples had a civil ceremony on site at the hotel. Just the opposite was true in Texas where most weddings are held in a church with only the reception following at the hotel.

Religious vs. Civil: It's All a Matter of State

Interestingly enough, the split between civil and religious ceremonies varies greatly from state to state. According to federal government statistics, the state with the largest number of religious wedding ceremonies is West Virginia. In that state, a whopping 97% of all weddings are religious ceremonies. On the other end of the spectrum, South Carolina leads the nation in civil ceremonies (54% of all weddings), perhaps due to the state's large military population.

So what happened to Nevada, where the large number of Las Vegas weddings probably would rank that state #1 in civil ceremonies? Well, Nevada was omitted from this study for reasons unknown. Other omitted states include Ohio and Iowa (both of which do not record the type of ceremony) and Arkansas, Oklahoma, Texas, New Mexico, Arizona, Washington, and North Dakota.

Other states with a high number of civil ceremonies include South Carolina (54%), Florida (45%) New Hampshire (40%), Hawaii (36%), New York (35%), as well as Maine, Georgia and Virginia.

Which states have a large number of religious wedding ceremonies? Besides West Virginia, those states include Missouri (91%), Nebraska (84.2%), Michigan (83.9%), Pennsylvania (83.7%), Idaho (83.5%), California (83.1%).

What Are You Buying?

When you book a ceremony site, you are not only purchasing use of the site for the wedding but also time for set-up and tear-down of the decorations. Now we say purchasing because many sites charge fees to use the facilities for a wedding. One bride we interviewed was surprised that the church they belonged to charged her over $600 in fees for her wedding. Of course, these fees often go to reimburse church staff and to pay expenses like utilities, clean-up, etc. Unfortunately, some churches use weddings to subsidize other less-profitable operations. Anyway, the fees vary widely from site to site but the charges tend to be more in larger cities.

What if you are not a member of a church but you want a church wedding? Well, a few churches allow non-members to use their facilities for weddings . . . but with a few catches. First, the fees are normally higher. Second, members get first shot at dates so non-members may not be able to book a wedding until, say, three months in advance. Obviously, this is a roll of the dice.

Whether you're planning a civil or religious service, the officiant typically gets paid an honorarium. Sometimes this is in the form of a donation to the house of worship. Other church employees (organist, choir) may require separate payment that covers not only their performance at the wedding but also any prior rehearsals.

Sources to Find a Great Ceremony Site

There are several great sources to use to find ceremony sites.

♥ **LOCAL VISITORS/TOURISM BUREAUS.** Many have a guide to local facilities that are available for weddings and receptions. A local Chamber of Commerce or Historical Society office may also have more leads.

♥ **LOCAL PARKS DEPARTMENTS.** Most city and county parks and historical areas are administered by a parks department. Ask them which sites are most popular for wedding ceremonies.

♥ **SURF THE 'NET.** We found an amazing number of web sites (including one reviewed on the next page) with local site information. Another idea: USA CityLink (www.usacitylink.com) links you to the web sites run by local, municipal and other government agencies. Want to find a public rose garden in Austin, Texas for your ceremony? Or a ceremony site in Walla Walla, WA? This web site opens the door to municipal-owned sites that great bargains.

Sources to Find an Officiant. If you're planning a civil ceremony, where do you find an officiant? Here are some thoughts:

♥ **VENDOR LISTS.** Many reception sites (including parks departments) have "vendor lists" that list everything from florists to photographers. Often, you can find officiant names on such lists.

♥ **THE WEB.** Finding obscure information is what makes the web so much fun. Many of the Big 7 Wedding Portals (reviewed in the Etcetera chapter) have search engines to find wedding vendors (including officiants).

♥ **CHECK THE YELLOW PAGES.** Under "Clergy" and "Wedding," you may find officiant listings.

♥ **NON-DENOMINATIONAL CHURCHES.** Such houses of worship (example: Unitarian churches) may have officiants who are willing to conduct religious ceremonies for couples who are not members of the church.

Brides in Cyberspace: What's on the Web?

Finding a ceremony site on the web can be a bit tricky—many religious and smaller sites don't have web pages. But many sites that offer both ceremonies and receptions (so-called catering halls and facilities) can be found online. One of the better sites to do this: The Knot (www.theknot.com) has a local vendor search function that lets you zero in on ceremony and reception sites (and other wedding vendors) by local region. We did a search for sites in the Northern New Jersey area (see Figure 1) and came up with 100+ options.

Getting Started: How Far in Advance?

Especially for popular wedding months, start your search for a ceremony site as soon as you have selected the date. Prime dates can book up to a year in advance—you know, there are only so many Saturdays in June. However, be aware that popular months vary by region. For example, in the South, December is a particularly popular month. In Arizona, and many areas of the desert Southwest, the spring months (such as May) are almost as popular as the hot summer months. See the chart later in this chapter for a list of the most and least popular months for weddings by state.

Be aware that religious restrictions may rule out certain times of the

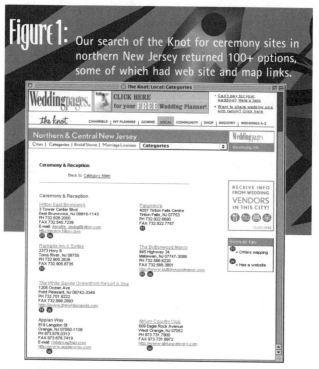

Figure 1: Our search of the Knot for ceremony sites in northern New Jersey returned 100+ options, some of which had web site and map links.

year. For example, Catholics and Greek Orthodox avoid marrying during Lent in March. Jews don't have weddings during the High Holy Days (usually in September or October).

Questions to Ask of a Ceremony Site

1 **Do you have my wedding date available?** Yes, it's an obvious question, but probably the most important one. Many brides forget there are many other brides competing for the same slots on a Saturday afternoon.

2 **What are the restrictions, set-up times and clean-up requirements?** Many sites have put these items in writing. One local church we know has so many guidelines that they filled a 72-page book! Make sure you are fully aware of these details to avoid any surprises.

3 **Are there any rules regarding candles or flowers?** Some facilities ban candles outright. Others forbid the throwing of rice or birdseed after the ceremony. We've even heard of one church that required the altar flower arrangement to be "donated" to the church after the ceremony.

4 **Who will be my contact?** In order to prevent miscommunications, make sure you find out who is the wedding coordinator. This

---

REAL WEDDING TIP

Church ceremony fees can add up

"I would just like to comment on a substantial wedding cost which I did not see addressed in your book. After I got engaged, I called the Episcopal church I have attended since I was a little girl and booked a date in May. I have always assumed that I would be married there, and so I did not give this aspect of planning the wedding much thought. Recently, I received an information packet from the church that included a price list. Imagine my surprise to learn that getting married at my local church will cost approximately $2,000 ($750 for rental of the church and the rest in fees to various people needed to perform the service). I had not counted on this expense, and frankly, I feel a little angry about it. To make matters worse, when I tried to call other Episcopal churches in the area, the wedding coordinators refused to disclose any prices unless I had the rector of my official church call and give permission for me to be married there."

person will be an invaluable referral source of other wedding services. Ask if the coordinator will be there the day of the wedding.

5 **What kind of equipment must be rented for my wedding?** Don't assume that something in the sanctuary or at the site is included in your rental of the facility.

6 **How early will the site be available for decorating?** Will the air conditioning or heat be turned on that time? Your florist may

MOST/LEAST POPULAR MONTHS

STATE	Most Popular	Least Popular
New England:		
Maine	August, July, June	Jan., Feb., Mar.
New Hampshire	Oct., June, Aug.	Jan. Mar., Feb.
Vermont	July, August, June	Jan., Mar., Feb.
Massachusetts	Oct., Sept., June.	Jan., Mar., Feb.
Rhode Island	Sept., Oct., June	Jan., Feb., Mar.
Connecticut	Oct., Sept., June	Jan., Mar., Feb.
Middle Atlantic:		
New York	Sept., Aug., June	Jan., Feb., Mar.
New Jersey	Oct., Sept., June	Jan., Feb., Mar.
Pennsylvania	Oct., June, Sept.	Jan., Feb., Mar.
East North Central:		
Ohio	June, July, Sept.	Jan., Feb., Mar.
Indiana	June, July, August	Jan., Feb., Mar.
Illinois	June, Sept., Oct.	Jan., Feb., Mar.
Michigan	August, June, Sept.	Jan., Mar., Feb.
Wisconsin	June, Sept., Aug.	Jan., Feb., Mar.
West North Central:		
Minnesota	June, Sept., Aug.	Jan., Mar., Feb.
Iowa	June, August, Sept.	Jan., Feb., Mar.
Missouri	June, May, Oct.	Jan., Feb., Mar.
North Dakota	June, July, August	Jan., Mar., Feb.
South Dakota	August, June, July	Jan., Mar., Feb.
Nebraska	June, July, August.	Jan., Feb., Mar.
Kansas	June, July, May	Jan., Feb., Mar.
East South Central:		
Kentucky	June, July, May	Jan., Feb., Mar.
Tennessee	June, July, Dec.	Jan., Feb., Mar.
Alabama	June, July, August	Jan., Feb., Nov.
Mississippi	June, July, Dec.	Jan., Feb., Nov.
West South Central:		
Arkansas	June, July, August	Jan., Feb., Nov.
Louisiana	July, June, Oct.	Mar., Feb., Jan.

‖‖‖

need to access the ceremony site several hours before your wedding. Confirm that heat or A/C will be running to make it easier for vendors to work (and to avoid damage to delicate blooms and other décor).

Questions to Ask an Officiant

1 **What is the expected honorarium, donation or fee?** When is this normally paid?

FOR WEDDINGS BY STATE

STATE	Most Popular	Least Popular
Oklahoma	June, August, May	Jan., Feb., Oct.
Texas	June, July, August	Jan., Nov., Feb.
South Atlantic:		
Delaware	Oct., Sept., June	Jan., Feb., Mar.
Maryland	June, Sept., Oct.	Jan., Feb., Mar.
Wash. D.C.	June, Sept., Oct.	Feb., Jan., Mar.
Virginia	June, July, May	Jan., Mar., Feb.
West Virginia	June, July, Aug.	Jan., Mar., Feb.
North Carolina	June, July, May	Jan., Mar., Feb.
South Carolina	July, June, May	Jan, Feb., Mar.
Georgia	June, July, April	Jan., Feb., Mar.
Florida	Dec., June, April	Jan., Mar., Sept.
Mountain:		
Montana	July, June, August	Jan., Feb., Mar.
Idaho	August, July, June	Jan., Mar., Feb.
Wyoming	July, August, June	Jan., Mar., Feb.
Colorado	June, August, July	Jan., Mar., Nov.
New Mexico	June, August, May	Jan., Sept., Feb.
Arizona	June, May, Apr.	Feb., August, July
Utah	July, August, Sept.	Jan., Feb., Oct.
Nevada	July, August, April	Jan., Mar., Nov.
Pacific:		
Washington	August, Oct., July	Jan., Feb., Dec.
Oregon	August, June, July	Jan., Feb., Mar.
California	June, Sept., July	Jan., April, Feb.
Alaska	August, June, July	Jan., Mar., April
Hawaii	May, July, August	Jan., Mar., Feb.
US (TOTAL)	*June, July, August*	*Jan., Feb., Mar.*

Note: Months are listed in order of popularity. For example, "July, August, June" means that July is the #1 month, followed by August and so on. The least popular month is listed first, followed by the second least popular and so on. Source: US Dept. of Health report issued 1996 (based on 1988 data).

2 **Are there any travel charges or other costs?** If you're planning a wedding at a non-religious site (hotel, home, etc.), you may want to confirm these details.

3 **Is any pre-wedding counseling required?** Some churches require couples to attend pre-wedding counseling. Others require the couple to promise to raise their children in that religion. Before you are asked to make any commitments, ask the site coordinator about this matter.

4 **Do you provide the ceremony/vows or can we write our own? Are you familiar with the wedding site?**

5 **Are you licensed to perform wedding ceremonies in the county?** And will you file all the necessary paperwork (marriage license, etc.) with the county?

6 **Will you attend the rehearsal?** If so, is there an extra charge for this time? Another issue: ask the officiant when they arrive at the ceremony and how long they stay afterward. This is important to coordinate with your photographer. If you are marrying in your or your family's church or synagogue, it is customary to invite the clergyman (and his wife) to the reception.

Top Money-saving Secrets

1 **Consider a civic site.** Many sites run by your city (parks, rose gardens, etc.) have lovely facilities available for wedding ceremonies. Best of all: most of these sites are available for a very small fee. For example, we've found rose gardens and historical parks (complete with gazebo or chapel) that cost under $100.

2 **Call around to different sites.** You wouldn't believe how widely fees vary from facility to facility.

3 **Consider becoming a member.** Many churches charge less for weddings of members than non-members. Hence, consider joining the church where you'll be married. Another bonus: dues/membership fees are tax deductible.

4 **Ask about discounts.** For example, some churches and temples offer discounts on wedding invitations as a fund raiser.

5 **Have a friend officiate.** In most states it is fairly easy to become licensed to perform weddings. Have a friend or relative get licensed and perform the ceremony as a gift.

A rose is a rose . . . except when you're shopping for flowers for your wedding. Then a "bridal" rose is suddenly eight times more expensive than a regular rose. With the average floral bill for weddings topping $900, there have to be some creative ways to stretch that budget. We came up with 17 cost-cutters. Plus, in this chapter, we also cut through the "floral speak" and give you eight floral "best buys."

What Are You Buying?

Flowers are more than petals, stems and leaves. When you contract with a professional florist, you are buying their expertise and creativity. Not only is the florist's knowledge of flowers important but also their understanding of colors and contrasts. Florists must be able to come up with a floral motif to best complement the bride, the bridal gown, the bridesmaids' colors, the ceremony and the reception. To synthesize these elements and the "feel of the wedding" (a formal sit-down dinner versus an informal barbecue) takes talent. Lots of it. Your tastes and desires are key here, and a florist who understands a couple's individuality is the best choice.

There are three basic categories of flowers that you are buying:

♥ **PERSONAL FLOWERS.** The bride's and bridesmaids' bouquets, corsages for the mothers and house party, and boutonnieres for the men.

♥ **CEREMONY SITE FLOWERS.** Altar flowers and/or aisle arrangements (ribbons, candles, pew markers).

♥ **RECEPTION SITE FLOWERS.** Guest book table, table centerpieces and the cake table. Other floral expense areas may include the rehearsal dinner and any other pre-wedding parties.

Average total costs: About $900 covers the total floral bill at most weddings, according to industry estimates. In the largest cities (such as New York or Chicago), the flower budget can easily zoom past $1000 or even $2000 for lavish affairs. Deposits range from nothing (the exception) to as much as 50% of the estimated bill. Many florists ask for $50 to $100 to reserve the date. The balance is usually due one to two weeks before the wedding (because many florists must order the flowers in advance from their suppliers).

Sources to Find an Affordable Florist

Since there are three general types of florists out there, we thought it might be helpful to explain the differences, then detail where to find the one that will work best for you:

1 **Cash 'n Carry.** These shops basically specialize in providing an arrangement for Mother's Day, or a friend's birthday. They usually don't do many weddings and may not have as much experience with such a special event.

2 **Full service.** Weddings, wire service arrangements, and special events are within a full-service florist's repertoire. A majority of florists fit in this category, although some are better than others at weddings.

3 **Specialists.** Some florists specialize in one aspect of the floral business, such as corporate affairs. Obviously, those who specialize in weddings are your best bet. Those that don't may have little incentive to do a good job since they don't target that market anyway. Don't assume that your neighborhood florist, who has done great arrangements for you at Christmas and other times, will be best for your wedding.

Where to Find Florists Who are Wedding Specialists

♥ CEREMONY SITE COORDINATORS. Ask the person who coordinates (or books) weddings at your church, synagogue, etc. for florist recommendations. This is a great source since they often see florists' work up close and personal. They also know the florists who have been late to set up and those who have not provided the freshest flowers or best service. If your ceremony site coordinator doesn't have any recommendations, call around to a few popular churches in your area. Odds are you'll turn up some valuable referrals.

♥ PHOTOGRAPHERS. Many have opinions as to which florists offer the best service and which don't. However, since a photographers contact with florists is limited to the final product at the wedding, their opinions could be somewhat biased.

♥ IF YOU PLAN TO PRODUCE YOUR OWN ARRANGEMENTS or have a friend do it, look under the Yellow Page heading of "Florists-Wholesale" for supplies. Some wholesalers refuse to sell to the public while others don't have such restrictions.

Also consider contacting the Association of Specialty Cut Flower Growers (ASCFG) at (440) 774-2887. Often these growers will even design your wedding flowers for you. Janet Friedman of Flinthill Flower Farm in Maryland (301-607-4554) emailed us about this tip. She told us you'll find the freshest flowers from local growers and "many of them can design masterpieces" as well.

Brides in Cyberspace: What's on the Web?

Don't know a gladiolus from a glamelia? Does the word "phalaenopsis" make you think of a rare skin condition? (Actually, it's an orchid). Don't fret—you can get a crash course in bridal flowers by surfing the web. Here's the best site we found to answer these and other floral questions:

Flowersales.com

Web site: www.flowersales.com
What it is: A flower wholesaler that has extensive links to floral picture web sites (see Figure 1 on the next page).
What's Cool: What's the current wholesale price for tulips? Wonder what those tulip colors really look like? This web site has the answer. We liked the wholesale flower prices, updated weekly for hundreds of flowers from California, Hawaii and Europe. The links on this site (under "Floral Picture Gallery") are fantastic. You can check out the International Floral Picture Database (7000 images, www.flowerweb.com), the European Rose Gallery List, the Orchid Photo Page and more. The site

also has care and handling tips for cut flowers as well as a list of flowers and their meanings. And, of course, you can also order flowers at wholesale, shipped to you overnight via FED-EX.

Needs Work: The site quotes prices in floral speak, such as Agapanthus for 1.40st (that is, $1.40 per stem) or Feverfew for 4.40bu ($4.40 per bunch). Flowersales.com isn't a pretty site to look at—their main page is just a long list of links to prices, general info and picture galleries. A little more organization would be helpful.

♥ Another great site: **C.O.D. WHOLESALE** (www.codwholesale.com), which sells ribbon at unbelievable prices with no minimum order. For example, we saw wired organza ribbon in 29 colors and eight widths starting at $4.10 for 50 yards. Wow. You'll also see satin ribbon, corsage ribbon and more. You'll even find bouquet holders and tulle if you're really ambitious. C. O. D. also offers a free catalog and will send a swatch card of all their colors for $15.

♥ Online bridal magazine **BLISS' "WEDDING FLORAL CHART"** (www.blissezine.com/weddingfloral/) lets you search for flowers by color, season, where they are grown and more. The site even suggests flowers given a selected bridesmaid' dress color. The coolest part: not only do you get a list of blooms, but the site has small pop-up windows with flower pictures.

Getting Started: How Far in Advance?

Book a florist up to six months in advance of your wedding. In larger cities, some florists may even require more time. For most towns, however, many florists consider three

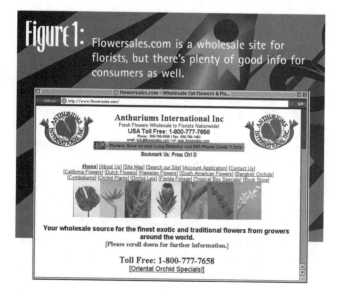

Figure 1: Flowersales.com is a wholesale site for florists, but there's plenty of good info for consumers as well.

to six months notice adequate. Remember that you can put down a small deposit further in advance and then talk specifics at a later date.

Step-by-step Shopping Strategies

♥ **Step 1**: First, you must have the time, place and apparel selected before you can get an accurate bid from a florist. The bridal gown is crucial—everything flows from this design element. The colors of the bridesmaids gowns are also important.

♥ **Step 2**: Choose two to three florists from the sources mentioned earlier to visit. Make an appointment with each and leave about one hour's time to discuss the details.

♥ **Step 3**: Be sure to bring swatches of the bridesmaids apparel and a picture of the bridal gown you have selected. A magazine ad or rough sketch will suffice. Give this to the florist so they'll remember what the dress looks like when they actually make the bouquet. Also, it will be helpful to bring any pictures of flowers/designs you like.

♥ **Step 4**: Look through actual photographs of previous work. Don't settle for FTD design books or floral magazines. Identify flowers and designs that fit your wedding's style—unadorned wedding gowns can be set-off by a lush bride's bouquet. Similarly, a simple bouquet may better compliment an ornate wedding dress. See if the florist attempts to understand your tastes and desires instead of merely *telling* you what you must have.

♥ **Step 5**: Get a written proposal specifying exact flowers to be used. Each item (brides bouquet, corsages, etc.) should be priced individually. Get this *before* you place the deposit.

♥ **Step 6**: Pick your top florist choice and ask to visit one of their weddings during set-up. On your visit, check to see if they are on-time and organized. Also, look to see how fresh the flowers are. Do you find the designs pleasing (keeping in mind that the other bride's taste may be different from your own)?

♥ **Step 7**: If you believe an on-site meeting at your ceremony or reception site is necessary, now is the time. Finalize the details.

♥ **Step 8**: Get a written contract that spells out the date, set-up time, place, and specific flowers and designs to be created. Details (if you want open roses, for example) need to be *clearly* spelled out. As you get closer to your wedding, there may be some modifications (more corsages, etc.). Make sure any changes are in writing.

♥ **Step 9**: If you're having a large or complex wedding, a pre-wedding floral check-up may be necessary. Here you'll meet with the florist about one to two weeks prior to the date to iron out any last minute details/changes, etc.

Questions to Ask a Florist

1 **Is my date available?** If it is, check to see if a deposit is necessary to hold the date. Also ask if there is any consultation fee. Inquire as to whether you can receive a price proposal before a deposit is placed.

2 **Do you have actual photographs or samples of your past work?** It's important to see the work of your florist, not airbrushed photos from an FTD book. There is no better way to see if their style complements your tastes and verify just how skilled they are.

3 **Do you offer any silk or dried flower arrangements?** This may be important to you if you want to save your bouquet or want an unusual look for a table centerpiece. Sometimes these two options may be less expensive than fresh flowers, especially for some exotics like orchids. A table centerpiece idea: dried rose topiaries (see right) double as an elegant keepsake.

4 **Is there a delivery or set-up fee?** Watch out—this can be a substantial extra charge. Most florists will charge a delivery/set-up fee especially if you have either complex flower arrangements or a site that is a long distance from their shop. If the charge is high, consider finding a florist closer to the site or cut back on the complicated decorations.

5 **How many weddings do you do in a day?** The biggest problem with some florists is that they become "overextended"—trying to do too many weddings in one day. A florist can probably do two or three weddings a day if the events are held at different times and/or the florist has plenty of help. If the florist's schedule looks crowded for your wedding date, they may arrive late or deliver the wrong flowers (or worse). Look for someone focused on your wedding.

6 **Are you familiar with my ceremony/reception site location?** If not, will you visit it with me? It may be a good idea to introduce your florist to the ceremony or reception site if they've never seen it. Ask if there is any charge for this on-site visit.

7 **What rental items do you have?** How are they priced? Some things you may want to rent include candelabrum, aisle standards, or urns. We prefer florists who don't over-charge on rentals. One way to find out is to compare prices with a local rental store. A common mark-up for florists is about 10% for their time to coordinate this detail. If you would prefer to rent the items yourself because you can get a better price, be sure you have the time to pick-up and return the items.

8 **Can I attend one of your weddings during set-up for a look at your designs?** Here is another way to determine how profes-sional and talented your florist is. You'll need to visit during set-up and leave before the wedding party arrives. Look for timeliness, freshness and beauty of the flowers, and how well the florist and staff work together.

9 **What time will you be at my ceremony/reception sites to set-up my wedding?** Confirm this time constantly throughout your planning. Many florists set up weddings a couple hours in advance. If this is the case with your wedding, be sure the temperature at the site is not too hot for the flowers—you want them to look fresh at wedding time. Some ceremony sites might have a refrigerator to store flowers until you arrive. Confirm this detail with both your site and florist.

10 **Will you merely drop off my flowers or stay through the ceremony?** The degree of service here differs dramatically from florist to florist. Some just drop off the flowers at the ceremony and leave, while others stay to pin on corsages, make sure nothing is missing, etc. There may be an extra fee ($50) for this service—for large weddings, however, this may be a worthwhile investment.

Top Money-saving Secrets

1 **Don't use a florist who charges a consultation fee.** Most florists do NOT charge a consultation fee, however, beware of those who do. You can find plenty of great florists who will talk to you for free; don't spend time with the few that charge such fees. (Some florists tell us they charge consulting fees to "weed out" brides who are just window shopping.)

2 **Choose a wedding date that is not near a holiday.** As you may well realize, all roses are outrageously priced in February thanks to Valentine's Day. So if you want roses, don't plan on a wedding at that time. Also, December is an expensive time to buy fresh flowers since the supply is limited and the demand from holiday events is high. On the other hand, brides have found Christmas weddings are less expensive for ceremony flowers since the church may already be decorated.

3 **Seasonal and regional flowers can be great bargains.** For example, in California, certain orchids and other tropical flowers grown locally may be available at affordable prices. Also, seasonality often affects floral prices. For example, tulips are abundant from December through April and as such are fairly inexpensive. If you want them in July, however, they will be extremely expensive (three times the price) if they are available at all.

4 **Avoid exotic flowers.** Of course, what's considered an "exotic" flower may vary from region to region. For example, in the Southwest, lilies of the valley (see picture) are very expensive and difficult to find. Yet in the northern part of the US, where they are common, they may be very reasonable. Exotic flowers such as pricey orchids from Hawaii are usually expensive no matter where you live.

5 **Instead of big (and expensive) bouquets, carry a single flower.** This is extremely elegant especially with long stem varieties like calla lilies and roses. If you (the bride) want to carry a bouquet, consider having the bridesmaids carry single flowers.

6 **Use silk flowers to replace expensive, fresh varieties.** Even dried flowers may be affordable alternatives. All-silk arrangements may not be much less expensive if you have them made by a florist—their charge for labor may be expensive no matter what type of flower they use. However, you can save money doing it yourself or substituting silk exotics (like orchids) for real ones.

7 **Limit the number of attendants.** This is just basic math: the more attendants, the more flowers, the higher the final cost.

8 **Spend your money where people will see it.** Most wedding ceremonies are relatively short (about 30 minutes), therefore your guests will be spending most of their time at your reception. We suggest that you spend money on flowers at the reception rather than at the ceremony. You'll be able to enjoy them more at the reception and so will your guests. At a typical wedding, ceremony site flowers are the biggest expense, but you see them for the shortest amount of time!

9 **If there is another wedding scheduled for the same day at your ceremony site, share the floral arrangements with the other bride!** Splitting the cost here could be a major savings. Use neutral hues like whites and creams to avoid any color clashes.

10 **Balloons!** Forget the florist and call a company that does balloon arrangements. You might be surprised at how inexpensive balloons can be. We priced balloon table centerpieces at $30 to $50 each—you'd have to spend twice or three times that amount to get a similar look from fresh flowers. One tip: balloon centerpieces look best in reception sites with high ceilings. For more ideas on affordable table centerpieces, check the box on the following page.

11 **Renting plants and other greenery as filler.** A great money-saving option, this may save you from buying tons of flowers for a reception or ceremony site that needs lots of decoration. Check local nurseries and party stores for rental greenery. Another idea: buy cheap greenery at places like Home Depot. Many sell large potted plants for a fraction of what a florist would charge. Use blooming plants as table centerpieces or larger greenery (trees) to fill in blank spots at the ceremony or reception sites. Best of all, at the end of the reception, you can give them away to guests or reuse them in your own garden.

12 **Re-use some of the arrangements and bouquets.** The bridesmaid's bouquets can be used to decorate the cake and guest book tables. Some altar arrangements can be moved to the reception site (although there may be a delivery fee).

13 **Consider arranging the flowers yourself.** It's not that hard, especially if you have a friend or relative who can lend a hand. An entire package of wedding flowers can be ordered online (see later in this chapter for sources) for as little as $100 or $200. Silk flowers are another option; many craft stores like Michael's (reviewed later) sell do-it-yourself supplies or you can use their in-house arranging service. Another idea: farmer's markets. In our home town, we found local growers selling flowers at prices that can only be described as a steal—a dozen roses for $6, a large mixed bouquet for $7. Pop into Home Depot for some containers (a steel watering can for $10? a galvanized bucket for $5 to $8?) and you've got ceremony or reception site decor on the cheap.

14 **Scale-down the pew decorations at the ceremony.** Consider using just greenery or bows instead of fresh flowers. Some brides have eliminated this decoration altogether. Another option: craft stores will teach you how to make the bows yourself. One handy product is the EZ Bowmaker. This simple $10 device enables you to make professional-looking bows for pew decorations, table centerpieces and more. Why pay a florist hundreds of dollars when you can do it yourself for pennies? Made by EZ Bowz (call 800-311-6529 or 423-453-3060 for a store near you), the EZ Bowmaker is available in craft stores like Michael's (800-Michaels; www.michaels.com). Michael's web site even has free projects with the EZ bowmaker posted online to help inspire you.

15 **Pick the general color scheme and let your florist buy the most affordable flowers available the week of your wedding.** Obviously, you must feel very confident in your florist to go this route. Specifically rule out any flowers you don't want but try to remain flexible—this isn't a tip for control freaks. Flower prices fluctuate so greatly from month to month; take advantage of this by having your florist pick the best bargains.

Table centerpieces on the cheap

Talk with any florist and you'll quickly realize how table center-pieces can greatly inflate the final bill. If you've got ten tables to decorate, the cost of flowers, greenery and a vase can easily run $50 per table. And elaborate centerpieces with extensive flowers and rented pillars can soar above $100 each.

How can you save on this item without looking cheap?

♥ **POTTED PLANTS AT HOME DEPOT.** Five bucks goes a long way at Home Depot. One reader decorated her tables with $5 pots of spring flowers like daffodils and tulips. Obviously, what plants and flowers are available will vary depending on the time of the year. Tip: ask a Home Depot manager what flowers are set to arrive the week of your wedding. Ask them if they can order in specific colors or plants you want, plus set them aside when they arrive so you can get first choice.

♥ **BASKETS WITH GOURDS AND SILK LEAVES.** For a fall wedding, this would be a fitting theme. One bride in Massachusetts told us she found baskets on sale at Pier One for 50% off. By scouting out grocery stores, craft stores, and nurseries, she found gourds, mini pumpkins and silk leaves in fall colors to fill the baskets. Total cost: $21 per basket.

♥ **GOLDFISH BOWLS.** Go to a pet store and buy fish bowls and gold-fish. Place them on mirrored tiles (available at any hardware store) and scatter votive candles nearby. The light will flicker off the water, creating a shimmering effect. Total cost: about $7 per table.

16 **Call a local horticultural school.** A bride in Ohio wrote to us with this great tip–she found that the students at a local horticultural school would arrange the flowers for her wedding for free. She paid for the flowers (only $200) and they did all the labor–a great deal! Check the local phone book for any schools in your area. Another idea: craft stores and community colleges often have classes in flower-arranging. If you don't have time to take a class, see if the students will take on your wedding as a class project.

Another thought: hire an instructor from a local horticulture school to design your wedding flowers. They often moonlight for private parties and are very experienced as well.

17 **Surf the net.** Yes, you can order flowers at wholesale over the web. Check out the Spotlight: Best Buy on 2G Roses later in this chapter for more info on this tip. You (or a friend or relative) have to do the arranging, but this can be a substantial savings.

♥ **EDIBLE CENTERPIECES.** Instead of flowers, have your caterer stack piles of fruit (in coordinating colors, of course) in the center of the table. For example, an arrangement of strawberries with chocolate dipping sauce or powdered sugar would be nice. Another idea: cheesecake centerpieces. Elegant Cheesecakes of Half Moon Bay, CA (650) 728-2248 (web: www.elegantcheesecakes.com) sells cheesecake centerpieces that serve 10 to 12 guests for $75 to $200—not cheap, but since these elaborate designs double as dessert, you save on a the expense of a wedding cake.

♥ **CYBER FLOWERS.** Yes, you can order fresh flowers from the Internet delivered to you via Fed Ex the day before your wedding. You may not want to design and arrange *all* your flowers for your wedding, but you could buy 100 gerbera daisies from the Get Fresh Company (www.getfresh.com) for $144. Find affordable containers and you've got casual, fresh floral centerpieces (at just $14 per table, assuming 10 stems per arrangement) to brighten up your reception site.

Of course, that's just the tip of the iceberg. If you think you're up to making your own centerpieces, check your local library or bookstore for decorating books. We searched Amazon.com's web site and found quite a few titles under the headings "Flower arrangement" and "Table setting and decoration." One book that looked quite interesting was *Tabletops: Easy, Practical, Beautiful Ways to Decorate the Table* (by Barbara Milo Ohrbach, CN Potter Publications, 1997, $24). This hardcover book featured color photos and how-to instructions on creating beautiful, yet affordable table centerpieces.

Flowers

For some lovely yet affordable flowers that won't bust your budget, we've compiled a short list of flowers that can be used to fill out arrangements. Be aware that certain flowers may be more affordable in various regions of the US. Ask your florist for local recommendations. Also, seasonality may affect the prices of certain flowers.

♥ **GERBERA DAISIES.** These giant-sized versions of common daisies make wonderful and colorful bridesmaids' bouquets. They also have long stems and can be used successfully in table and altar arrangements. They come in incredible colors from plain white to deep fuchsia. Pastels are also available; there are even "miniature" gerbera daisies that can be used in boutonnieres.

♥ **STATICE.** A fabulous filler flower for bridal bouquets, these bunches of tiny white or purple blossoms are reasonably priced options. Other fillers that are inexpensive include Queen Anne's Lace and "stock," a long-stalked flower with copious blooms.

♥ **ALSTROEMERIA LILIES.** These are miniature lilies that come in over 20 different shades. Some flowers are even multi-colored. Because they are small, they look best in bouquets, hairpieces, on wedding cakes or in table arrangements.

♥ **CARNATIONS.** Ah, the old standby. These are a great pick for altar arrangements since they stand out without great expense. They come in every color variety, but we don't recommend the dyed ones—stick to natural colors. Some varieties are also available as miniatures if you want to add them to table arrangements or bouquets. These are very "heat-hardy" too for those of you in hot climates.

♥ **CHRYSANTHEMUMS.** More commonly referred to as mums, these flowers are also great filler for altar arrangements. They add oodles of volume to your arrangements without costing a great deal. These flowers are available in a wide range of colors from white to bronze. Some even look like simple daisies in pinks, yellows and white.

❤ GLADIOLUS. These long-stalked flowers are covered in bright blooms. They look especially nice in altar or buffet arrangements to add height. Individual blooms can be used as glamelias (ask your florist to see an example). Colors range from white to pink to deep, true red.

 ❤ FREESIA. Another small delicate flower with a pleasant scent, freesia can be used as a wonderful substitute for the more expensive stephanotis (a traditional "bridal" flower). They come in white, yellow, pink, orange, lavender, and red.

❤ HEATHER. This dusty-pink flower has tiny spikes of bell-shaped flowers. Many florists use heather as an affordable boutonniere or in corsages. The price is about $1.50 per stem.

Biggest Myths about Wedding Flowers

MYTH #1 *"My mother insists that we have lots and lots of flowers at my wedding. Is this really necessary?"*

Bridal magazines often picture weddings with flowers dripping from the ceiling and crawling along the floor. Some florists feed this perception by suggesting superfluous floral items like "cake knife corsages" (believe it or not, a special flower wrapped with a bow around the knife you cut the cake with), "hairpiece flowers" and arrangements for the gift table. We are not making this stuff up. Does the gift table really need a floral arrangement?

Among the more ridiculous examples of floral price gouging: $20 for *petals* for a flower girl's basket (that doesn't include the basket, nor rose petals—just regular flower petals) and $50 for a small floral wreath for the flower girl's hair. Those were actual prices quoted to a Chicago bride by a Winnetka florist. The same bride told the florist to keep the quote under $1500. The florist's bid: $1900.

Another example of floral excess: the Martha Stewart "bouquet eats bride" look. We've noticed Martha's magazine has recently featured monster bridal bouquets that look like they could swallow a small child. Of course, these "fabulous" bouquets make a "bold statement"—and a big dent in your wallet at a cost of hundreds of dollars each.

MYTH #2 *"I figured on spending only about $250 on my wedding flowers. Given the cost of arrangements I've sent friends, I assume this is a good estimate."*

Most flowers are cheap. Most *florists* aren't. What you are paying for is the florist's talent, skill and overhead. The manual labor needed to create beautiful bouquets and arrangements (not to mention delivering them) is what costs big money. We should note that some exotic flowers (orchids, etc.) are pricey exceptions: they virtually guarantee an astronomically high floral bill.

Helpful Hints

1 Put your deposit and balance on a credit card. We have heard occasional stories of couples who hired a florist to do their flowers only to have the wrong flowers delivered. Or worse, the florist went out of business. Although these are rare occurrences, its best to be safe. Payments on credit cards are protected by special consumer protection laws. See the Apparel chapter for more details.

2 Keep an open mind. Instead of setting your heart on a particular design or flower, let your florist come up with some suggestions. Because florists works with flowers so closely, they may be aware of some options that are really terrific. Especially with regards to colors, listen to your florist's ideas and look at some of their past work before you make up your mind. You might be surprised!

3 Confirm any restrictions on flowers/decorations. Some churches prohibit candles and still others "request" that you donate the altar arrangement to the church. Reception sites may also have similar rules, especially regarding the throwing of birdseed or flower petals.

4 Go European. Check out European bridal magazines (available on most newsstands or in bookstores) for creative ideas. We've noticed those publications feature more unique designs than their American counterparts.

5 Mail order catalogs. These are great for tracking down hard to find items. An example: Illuminations (800) CANDLES (www.illuminations. com) sells dozens of varieties of (what else?) candles, holders and other supplies. Quantity discounts are available for bulk purchases. Another catalog to have is Linen & Lace (800) 332-5223 (www.linen-lace.com). They specialize in lace curtains and tablecloths, but we were surprised to see some bridal accessories such as a silver "Tussie Mussie" bouquet holder that was $38.50. Not cheap, but, it is sterling silver.

6 Head measurements for floral wreaths. One bride emailed us this tip: if you order floral wreaths for the flower girls or bridesmaids, make sure you give the florist head measurements so they have an idea how big (or small) to make the wreaths. Her florist failed to get this detail, and the resulting flower girl wreaths were so big they could be worn around the girls' necks.

7 Label the personal flowers. Here's a tip from a bride who learned this lesson the hard way: have your florist label the personal flowers (bouquets, corsages, boutonnieres) with the names of the intended recipient. That way you know who gets what at the wedding— and you avoid that messy scene when Aunt Bunny "accidentally" takes that special corsage you had made up for your mother-in-law. Don't laugh, this can happen to you.

8 Check out floral arrangement books. In the library or at the bookstore you can find many books on floral arranging or entertaining. You may find some great ideas that you can take to your florist or do yourself. You can also educate yourself a bit on types of flowers and good design tips.

Pitfalls to Avoid

PITFALL #1 THE MERCEDES SYNDROME

"I was at a florist the other day discussing my wedding when another bride pulled up in an expensive car. All the sudden, the florist's employees started chattering about how rich she was and how they'd have to triple the bill for her flowers! They were kidding, right?"

Maybe not. We once interviewed a florist who admitted charging more for wedding flowers depending on what type of car the bride drove up in! Apparently, brides who arrived at the florist's studio in fancy wheels looked like they could afford to pay more for their wedding flowers. While that sounds absurd, think about it—when you walk into a flower shop, do you see any prices for bridal bouquets? Nope, most flower proposals are worked up on the fly, where a florist "estimates" what items cost due to the flowers used. Or perhaps how deep the client's pockets appear.

We've never tested this theory scientifically, but we wonder what would happen if two brides arrived at a floral shop to price bridal arrangements. One drives a Mercedes; the other a Ford Pinto. Who gets charged more? We sense this happens based on email we've received from readers. One bride in Oklahoma told us her florist's eyes lit up when the bride slipped and mentioned her fiancé was a doctor. Suddenly, the florist *insisted* she fly in exotic Asiatic lilies for the wedding. And the bill soared concurrently.

So a word of advice when floral shopping: don't flash that big diamond engagement ring. Dress in baggy clothes. And take the bus.

PITFALL #2 "FTD COOKIE-CUTTER" WEDDINGS

*"I met with a florist for my wedding and was extremely disappointed. All
they showed me were boring FTD design books. The few real photos I saw
featured bouquets that all looked the same."*

Some florists try to make every wedding fit a "cookie cutter" mold.
Instead of keying on the individuality involved, they merely suggest stiff,
formulated designs that are uninspired at best and dreadful at worst. We
find "cash and carry" florists most guilty of this offense—they simply
don't care enough about weddings to try harder.

PITFALL #3 PLASTIC BOUQUET HOLDERS

*"We attended a fancy wedding and were surprised at the bouquets.
Beautiful flowers were stuck in plastic holders that just looked cheap!"*

Plastic bouquet holders have become a crutch for many lazy florists.
Instead of hand-tying and hand-wrapping the bouquets, some florists
simply stick flowers into floral foam inside plastic holders. Besides looking
cheap, poorly-inserted flowers can actually drop out of the plastic holder!

Some florists insist plastic holders are necessary since they provide a
water source for delicate flowers. Other florists point out plastic holders
are a cost-cutter for crescent or cascade bouquets, since they don't have
to wire each individual bloom. That's great, but as they say, show us the
money—we often found little savings with florists that use plastic holders.

If your florist uses plastic holders, insist the plastic be covered with
green floral tape and/or ribbon. Another idea: you can camouflage a
holder by wrapping it in satin fabric or by using leaves. Or choose a
florist that hand ties and hand wraps the bouquets. A small tube of
water can be attached to delicate flowers needing moisture.

PITFALL #4 HEAT-SENSITIVE FLOWERS.

*"My friend got married last summer in an outdoor ceremony.
Unfortunately, the heat caused the flowers to wilt and even turn brown."*

If your wedding is in the summer, watch out for flowers that are vul-
nerable to extreme heat. Some flowers with this problem include
stephanotis and gardenias. Ask your florist for flowers that can withstand the heat and still look fresh. As a side note, we heard from one
florist who uses an "anti-transpirant" spray such as Bloomlife Plastic
Wax or Crowning Glory on delicate blooms. These products seal in the
moisture so flowers don't wilt as fast.

REAL WEDDING TIP

Beware the Surprise Consulting Fee

A reader in Richardson, TX gave a florist a $100 deposit to hold the date for her wedding. The florist said she could work within the bride's specified budget, promising to mail a detailed proposal in short order.

Two weeks later, the proposal came in—at twice the amount the bride had budgeted. Obviously, the bride wasn't very happy. When she told the florist she was going elsewhere for flowers, the florist said she was keeping the $100, calling it a "consulting fee." To make matters worse, she had the gall to send the bride another bill for $62, for "additional labor" to prepare the proposal.

What's the lesson? Whenever you give a deposit, make sure you get a written receipt that states any refund/cancellation policies. Even better: put it on a credit card. Then, if the florist decides your refundable deposit is now non-refundable, you can go to your credit card company to dispute the charge. While it may be tempting to place deposits to hold dates, make sure you first get written documentation spelling out the refund policies.

PITFALL #5 MARTHAHOLICS.

"I fell in love with a bouquet I saw in the Martha Stewart Weddings magazine. The flowers were phenomenal and I wanted my florist to copy it exactly. But when my florist called to find the source for the flowers, they told him they are from Martha's garden and not available commercially! Shoot!"

While Martha is an arbiter of taste and trends these days, sometimes she forgets to let brides in on a secret: the supplies are often hard or impossible to find. Or the "Martha look" may be impossible to replicate without hours of labor by a florist. If you've got your heart set on a Martha design, realize you may have to make compromises or shell out big bucks.

PITFALL #6 THE MARRIAGE MARK-UP?

"I went to a florist to price wedding arrangements. Among other items they quoted me $13.50 for a corsage with one rose and some alstroemeria. Later that week my sister called to order corsages for another event and they quoted her $8 for a corsage with three roses, filler flowers, greenery and a big bow! Why do brides have to pay more to get fewer flowers?

Wonder if you say the word "wedding," and the price rises for flowers? We have always been suspicious of some florists, who seem to view brides and grooms as automatic cash machines. To test this theory, Boston NBC-TV affiliate WHDH called Massachusetts area florists to price wedding flowers. Then they called back to price flowers for a retirement party. Guess what? Eight out of 11 florists they called quoted them the "marriage mark-up." The same flowers, just a different event. . . and a different price. One example: a table centerpiece that is $30 for a retirement party, but $50 for a wedding. Another said flowers would be $25 for a party, but $80 for a wedding. "As soon as they hear wedding, they'll jack up the price," a Boston wedding planner told the TV reporter.

So, what's a bride to do? Well, while it is tempting to not tell the florist you are planning a wedding, this may not be very practical. Brides need items like bridal and bridesmaids bouquets that are hard to fake as items for a birthday party. The best advice may be to just get several competitive bids. Not all florists charge a marriage mark-up—take some time to get a few bids to make sure you are getting a good deal.

Trends

♥ TWO WORDS: MARTHA STEWART. Just about whatever Martha features in her bridal magazine or TV show, brides want. Lately she's been showing nosegays using one type of flower. But no more the loosely constructed designs. Instead she's using as many blooms packed together as tightly as possible. The look has an almost Victorian feel with its emphasis on masses of blooms.

♥ ROSES ARE BACK. Out of favor for several years, the sweet simplicity of roses is making a come back. But no more the solid cream or white blossoms. Now bi-color looks such as pink and white or red and white are popular. And rich reds are no longer relegated to table centerpieces. You'll see brides carrying whole bouquets of bright color.

♥ MASSIVE BLOOMS. Flowers like hydrangeas are becoming popular. With such a mega bloom you get lots of bang for the buck in lavenders, pinks or whites. Other giant blooms include lilies and gerbera daisies.

♥ TEENY TINY BLOSSOMS. On the other hand, miniature calla lilies and gerbera daisies are a hit when massed together in bright colors for bridesmaids bouquets.

♥ CUTTING EDGE BOUTONNIERES. Forget those single rose or carnation boutonnieres. Today's couples are choosing tiny blooming sprigs like heather or even fragrant herbs such as rosemary, basil and lavender to adorn the guys.

SPOTLIGHT: ROSES

Roses are still by far the most requested flower in wedding arrangements and bouquets. In the mid to late 1990's there was a trend away from roses in bridal bouquets, but they've seen a resurgence in recent years. Here is some more background on this venerable bloom:

Types of Roses
"Where do florists get roses? Will they look like roses at the grocery store? How can I be sure to get the best quality?"

Florists buy roses from wholesalers. Wholesalers, in turn, buy them from a variety of sources. California is the largest producer of roses for the US, but roses also come from Colombia (Visa roses) and Mexico (Vega roses). Another big supplier of roses to the US is Ecuador, not to mention Holland and France which also export some varieties. Some of the best roses are Vegas, whose blossoms tend to be bigger than California roses and better shaped than Visas. Each florist typically has his or her own preference.

Roses also come in a variety of qualities, similar to eggs at the grocery store. California roses, for example, come in Select (the best), Extra Fancy (middle quality) and Fancy (cheap). Most of what you see in grocery stores are Fancy roses. Few professional florists sell Fancy roses, but it is difficult to determine yourself which grade your florist buys. If you are concerned about the quality, ask the florist which grade is used. Hopefully, they'll say Select. Select roses will be more expensive, but the quality will be better.

Color Options
"I requested bridal white roses from my florist for my bridal bouquet, but the bouquet I saw on my wedding day looked pinkish rather than white. Was my florist substituting the wrong flowers?"

Definitely not. One thing brides should understand about colors in the floral business is that they can be very deceiving. For example, a red rose isn't actually a true red. And a "bridal white" rose isn't really all-white, rather it's a creamy white hue with a pink- or peach-tinged center. Gather several bridal white roses together in a bouquet and the overall look may be more pink or peach than you expected.

Here are some examples of other popular wedding roses:

♥ **Champagne**
A creamy, antique ivory colored rose.

♥ Candia

Creamy white with dark pink edges to the petals. This would be a truly unusual look.

♥ Darling

A creamy peach rose suitable for a touch of color in the bride's or bridesmaids' bouquets.

♥ Bridal Pink

These are definitely all-pink roses. Many brides assume they will be soft pink, but they are actually quite a bit brighter.

♥ Delores

This is a soft pink rose.

♥ Jacaranda or Purvey

A hot pink rose; perfect with the jewel tones of bridesmaids' dresses.

♥ Lady Diana

Named after the late Princess of Wales, these are pale peach roses. They are beautiful for bridal work and may even look pinkish rather than peach against a pink background.

♥ Sonia

A brighter peach rose with a little more vibrant color than the Lady Di.

♥ Jacqueline Kennedy

One of the few true red roses but tends to be rather small in size.

♥ Madame Delbard

This is a French rose with a rich velvety red color. It opens well but can be expensive.

♥ Sterling Silver

Also called an Elizabeth Taylor, the color is a lovely lavender. It tends to have a small blossom than other roses.

♥ Ranunculus

These flowers aren't actually roses, but they do look a lot like a fully open rose. They make a very inexpensive alternative to roses especially since they are available in February and March, the time of year when roses are most expensive. They come in reds, pinks, and yellows.

One interesting final note on roses: color has little or nothing to do with prices. You might expect more unusual hues (lavender, for example) to cost more but in reality the wholesale price is often the same.

Unique Ideas

♥ Hold the rice. The traditional rice thrown at the newlyweds has been declared "environmentally-incorrect" (birds eat the rice; birds die). So, couples have been replacing rice with flower petals, bubbles and so on. Another alternative to rice to consider: The Butterfly Celebration (800) 548-3284 (www.butterflycelebration.com) sells butterflies for live release as the bride and groom make their get-away.

SPOTLIGHT: BEST BUY

2G ROSES
(800) 880-0735; Web: www.freshroses.com

Ever wish you could order flowers at wholesale prices direct from the grower? Thanks to the 'net, you can—2G Roses is our pick as a best buy for brides who want to do their own flowers. The Watsonville, CA grower has been in business since 1974, but just recently branched out into cyberspace.

Their web site is a floral bargain hunter's paradise. 2G sells much more than roses—you can order lilies, orchids, tulips or hundreds of other available varieties. And the prices? Roses start at as little as 50¢ a stem. You can order flowers in individual bunches (say, calla lilies, 10 stems for $10 to $15) or select one of several bridal packages. For example, the "All Rose Wedding" features enough roses, greenery and filler flowers to make ten table arrangements, eight boutonnieres, four corsages, four bridesmaids bouquets, one bride's bouquet and a head table arrangement. Price: $355, including shipping (FED-EX overnight to insure freshness). Order that many flowers from a retail florist and you'd easily spend two or three times that amount of money.

If that's too much, consider buying a la carte items. For example, enough flowers for a bride's bouquet (25 roses, filler flowers) is just $25 (plus shipping). That might be perfect for a smaller wedding where you just need a bouquet or two. While there is no minimum order, the overnight shipping charges on small orders can be substantial.

Of course, once you get the flowers, you'll need someone to arrange them. If you don't have a friend or relative skilled to do that, consider just doing table centerpieces. 2G's "Simple Elegance" package includes enough gardenias, smilax (greenery) and rose petals for 10 table centerpieces. Price: $155, including shipping. At $15.50 a table centerpiece, that's a steal.

2G's web site clearly explains their packages and how to order, or you can call for a brochure and price list. Most handy was a chart that listed flower availability by month—that way you can tell exactly what blooms are available for, say, an October wedding.

In order to test out this concept, we ordered a sample bunch of 25 mixed color roses from 2G. The short (14" to 18") table roses were $14, with shipping adding another $16 to the tab. 2G sent us an email to confirm our phone order; they were professional and courteous on the phone.

The box arrived on time with an ice pack, bubble wrap and little tags noting the rose names/colors. We should note the roses came tightly budded, with instructions on how to care for them. It took about two to three days for the buds to fully open; unfortunately, four or five roses were duds (they didn't open at all). Nonetheless, we were impressed with the overall quality of the roses, which perfumed our office for quite a few days thereafter.

Of course, 2G Roses isn't the only grower selling flowers at wholesale over the web. Another interesting site is the **Get Fresh Company** (web: www.getfreshwithme.com), which has extensive price lists on-line that are updated weekly. They also offer four wedding packages ranging from $330 to $1000. The "Elegant" package for smaller weddings, includes 50 roses, 10 spray roses, Asiatic lilies, various filler flowers like snapdragons and ranunculus, and greenery for a mere $330.

Our biggest frustration with GetFresh.com's site is its lack of organization. While they do offer wedding packages, they don't call them out very clearly on the site. You can click on the catalog button to get to those options, or choose the Browse and Buy category.

Tips for mail order flowers

♥ **Do a small test order first, a few months before your wedding.** That way you can evaluate the flower quality, color and delivery. You can also see how long it takes certain flowers to open. A multi-color bunch is a good idea to see variations in hues.

♥ **Plan in advance.** You may need the flowers to arrive a few days before your wedding to insure they open in time. Warm water speeds this process, but it can still take a few days.

♥ **Remember you don't have to go whole hog.** If the thought of doing ALL your floral arrangements via the web is scary, consider doing merely the table centerpieces or other decor at the ceremony or reception site. Then hire a professional florist to do the personal flowers (bouquets, corsages, etc.).

CYBER FLOWERS

Here's how two major floral web sites for weddings stack up:

COMPANY	# OF WEDDING PACKAGES	PRICES
2G ROSES WWW.FRESHROSES.COM	3	$110-355
GET FRESH	4	$256-1000

Spotlight: Craft Stores

MICHAELS ARTS AND CRAFTS STORES
(800) MICHAELS
www.michaels.com

One of the best sources for silk flowers and wedding supplies in North America has got to be Michaels Arts and Crafts stores. With over 450 stores in the US and Canada, Michaels provides not only a large number of attractive, affordable silk flowers, but they also have in-store arrangers who can do all the arrangements at affordable rates.

For example, when we visited a Michaels store, the floral department told us most custom silk bouquets range from $25 to $65. Pre-made silk bouquets are just $10 to $15. Wow! This is a great savings when compared with the average fresh bouquets from a retail florist—which can range from $75 to $200 and more.

Michaels stores also carry other accessories for do-it-yourself brides. They have supplies with which to make veils and headpieces($3 to $20), wedding cakes toppers, favors (Jordan almond 16 oz. Bag $5), unity candles ($13-$25) and other wedding items. They carry accessories ranging from ring pillows to do-it-yourself invitations to cake knives as well.

If you have access to the web, check out Michaels excellent web site (www.michaels.com). Besides the standard store locator, you'll also find craft projects posted on-line, complete with supplies lists and instructions. We saw several bridal projects that could be used to make favors, table centerpieces and more. There's also a "crafts calendar" that lists in-store classes.

Shipping	Comments
Included (Fed-ex)	Wedding sampler available
$37-$47	$50 late fee for last minute orders

HOBBY LOBBY
(405) 745-1100; web: www.hobbylobby.com

Hobby Lobby is an expanding national chain of craft stores with some unusual offerings. We were surprised to find that Hobby Lobby rents an amazing variety of arches, columns and greenery. For example, you can rent a brass heart-shaped arch for a mere $40. How about 7-candle candelabras? $25 per pair. Wrought iron stands with greenery are only $35 per pair. For an extra charge, you can customize the greenery used to decorate arches and columns.

Of course, Hobby Lobby still carries all the usual bridal supplies like silk flowers and ribbon. We also saw throw away silk bouquets for $10, headpieces for $10 to $20 and unity candles for $5 to $15. Favor supplies were extensive including bags of Jordan almonds for $7 per 16 oz.

But don't limit yourself to the wedding aisles at this store. We discovered clay pots (for garden style table centerpieces) for only $5. Looking for gifts for children in your wedding party? Don't pass up the funky picture frames and craft kits for kids. Overall, we think Hobby Lobby is one of the best do-it-yourself wedding resources you'll find in the country.

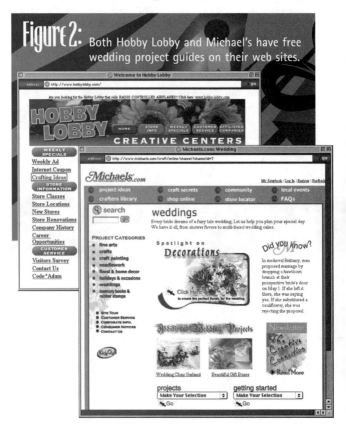

Figure 2: Both Hobby Lobby and Michael's have free wedding project guides on their web sites.

MJDESIGNS
(817) 329-3196; web: www.mjdesigns.com

MJDesigns is an excellent place for wedding accessories and supplies. Yes, the company has scaled back their stores to a handful in Dallas/Ft. Worth, but they still have a huge selection of fine quality silk flowers and supplies for the do-it-yourselfer. If you prefer to have your wedding flowers arranged for you but can't afford the high prices of retail florists, MJDesigns has the answer.

Each store carries a catalog of ten different designs for brides' and bridesmaids' bouquets ($15 to $60). Besides bouquets, there were ten possible corsage designs, and five boutonniere options. We also saw pew bows, hairpieces, flower girl baskets and veils—all at very affordable prices.

To order a bouquet from MJDesigns, you first pick a color from the display in each store. Then, you choose a style from their catalog. MJDesigns then sends your order to their main design studio where it takes about seven days to produce. The store also provides other wedding accessories, including cake decorating supplies, toasting glasses, cake toppers and veil supplies. Their web site includes craft ideas and directions as well (see Figure 3 below).

Figure 3: We downloaded this reception favor project guide (a PDF file) from MJDesigns.com.

Floral Dictionary

Lilies

♥ **Calla**

Huge, long white flowers on thick stalks (as in Katherine Hepburn's ". . . the calla lilies are in bloom.") Smaller versions (called posy calla lilies) come in a variety of colors.

♥ **Rubrim**

Star flowers, come in colors from white to peach to deep maroon.

Rubrim Lily.

♥ **Lily of the Valley**

Small, white blooms that look like tiny bells. This flower is affordable in the northern climates but quite expensive in other parts of the U.S. For a picture, see "Top Money-saving Secrets" earlier in the chapter.

Orchids

♥ **Dendrobium**

Miniature orchids that come in sprays, may be used individually or as trailing pieces.

♥ **Cymbidium**

Smaller than Japhet orchids with a curly edge only at the center.

♥ **Japhet**

Large orchids with a curly edge all over, often have yellow throats.

Dendrobium Orchid.

♥ **Phalaenopsis**

These are round-edged orchids that are white with reddish throats. Their delicate nature makes them best for corsages as opposed to bridal bouquets.

Miscellaneous

♥ **Stephanotis**

Small, white flowers with star-like petals and a deep throat (we've been told that these can discolor in extreme heat.)

♥ **Anthuriums**

One of the few "true red" flowers, this has a heart-shaped bloom with a large stamen.

Stephanotis

Chapter 6

INVITATIONS

In this chapter, we'll tell you about a printing process that can save you 50% or more on your invitations. Then check out discount sources for invites, from catalogs to web sites. Next, we'll show you the five-step shopping process for finding invitations, and share several unique ideas such as letterpress invitations.

What Are You Buying?

Buying invitations is a little like buying a meal at an à la carte restaurant. In other words, everything is priced separately: the appetizer, salad, entree, and dessert. With invitations, the entree is the basic invitation design itself (the paper style and the printing). Thankfully, the price does include the envelopes (two for very formal invitations or one for more informal options).

There also are other "accessories" available but these are priced separately in addition to the original invitation. Here are some options and a short description:

♥ RECEPTION CARDS announce to the guest the location and time of the reception.

♥ **RESPONSE CARDS** (also known as R.S.V.P.'s) are just as they sound—a card that asks guests to tell you whether or not they can attend. An envelope (with your return address printed) is included with each response card. Most brides put postage on the response card envelopes to encourage their guests to respond.

♥ **ENVELOPE LININGS** add a little flair and color to invitations.

♥ **YOUR RETURN ADDRESS** can be printed on the back flap of the envelopes.

♥ **INFORMALS**, used mainly as thank-you notes, usually are blank cards with your names printed on the outside.

♥ **EXCLUSIVE (OR PHOTO) LETTERING VERSUS REGULAR LETTERING** refers to the style of lettering you choose for your invitation. Most invitation books offer you a choice between styles of script. Some, however also offer two separate lists to choose from called "exclusive (or photo)" and "regular." Exclusive lettering is more expensive than regular lettering but we recommend using exclusive lettering anyway. Why? Exclusive lettering gives you a wider choice of type-styles. Also, the *size* of exclusive lettering can be adjusted to fit the size of your invitation—a plus if you want a more intricate invitation design. The choice is up to you but the added expense is very small (about $4 or $5 per 100 invitations).

♥ **PROGRAMS, PEW CARDS, AND OTHER ENCLOSURES** may be additional items you'll see in invitation books. Programs ($30 to $100 per 100) list all the participants in the wedding ceremony and tell guests the order of the service. Pew cards are used to differentiate between guests who are to be seated up at the front of the church (reserved seating) from those who should be seated farther back (general admission). Maps are used at weddings with many out of town guests or if guests are going to a separate reception site after the ceremony.

A word on invitations sizes. Most wedding invitations are rectangles; a typical size is 5" by 7". In recent years, new hip styles include square invites (7" by 7" or their smaller cousins, marquis 5.5" by 5.5") and something called "tea length" invites that are the size of this book (4" by 9"). Remember that larger square invitations may require additional postage.

Average total costs. The average couple pays about $390 for invitations and other stationery needs (for a wedding with 150 guests). But you can spend as little as $100 . . . or as much as $800 for top-of-the-line engraved options. The average deposit is 50% down with the balance due when you pick up your order.

Where to Buy Invitations

Fortunately, there is no national shortage wedding invitations; not only are the styles endless, but the suppliers are equally plentiful. How does this process usually work? Well, most wedding invitations are printed by big, national printers. Some of these printers have a network of retail dealers (stationery shops, department stores, etc.). Others market invitations through the mail—they print up full-color catalogs and do business over an 800-number. You can also buy invitations through discount buying services. And, of course, you can also buy invites online.

Here's a little secret about the invitations industry you won't hear from anyone else. Ironically, the same company owns both the major mail-order catalogs *and* many of the invitation brands sold through retail stores. Taylor Corp. is the 800 lb. gorilla in this business—this private printing company with $826 million in annual sales has over 70 subsidiaries in the US, Europe and Australia. We guess that Taylor long ago must have realized brides don't want to buy their invitations from some giant company. So instead, Taylor has a Byzantine collection of brands and catalogs that operate more or less like autonomous business units.

Taylor owns such major invitation brands as Regency (and its upscale division Elite), Carlson Craft, Celebration, Chase, Nu Art/Pacific Thermographers, Stylart, Royal, Masterpiece and Tatex among others. Taylor also owns major mail order invitation mail-order catalogs like Rexcraft and the American Wedding Album. Taylor also owns Current, the mail-order specialty catalog. And here's the crazy part: you can often find the very same invitations styles sold through retail stationer shops in a Taylor-owned mail order catalog at HALF the retail price.

Of course, you can bypass the standard invitation brands entirely if you wish—all you need is a computer and printer. More on this later. Here are some common (and not-so common) places to find wedding invitations:

♥ RETAIL SOURCES.

1 **Stationery shops.** Look under "Invitations" or "Wedding Invitations" in the phone book and you'll find a smorgasbord of places, from party stores to gift boutiques. As dealers for the major invitations printers, they carry a selection of sample books containing examples of each invitation. Brides choose a design from these sample books and then place an order. The hands-on service is one of the chief advantages to this route—most stores can help you with etiquette/wording questions and, perhaps more importantly, deal with any problems that crop up with the printer. Of course, you pay for this service with full-retail prices and few discounts.

2 **Places you wouldn't think of.** Some churches and synagogues offer invitations at discounted prices as a fund-raiser. We've even

heard of several companies that offer invitations as a perk for their employees. One bride who worked at Xerox told us she was able to order invitations through the company at a substantial discount.

Another great source is "out of home" stationers. These businesses operate from home-based offices and, thanks to low overhead, usually pass along savings from 10% to 20%. You still get service with these stationers, just no fancy retail shop. As with any merchant you deal with for your wedding, you'll want to make sure the company is reputable by calling the Better Business Bureau, checking references, etc.

Some department stores with bridal registries also sell invitations, as do off-set printers. Some local printers actually print their own invitations, while most send the orders along to the same national printers you'll see in stationery shops.

♥ Mail-order/Web catalogs

Of course, you can also order wedding invitations from the comfort of your home. Over 20 companies have sprung up in recent years to offer wedding invitations via mail (later in this chapter we'll review some of the best).

How do the catalogs work? First, you call the 1-800 number and wait two to four weeks for the catalog to arrive. The glossy four-color publication will have pictures of invitations, accessories and generic etiquette/wording advice. Most will also send along a sample or two of various invitation styles.

Ordering from the catalogs is rather easy. Prices (at least on the invitations) are hard to beat; we've found the same designs in catalogs for 40% less than at retail stores. Yes, we are talking the SAME invitation. Most take credit cards and are quick to fill the order—it takes as little as two to four days (plus another week shipping time). Expedited or overnight delivery may be available, but at a steep extra cost.

Later in this chapter we'll go into more details on mail-order invitations, including pitfalls to avoid.

Don't forget the Internet either. Invitations web sites abound with catalogs of major manufacturers online and online shopping as well. Even small, custom designers are using the web to attract customers by offering the offbeat and the unusual. You'll see some of these sites later in this chapter.

We do have to admit using the 'net to shop for invitations is often an exercise in frustration. With a few exceptions, most major catalog's web sites are poorly designed and hard to navigate. Slogging through page after page of invites to look at tiny thumbnails of invitations is a pain. Like everything on the web, we realize much of this will be fixed over time but we can't wonder if the old-fashion printed catalog or stationery store is a better way to invitation shop for the time being.

♥ Discount buying services.

Later in the chapter, we review Invitation Hotline, an example of a discount buying service for invitations. What do they discount? Basically, the same premium brand names you'd see in full-price stationary shops (examples of such brands are reviewed later in this chapter) at discounts from 15% to 25%!

Discount buying services are a hybrid between mail-order and retail dealers. They don't have any catalogs—you do the shopping and then call them for a price quote, once you've decided on the invitation (a page or style number will work). Once you place the order over the phone, the invitations are mailed back to you within a few weeks time. In a way, discount buying services offer the best of all worlds—the high-quality of premium brands at discount prices, combined with the convenience of mail-order.

Sources to Find Stationers

♥ Friends. Recently-married couples may be your best resource to find a good stationer.

♥ Bridal shows. Bridal shows are a great place to find little-known stationery companies. You may be able to look through some of their sample books at a show too.

♥ Other bridal businesses. Many other bridal businesses such as photographers, florists and bridal shops may be able to suggest a good local stationer. Some wedding vendors even sell invitations at steep discounts as a perk for their customers.

♥ Discount Bridal Service. Besides gowns, most DBS reps also sell invites at discounts. For a list of their representatives who also discount invitations call (800) 874-8794, web: www.DiscountBridalService.com.

 Brides in Cyberspace: What's on the Web?

OurBeginning.com
Web: www.ourbeginning.com
What it is: An online wedding stationary superstore.
What's cool: The company offers hundreds of styles and some interesting interactive features, including enlarged pictures of any invite. The "Personal Preview" area lets you store invites that you or your friends can look at. Click another button and get an online price quote. Overall, we found this site very well-designed and easy to use. While we didn't have time to do an in-depth analysis of the site's prices, they looked in line with those from mail-order catalogs (they claim a 20% discount off retail).

Figure 1: Cluttered, yes, but OurBeginning.com offers hundreds of invitation styles to view online.

Needs work: Talk about a cluttered site! (See Figure 1 above). Another negative: they don't list invitations by manufacturer, making it hard to locate a specific design. Instead, they list options by style, theme, presentation and color.

Wednet's Engaging Questions and Library

Web: www.wednet.com/questions/default.asp or go to www.wednet.com and click on "Engaging Questions" or "Library"

What it is: One of the best wedding FAQ's with detailed, accurate info.

What's cool: This site is easy to use with simple search functions. The "Engaging Questions" page is divided into categories and includes answers to questions about family difficulties, clothing and beauty, and even theme weddings. We like the tone of the "experts" and found their answers thoughtful and helpful. WedNet's "Library" is a compendium of articles on various planning aspects of a wedding. A quick search for info on invitations turned up six different invitations wording samples. The search options seem endless with hundreds of articles available.

Needs work: This may be a minor quibble, but we couldn't find a way to send the site's etiquette expert a question. Isn't "interactivity" what is supposed to make the web so cool? Yea, there is a general email address, but no direct email link.

eInvite

Web: www.einvite.com

What it is: An online invitation source affiliated with the Wedding-Channel.com (see Figure 2).

What's cool: This site with its 1000 invitation designs (from Traditional to Layered to Superb Value and more), offers a unique option: "display proofs." Simply select any design, enter your personal wording, choose an ink color and letter style, then click on "display proof." Immediately you'll see a life size version of your wedding invitation exactly as it would be printed. If you like it, it's simple to order the design online.

If you have any etiquette concerns eInvite offers a wedding etiquette guide, FAQ and email access to human experts. Shipping is a mere three days, according to the site, and brides can request up to six samples for free ($2 thereafter).

Needs work: Perhaps our biggest complaint about eInvite is the price. For a basic panel invitation ("Simplicity" in the Tradition section) the invitation itself was $229 per 100. Ouch! We thought the advantage to buying on line was cheaper prices because overhead is lower! We weren't able to view the paper quality so it's hard to say if the actual invites justify the high price.

Other web sites to consider. If you're looking for general articles on invitations, the **Wedding Channel** (www.WeddingChannel.com) offers quite a compendium. From the "History of the Wedding Invitation" to "Mastering the Art of Mailing Invitations," site cover a broad range of topics. Remember, however, to take some of their advice with a grain of salt.

What about etiquette? The Internet age has raised a whole new set of questions about wedding invites. Should you use your computer to print address labels for invitation envelopes? Should you put the web site where you're registered on your invitation? Fortunately, sites like **TheKnot.com** provide answers to these thorny questions.

Figure 2: eInvite's cool "online proof" lets you create and customize invites to your heart's desire—but at a stiff price.

Finally, check out **Catalog Orders Headquarters** (www.catalog. orders.com), which offers free catalogs of invitations (most of which are reviewed later in this chapter) for brides in the US and Canada.

Getting Started: How Far in Advance?

There are five steps in the shopping process for invitations: Overall, we recommend you order invitations at least three to four months before your wedding.

1 Shopping. Take a couple of weeks to visit two or three stationers in your area. If you are interested in mail-order, remember it takes two to four WEEKS (or more) to receive most catalogs.

2 Ordering. This varies greatly by printer. Generally, it can take anywhere from ten days to two months to order invitations. Most orders take two to four weeks, although some companies offer rush service.

3 Mistakes. We suggest you leave a two week "buffer zone" in case your invitations come in with errors. One stationer told us that one out of every three orders comes in with mistakes from the printer. "Quality control" seems to be a fuzzy concept with some invitation printers.

4 Addressing. Considering how busy you probably are with work and wedding planning, leaving four weeks here is prudent. If you choose to hire a local calligrapher, most take between one and three weeks to complete a job.

5 Mailing. Everyone knows how wonderfully efficient the US Postal Service is. Give yourself plenty of time. Mail invitations to out-of-town guests *at least* six weeks before the wedding. For in-town guests, mail at least four weeks before the event. If your wedding is on near a holiday, consider mailing even earlier so your guests will have time to make plans.

Step-by-step Shopping Strategies

♥ **Step 1:** Determine the number of invitations needed. Here's a quick quiz: if you're inviting 200 people to your wedding, do you need 200 invitations? Answer: no—you send only one invitation *per household*. And since most of the folks you invite will be couples, you probably need about 100 invitations. (There is one exception to this rule, however: if a guest's child is over 18 and living at home, he receives his own invitation.) This step, of course, involves the groom. You must compile a list of his, yours, theirs (parents' friends) and ours.

♥ **Step 2:** Confirm the place and time of the wedding and reception. Also, verify the spellings of the facilities and names of participants. (We heard one story of a bride who didn't know how to spell her fiancé's middle name—the resulting invitation was misspelled! Doing your homework here is obviously helpful.)

♥ **Step 3:** Determine your overall wedding style. For example, an outdoor afternoon wedding followed by a barbecue reception will probably not have a formal, engraved invitation. On the other hand, a formal wedding with a sit-down dinner reception at the Waldorf-Astoria isn't the time for embossed hearts and flowers on parchment paper. The invitation is your guests' clue about what to expect. To decide how formal your wedding is, consider time of day, formality of dress, and reception style. At the same time, you and your fiancé's personalities should also be reflected in the wedding invitation.

♥ **Step 4:** Decide on an invitation budget. Prices range from $25 to $900 per 100 invitations, so have some amount in mind.

♥ **Step 5:** Once you find a stationer (either retail or mail-order), look at their sample books or catalog. First, decide on the paper. Forget the wording, type styles, and ink colors. Instead, look at the paper design and quality. (If you are shopping mail-order or online, request a sample of the paper to see it in person). Any style of type, wording and colors can be put on any paper design, so focus on the paper first. Paper grades and weights largely determine the price—inexpensive mail-order catalogs use lightweight 24 lb. paper, while more expensive brands use heavier (up to 80 lb.) stock. Papers made of 100% cotton are usually more expensive than wood pulp options, but give a more elegant look.

♥ **Step 6:** Next, consider the printing. Decide on the ink color, lettering style and printing method (engraving or thermography). Some invitation designs limit choices in these areas.

♥ **Step 7:** Given the paper design and printing that best fits your reception, choose an invitation in your price range. Don't forget to factor in the cost of extras including napkins, place cards and maps if you want them.

♥ **Step 8:** Order at least 25 more invitations than your actual count in case you decide you need more later. Also, order extra envelopes in case of addressing goofs (calligraphers often ask for 10% extra for mistakes). After the order is written, proofread very carefully before the order is sent off. This is a critical step to catch any errors.

♥ **Step 9:** When the order comes in, proofread again and count the number of invitations to be sure you received the amount you ordered. Do this *before* you leave the store or as soon as the invites arrive by mail. Stationers have only a three- to five-day window allowed by printers to catch mistakes. Mail order catalogs have varying return policies, but most only allow 10 to 15 days.

Questions to Ask a Stationer

1 **How many different lines do you carry?** A wide assortment of styles and brands not only gives you more choices (and price ranges) but also a clue to how seri-

---

REAL WEDDING TIP

How many people should you invite?

Here's a classic dilemma: Your reception site holds 150 people ... so, how many guests should you invite? 200? 175? Or just 150?

This issue points up one of the mysteries of wedding planning: estimating possible response rates to a wedding invitation. The answer: it's anybody's guess.

Your response rate will be based on several factors. How many out of town guests are invited? Odds are you'll have a higher rejection rate from folks who have to travel a great distance. What about the time of year? Weddings near major holidays may also suffer from lower response rates, since guests may be out of town on vacation.

A parallel issue to this is the response (or RSVP) card, where folks are asked the simple question "will you be attending?" Yes or no? Heck, they even get a postage-paid envelope that makes a response painless. The sad fact: many guests simply don't pay you the courtesy of using them. Perhaps they're too busy; perhaps they don't want to offend you by saying no. Whatever the reason, it can be very hard to tell just HOW MANY people will actually show up to your wedding.

We think it's fair for the bride and groom to contact wayward guests to see if they are coming. Blame it on the caterer, who needs an approximate count two weeks before your wedding. If the acceptance rate seems lower than expected, consider sending off a second wave of invitations to those friends or relatives on the B list.

---

ous the retail stationer is about their business. Since stationers must purchase those sample books (at a cost of $35 to $250 a book), the number they carry indicates their commitment to wedding invitations.

2 **Given my wedding and reception, what is your opinion of having response cards?** Response cards (an extra expense) encourage your guests to let you know whether they will attend the wedding. However, in some regions of the country (parts of the South and Southwest) guests often don't send in their response cards because they prefer not to "disappoint" the bride by saying no. In other regions, particularly the Northeast, response cards are considered a must and are routinely returned by guests.

A retail stationer in your area should be able to give advice on this if you are uncertain . Even if you do choose to send response cards, you may only receive as few as 30% back. We recommend response cards when you are inviting a large number of guests and/or are having a very expensive meal. If you are only planning a cake and punch reception or are having fewer than a hundred guests, response cards may not be needed. Remember that response cards also require their own stamp, raising your expenses accordingly. Yes, you can put your email address on the RSVP card, but always give guests the option of responding by mail.

3 **Can I see some samples of actual invitations?** This is one way to separate the part-time stationer from the full-time professional—the latter typically has many actual samples on hand. The best mail-order and web sources also provide samples of invitation designs upon request (either for free or at a nominal charge). Don't look at the style or color of the samples. Instead key in on the wording and the overall composition. Is the effect pleasing? Are the lines of type proportionate to the paper size? Is the type correctly aligned on the paper? If the invitation wording looks awkward, you may not want to trust your invitation to this business.

4 **Who is responsible for any errors that occur?** Some retail stationers may not offer to fix errors, whether you made them or they did. The true professional will take care of anything that goes wrong, regardless of who is responsible. If ordering from a catalog, be sure you get a written copy of the return policy and guarantee offered.

5 **Can I see a proof of the invitation?** Some printers offer this at a very small cost ($20 or less). If you have a large order or complex invitation, this might be a prudent way to go.

Top Money-saving Secrets

1 **Choose thermographed invitations instead of engraved.** Right about now you may be wondering what is thermography. Let's take a quick look at the difference between the two printing processes. Note: we aren't talking about the style of script or the quality of the paper, this is just the actual printing process.

Engraving is the Rolls Royce of printing. Until 1970's (when thermography became widespread), this was your only choice for invitations.

Both engraving and thermography create raised printing. However, with engraving, a copper or steel plate is etched with the type and design. These etchings fill with ink and are forced against a die, lifting the ink out of the plate and creating a raised image on the paper. The paper is left with an impression from the back (called a "bruise').

Thermography is often used to simulate engraving. A resinous powder is dusted over the ink while it is still wet. The paper is then heated, the powder melts and fuses with the ink, swelling to create a raised surface. While metal plates may be used, this process is much less expensive (up to 50% or even more!). Another advantage to thermography: this process also allows you to use a wide variety of ink colors. Thermography has become extremely popular, thanks to better production processes. The process is virtually indistinguishable from engraving, except there is no dent (or bruise) on the back of the invitations. All the mail-order catalogs listed later in this chapter offer thermographed invitations.

2 **Order from a professional stationer who discounts.** Discount Bridal Service (800) 874-8794 has many representatives around the country who regularly discount invitations 10% to 20%.

3 **Check the local newspaper for sales.** Some professional stationers have periodic sales.

4 **Don't buy all the extras.** As you've read above, there are quite a few different accessories and extras available to match your wedding invitation. Instead of ordering separate reception cards, consider printing "Reception Following" at the bottom of your actual invitation. This could save about 15% off your bill. Also, skip envelope linings and response cards if you don't see a need for them. To see how all these charges add up, let's look at the sample costs for an invitation with black ink from Regency, a major brand we'll review later in this chapter.

Invitation Pricing Example
Regency Invitation
(Price for 100 Invitations)

Basic Invitation	$71.90
Return Address on Flap	29.90
Reception Card	40.90
Response (RSVP) Card	48.90
Lined Envelopes	19.60
Informals (Thank You Notes)	40.90

TOTAL	**$252.10**

As you can see by this sample, the original invitation is a fraction of the total bill; note how the "options" can double or triple your final bill.

5 **Buy an embosser with your return address instead of paying extra to get this printed on the back flap.** The cost of an embosser is about equal to or less than the return address charge in many cases—the advantage here is you can use the embosser again.

6 **To save on postage, don't buy an oversized invitation.** Oversized invitations require more postage. Also, an invitation with lots of enclosures (reception cards, response cards, maps, etc.) will be more expensive to mail. Remember that response cards require their own stamp, too.

7 **For engraved invitations, consider alternatives to Crane.** The Cadillac brand of engraved invitations, Crane (see review in the next section) charges $400 for 100 engraved invitations. But what if you desire engraved invitations, yet can't afford the Crane price? There are several affordable alternatives. For example, the Reaves Engraving mail-order catalog (877-9REAVES or 910-369-2260; web: www.reavesengraving.com) charges just $249 for 100 engraved invitations on Crane paper. (It's even less for engraved invitations on their own in-house stock—$102.75 per 100). Another alternative: use a discount buying source like Invitation Hotline (800) 800-4355 (see review later in this chapter). They'll sell you 100 engraved invitations by Encore (on 100% cotton paper) for just $248.

8 **Postcards: a great way to save on money and postage for RSVP's.** Instead of a response card (which needs a separate envelope and a 33¢ stamp), consider a response postcard. 25 postcards cost about $15 from mail-order catalogs like Jamie Lee (800-288-5800, see review later in this chapter)—that's nearly a 50% savings over standard response cards-with-envelopes. Another bride told us she whipped up a response postcard on her computer and had it copied on double-sided cardstock at Kinko's (a national chain of copy shops). Total cost: $12 per 100. And then the postcards only require a 20¢ stamp. That's a $13 savings for every 100 invitations you send out.

9 **Design it yourself on a computer.** Got a computer and printer? Check out the Best Buy later in this chapter for info on software that lets you design invitations on the cheap. We'll also discuss sources for laser-compatible invitation paper. Another good source for do-it-yourselfers: Crane's Wedding Blue Book by Steven Feinberg (on line at www.crane.com or in your local library). This 150 page paperback answers just about every wedding etiquette question there is when it comes to invitations—wording, addressing, assembling and more. The book is available in libraries or online for free at Crane's web site (web:www.crane.com/wedding_blue_book.html). See figure 3 below.

10 **Get creative on the accessories.** When you buy invitations, you're more than likely to be pitched on buying all those little bridal accessories like guest books, plume pens and other doo-dads. Our

Figure 3: How do you word a wedding invitation? Address envelopes? Crane's online wedding blue book provides excellent advice and tips.

advice: get creative. One reader from Toronto, Ontario told us her inventive idea for a guest book. She went to an arts and crafts store and purchased a picture matte (16x20) and an archival-quality gold pen. "At the wedding, each guest signed their name on the matte. I used the matte to frame a photo of us and got a beautiful and unique keepsake." Total cost: $16 Canadian (or $11 US). Compare that to fancy guest books that can run $30 to $50.

11 **Compare prices on mail order invites.** One of our readers noticed that mail order companies often sell the exact same invitation at different prices. In her case, she noticed that The American Wedding Album offered the "Fresh Beginnings" floral invite at $65.95 per 100 while the same invites from Wedding Invitations by American Stationery were $46.95, a savings of 30%.

Our guess for the reason behind these price differences: the same parent company, American Stationery, owns both catalogs. The price difference may be because each catalog is targeted toward a different audience. Regardless of the reasons, as you can see, it pays to shop around with mail order.

12 **Check out warehouse clubs.** An example: some Cosco warehouse stores (web: www.cosco.com) offer name-brand invitations at a 10% to 30% discount off stationery stores. Call your local Cosco to see if they offer this service.

Helpful Hints

1 **For large weddings, engraved invitations may be a better bargain.** While thermography is generally cheaper than engraving, there is an exception. After you get beyond 300 to 350 invitations, the reverse is often true. For example, we priced 400 thermographed invitations from a major printer at $575. The same number of engraved invitations from a discount buying source was $566. Not only is it cheaper, but you also get a bonus: some printers like Jenner (see review later in this chapter) will fold and stuff the invitations into envelopes—that's no small task. Another tip: while mail-order catalogs have great prices on orders of 100 or 200 invitations, their price advantage drops as the quantity grows. You may find a better deal on large orders (over 300) from a local stationer.

2 **Consider addressing options.** Many stationary shops and even mail-order catalogs today offer envelope addressing services for busy brides and grooms. They'll take your guest list, feed it in the computer and then voilà! Addressed envelopes ready to stamp and mail.

While some services use a pen-based addressing machine (like Inscribe), more and more are turning to computerized output from laser and ink jet printers. Which is best? Consider the paper type before making a decision. If your envelopes are not made from paper that is laser-printer compatible (ask the stationer or catalog to find out), go with an ink jet printer service. Why? The laser printer toner might rub off at the post office, making the invitation undeliverable. Ink jet printing is preferable since it sticks to the envelope better.

3 **Recognize the limits of the postal system.** Invitation printers love to sell brides all sorts of new looks. But before you pay, make sure your invitations are post-office friendly. An example: wax seals. They sure look neat on envelopes, but they can gum up the post offices processing machines. The result: at best, the wax will smudge. At worst, the invitation gets jammed in the machine, shredding it beyond recognition. The best advice is to only use wax seals on the inside envelopes.

Along the same lines, watch out for the new invitation fad of bows, ribbons and fabric appliqués that extend off the card. Sure, they look neat . . . BUT they have to be stuffed into an envelope and sent through the postal system. The result may look nothing like those glossy catalog books.

Finally, ask the post office to hand cancel your stamps. That way your invitations aren't machine canceled with an ugly post mark advertising Fred's Shrimp Shack.

4 **Beware of brazen bridal registries.** In the category of overzealous marketing hysteria, some bridal registries are providing brides with special cards that they're suppose to stuff with their invitation. Online registries offer to send emails to your guests. The cards/emails "inform" guests where the bride is registered, with a handy web address or phone number. Nifty, eh? No, it's in bad taste. You are NEVER suppose to send guests an invitation that suggests or demands a gift. Even for us etiquette minimalists, we're appalled at the attempt of bridal registries to shamelessly shill for business. Guests should find out where you are registered the old-fashioned way—by word of mouth. Trust us, if they want to know, they'll ask.

5 **If you don't like the flimsy paper from mail order catalogs, check out single panel cards.** The card stock used to make single panel invitations is much more substantial than many of the papers used for the folded designs in mail order catalogs. You'll give your guests the illusion of better quality invitations and spend a fraction to do it. Rexcraft, reviewed later in this chapter, sells a simple single panel invitation for just $50 per 100.

Biggest Myths About Invitations

MYTH #1 *"My aunt, who is a real stickler for etiquette, says engraved wedding invitations are the only option to consider. She says the quality of thermographed invitations is awful."*

Unfortunately, your aunt has been reading too many outdated etiquette books. In reality, thermography printing has improved so much in recent years that even Crane, the number-one seller of engraved invitations, now offers thermography. The only visible difference between thermography and engraving is the dent on the back of your invitation— and in your pocketbook.

MYTH #2 *"I thought it would take 15 minutes to write up my invitations order at the stationer. Boy was I surprised when it took nearly two hours!"*

That's right! Many folks think writing an invitation is easy—until they actually try it. In reality, finding the right combination of words and type styles that make an aesthetically attractive invitation is challenging. That's why just writing up an invitation order can take an hour or more. Using a professional retail stationer or calling a catalog's customer service department will make this process go easier.

MYTH #3 *"I assumed when we ordered our invitations that extra envelopes would be included—is this true?"*

Nope, many printers send the exact compliment of envelopes as invitations ordered. If you want extra envelopes, they must be ordered in advance (there is a small additional cost). Why is this important? Well, if you're addressing your own invitations, it pays to have extra envelopes in case of mistakes. Even calligraphers will request you supply extra envelopes.

Pitfalls to Avoid

PITFALL #1 UNDER-ORDERING OF INVITATIONS.

"When I first ordered invitations, I ordered exactly enough for the people on my list. Later, my mother came up with some long-lost relatives, and I had to go back and reorder another 25. I was shocked at the extra expense!"

If you guess wrong and need more invitations, the set-up charge to reprint will be tremendous. For example, let's look at a sample invitation order from a popular brand. The total for 100 invitations is $204.50. Let's say you're a smart bride and decide to order extras, say 125 invitations. The total would be $246.20—a $41.70 difference. However, if you order only

100 and find out later you need 25 more, the total cost will be $363.50. Wow! Ordering 125 in the first place would have saved you $117.30! As you can see, ordering extras in your original order is much more cost effective. That's because the set-up charge for additional orders is the same as for the original order. There is no cost savings on invitations if you go back later to order more. Also keep in mind that if you "go back to press" later, the ink color and paper may not match the original order.

Pitfall #2 Mail-order snafus.

"I ordered invitations from one of the catalogs advertised in a bridal magazine. Boy, am I sorry—the order came in with several mistakes and the whole design looked out of whack."

Sure, mail-order invitation catalogs offer great prices, but do you get what you pay for? We've heard stories from brides who felt burned when their invitations arrived, looking nothing like they expected.

The reasons for this are many. In some cases, the composition (how the type is aligned) is off, due to a mistake in the printing process. Other times, the catalog made a goof with the spelling or wording. Later in this chapter, we'll review the companies we think are most reliable—including those who offer an unconditional guarantee, the best bet for getting what you want.

Of course, the mail-order companies sometimes have themselves to blame. At some catalogs, quality control is so bad they actually send out samples to prospective customers that include spelling errors and bad composition! In other cases, we've seen catalogs recommend invitation wording that is awkward at best. If you go the mail-order route, you may want to look up *Crane's Wedding Online Blue Book* (see Figure 3 earlier in this chapter for details).

Pitfall #3 When invitations are just a sideline.

"The bridal shop where I bought my gown offered to order invitations for me at a 10% discount. However, the salesperson who helped me didn't seem to know much more than I did about how to write up the order or word the invitation."

Competition in the invitation business is intense. Many bridal businesses (particularly bridal shops and photographers) now offer discounted invitations as an enticement to order a gown or purchase photography. The discount is usually 10% to 20% off retail. The problem: many of these businesses are inexperienced with invitations. Their selection and knowledge of invitation printers is limited and service by low-paid clerks is lackluster. Many also lack the skills to word the invitations correctly.

Another twist on this pitfall are stores that advertise "up to 50% off" wedding invitations, as one bridal shop in Ohio recently promoted. As it turns out, you have to order five bridesmaids dresses (or rent five tuxes) to get the discount, which only applies to the invitation itself—response cards, napkins and other accessories are full price. Hence, you might get a better deal on the *whole* invitation order from a mail-order catalog or retail stationer who discounts.

PITFALL #4 LAST MINUTE CHANGES.
"My church just called to say that we have to move up the time of our ceremony by one hour. The problem is I've already ordered invitations. Can I make a change?"

Not without incurring some big charges. First, understand that most invitations orders are faxed/emailed to the printer within 36 hours. Once received by the printer, it is very difficult to change or stop the order. If changes can be made, there is always a charge. For example, one big printer we researched charges $10 "per inquiry" and another $10 per change.

PITFALL #5 CRANE SWITCHEROO.
"I ordered Crane invitations from this store in the mall that was advertising a special deal. Yet, when the invitations came in, they didn't feel anything like what I expected. Did I get ripped-off?"

It's possible. Crane is one of the best known (and most expensive) brands of wedding invitations. This notoriety has a down-side—some Crane dealers, desperate to compete with lower-cost alternatives, use tricks to discount the brand to brides. One common example is the "Crane envelope switcheroo:" sure, you get Crane engraved invitations, but the stationer substitutes cheaper, non-Crane envelopes without telling you. How can you spot this? Most (but not all) Crane envelopes have the distinctive Crane watermark—check for this when you pick up the order. Also, make sure you specify in writing that you're to get Crane envelopes.

Another Crane scam: we've documented several cases of stationery dealers who use Crane's "commercial" stock instead of the 40 lb. social paper more commonly used for wedding invitations. Why? The commercial stock is thinner and less expensive, enabling the dealer to give a "discount" on the order. Our advice: don't use it—this stock just doesn't look right for wedding invitations. Ask the dealer what type of stock they use for their Crane orders.

PITFALL #6 THE REVENGE OF THE ETIQUETTE POLICE.
"I just got in my invitation order and got a big surprise. With no warning, the printer had changed my order to fix an alleged 'etiquette error' in the wording! This is ridiculous."

Hard to believe, but it is true that some printers will change the wording on invitations to conform to "proper etiquette" as they see it. The only way you can avoid this problem is to tell the stationer or catalog that you want the wording (and any capitalization) to be exactly as you specify. This is usually accomplished by checking a box on the order form (which can be in very small type buried at the bottom) or noting it in some other way. You must also indicate if unusual spellings of names (like Henri instead of Henry) are correct. That way the printer won't substitute their etiquette rules or spelling corrections for your finely-crafted prose.

PITFALL #7 PET POSTAL PEEVES.

"My stationer told me the invitations would cost just 33¢ to mail. However, after I added two maps and took the invitations to the post office, they said it would be 55¢. As a result, we have to shell out another $50 in postage. Is that fair?"

This is why we recommend taking your invitation (and all the enclosures) to the post office and getting it weighed *before* you buy all those cute "love" stamps. Start adding maps, response cards or other enclosures and you'll notice the postage bill soars.

Another interesting twist on this problem is a story we heard from Austin, Texas. A local company there was advertising an "addressing, stuffing and mailing" service for just $1 per invitation. Sounds great, eh? The problem was the service didn't tell brides they were mailing their invitations *bulk rate*. The post office treats bulk rate mail as a very low priority, to put it charitably. As a result, some of the brides' invitations arrived six weeks after the wedding—others didn't arrive at all. As it turns out, it's illegal to mail invitations (or any personal correspondence) bulk rate and the post office may have confiscated the invitations. The best advice: *always* mail invitations first class.

PITFALL #8 OUTRAGEOUSLY PRICED ACCESSORIES.

"I was so excited with the savings on invitations from a mail-order catalog, I decided to order a slew of accessories too. Yet when I visited a local shop, I saw some of the same products at much lower prices. What's going on here?"

Ah, you've discovered the secret money-making machine behind the mail-order invitation catalogs. While the invitation itself is very affordable (perhaps as much as 50% less than retail), the prices on accessories can go through the roof.

Look through any of the mail-order invitation catalogs and you'll see plenty of superfluous stationery items (pew cards, save-the-date cards) as well as pictures of "suggested accessories," including matching nap-

kins, programs, unity candles, cake toppers, toasting glasses, garters—
even swizzle sticks printed with the bride and groom's name. Yet the
prices can be amazingly high. We found much better deals on these
items at party stores, gift shops, and other local stores. And then there's
the whole question of whether you really need a matching "gold guest-
book pen with heart-shaped, rose-etched Lucite base" for $17. The best
advice: comparison shop before you buy.

Reviews of selected invitation brands

Through our research for this book, we have identified a few "best
brands" in wedding invitations—these are printers who sell their designs
through retail dealers. These printers do NOT sell directly to the public;
nor do they have catalogs for consumers. We provide their phone numbers so you can find a dealer near you who has their sample books.

THE RATINGS

A	EXCELLENT . . . .OUR TOP PICK!	
B	GOOD . . . . . . .ABOVE AVERAGE QUALITY, PRICES AND CREATIVITY.	
C	FAIR . . . . .COULD STAND SOME IMPROVEMENT.	
D	POOR . . . . . . .YUCK! COULD STAND MAJOR IMPROVEMENT.	

Carlson Craft One of the largest invitation printers in the country, Carlson
Craft has something for everyone. Their "blue book" catalog features a wide
variety of styles that range from $52 to $90 per 100. The quality of their
thermography is very good. As far as the paper goes, stand-outs include
their 100% cotton (40 lb.) paper designs, which are a good value. Newer
additions to the Carlson Craft lines include the "Heritage Collection," with
African American motifs and artwork. The company also markets the
Exclusive Collection, which features "high-end, exclusive designs." This collection showcases such hip looks as "tea length" invitations (which are long
and skinny, sort of like the shape of this book). Prices for that collection are
$60 to $80 per 100. While these offerings were winners, we have to give a
thumbs down to Carlson Craft's "Imprintables" line of laser-friendly blank
invites. While the designs are great, the paper doesn't come in 8.5 x 11"
sheets, making them very difficult to align correctly in a desktop printer. *For
a dealer near you who carries Carlson Craft, call (800) 328-1782. Web:
www.carlsoncraft.com.* **Rating: B–**

Chase Paper From plain traditional to glitzy contemporary, Chase Paper
has a wide selection of unique papers. The quality of the thermography
is top-notch, say our stationery experts. Prices run $80 to $200 per 100
invitations. Best of all, the lower-priced options are a definite step up in
quality compared to other companies. Chase also offers an upper-end

line of exclusive paper designs called the Chase Collection, with prices ranging from $180 to $400. This group featured current fads like invites with ribbons and bows, as well as printing on velum paper. While we liked the look of this collection, if you plan to spend that much money, you might as well go with an even better brand like William Arthur. Shipping takes about two weeks. *For a dealer near you who carries Chase, call (508) 478-9220.* **Rating: B**

Checkerboard Invitations Checkerboard's sample book features a wide assortment of designer invitations—you can even mix and match type styles (most printers don't let you do this). We saw designs with splattered ink, mylar prisms and marbled paper; they even have several recycled paper designs. Funky envelope linings complete the looks. New in recent years is "Love Knots," a collection of ten invitations printed on translucent parchment, then layered with custom-made papers and topped with a bow. The innovative catalog features a velcro system that lets you swap bows, rearrange layers and more. Love Knots invitations average $298 per 100; that's a bit more than Checkerboard's regular invitations (which average $220 per 100, but range from $129 to $595). *For a dealer near you who carries Checkerboard, call (508) 835-2475.* **Rating: B+**

Crane Pull out a dollar bill and you'll feel some Crane paper. Yes, this is the same company that provides Uncle Sam with stock for greenbacks. Their wedding invitations are equally legendary—"Crane engraved" invites were the preferred (some say only) method for announcing a high-society wedding in the past. Today, 200 year-old Crane bows to modern times by also offering thermography. No matter which printing method you choose, however, a Crane order will require bushel loads of those aforementioned greenbacks. The *average* engraved invitation runs $400 per 100 invitations (thermography is about 20% less). Add in pricey extras like response and reception cards and you can easily see how the average order for Crane tops $850! So, is it worth it? Well, the paper (heavyweight 100% cotton) is exquisite, but we're turned off by the limited options to customize your invite—you can only choose from three sizes, basically plain panels in white or ecru. Yes, there are 72 different typefaces, but there aren't many ways to add your own personal stamp on these invites. And we found Crane prices vary dramatically from dealer to dealer (see Pitfalls to Avoid earlier in this chapter for more info). If you do decide Crane is right for you, pick a dealer that has their "Paper Emporium" system, a computer that lets you (and the store) word the invitation in perfect etiquette and see a preview of it on screen, letting you swap typefaces, paper options and more. Then, you get a laser print of your invitation, composed exactly as it will be printed—that's a concept other printers should (but don't) offer. *For a dealer near you who carries Crane call (800) 472-7263. Web: www.crane.com* **Rating: B**

Elite Elite is Regency's sister division that offers high-end invites that are equal parts quirky, elegant and stylish. Of course, this comes at a price. Pearlized, embossed and glittered designs can cost as much at $950 for 100 invitations (they start at $139, but most average $300 to $400). Elite's designs are always on the cutting edge: their current catalog features many mixed media invites, combining fabrics, ribbons, translucent papers, embossing and more. The separate "In Folio" collection features "invitation ensembles" that are presented as theme concepts, all engraved or thermographed on 100% cotton paper. If you want something more conservative, the Elite "Fine Papers" designs are more restrained both style and price wise (starting at $158 per 100 for thermographer, $248 for engraved). While we like Elite (it's hard to believe they're even related to Regency), the print quality and customer service are a few steps behind rival brands like Encore. *For a dealer near you who carries Elite call (800) 354-8321.* **Rating: A-**

Embossed Graphics If you're planning a large wedding, Embossed Graphics should be at the top of your invitations shopping list. That's because the company has incredible prices for large quantities of ther-

---

REAL WEDDING TIP

'Net expands invitation options

Recent bride Shannon Crotts pointed out that the web offers great options for brides looking for unique invitations:

"I wanted to share with you a company that I found for custom invites: Gaddis Design (www.gaddisdesign.com). Her invites are beautiful and unique and reasonably priced. I was getting frustrated looking through the books of invites at stationary stores, seeing the same thing over and over. I had a hard time choosing between all of the gorgeous designs that Gaddis had to offer."

We checked out Gladdis' web site and have to agree. They offer papers and designs you won't see in the usual mail order catalog or stationery store. You'll find see-through vellums, unusual ribbon treatments and gorgeous papers. A calla lily design runs about $250 per 100. Not cheap, but not run-of-the-mill either. Another plus: they sell their paper to readers who want to design their own invitations as well. Do-it-yourself kits are $12 for 10 invitations plus envelopes (for the calla lily design).

mographed invitations. For example, 400 invitations from Embossed Graphics cost just $322! Compare that to Carlson Craft or Regency, where the same quantity would set you back $400 or $500—on paper that's much lower in quality. In fact, it's Embossed Graphics heavyweight paper that is the star here; the type styles (48) and extra options are more limited compared to the competition. Yes, they've tried to jazz up the line in the past few years (new styles feature embossing, foil borders and bonded envelope linings), but this line is more the understated classy look than glitz. Prices range $135 to $195 per 100 invitations (an excellent value for a quality product) and shipping is fast. *For a dealer near you who carries Embossed Graphics, call (800) 362-6773 or (630) 236-4001. Web: www.embossed.com* **Rating: A**

Encore Cutting-edge invitation printer Encore combines the best of both worlds: high-quality paper, innovative designs and, most of all, excellent quality. If you're going to spend $400 per 100 invitations (Encore's average order), you might as well go for the gold standard—choose from designs trimmed with ribbons, flecked paper overlays or round borders with gold or silver edges. Want flowers? Choose from embossed lilies, roses and more on textured papers and card stock. All the Encore invitations are thermographed and a wide variety of ink colors is available. Encore's prices range from $199 to $679 per 100—no bargain, but, as mentioned earlier, their engraved invitations on 100% cotton paper (the Classic Collection) are much less than Crane's offerings. New to the Encore line is an envelope calligraphy service that matches the type face on the invitation. Brides and grooms can download a calligraphy database program off Encore's web site, enter their guest names and address and then email the list back to Encore. The company then does the calligraphy for $1.50 per envelope. Encore can now even add the guest's name(s) right onto the invitation. Also new: a translation and type-setting service for foreign languages. "Encore's quality is the best in the industry," an industry source tells us. "They have an artistic flair when it comes to typesetting—and they rarely make mistakes." *For a dealer near you who carries Encore, call (800) 526-0497. Web: www.weddinginvitations.com or www.encorestudios.com* **Rating: A**

Jenner Here's a little secret of the invitation business: if you want Crane engraved invitations, there are other sources than just Crane itself. For example, Jenner, a Kentucky-based printer, engraves invitations on Crane paper . . . and for much less than Crane. 100 engraved invitations on Crane paper from Jenner are $306 (that's about 25% less than Crane's prices). You can save even more by using Jenner's in-house stock, which runs $244 for 100. Best of all, Jenner includes folding and stuffing of invitations into the envelopes (most printers don't offer this service). The printer also offers thermographed invites as well. (The only bummer: some states like California have very few Jenner dealers; call the company for a list of local dealers). *For a dealer near you who carries Jenner, call (502) 222-0191. Web: www.jennerco.com* **Rating: A-**

NuArt/ Pacific Thermographers Unimpressed with the flimsy, boring designs of the low-cost printers—but you can't afford the fancy designs of the super-expensive brands? Here's a solution: check out NuArt/Pacific Thermographers. (It's the same company; in the Eastern US, they go under NuArt. In the west, it's Pacific Thermographers). This printer offers excellent printing on incredibly heavy paper. And best of all, the prices are very down to earth—just $85 to $205 for 100 invitations. The "Elegant" catalog (sold by both brands), features intricate embossing, linen and silk-finished papers and a choice of 37 type styles. NuArt's "Diamond Boutique" catalog is only sold in the Midwest and features more traditional designs at $38 to $100 per 100. Fool your friends in thinking you spent hundreds of dollars on invitations! With both stylized and traditional paper designs, NuArt/Pacific Thermographers is definitely a best buy. *For a dealer who carries NuArt, call (800) 653-5361; for Pacific Thermographers, call (800) 423-5071 or (818) 998-2000.* **Rating: A-**

Regency This invitation printer behemoth has just about something for everything. Their three invitation books (the names of which—Flower, Rainbow and Tempo—sound like '60's love children) feature just about every style known on Earth. Prices range from $44.90 to $115 per 100. New to the line are several combo letter style looks that combine two typefaces for no extra charge. The quality of this line (paper, printing) is only average. On the plus side, this brand is one of the few that offers Hebrew invitations—at prices that are much lower than other Jewish specialty printers. *To find a dealer near you, call (717) 762-7161. Web: www.regencythermo.com.* **Rating: B-**

William Arthur Our pick as a best bet for invitations is Maine-based William Arthur. Their fabulous collection of thermographed invitations offers a sophisticated and classic look for brides who want an alternative to the plain, traditional invitation. With a variety of unique type styles and card-type designs, Arthur's line runs $190 to $334 per 100 invitations. Included in that price is return address printing, which is a nice plus. In recent years, William Arthur added engraved invites to their line, at prices that range from $320 to $464 per 100. Unlike Crane's limited offerings, Arthur's engraved invites feature delicate touches like an embossed design on the envelope, different ink colors and hand-lined envelopes. Arthur's customer service is excellent, according to stationers we interviewed. "They're in a class by themselves," one told us, adding that their shipping (24 hours for thermography, 7-10 days for engraved) is incredibly reliable. One and two day rush service is also available. *For a dealer near you who carries William Arthur, call (800) 985-6581 or (207) 985-6581. Web: www.williamarthur.com.* **Rating: A**

Do It By Mail

When we first researched this topic back in 1990, we were not very impressed with the mail-order wedding invitation catalogs. The designs were bland and the samples we viewed left much to be desired.

Well, there is good news to report. In the last several years, the catalogs have improved their offerings and quality. And, not too surprisingly, their popularity has soared—now nearly 50% of all wedding invitations sold in North America are through the mail order catalogs.

The big reason: price. Catalogs sell some of the very same designs you see in the stores for 40% less than retail! How do they do that? Well, here's a little secret of the wedding invitation business: the same giant company (Taylor Corp.) that owns most of the big invitation brands sold in stores (such as Regency and Carlson Craft) also produces the catalogs. Sneaky, eh?

How they get away with this is beyond us—why would anyone walk into a store and order invitations at full retail when the very same design can be had for 40% less through the mail? Well, the invitation printers tell us some brides like the "hand-holding" (that is, etiquette advice, wording suggestions, etc.) they get from a retail stationer. It comes down to personal choice.

So, here's our research on the best mail-order invitation catalogs—and some comments on how we came up with this list. First, we pored over samples and catalogs from 20 mail-order companies. Then we looked at the feedback we've received from brides over the past several years (our e-mail address is in the back of the book, by the way). Finally, we think we've come up with a list of the best resources for discount mail-order invitations.

A couple of thoughts before we get to the reviews: we noticed many of the catalogs carry some of the same designs. Yet comparing prices can be difficult—some catalogs charge more for fancy type styles, while others throw this in for free, for example. Also, the prices can be all over the board: some catalogs offer great deals on small quantities, while others give better discounts on large orders.

The big bummer with most mail order invitations: paper quality, or lack thereof. Most catalogs sell invitation papers that are quite thin (24 lb. is a common stock weight). If you want a heavier weight, you may have to go with a brand we review earlier that is sold through retail stores.

Even more offensive than paper weight were the samples we got from some of the catalogs—one had printing that was off-center and the wording was incorrect (etiquette-wise). And this is an example of their best work?

On the other hand, the prices were hard to beat—sometimes 40% below retail for the exact same invitation. Mail-order (and the web) is also a convenient option for many brides; you can shop in the comfort of your home and don't have to drag the groom to yet another wedding-related appointment.

One note for Web surfers: we noted many of the Taylor-owned mail order catalogs had web sites that behaved strangely when viewed with Internet Explorer (yes, we were using the most recent version). Using Netscape seemed to solve these problems. As we mentioned earlier in this chapter, using the web to invitation shop can be an exercise in frustration thanks to poorly designed web sites.

So our advice is to shop carefully. Request a sample of the design you're thinking about ordering. Visit retail stationery shops to compare paper quality and prices. Make sure the mail-order company has an unconditional guarantee that allows you to return the invitations, no questions asked. Finally, we recommend paying with a credit card (in case a dispute develops, you may be able to get a refund from your bank).

The prices quoted on the next page are for invitations with black ink and regular lettering. Our round-up of the best mail-order invitation catalogs can be found on a chart on the next page.

Trends

♥ **LETTERPRESS DESIGNS.** What's on the cutting edge of invitations today? Actually it's a printing process that was invented in 1450 by Guttenberg: letterpress. This printing method is creeping back into the mainstream today, especially among brides who want something different . . . and have the budget to afford it.

So, what is letterpress? Often confused with engraving, letterpress uses a raised surface that is inked and pressed into the paper, so the letters and design are impressed (instead of raised). Contrast that with engraving, where letters are etched into a flat plate. Then, the paper is pressed against the entire plate, creating raised lettering. As a result, all engraved invitations feature rather plain panel paper designs; letterpress enables the printer to use textured papers and backgrounds. Letterpress is a very time-consuming process, which explains why it is so expensive.

Julie Holcomb Printers has been creating custom letterpress invitations since 1981 in San Francisco (call toll free at 877-877-8905 for a dealer near you; web: julieholcombprinters.com). The company imports

Continued on page 208

MAIL ORDER INVITES

Catalog	Taylor?	Price*	Turnaround
AMERICAN WEDDING ALBUM (800) 428-0379 WWW.THEAMERICANWEDDING.COM	No	$67.95	10 DAYS INCLUDES SHIPPING
DAWN (800) 332-3296 WWW.INVITATIONSBYDAWN.COM	Yes	$47.80	2-3 DAYS PLUS SHIPPING
DEWBERRY ENGRAVING (800) 633-8614	Yes	$109.90	5-6 DAYS PLUS SHIPPING
EVANGEL CHRISTIAN INVITATIONS (800) 457-9774 WWW.EVANGELWEDDING.COM	Yes	$41.90	48 HOURS PLUS SHIPPING
HEART THOUGHTS MUST (800) 648-5781 WWW.HEART-THOUGHTS.COM	No	$76	2 DAYS PLUS SHIPPING
NOW & FOREVER (800) 521-0584, (800) 451-0610 WWW.NOW-AND-FOREVER.COM	Yes	$55.90	2-3 DAYS PLUS SHIPPING
PRECIOUS COLLECTION (800) 537-5222, (800) 553-9080 WWW.PRECIOUSCOLLECTION.COM	Yes	$39.90	3 DAYS PLUS SHIPPING
REAVES ENGRAVING (877) 9REAVES OR (910) 610-4499 WWW.REAVESENGRAVING.COM	No	$102.75 (IN-HOUSE PAPER)	4-5 WEEKS FOR ENGRAVING
REXCRAFT (800) 635-3898 WWW.REXCRAFT.COM	Yes	$94.95	2 DAYS PLUS SHIPPING
WEDDING TRADITIONS (800) 535-1002 WWW.WEDDING-TRADITIONS.COM	Yes	$50.95	2 DAYS PLUS SHIPPING
WILLOW TREE LANE (800) 219-1022 WWW.WILLOWTREELANE.COM	Yes	$29.90	3 DAYS PLUS SHIPPING

*Key: **Taylor?** Is the catalog owned by giant printer Taylor? **Price:** Single panel price is

Guarantee	Comments
10 days	A nice mix of traditional and contemporary styles. Customer service is OK; we noted they had a melt-down during the last UPS strike but that was the exception.
No specific time limit	Has both US & Canadian version. These invites seemed a bit more traditional and frilly to us than other catalogs.
Return within 90 days	This catalog specializes in affordable engraved invites. But . . . there is no web site, pricing is confusing and Dewberry only sells in a limited number of states.
Return within 10 days	Evangel specializes in Christian themed invites. They carry quite a few Precious Moments invites and accessories.
Return within 10 days	Web site does not include catalog photos or prices. Order catalog to see the line. Allow one extra day for invitations for ribbons.
Return within 3 months	Carry a large selection of square cards and other unusual shapes and sizes. About 88 different invitations.
Return within 15 days	Lots of layered invitations and bow accents. Floral motifs abound.
Return within 30 days	$249 for engraved invites on Crane paper, a 50% discount. New: they accept MasterCard and Visa now.
Return within 30 days	Huge catalog and excellent web site. Great customer service and decent prices.
Return within 90 days	Web site had no online catalog or ordering capability. General advice and FAQ is available.
Return within 15 days	Some of the cheapest invites around. Also very popular— web site was slow and phone lines had long holds. Web site is VERY primitive.

the cost for 100 single-panel invites printed with black ink.

its textured paper from England. The prices: $600 to $700 per 100 invitations. Turnaround time is about two to three weeks.

Vermont-based **Clover Creek** (call 800-769-9676 or 802-425-5549 for a catalog) recently debuted a letterpress line that runs $1200 to $1800 per 100 invites. The company specializes in hand-made invitations that use natural papers, silk ribbons and dried flowers. Their non-letterpress invites run $800 to $1150 per 100.

♥ **UNIQUE PAPER FOR DO–IT–YOURSELF KITS.** Invitesite (www.invitesite.com) offers brides unique papers in a do-it-yourself kit. With a kit such as the Ethereal Invitation set, couples receive a clear vellum wrapper, lavender printing paper, a lavender response card and envelope and translucent envelope for $2 per set (24 set minimum). What excited us about Invitesite is, finally, a company has made sets of invitations that are compatible with personal printers but also look truly unique. Invitesite's parent company, Fine Paper Co. of Old Pasadena, California (626) 584-9804) has years of experience with fine paper and letterpress printing. If the kits don't interest you, Invitesite can create a one-of-a-kind design. They also offer letterpress printing as well.

♥ **SMALL CUSTOM DESIGNERS.** The web is a great place to find small, custom designers. One reader emailed us about Dreamland Designs (www.dreamland-designs.com), a custom invitations designer in Minnesota. She told us owner Gina Selelsky hand draws all her invitations and announcements. She praised Gina's calligraphy and hand coloring. Although the site itself doesn't show any of the designs, you can order a sample box of 20 invitations for a $100 refundable deposit. While they aren't cheap ($2 to $10 per invitation), the quality of the work might be worth a look.

♥ **PERSONALIZE IT.** Among the bigger general trends in the invitations biz, personalization seems to be the craze. Printers have moved toward allowing more customization with paper, see-through vellum, ribbons and more. You may even be able to add a small dried flower or use an unusual type face to set off your invitation.

Of course, the ultimate in personalization is to create your own invites. Some brides and grooms make their own paper (yes, you can with a paper making kit from a craft store), while others buy unusual or unique papers from art stores. Zap this through a laser or ink jet printer and pressto! Instant invitations. (We have sources for unique papers later in this chapter).

Spotlight: Best Buy #1

Wedding Invitations kit CD-ROM

Like the idea of doing your invitations yourself on a computer, but feel a bit intimidated? After all, maybe you're *not* a graphic artist. Even if you could track down laser-compatible invitation paper, what's the correct way to word an invitations, etiquette-wise?

We found a great answer to those questions: the Wedding Invitation kit, a CD-ROM from the Creative Card Company. This handy software program is $20 to $25 (available nationwide in office supply stores like Staples or online at Bridalink.com). Call 888-727-3772 for a store near you; web: www.pcpapers.com.

If you've got a Windows PC (version 3.1 or later) and a laser or ink jet printer, that's all you need to print out professional-looking invites. The CD-ROM guides you through the process of setting up an invitation—you enter the bride and groom's names, the date, location and other details . . . and the computer words the invitation in perfect etiquette.

Best of all, the kit contains heavyweight-paper stock to print 25 invitations, 25 envelopes, 50 "accessory folders" (for reception cards, response cards, maps, etc.), 50 companion envelopes for the accessory folders and several sample sheets to verify the printing. There are several invitation designs available and you can order refill packages in case you need more than 25 invitations. You can choose from five fonts (various cursive typestyles) and eight colors; there's even a module to track gift information and keep a count of guests who will be attending the wedding.

We were skeptical about this concept until we actually saw some samples—they were impressive. The card stock is equivalent to what's available from mail order catalogs and the typefaces look very professional. The only bummer: there is no Mac version of the kit; Windows only. Of course, the quality of your printer may also affect your results. While the typefaces are excellent, the printing isn't raised (as you'd get from mail order or a stationary store). If you can live with that trade-off, then you'll love this software.

"My laser printer did such a beautiful job, you would never know it wasn't done by a professional," a reader told us after using the Wedding Invitation kit. "Total cost? $42. I figure the same design from a mail order catalog would have been close to $200."

One caveat to this review: In May 2000, invitation behemoth Taylor Corp bought the Wedding Invitation Kit's parent. We are not sure what Taylor plans to do with this product, if it will continue to be updated or allowed to die a slow death. Check our web page for updates on this.

SPOTLIGHT: BEST BUY #2

INVITATION HOTLINE

If you love the quality of designer wedding invitations but not the designer price tag, consider the **Invitation Hotline** (800) 800-4355, (732) 536-9115, fax (732) 972-4875. The Manalapan, New Jersey-based company offers a 25% discount on such well-known brands as Carlson Craft, Elite/Infolio, Encore, Embossed Graphics and more. Over 90 albums are available to chose from and the company does take all major credit cards. Owner Marcy Slachman told us that all brides need to do is call her with the book name and style number. She'll help troubleshoot any etiquette or wording questions. Delivery takes about two weeks from the date the order is placed. Faster delivery is available via overnight services.

New this year Invitation Hotline is going online with a web page at www.invitationhotline.com. They'll continue to offer the same discounts with the advantage of ordering online. But what really makes the site cool: you'll find catalog pictures from many of those name brand invitations makers listed above.

The Invitation Hotline also carries favors, including a few more eclectic offerings. For example, we noticed their price list included a silver-plated dolphin bottle opener ($3.95) and a silver-plated ice cream scoop ($4.15). Other wedding accessories and calligraphy are available as well.

SPOTLIGHT: BEST BUY #3

PAPER SOURCES FOR DO–IT–YOURSELF INVITATIONS

If you have a computer, laser-printer and desktop publishing know-how, you can easily design your own invitation. But how do you find the appropriate paper?

There's good news: laser-compatible papers (called "imprintables") are now one of the hottest-selling items at stationary stores and copy centers like Kinko's (with prices as low as 20¢ per invitation, including envelope). If you can't find imprintables through a retail source, check these mail order catalogs:

Paper Direct (800) 272-7377 (www.paperdirect.com) has an amazing collection of laser-compatible stationery, notecards, placards, and more. For a rehearsal dinner, bridesmaids luncheon or informal wedding invitation, Paper Direct's "Themes" collection has several fun options. The catalog even sells "Festive" papers with embedded silver and copper flakes.

Paper Journey (800) 827-2737 or (203) 744-2949 is a wonderful catalog of "unique papers and accessories." The "Exotic Printables" are laser-printer compatible, hand-made papers in two styles: off white with indigo or mauve flecks. A couple of other hand-made paper options are also available, including a 22x30 sheet (you can get 10 invites out of that) for just $5 per sheet. Sample packages are available for $5. The catalog also features guest books, photo albums, notecards and even custom invitations.

Paper Showcase (800-287-8163; www.papershowcase.com) is a 47 page catalog with an wide range of laser-imprintable papers. Quite a few selections here would work for weddings, including their fold-over cards in white or ivory at $21.95 for a pack of 50 invitations and envelopes. They also sell "Ibifoil," a laser-compatible foil in six colors that can add zip to any invitation.

Another idea: print up a basic invitation on a plain panel white or ecru card. Then wrap the invite with a fancy paper cover. All the above catalogs sell a variety of beautiful stock that would work. The cover adds a splash of color and dresses up a plain invite.

SPOTLIGHT: FAVORS

Like many wedding traditions, favors have a colorful if not somewhat mysterious history. Here is some background:

♥ **WHERE DID FAVORS ORIGINATE?** Popular mainly on the East Coast and in California, wedding favors have had a long, rich history. When we say rich, we really mean royal. In fact, in France in the 16th century, nobility and royalty gave valuable gifts (usually of porcelain) to their wedding guests as mementos of the occasion.

In the middle of the 16th century, almonds came to Italy from the Far East. These almonds were very expensive and became popular to give as favors to guests at royal weddings. To preserve these almonds, a sugar-coating was invented—Jordan almonds were born.

In the 17th century, three almonds, painted in bright colors and wrapped in bridal veiling, were given to guests as a symbol of fertility. The significance of three almonds is this: from the union of two comes one—a baby. The veiling meant that the guests shared the couple's happiness.

♥ **WHAT ABOUT FAVORS IN THE US?** In the US, favors are most popular with ethnic communities (particularly Italians). Favor manufacturers tell us that nearly 25% of their orders come from Pennsylvania, New York and New

Jersey. Couples there order more expensive favors with almonds inside a porcelain swan or champagne glass—these can cost as much as $20 each! In other areas, potpourri is a more popular choice. While favors are also common in the Southeast (Georgia, Florida, the Carolinas in particular), brides in the Midwest, Northwest and Southwest rarely give favors to guests.

♥ SOURCES FOR WEDDING FAVORS. **Favours Internationale** (781) 383-1065 (PO Box 205, Cohasset, MA 02025) is a Massachusetts-based company that makes favors. Their showroom in Cohasset features over 200 items. They can even design a favor from a verbal description. Call or mail for a price quote or catalog sheets ($3, which is applied to any order).

Hercules Candies (800) 924-4339 or (315) 463-4339 (web: www.her-culescandy.com) is a New York-based candy maker that's been selling handmade chocolates for 90 years. Their extensive brochure lists dozens of chocolate favor options. Each is customized with the bride and groom's name and wedding date on the box holding the chocolates. Prices range from 40¢ to $1.50 per favor. The samples we tasted were great.

Another idea: an Ohio bride told us she gave away flower seed packets as favors to her guests. Cost: 17¢ per packet. One source: the **Tender Seed Company** (web: www.tenderseedcompany.com) sells customized seed packets, some with ribbons and pearls, for $1.70 to $2. Another eco-conscious bride in Pennsylvania gave 8" pine seedlings (in white plastic bags with white bows) she found at a local nursery for $2 each. **Nelson Trading Company** (800) 699-1859 (www.nelsontrading.com) sells tree seedling wedding favors for about $2.50 each. And what about candy bar wrappers with the bride and groom's name and wedding date? **Moosie Wrappers** (web: www.moosiewrapper.com) sell the wrappers for only 65¢ each for 175 to 200 wrappers. You buy the candy bars then slide the wrappers over them. If you want to go the do-it-yourself route, check out the book *Craft An Elegant Wedding* (by Naomi Baker and Tammy Young, Chilton Books, 1995, $17.95). The 30 projects in this book are easy and affordable.

Do yourself a favor—and save money

If there is one aspect of a wedding where you can put that do-it-yourself energy to work, consider making your own favors. Heather Remer of Pittsburgh told us she "didn't want to give my guests a dust collector that they throw away. I wanted something simple and sweet—chocolates! Yet, when I looked at the prices some places were charging for a box of chocolates, I thought I would have to starve for a month (okay a little drastic) just to scrounge up the money. Then I got an idea—why not make them myself? A few weeks before the wedding, my four bridesmaids and I had a "chocolate party" to make my favors. The molds, chocolate and netting are all inexpensive—I figured my total savings to be $150."

Chapter 7

RECEPTION SITES

The choice of a reception site can make or break any wedding budget. In this chapter, we'll explore 13 ways to save—including some ingenious places that brides have discovered to hold their receptions. Plus, we'll give you the five most common pitfalls with reception sites and how to avoid them. Finally, we'll take a candid look at the pros and cons of the five most common sites.

What You Are Buying?

There are two basic categories of wedding receptions sites: places where you just rent the hall (and bring in an outside caterer) and others that have on-site catering, like hotels, country clubs or catering halls. Therefore, you are basically buying the following services:

♥ **EXCLUSIVE USE OF THE FACILITY.** Either you are charged a flat fee for a certain period of time or there is an hourly rate. Obviously, rates vary with the amount of ambiance. An historic restored mansion will cost much more than a local union hall. Most places require a booking deposit which can be several hundred dollars. A second deposit (to cover any damage or clean-up) may also be required at some sites.

♥ **CATERING** (food, beverages, service and rentals). You typically have two choices: use the site's in-house caterer or bring in an off-site caterer. When a site has an in-house caterer, there is often no "room charge"—the facility makes its money from the catering. Unfortunately, some sites not only charge you for the catering but also tack on a facility rental fee. We cover wedding catering in-depth in a separate chapter later in this book.

The Big Trade-off: Ambiance vs. Great Food. In a perfect world, a reception site would offer both beautiful ambiance AND great food. In reality, there are typically trade-offs. A restaurant may offer a stunning view of the city, but only offer mediocre food choices. On the other end, catering halls may have a sterile "wedding factory" atmosphere, but they have receptions down to a science. A site that lets you bring in an outside caterer (and hence, allows you more control over the food that's served) may be the perfect compromise, but these sites can be hard to find.

Average costs. What does it cost to hold a wedding reception? As you might remember from Chapter 1, we quote the average cost as $8400 for 200 guests. That figure covers not only the facility but also all the catering (food, beverages, labor, rentals, etc). What makes this confusing is that some sites include the site rental fee with the catering (hotels, for example). Of course, you often have to meet a rather hefty minimum spending charge. Other sites charge you a flat or hourly fee and let you bring in your caterer. Prices for those types of sites are all over the board, from free (a church hall in some cases) to $1000 or more for a historic inn or home.

The basic rule is that money buys you more ambiance—the prettiest sites always cost more than a nondescript hall.

Sources to Find a Reception Site

Finding the right reception site for your wedding may be the most challenging task you face. That's mainly because of the big bucks involved here—the reception (and, specifically, the catering) is the most expensive part of getting married. Here are some top sources to find affordable sites.

♥ **WEDDING COORDINATORS AT YOUR CEREMONY SITE.** Yes, these folks probably have talked to hundreds of brides over the years. They might be able to give you the "word on the street" for several reception sites.

♥ **CATERERS.** Most off-site (or independent) caterers are well aware of the best local wedding reception sites. That's because their livelihood depends on the existence of facilities that let outside caterers come in for receptions. Call around to a few local caterers to find leads.

♥ **RECENTLY-MARRIED COUPLES.** Ask your co-workers or friends if they know anyone who was recently married. These couples are often more than willing to share their research and experiences about reception sites.

♥ **VISITORS/TOURISM BUREAUS AND LOCAL PARKS DEPARTMENTS.** If you are looking for a civic site (such as an historic home), your local visitors/tourism bureau or chamber of commerce may have some suggestions. Many civic sites (like gardens and parks) are booked by local parks departments.

♥ **BRIDAL SHOWS.** Yes, bridal shows can be a source for reception sites. Large expos with many vendors are your best bet. Reception sites often set up booths and hand out food samples and menus.

♥ **OUR WEB PAGE.** In the back of this book, we'll give you information on how to access our web page. Once there, go to the Bridal Bargains update section and check out the links area—we have links to many other sites that provide local wedding and reception site info. Some sites are focused on a particular city or state, while others are national in scope. Also check the "reader mail" section of our site. There we post stories about reception site searches from brides in many cities.

Brides in Cyberspace: What's on the Web?

Yes, the big wedding portals like the Knot.com and the WeddingChannel.com have large databases of reception sites and other wedding vendors. (And the Knot's listings just grew with the recent acquisition of the Wedding Pages, a regional bridal magazine publisher). However, we found better reception site information other places on the web.

Instead, check out city directories that are have hundreds of links to other sites. Look for lists of meeting sites, historic homes, museums and other reception facilities. Here's a selection of some of the best:

♥ **CITYSEARCH.COM** has a cool "Wedding Bells" section (see Fig. 1 on the next page) that lets you search for sites and other vendors in 40 different cities. Even if you just enter "wedding" into their search engine, CitySearch.com will generate dozens of possible sites. We were impressed that many listings offer reviews (even "recommending" certain facilities!), as well as thumbnail photos, contact info and online maps. This site is a winner.

Figure 1: CitySearch.com "Wedding Bells" is customized for 40 cities with reception site ideas.

♥ **DIGITALCITIES.COM** allows you to access incredible information for over 60 cities. Check out their Visitor's Guide, Maps and Directions, Attractions, and Local Links sections to find ideas for reception sites.

♥ The goal of **USA CITYLINK** (www.usacitylink.com) is to help web surfers find local, municipal and other government web sites. Unlike other sites with info on a limited number of cities, you can use this site to access web sites for almost any town in any of the 50 states. Granted, there may not be a ton of entries under small, rural towns like Round Top, Texas, but even for this small burg we found several sites. Once you choose a city, you'll find lots of areas to research. Hint: try local Chamber of Commerce sites or local Visitor's/Tourism Bureau sites to get lists of "meeting facilities." These often double as reception sites in most towns.

And that's just the tip of the iceberg. Many sites are experimenting with "virtual tour" technology which lets you take a virtual walk-through of a reception site via the 'net. One of the leaders in this category is 1800wedding.com, although the site only has limited listings in California so far. The Knot has also signed deals with streaming video companies as well, so we expect to see most of the major wedding portals offer this technology soon.

Our new book *CyberBride* has several more options to find local sites on the 'net. See the back of this book for details.

Getting Started: How Far in Advance?

Don't delay the search for your reception site. As soon as you have confirmed your ceremony site, start the search for a reception facility. Time is of the essence. Most cities have a shortage of great reception sites; prime dates in the spring and summer often go quickly. In the South, December can book up to a year in advance for popular Christmas weddings. For spring/summer dates, booking a site nine months to a year in advance may be necessary.

Step-by-step Shopping Strategies

♥ **Step 1:** Figure out how many guests you want to invite. Then look for a site that fits that capacity. Many brides make the mistake of doing this the other way around—picking a site first and then having to adapt their guest list around its size.

♥ **Step 2:** Using the above sources, make appointments with three to five of the top prospects. Confirm the availability of your date before making any trip. Bring a friend or your fiancé along to help inspect the facilities.

♥ **Step 3:** When you visit a reception site, look carefully at the facility. Can the room really hold all your guests comfortably or does it looked cramped? Is the lighting on a dimmer system? How will the traffic of guests flow around buffet tables, the dance floor, etc.?

♥ **Step 4:** Try to meet the catering manager (if the catering is done in-house). Honestly discuss your budget and suggest the manager custom-tailor a menu for your reception. Read the catering chapter to make sure you cover all of those details. Get a detailed price breakdown—in writing—on *everything* (food, beverages, service, centerpieces, linens, china, etc.).

♥ **Step 5:** Ask to see the site set-up for a wedding. It's sometimes hard to imagine an empty ballroom dressed to the nines for a wedding reception. Here's a good way to get a more realistic impression. Ask to visit just before a reception is about to start. Check the traffic flow—for buffets, see if the lay-out of the food stations makes sense. Does the staff seem organized, or are they running around at the last minute like chickens with their heads cut off?

♥ **Step 6:** If the site has in-house catering, ask for a taste-test of the food. The quality of food varies greatly from site to site, so asking for this is a wise precaution. Most sites offer taste tests at no charge; of course there are exceptions. Some brides have emailed us with stories of sites that refuse to do tastings. We usually wonder what those facilities are trying to hide.

♥ **Step 7:** After visiting several sites, make your decision and put down as small a deposit as possible. Sign a contract that includes the date, the hours, the rental fee and any other charges and approximate guest count. Be very careful to get any verbal promises by the site ("oh, sure we can decorate that landing with flowers for no charge") in writing in the contract. As with any wedding, details may change. Make sure you get any alterations to the original menu or site plan in writing (keep a log of conversations, send a letter to confirm changes, etc.).

♥ **Step 8:** Get the site coordinator/catering manager's name in writing in the contract. Confirm that this person will be there at your reception. If there are problems, you'll need this contact to troubleshoot any last minute issues.

♥ **Step 9:** Keep the lines of communication open. Remember you might book the site up to a year (or more) before your wedding. Checking back periodically with the site's manager (a call every month or so) is prudent to avoid any surprises (oh, did we mention we sold the facility to the Society of Professional Motorcyclists last month?).

Questions to Ask of a Reception Site

1 **How many guests can the space accommodate?** Typically, the capacity is given in two numbers, one for a buffet/hors d'oeuvres (or standing) reception and one for a sit-down (seated) dinner. Be careful about these figures—sites often fudge capacity numbers or give "approximate" guesses. Don't forget to account for any buffet tables or dance floors; these all take space.

2 **How many hours does the rental fee cover?** What are the overtime charges? Be sure to ask about whether set-up and clean-up time is included in the stated hours. Some sites don't count this time "on the clock," while others do. Because some sites do more than one wedding a day, be careful there is adequate time between events. A money-saving tip: book the time you realistically need for your reception and avoid costly overtime charges.

3 **Is there an in-house caterer or a list of approved caterers?** Or can you bring in any caterer? Obviously, hotels have in-house caterers (that's how they make the big bucks). But many other sites are also picky about this—after they get burned by a sloppy caterer, a site may restrict brides to a list of "pre-approved" caterers. In case you can't find a caterer on their approved list who meets your specifications, ask if you can bring in another one.

4 **Are there any cooking restrictions?** For a site where an outside caterer is brought in, check the kitchen facilities. Some sites restrict caterers from cooking on-site and just allow the warming of food that is prepared elsewhere. Make sure you confirm with your caterer to see if the kitchen facilities are adequate.

5 **Is there a piano available?** How about a dance floor? Obviously, bands don't cart around a baby grand with them to every reception, so ask the site coordinator. Don't assume anything is free. Ask the site about any extra charges to prevent surprises.

6 **What else is happening at the site the day of my wedding?** Greed drives some sites to book multiple events during one day, even when the site can't realistically handle that many people. And we're not just talking about hotels. We've even seen smaller sites (restored mansions, catering halls) try to cram two or more weddings into a facility. Any site that tries to do more than one wedding a day is a wedding factory; approach any such facility with caution. Will you have to compete with a noisy convention of insurance agents that has a 10-piece band in the next room? Will your party have to share a bathroom or other facilities with the other party? Press the catering rep to give you exclusivity over the facility. Or at least, insist on a layout of the parties that minimizes overlapping noise.

7 **Are there any union rules we must follow?** In some states (particularly the Northeast), union work rules may force certain restrictions on sites, including the serving of food and set-up of any audio equipment.

8 **What are the minimums?** Watch out—some sites may require you to pay for a minimum amount of catering, no matter how many guests you have. Such minimums are common during peak wedding months (typically, May through September).

9 **How late can we play music?** Some sites have a curfew for music. Be sure that doesn't conflict with your plans to dance the night way.

10 **Are there any insurance requirements?** According to our reader email, there are some reception sites out there that require other wedding vendors present at your event (DJ, band, photographer) to carry liability insurance. We're not sure why this is the responsibility of the bride and groom to check out, but it might be a good question to ask. If a vendor you want doesn't have liability insurance, inquire as to whether your (or your parent's) homeowner's insurance will cover the event.

11 **Are there any "caterer surcharges"?** Some sites that let you bring in a caterer will slap that caterer with an extra surcharge that is a percentage of what you are spending on food and beverage. This fee is a major rip-off and rarely disclosed–that is, until the caterer passes it along to you in the form of an additional charge of 7% to 15%. We'll discuss this more in the Pitfalls section later in this chapter.

Top Money-saving Secrets

1 **City Sites.** Fortunately, most sites run by municipal governments aren't trying to make a killing on weddings. Hence, city sites are the most affordable reception sites you can find. For example, in one town we researched, a nice city-owned clubhouse in a park that offered stunning skyline views was available to rent for just $125 for five hours. That's no typo—$125 and you bring in your own caterer. Another similar-sized facility run by a private company in the same town cost $750 to rent for four hours. Obviously, the ambiance of these city sites (clubhouses, recreation centers, parks, gardens) is different than a downtown hotel or catering hall, but, hey, they are great bargains.

2 **Choose a site where you can bring in a caterer.** In every city we've researched, there are always a handful of sites where you can rent the facility and then bring in an "off-site" caterer. Often, this is where the big savings are found—see our chapter on catering for more details.

3 **Consider an off-peak time.** Everyone wants to get married on a Saturday night in June. Now, if you pick a time with less competition, you can often negotiate better rental rates. Many sites have stated discounts for Friday or Sunday weddings. (The down side to this tip: some wedding vendors like photographers may charge an extra fee to work on Sundays). If you still have your heart set on a Saturday wedding, consider less popular months of the year (basically anytime other than the summer). Many sites have stated discounts for such off-months.

4 **Your house.** Hey, at least the facility is free. Be aware that you may have to rent chairs, tables, etc. and this will add to the tab. You may also have to pay a mover to store your furniture for the weekend. If you plan to pitch a tent in the backyard, the expense can go even higher (see the box Tent Rental 101 tips and advice). Of course, even when you factor in all these expenses, the savings of a home wedding instead of holding the reception at a pricey hotel may put you ahead overall. Between 10% and 20% of all receptions are held in private homes.

Tent Rental 101

Yes, renting a tent for a home wedding can be pricey, but there are some basic points to remember:

♥ There are four types of tents: frame tents, pole tents, pop-up and party canopies. **Frame tents** have no center poles, using a lightweight metal frame covered with vinyl for support. Since they require minimal staking, frame tents are best for decks and patios. **Pole** tents are more traditional, with pole supports both on the perimeter and in the center. These types of tents require extensive staking. Some folks think pole tents are more festive looking; pole tents are probably the best option for large receptions. **Pop-up** and **party** canopies are do-it-yourself alternatives to pole tents with collapsible frames and offer shelter against sun or light rain.

♥ Which is the most affordable? Pop-up and party canopies are the cheapest options. Frame tents tend be more expensive than pole tents. A large company that rents tents in New England charges $625 for a frame tent that is 30' by 60' feet (this would hold 144 people seated for dinner). The same size pole tent is $545. Other elaborate pole tents with sidewalls can top $1000 and even $2000 depending in the options. At the top end, in the Northeast, it can cost $6000 to $9000 to rent a 50x70 tent that holds 200 guests—that includes lighting, flooring, heating, delivery, set-up and tear-down. While it might run $4000 for the same tent without all the extras, remember that a tent for large crowds will probably be more expensive than holding the same event in a hotel or catering hall.

♥ How big of a tent do I need? A good general rule is to leave 15 square feet per guest at receptions; for ceremonies the suggested size is eight square feet per person (assuming chairs, a center aisle, podium and/or stage).

♥ Accessories can add comfort—for a price. Sidewalls with windows are an option for larger tents, as are air conditioning and heating. If a tent is placed on a lawn, subflooring and carpeting can protect sod. Most folks rent a dance floor and add some basic lighting to create a mood.

♥ Key questions to ask: What exactly is included in the price? What are the extras? Some companies include set-up and take-down in their fees; others price this separately. Be sure to confirm any extra charges for weekend delivery and special fees like a "drying charge" should it rain on your event. Also ask: Are tents deodorized? How early is the set-up? Do you have insurance? Get a written agreement that covers ALL these details.

5 **Consider your ceremony site.** Many houses of worship have attached reception halls. In fact, almost one-quarter of all receptions occur at churches or temples. Perhaps this is because rental rates are particularly affordable. We'll have more on this option later in this chapter.

6 **Have a reception lunch or brunch instead of dinner.** The biggest expense of most receptions is catering, and the most expensive meal to serve is dinner. Wedding lunches or brunches often are much more affordable. What's the cheapest time of day to tie the knot? A two o'clock wedding—guests will already have eaten lunch and are not expecting dinner. Hence, a reception with cake, punch and light hors d'oeuvres is all that's needed . . . and 40% to 60% less expensive than a full dinner. Check the catering chapter for more tips to save money on this big budget item.

7 **Restaurant receptions.** Many restaurants have banquet rooms, some that can hold large crowds. These may be a great alternative to pricey hotels or catering halls. A bride in Chicago provided us with some cost comparisons: she priced a reception at a gourmet French restaurant called Cafe Le Cave (in Des Plaines) at $55 per person. That's for a chicken or filet mignon dinner. Compare that to fancy Chicago downtown hotels, where a similar reception starts at $75 and can go up to $200 per guest. Another bonus: most restaurants don't charge "room fees" or other bogus charges that pricier facilities do. And the food may be higher quality than a hotel or catering hall.

8 **Join the Navy.** Just kidding. But, do you have any relatives or friends that are active duty or retired military? If so, you may have access to a wide range of possible reception sites at military bases. One bride in Cape May, NJ discovered she could rent the Officer's Club of the local Coast Guard base since her father was a retired naval officer. The cost? A mere $25 per hour.

9 **Check nearby small towns.** A bride in Lexington, Kentucky emailed us this tip. She found a reception site in nearby Paris (a 15 minute drive) that was charging 40% cheaper rates than in-town options. "The historic building offered the outdoor intimate garden we were looking for," she said. Another tip for historic sites: barter. If you've got any skills, offer the caretaker of these sites a trade. One groom offered to fix some broken doors and shutters on a historic site and received a reduced rental rate.

10 **Tell them you are planning a retirement party.** A Connecticut bride called in this tip: she found a restaurant with a nice banquet room that was perfect for her 50-guest reception. Instead of telling them it was a wedding reception, she said the party was a family reunion. The result: she was able to get a great price for a complete sit-down luncheon, estimating she saved about 20% off a similar "bridal" package. Two weeks before the reception, she told the restaurant it was actually a wedding—too late for the restaurant to raise the price!

11 **Consider a business hotel.** If you like the convenience of a hotel reception but not the costs, check out hotels that cater to business travelers. Why? Most are dead on the weekends . . .and may be

The Marriage Mark-Up

Do you wonder if you mention the word "wedding" to a reception site that the price suddenly goes up? We've always been suspicious that folks planning retirement parties, birthdays or any other type of event get LOWER prices than brides and grooms.

Our suspicious were confirmed recently when Boston NBC affiliate WHDH-TV did a story on the "Marriage Mark-Up." The TV station did a simple test—they called 11 Boston-area reception sites and asked how much they charge for a wedding. Then they called back and asked for a retirement party. Now, to be fair, the station made sure it was asking for the same date and size party.

The results? Eight out of 11 places quoted the station the "marriage mark-up." One said the party would be $65 per person, but $90 for a wedding. Another said brides and grooms have to shell out 20% more. And those prices didn't include any special wedding-only items like a cake, just food and beverage.

In Atlanta, one major hotel quotes a $10,000 minimum for a wedding, but just $7500 for retirement parties. Another facility in San Francisco quoted us an $18,000 estimate for a wedding with 125 guests; the same size party for a family reunion was just $9000.

So, what can you do? While most couples don't want to perpetuate a major hoax on sites, it is rather tempting. Perhaps the best path would be to just "forget" to mention you are planning a wedding when you request menu packages. It's very possible that hotels and other reception sites have special "bridal package" menus that are quite pricey. What they DON'T show you is their regular menu packages with lower-cost food options.

Of course, you could go all the way. In Boston, we heard of one couple who planned an entire "retirement party" at reception site. And then, the day of the event, they walked in as bride and groom and told the site it was a "surprise wedding"! Yes, the site was livid but they stuck to the lower price quote.

willing to cut a deal for a wedding reception. A bride in Los Angeles discovered the savings can be dramatic. She priced a 250 guest reception (four-course sit-down dinner, cocktail hour with open bar and appetizers, beer, wine and a champagne toast) for $7500 at a Wyndham hotel. "That's pretty amazing considering that this is in Los Angeles," said the bride, adding that "I don't feel that we are giving up on the quality either. The food is excellent." An additional bonus: she got a special weekend hotel room rate of $75 for out of town guests, which is a steal in LA.

12 Go to college. Got a university or college in town? If so, that's a great place to look for reception site bargains. Many such institutions have alumni halls, faculty clubs and other facilities that are available at very affordable rates. And you don't always have to be a student or alum to book a site.

13 Get creative. We're constantly amazed at the inventive sites couples can find to hold their receptions—aquariums, airports,

---

REAL WEDDING TIP

Frequent flier nuptials; Zoo I Do's

We never cease to be amazed at the sheer creativity of brides who unearth some very amazing receptions sites. Like the airport in Chattanooga, TN. Apparently, it's not so busy, so the airport rents the brand new terminal for weddings. Cost: a mere $250— you bring the caterer.

Museums (like the Museum of Life and Science in Durham, NC or the Museum of Natural History in Cleveland, OH) make a creative backdrop and are usually very affordable. Finally, don't rule out oddball places like . . . breweries. In Memphis, the Coors Brewery (901) 375-2100 has two large rooms available for receptions (the Texas Deck and the Coors Belle). For $1000 to $1250 for four hours, your guests get all the Coors, soft drinks and coffee they can drink—and the room can hold up to 300 guests. Yea, food is extra, but who will notice? Meanwhile, a bride in Apple Valley found the Minnesota Zoo to be a great reception site bargain:

"The Minnesota Zoo (612) 431-9215, www.wcco.com/partners/ mnzoo/rentals.htm) has various rooms for weddings, including an area surrounded by dolphin tanks. So you feel like you are under a huge coral reef. The rental is $1500, which includes tables, chairs, linens and china! You bring in your own caterer."

zoos, laundromats, you name it, it might be possible. Another major money-saver: if the site you are renting from is a non-profit, see if the rental fee is tax deductible. One bride found the Minnesota's Zoo's $1500 rental fee is not only a decent price in that city, but also a nice tax deduction (see Real Wedding Tip for more details). If you want an off-beat site, the web is your best friend. Brides said they've found great sites possibilities from web sites such as FieldTrip.com (which focuses on such Eastern states as Connecticut, New York, New Jersey, Delaware, Maryland and Pennsylvania) and HereComesTheGuide.com (California).

Pitfalls to Avoid

PITFALL #1 UNWRITTEN PROMISES.

"I booked my wedding and reception at an historic home. The wedding coordinator there told me all the wonderful things they would do for my reception at no charge. For example, they said they would decorate the gazebo for free if I brought them the fabric. Then, wouldn't you know? My contact person left and the owner of the site refused to fulfill the promises she made! I was furious! The only problem was I couldn't prove a thing since nothing was written down!"

Well, this is perhaps the most common complaint we hear about reception sites: unfulfilled promises. To get you to book the site, some unscrupulous site managers will make wild promises they never intend to keep. Another problem: the person you first meet with quits or is fired before your wedding. This happens more than you might think (catering and site managers hop from job to job like rabbits). A word to the wise: get every last promise and detail *in writing* in the contract. This protects you from dishonest people or from changes in personnel. If promises are made after the contract is signed, get them to write a note (a fax or email will do) putting the promises in black and white.

PITFALL #2 MENU GOOFS.

"My wedding and reception was at a popular hotel in our town. We spent hours going over the menu but what was served at the reception in no way resembled what we ordered. Worse yet, then we couldn't find any-one from the catering department to fix the problem! What happened?"

Sometimes the bloated bureaucracy at hotels and other reception sites can lead to snafus. Perhaps the catering manager "forgot" to inform the kitchen of your menu. Maybe the chef just had an extra 200 Chicken Cordon Bleus left over from a banquet the night before. In any case, you deserve a refund or the site should offer a fair reduction in the bill as compensation for their mistake.

As for fixing a problem the night of the wedding, good luck. While you might be able to have the maitre d' contact the catering director, there may be little that can be done at that moment. Another wise idea: if the catering director or representative won't be at the reception, get their home phone, pager and cell phone numbers.

PITFALL #3 KICK-BACKS AND CATERING MANAGERS.

"I picked a band for my reception based on the recommendation of my site's catering coordinator. It was a disaster—the band was a flop! To add insult to injury, I later found out the catering coordinator received a 'commission' from the band!"

One scam we uncovered in this field is catering managers/coordinators who take kick-backs from bands (or other wedding merchants) they recommend. In California, one musician blew the whistle on a site that was charging a $200 fee to get on their "recommended list." We've also encountered this on the East Coast. Protect yourself by thoroughly checking out any of these "recommended" services before hiring them.

PITFALL #4 BETTER SAFE THAN SORRY.

"My fiancée and I wanted to book this civic site since it had sentimental meaning to us. The site coordinator told us we 'had dibs' on the site because we had inquired about it first. They only book one year in advance, but we were told we didn't have to get our deposit in immediately. Guess what? We just discovered they then booked our date to another bride who came in on the first day it was available!"

Some site coordinators may tell you "there's no need to rush" to put a deposit on a site, but you might want to do otherwise. There's no guarantee that a date will be held for you ... especially when another bride shows up with deposit money in hand. The best advice: book it now, show them the money (place the deposit) and get it in writing.

PITFALL #5 CATERING SURCHARGES

" I was perturbed to learn recently that the reception site I have booked for my wedding charges caterers a % fee for "use of the site." In other words, once the total catering fee is determined, an extra 7% of this total must be paid to the reception site. This cost of course, is passed on to me. This was no where reflected in my contract with the reception site and it seems pretty underhanded to me. The caterer I'm working with however, explained that really the fee is imposed on the caterer as the price of doing business at the site, that all sites do this and that in fact 7% was very reasonable. Is this typical? Is this LEGAL when I've already paid $2000 to rent out the space!"

This is a new rip-off we've started hearing about in recent years. The words "sneaky, underhanded and unethical" have been used by brides and grooms to describe these new charges and we agree—many sites "forget" to disclose this fee when booking. It also appears nowhere in the site's contract. And, of course, many caterers simply pass this fee along to you as an extra charge. (In one case, a caterer simply refused to work with a bride at a site that charged a 15% commission, since she didn't want to pay it either).

How can you prevent this from happening to you? Be sure to ask about any catering surcharges or commissions BEFORE you book a site that allows outside catering. And if a site fails to disclose this fee, you should be entitled to a full refund on your deposit if you decide to cancel. From a legal point of few, such sites are on very shaky ground. The sites cannot impose a fee on a third-party (the caterer) because you've contracted with the site for a reception. What's next? Charging the DJ a "electricity fee" when he plugs in a CD player? Slapping the baker with a "cake fee" because they are delivering a wedding cake to the site?

Helpful Hints

1 Kid's buckets. If you plan to have children at your wedding, consider doing what one reader did: she made up kid's buckets (cheap, plastic sand buckets) and filled them with 99¢ coloring books, crayons and small games. "They were waiting on the tables at place settings for kids. As a result, moms and dads didn't have to entertain their kids. I still hear thank you's to this day!"

2 Check back occasionally. Bridal shops aren't the only ones to go out of business suddenly; sadly this can happen to reception sites too. We heard from a Michigan bride who reported two sites near Ypsilanti closed during a six-month period; couples were left scrambling to find alternatives. While this is still rare, it might be prudent to call your reception site every other month to make sure they're still around.

3 Box up meals of guests that don't show up. If you paid for 100 prime rib dinners and only 97 guests showed up, then ask the caterer to box up those extra meals! If not, they go into the trash (or into the mouths of waiters).

4 Choice can be a pricey option. Some folks like to give their guests a choice of entrees—say fish or chicken. That's nice, but watch out: some sites will charge you the HIGHER meal price no matter what option the guest chooses. It might be less expensive to just pick one menu and forget the choice.

A Look at the Six Most Common Reception Site Types

This section will explore the pros, cons and costs of the five most common places for receptions: hotels/catering halls, private and country clubs, civic sites, home weddings, church weddings and (our favorite) miscelleanous sites.

HOTELS/CATERING HALLS

Catering halls and hotels may seem like an obvious choice as the site for a reception—both have spacious banquet rooms and full-service catering staffs to take care of every detail. On the East Coast, catering halls host as many as half of all wedding receptions. Meanwhile, in the South, hotel ballrooms are often the only choice for a bride who is inviting 300 or 400 guests. While hotels may only account for 10% to 20% of receptions nationwide, they often host the biggest and most lavish receptions in many cities. Here are the pros and cons of having your wedding reception at a hotel or catering hall.

The Good News

♥ **ALL-INCLUSIVE PACKAGES.** When you have a reception at these facilities, all the rentals (tables, chairs, serving pieces, bars, dance floors, etc) are generally included in the price.

♥ **LARGE WEDDINGS.** For large weddings, hotels or catering halls may be the best choice. That's because their big ballrooms can accommodate large parties up to or over 1000 guests. Most other sites have peak capacities at about 200 to 300 guests.

♥ **CLIMATE CONTROL.** In areas of the country with harsh weather, climate-controlled ballrooms are a plus.

♥ **DISCOUNTS ON ROOM RENTALS, HONEYMOON SUITES.** Most hotels are willing to negotiate a discounted rate for a block of rooms. If you have many out-of-town relatives, this may be a big plus. Some hotel packages also throw in a honeymoon suite gratis—a nice touch. One caveat: make sure to double-check the hotel's "special" rate to see if you're really getting a deal. More than one bride has told us they discovered the "special group rate" was no different than the regular room fees.

♥ **SPECIAL WEDDING RECEPTION PACKAGES.** Many hotels and catering halls have special catering packages for wedding receptions. Unfortunately, these are sometimes more expensive than their à la carte choices! Why? The extra labor needed for a reception versus other functions might be one answer. Or maybe it's just pure greed (call it a "bridal" package and the price rises 30%). Be sure to crunch the numbers for different packages to see which is the best deal. On the other hand, some facilities aggressively pursue weddings by offering many freebies—you'd be surprised at the big difference in costs from one site to another.

♥ **DIETARY RESTRICTIONS.** For those couples who need Kosher catering, hotels are often a best bet. Hotels must meet certain standards before they are certified Kosher. Call a local synagogue or rabbi to get a list of approved facilities._ Some hotels and catering halls can also host a lovely ceremony. One West Coast hotel has an outdoor garden and gazebo for ceremonies. At a catering hall we visited in New Jersey, lush gardens offered several ceremony site options. The convenience of having everything at one location may be a big plus.

♥ **ADVICE ON ENTERTAINERS, FLORISTS, BAKERS, ETC.** Catering managers at hotels and catering halls often have their pulse on the best wedding bands and entertainers. Use their experience, but be careful of unscrupulous managers who take kick-backs from "recommended" services. (See Pitfall #3 earlier in this chapter for more info.)

The Bad News

♥ **DRAB INTERIOR DECOR.** Some sites look like they were decorated in Early Eisenhower.

♥ **THESE SITES CAN BE DARN EXPENSIVE.** While hotels and catering halls offer all-inclusive packages, you definitely pay for this convenience. Case in point: sky high minimum food and beverage fees for premium nights. A bride in Chicago told us one exclusive hotel there has a $30,000 minimum charge for a Saturday night in May! The Drake in Chicago charges $150 to $250 per guest just for food and beverages. And that's before they slap you with a 18% mandatory gratuity and 9.75% sales tax. Even if you don't get married at the most chic hotel, your wedding budget at any hotel can suffer death by a thousand cuts. Hotels are skilled at taking $8 bottles of wine and charging you $30 in their "bridal package." Another facility charged couples $35 for a gallon of fruit punch. And don't forget about those high minimum charges for food and beverage.

♥ **FROZEN FOOD.** Perhaps the biggest problem that plagues many hotels and catering halls is poor quality food. These sites often buy frozen food that can be quickly prepared. Ever seen those mini-quiches at a hotel wedding reception? Hotels can buy these and other popular buffet items in bulk. Pop them in a warming oven and presto! Dinner's ready! Obviously, pre-fabricated, frozen hors d'oeuvres simply don't compare to freshly-prepared dishes.

♥ **BUREAUCRACY OF CATERING DEPARTMENTS.** From busboys to waiters to captains to catering assistants to managers, the multi-layer management of catering departments can be vexing. Ask if the catering manager (or the contact person whom you have dealt with) will be at your reception.

♥ **WEDDINGS CAN BE LOW ON THE PRIORITY LIST.** Especially in December, hotels are distracted with corporate holiday parties on large budgets. Competition with convention and reunion business can also be a headache.

♥ **REMEMBER THE CATERING REPRESENTATIVES ARE ON COMMISSION.** The more money you spend, the more money they make. Hence, we find many hotels and catering halls pushing exotic (and expensive) foods to jack up the tab. Many hotels also "suggest" expensive wines and other liquor.

♥ **BE CAREFUL OF NICKEL-AND-DIME CHARGES.** Never assume that anything is free. Extra charges could include valet parking, special table skirting,

REAL WEDDING TIP

Catering insider dishes the dirt on hotels

A bride-to-be emailed us with her "in the field" stories about hotel consumer abuse:

"I worked as a waitress/bartender for weddings in a five-star hotel in a major city and witnessed some incredible rip-offs. It was customary to remove an appetizer platter when it was only half-empty. The left-over food would be served in the employees' cafeteria. In the bus stations, it was not uncommon to see bus-boys and waitstaff having a drink on the customers' tab. In addition, the customer would be charged a tip on those drinks as well. Think you can complain to the management? Forget it. When working a large party as bartender, the food and beverage (F & B) director came up to my bar and asked me to fill several large pitchers with frozen margaritas. I thought he was going to deliver them to another bar. When I had to go into the kitchen for additional supplies, I saw the F & B director with the margarita pitchers. To whom was he serving them? The catering director, the chefs, the general manager. All on the customer's tab."

ice carvings, a dance floor, corking fees, cake cutting charge (see catering chapter), food station attendants, and any audio equipment (a microphone for toasts, for example). Also, silk flower table centerpieces and special linens or china may be extra. Compare the estimate on centerpieces with your florist's bid to get the best deal.

What Does a Hotel/Catering Hall Reception Cost?

Reception packages vary widely. Hotels and catering halls in downtown areas tend to be the most expensive (and also expect to pay extra for valet parking). In suburban areas, rates are somewhat less and these sites tend to be more aggressive in their competition for wedding business (since they can't rely on downtown convention traffic). In our research, we've found packages that start as low as $10 per person for a buffet at an Oklahoma hotel and go up to $200 per person for a complete sit-down dinner at a posh New York City catering hall. In general, most sites are in the $20 to $50 per person range for basic receptions (not counting liquor). In the biggest cities (New York, Los Angeles, Chicago, Philadelphia), you can expect to pay twice to three times more. Add in a big liquor tab and you'll see the total costs soar. In Chicago, we hear some top hotels now charge $15,000 to $20,000 minimums for food and beverage. And considering those same hotels charge $150 to $200 per guest for reception dinners, you'll be hitting those minimums real fast.

PRIVATE/COUNTRY CLUBS

Think you have to be a member of those fancy country clubs and private clubs to hold a wedding reception in their facilities? Not always. In fact, many clubs welcome non-members with open arms! That's because weddings often bring in badly-needed revenue. We define private and country clubs as any site that has membership requirements or restrictions. While you may have to be a member at some sites, others just require a "member-sponsor." Still others don't have any requirements at all.

Types of Clubs

1 **Business clubs.** Located downtown on top of skyscrapers, some business clubs have a restaurant open for lunch each day and space to host meetings and receptions. Various professional organizations (i.e., Engineers' Clubs, Doctors' Clubs) may own and operate these facilities. Such sites vary widely in appeal (we saw one Engineer's Club that looked like it was decorated by, well, engineers) but are generally more open to wedding receptions. Most likely, you must use the club's in-house catering.

2 **Country Clubs.** These sites normally have a golf course and several acres of landscaped grounds. Here, the clubhouse is the focal point for receptions. Some of these sites can be quite stuffy, with the snob appeal often spread rather thick. Nonetheless, lush grounds can make beautiful backdrops for photos. These sites may be the most restrictive; many require a member (who can be a friend or just an acquaintance) to at least "sponsor" the reception. Sometimes, this sponsorship is just a token technicality where the member assumes responsibility in case you don't pay the bill and move to Peru. In most cases, you must use the country club's in-house catering.

3 **Civic/Social clubs.** Elks Clubs, Garden Clubs, Federation of Women's clubs, Junior Leagues, Junior Forums—each of these organizations may have facilities they rent for receptions. Typically, you must bring in an outside caterer. Prices and quality are all over the board: Elks Clubs and Veterans of Foreign Wars (VFW) Posts, for example, are often quite affordable but offer rather Spartan decor. Other clubs are located in historic buildings that are beautiful but also carry a hefty price tag. Membership requirements are usually non-existent.

The Good News

♥ MORE PERSONAL SERVICE. These facilities have less of that "wedding factory" feel you find at hotels or catering halls. One reason: less bureaucracy. Many sites have fewer people to deal with and this sometimes improves customer service.

♥ BETTER AMBIANCE. Unlike the drab and sterile decor of many hotels, country and private clubs are usually set on beautiful sites—golf courses are definitely easier on the eyes than parking lots. Downtown business clubs perched atop penthouses may offer spectacular skyline views.

♥ SOME CLUBS PERMIT OUTSIDE CATERERS. While business and country clubs usually have in-house catering, some clubs let you bring in a caterer of your choice—this can be a fantastic savings (see our catering chapter).

The Bad News

♥ YOU MAY HAVE TO BE A MEMBER. Frequently this depends on the local economy. If the club is in need of funds, they may let non-members in to boost a sagging financial situation. However, if the club is flushed with members, they will limit the use of the club to members only.

♥ IF YOU AREN'T A MEMBER, SOME CLUBS REQUIRE YOU TO HAVE A MEMBER-SPONSOR. Here, a member of the club must "sponsor" your reception, agreeing to attend the event and pay for it if you skip town. If you have a friend who is a member, great. If you don't, some clubs may negotiate around this point—perhaps by requesting a larger deposit. We know one club that will find you a sponsor if you don't know one!

♥ **FOOD QUALITY CAN VARY WIDELY.** Some clubs have gourmet chefs on staff who create wonderful dishes. Other clubs may not be as lucky and their food quality is, at best, as good as that of an average hotel. Ask for a taste test to confirm this detail.

♥ **EXPENSIVE RECEPTIONS.** Some clubs can be just as, or even more, expensive than hotel weddings. Overpricing of liquor is a common problem. Just like hotels, club catering managers receive commissions based on the total amount you spend—giving them an incentive to inflate the tab. Many clubs also add on a high gratuity, similar to hotels.

What Does it Cost?

Well, it depends. Fancy country clubs may be just as expensive as the prices we quoted above for hotels and catering halls. Other clubs, that don't have in-house catering, just charge a rental fee for the facility. These can be a major bargain.

CIVIC SITES

A "civic" site is any reception facility that is owned and administered by a city or municipal agency. Almost always, you must bring in your own caterer. Some civic sites have a recommended list of caterers that you may have to choose from. Be aware that some sites may have time and beverage restrictions (no liquor) and others require you to hire security officers. Civic sites are usually the best bargains. Why? Subsidized by taxpayers, these sites aren't out to make big bucks like private facilities.

Types of Civic Sites

1 **Parks, gardens, amphitheaters.** Often quite affordable, these sites are usually administered by city parks departments. Some sites even have clubhouses. If you decide to have an outdoor ceremony or reception, make sure you have a backup plan in case of inclement weather.

2 **Recreation centers, civic centers, town halls, conference centers.** Quality varies greatly with these sites (some are spectacular while others are dumps), but they are usually quite affordable.

3 **Sites owned by universities or colleges.** These sites include faculty clubs, alumni halls, chapels, etc. You might be surprised at the sheer variety of spaces available for rent on a college campus—they are rarely advertised and can be great bargains. One limitation: you may have to be an alum (or know one) to book the site. Also, many of these facilities will require you to use their in-house caterer.

4 **Museums.** Rare but available in some cities, these sites may be quite expensive and even require you to be a "museum patron" (i.e. make a hefty donation).

The Good News

♥ LOW COST & UNIQUE LOCATIONS. Most of these sites are very affordable.

♥ BRING IN AN OUTSIDE CATERER. Off-site caterers can save oodles of money and offer creative, delicious menu options. However, you may be required to pick a caterer off an "approved" list.

The Bad News

♥ VERY POPULAR SITES BOOK UP QUICKLY. Since civic sites are so affordable, they are also very popular. Many book months in advance.

♥ EQUIPMENT RENTAL EXPENSE CAN BE HIGH. Some of these sites might require you to bring in tables, chairs, serving pieces, etc. This could be a significant expense.

♥ MAKE SURE THE CATERER IS VERY FAMILIAR WITH THE SITE. Some brides find hiring and dealing with an outside caterer challenging—increasing the complexity of the event by adding another person in the loop. Another limitation: civic sites' lack of kitchen facilities may affect a caterer's ability to do the function.

HOME WEDDINGS

Yes, we can always tell when it's wedding season in Boulder, Colorado. Pick any road that winds its way up into the foothills and you'll see several signs directing guests to a remote location for the nuptials of "Spense and Lisa," "Cheyenne and Bob," and so on.

Home weddings are big here, as they are in other parts of the Rockies. While only accounting for 6% to 10% of all receptions in the US, Boulder seems to be the center of the universe for home nuptials and receptions—half of all weddings here are at home, according to our estimates. Perhaps it's the nice summer weather or the views of the Continental Divide that convince brides and grooms to tie the knot at home. Or maybe we're just cheap—the price ($0) is right for many folks.

The Good News

♥ **AFFORDABLE RECEPTIONS.** Let's be honest: home weddings can be had cheap. Whether you have friends and family help with the food or order a meal from a restaurant or catering service, home weddings cost a fraction of receptions at traditional sites like hotels, catering halls and private clubs.

♥ **NO SCHEDULING CONFLICTS.** If you want to have a wedding in June on a Saturday night, you may discover that so do many other brides in your area. The competition for reception sites during popular months can lead you to consider a home wedding.

♥ **SMALL WEDDINGS.** Unless you live in Bill Gate's house, the average home can only hold a minimal number of guests (usually under 100). This is a plus and a minus. While you may not be able to invite everyone you'd like to, you do have the perfect excuse for cutting down that guest list.

The Bad News

♥ **RENTALS, RENTALS, RENTALS.** Planning a home wedding for 75 guests but you don't have tables and chairs for the crowd? You'll need to rent them, along with plates, silverware, glassware, serving pieces, bar set-ups and more. Afraid it might rain on your parade? Renting a tent can set you back $500 to $1000 or more. As you can see, the money you save on catering with a home wedding may be partially eaten up by a big rental bill.

♥ **SURPRISE EXPENSES.** Home weddings may entail several unexpected bills. At one home wedding we attended in Austin, Texas, the bride and groom hired a van service to shuttle guests back and forth—this cost an extra $250. You may also need extra insurance to cover liability at the event—call your homeowner's insurance provider to see what's covered.

Discount chair covers

Yes, most rental places rent chairs, but what if you want a fancier look? Some folks like the look of chair covers. But the price? A reader in New Orleans said a local rental company wanted to charge her $8 per chair for fancy covers. So she went online and found ChairCovers.com. This site has just about every chair cover fabric known to man—and the price is right at $3 or so per chair.

CHURCH RECEPTIONS

The classic mid-America wedding typically has a low-cost reception that follows in a church fellowship hall. Yes, they are cheap, but fellowship halls can be hard to look at. A mother of the bride in a small Arkansas town came up with some thoughts on how to make this work: "Beg, borrow, use that church family! If people want to lend stuff and help, then let them! Give them a list! We borrowed almost all of the decorations from church friends whose daughters have married in the last three years. Lattice work, columns, lights, artificial ivy, and flowers were used to cover up the ugly fellowship hall. We have friends that own a large restaurant who are letting us borrow silver serving pieces and 12 candelabras! We have other friends who are decorating the sanctuary and fellowship hall with tulle (very cheap and bridal looking), ivy, loose flowers, ferns, azaleas, etc. We have other friends who used to be caterers who are cooking all of the food at cost. We have another friend who is in food distribution who gave us free food for the reception. That's what friends are for!"

AND EVERYWHERE ELSE

Yes, you can have a wedding reception just about anywhere. Smiley's Laundromat, in Denver, Colorado has hosted weddings and receptions where brides and grooms have exchanged rings between the spin and rinse cycles. Other possibilities include theaters, ranches, private estates, chartered boats and yachts, bed and breakfast inns, and so on. Anything goes!

What's the message here? Don't think you must have your reception in a hotel or club just because all your friends did that. Every city has many romantic and beautiful settings for receptions—it may just take a little creative searching.

In fact, that's perhaps the biggest challenge to using a "non-traditional" site—finding one! (Perhaps the second biggest challenge is convincing parents and relatives that the site is better than the traditional options!) To find a non-traditional site, look in bridal editions of local newspapers and other local wedding advertising publications. Ask local caterers for suggestions. Don't overlook even the national bridal magazines—each has "regional" advertising sections that are full of ads from local sites.

Often you must bring in your own caterer (the exceptions, of course, are restaurants). As a side note, a recent survey in *Bridal Guide* revealed that 11% of all wedding receptions are held in restaurants.

If you read just one chapter in this book, make it this one. That's because we give you 20 ways to cut your catering budget, the biggest expense area for any wedding. Wonder what to ask the caterer? Check out our 18 questions to ask, plus six pitfalls to avoid with wedding catering.

What Are You Buying?

Wedding catering varies dramatically across the country. When food is the topic, the United States of America is hardly united. And such differences make weddings in one part of the country much different from others. Sometimes the differences are also social in nature. For example, in the Northeast, nearly all receptions are sit-down dinners—folks there like to have their own space to enjoy the meal. While in the South and West, almost all weddings have buffets or hors d'oeuvre receptions—people there like to mingle, instead of being in one chair for the entire reception. No matter where you have your wedding, however, here are the four basic things you buy from a caterer:

♥ **Food.** Everything from hors d'oeuvres to dessert. The typical method of calculating costs of wedding catering is based on a figure per guest. Cost can range from $4 to $6 per guest for a simple "cake, punch and mints" reception in North Dakota to over $200 per person for a full sit-down dinner with open bar at a posh hotel in New York City.

As you can see, food costs can vary dramatically from region to region. Yes, prices are less in the middle of the country and tend to be higher on the coasts and in major cities. In Oklahoma City, for example, a *simple* buffet dinner reception runs $10 to $15 per guest. In Seattle, that same meal is $35. But entry-level reception packages in catering halls in the Northeast can run at least $40 to $60 per guest.

In the mid range, a more elaborate meal (say a heavy hors d'oeuvre buffet or sit-down dinner of prime rib) is about $20 to $40 in a place like Houston, TX. On the coasts and major cities, you can see the tab soar to $50 to $150 for such a reception.

And what about the upper end? Once again, it depends where you live. In Oklahoma, $50 per guest will buy you one fancy reception, replete with a seated dinner of "surf and turf" and an open bar. Expect to shell out $100 to $175 for a top-end reception in Atlanta; up to $200 per guest in Boston and New York City.

In Chicago, a bride recently emailed us to say that she got proposals from six independent caterers for a meal consisting of six hors d'oeuvres per guest, salad, and a chicken entrée. The cost? Nearly $100 per guest. Rather amazing since that didn't include any appetizer, dessert, wedding cake OR the alcohol). Most fancy hotels in Chicago like the Knickerbocker charge $150 to $200 per person just for food and beverage.

According to the Washingtonian magazine, the starting price for most weddings (whether seated dinner or buffet) in the Washington DC metro area is $50 to $60 per person. Fancy events from top caterers run $100 to $150 per guest. Hotels in DC charge $55 to $75 per guest as a minimum, with prices up to $140 per guest at four-star properties.

♥ **Beverages.** Whether your reception will just have punch and coffee or a full open bar with premium well brands, the cost of beverages can be a significant part of the catering budget. For one hors d'oeuvres reception at a posh hotel with a full open bar serving premium liquor, the total bar tab for 400 guests was $9200—almost half the $19,000 total cost of the evening!

Of course, the charge for beverages depends on what you serve and how the reception site accounts for this. An open bar of modest-grade beer, wine, sodas and champagne (for a toast) averages about $12 per guest, according to national averages. Of course, costs can quickly soar above that for bars with mixed drinks and premium liquors—hotels in

Washington DC regularly charge $20 to $30 per guest for drinks.

Beverages can be priced one of several ways. One common method: the consumption bar. What your guests drink, you pay for. This can be by the drink or by the bottle (or tenths of a bottle consumed). Some sites have a flat charge for soft drinks and juices. If your guests aren't big drinkers, a consumption bar might be the most affordable way to go—just be sure to place a cap on the bar tab and get in writing that you are to be asked before they exceed that amount.

Another alternative method of beverage charging: flat pricing. Some sites might offer all-you-can drink packages for a specified period of time (an hour or so). This is a common option at sites that offer cocktail hours before a seated dinner. If your guests are heavy drinkers, this might be the way to go. Ask the site to only charge you for *adult* guests. If you have a 100 guests but 10 are children, be sure to get a flat pricing package that just covers the 90 adults.

Finally, you can sometimes bring in your own liquor—but quite a few sites slap on a "corking fee" to chill and serve the booze. This can be $10 or more per bottle, plus a gratuity and (in some states) sales tax.

REAL WEDDING TIP

Open vs. Cash Bars: Don't charge your guests for drinks.

One big controversy in the world of wedding etiquette is whether bars should be open or cash. In the latter case, guests pay for their drinks. Given the big expense of liquor at most reception sites, this can be $10 to $20 each guest must shell out at the bar. As you can imagine, this is a hot topic the bridal world. Yes, we realize some couples simply don't have the funds to stock an open bar for several hours. Some couples compromise by having an open bar for an hour at the beginning of the reception and a cash bar for the rest of the evening. This also discourages guests from getting smashed toward the end of the evening when they might get behind the wheel. The liability issue is also forcing many couples (and reception sites) to rethink serving alcohol altogether. Yet, despite all the pros to limiting alcohol consumption, our advice is simple—skip the cash bar idea. If you can't afford even a simple beer/wine/champagne bar, don't charge guests for drinks. Go non-alcoholic with creative ideas like juice bars, etc. If you insist on going the cash bar route, the least you could do is warn your guests in advance (perhaps putting notice of this on a personal wedding web site when you discuss the reception details).

♥ **LABOR.** Hey, don't forget those folks who actually serve the food. Of course, most sites won't let you forget to pay the staff—they impose a mandatory gratuity of 15% to 20%. This applies to the food and sometimes the liquor served at the reception. If you serve a buffet that costs $5000, you may pay as much as $1000 extra for the servers, bus boys, etc. Frankly, we think a percentage gratuity is slightly deceptive—most sites don't pay their staff anywhere near the amount of money they collect for "service." They pocket the difference as pure profit. For example, in the above case, let's assume the reception was for 150 guests. Using an industry rule of thumb of one server for 25 guests at a buffet reception, we would need six servers. Hence, each server would theoretically receive $165 of the $1000 service charge for the evening. If the reception lasts four hours (plus another two for set-up and clean-up), do you really think the site is paying the servers a wage that totals nearly $30 per hour? In most cities, we wouldn't bet on it.

Perhaps a more equitable way of paying for service is a method adopted by some independent caterers. This involves paying a flat per hour fee per waiter at the event—usually $10 to $20 per hour per server. No matter what the total tab of your function, you pay only for the number of people actually serving your guests.

How many bartenders do you need? It depends on whether you plan a full bar or just beer wine and soft drink service. The latter is much faster as you can imagine and requires less staff, say one bartender to 75 or 100 guests. A full bar might require a one bartender to 50 guest ratio.

♥ **RENTALS.** Certain reception sites may lack tables, chairs, silverware, china, glassware, table linens, etc. All these items must be rented separately and brought to the site. Some caterers have an in-house supply of rentals while others arrange the needed rentals through an outside company. Charges for this service vary greatly—sometimes the caterer will charge you what the rental company charges them. Other caterers may tack on an extra fee of 5% to 10% of the rental bill to cover the administrative expense of dealing with the company. Some caterers (who charge this fee) also absorb any charges for broken or missing rental items. However, in other cases, you may be responsible for any breakage.

♥ **COORDINATION OF THE RECEPTION.** In the past few years, many caterers have added a new service: coordination of the entire reception. This can range from simply referring names of good florists or entertainers to actually booking and negotiating with other services. Some caterers offer such coordination as a free customer service; others charge fees that are similar to that of a professional wedding consultant. The degree you will want your caterer to coordinate your reception will depend on how much you trust them.

♥ **AVERAGE CATERING COSTS.** So, what's the total tab? As we pointed out above, it highly depends on where the wedding reception will be. The exact menu (food and beverage) that costs $20 per person in Albuquerque could be as much as $90 in Detroit. For example, one bride told us she had to move her reception from Dallas, Texas to Washington, DC. In Dallas, she priced her complete reception at $32 per person. A very similar menu at a comparable hotel in Washington, DC cost $73 per person!

According to industry estimates, we peg the national average cost for wedding catering at $8400 for 175 guests—about $48 per guest. This includes everything: food, beverages, gratuity/labor, rentals and any fees for the reception site. Of course, that "average" combines both lower-cost areas like the Midwest with expensive major metro areas. If you are planning a wedding for a big city, the average is closer to $70 per guest (or a total of $12,250 for 175 guests).

Most caterers require a deposit that is as much as 50% of the total bill to hold a date. The balance is customarily due a week or two weeks *before* the date—some caterers will let you pay the final balance the day of the wedding. Get all payment policies in writing before you sign the contract.

Types of Caterers

1 **In-house or on-premise caterers.** These are catering operations that exclusively provide the catering for a site. Examples are hotels and many country clubs. Unless they're really desperate, most of these sites won't allow outside or "off-premise" caterers.

2 **Off-premise caterers.** These caterers bring in food to an existing site. The caterer's services can be limited to just providing the food or include the coordination of the entire event. Here, caterers become more like party planners or wedding consultants—either providing or contracting out for services like decoration (table centerpieces, table skirting, for example) and entertainment (DJ's, musicians, etc.).

Sources to Find an Affordable Caterer

♥ ASK FRIENDS AND OTHER RECENTLY MARRIED COUPLES FOR SUGGESTIONS. Finding a good, affordable caterer is by far the biggest challenge faced by engaged couples. The best caterers work strictly by word of mouth and hence, don't do much high-profile advertising.

♥ RECEPTION SITES THAT DON'T HAVE IN-HOUSE CATERERS. Most will have a list of local caterers they recommend. This will be an invaluable time-saver. Ask them for their opinions as to which caterer offers the best service or most affordable prices. Also, we have found some photographers who have recommendations on catering (they usually sneak a taste during receptions!).

♥ **DON'T LOOK IN THE PHONE BOOK.** Unlike some other categories, the best caterers do not have the biggest Yellow Pages ads.

Brides in Cyberspace: What's on the Web?
NACE
Web: www.nace.net

What it is: Home of the National Assoc. of Catering Executives.
What's cool: While much of this site is focused on the association, you can click on the "Local Chapters" button to find a caterer in your area. Or check out their extensive links to other catering-related sites.
Needs work: It'd be nice if you could search their membership directory on line to find caterers within X miles of your zip code. Instead, you just get the contact info for local chapters—you then have to call or email the chapter president for member listings.

Another site to consider: WeddingChat.com has numerous bulletin boards that let you swap tips with brides on catering, receptions, cakes—and a gazillion other topics. Yes, it can move quite slow at times but the boards are amazingly comprehensive.

Getting Started: How Far in Advance?

Book your caterer as soon as you confirm your reception site. Many book up far in advance (as long as a year) for popular summer wedding weekends. Also, December is extremely busy for caterers, thanks to holiday parties.

Step-by-step Shopping Strategies

♥ **Step 1:** Using the sources above, set up appointments with at least three recommended caterers. When you call for an appointment, notice how promptly the caterer returns your call. Within the business day is good—if it takes them more than a day, that's a red flag. Prompt attention is your first clue to the caterer's commitment to service. Before your meeting, discuss with your fiancé your likes and dislikes for catering.

♥ **Step 2:** Ask to see photos of each caterers' previous work. Look for colorful and creative presentations of food. Are they artfully arranged with flowers and garnishes or just piled up on mirrored trays?

♥ **Step 3:** Ask for sample menus. These may list some popular hors d'oeuvre choices or sit-down options. Hopefully, prices will be listed to give you a better idea of costs. While most caterers customize menus for each reception, they should provide basic cost parameters for certain items.

♥ **Step 4:** Be honest about your budget. If you're not sure, give them a range of costs per guest that you feel comfortable with. What one caterer will offer you for $30 per person may be vastly different from what another may propose. Also, be specific about your menu likes and dislikes as well as any dietary restrictions.

♥ **Step 5:** Ask for a proposal that details possible menu options. Also, the proposal should clearly identify costs for liquor, rentals, and labor. Call the caterer back and ask them to clarify any part of the proposal that isn't clear. Don't assume the proposal includes extra items like glassware, china, linens, etc.—always confirm that detail. One bad sign: caterers who promise to send you a proposal and then fail to do so.

♥ **Step 6:** Confirm any "minimums." Some caterers require you to purchase a minimum amount of food (in dollars or meals). Hence, you may have to pay for 125 meals even if only 100 people show up to your wedding. While some of this is negotiable (depending on the date and time of your wedding), never book a caterer who has a minimum you don't think you'll be able to meet. Check to see if the wedding cake will count toward the minimum—sometimes that helps put the figure within reach. Also ask the caterer about the opposite case: when more guests show up than expected. Most caterers make 5% to 10% more food than is ordered, but confirm this to be sure.

♥ **Step 7:** Given the different proposals from each caterer, pick the one you most like and ask to visit one of their weddings during the set-up. Look for how organized they are and how the staff is dressed. Just observe.

♥ **Step 8:** Ask for a taste test of proposed menu items. You are mostly likely planning to spend several thousands of dollars on catering, so this is the least caterers can do. You may be able to combine the taste test with the visit to one of their weddings. Another suggestion: take pictures of the food at the tasting, in case the chef or catering manager changes before your wedding. That way you'll be able to show the new staffers what you expect.

♥ **Step 9:** Once you select a caterer, get everything in writing—down to the very last detail. Food, labor, beverages, and rentals (if necessary) should be clearly stated in a written contract. Make sure you understand any price escalation clauses (where the caterer has the right to up the price within a certain time period) and get any price guarantees in writing. Also get a drawing of the physical layout of the room (placement of the tables, dance floor, buffet tables, etc.).

♥ **Step 10:** Before you sign anything, take the contract home to read it. Pore over any fine print like refund policies and cancellation fees. Remember that just because something is in the contract doesn't mean it's set in stone and can't be changed—ask the caterer to alter or change any wording that makes you uncomfortable. Make sure any modifications or cancellations are made in writing.

Questions to Ask a Caterer

1 **Can we have a taste test of the foods on our menu?** We positively loath caterers who expect you to pay thousands of dollars for food on faith. Equally reprehensible are caterers that say "why do you need to taste such basic items? Hors d'oeuvres are hors d'oeuvres." We suggest you find another caterer if you get this line. Should there be a charge for taste tests? Well, some caterers (especially restaurants) may have a minimal fee for tastings, which we can understand. While we'd prefer it to be free, it's better to pay for a taste test and know what you're buying. Ever better: taste two or three options for each course (if you plan a sit-down dinner).

2 **Can we see a wedding during set-up?** A truly organized and professional catering company should have nothing to hide.

3 **Do you provide a written estimate and contract?** Verbal agreements are a prescription for disaster. Make sure every last promise and detail is in black and white.

4 **Are you licensed?** Almost all municipalities (or counties) require caterers to be licensed. Local standards will stress clean and adequate facilities for food preparation and storage. Liability insurance on liquor and food may also be part of the requirements. Ask the caterer about insurance. Operating a catering business out of a residence is often illegal.

5 **Tell me about a wedding you did where something went wrong—how did you handle it?** Even the best caterers have things that go wrong—a crisis, accident or other unforeseen event that throws a wedding reception into chaos. How they handle the situation separates the professionals from the amateurs. We're always suspicious of caterers who say they "never" have problems with their weddings.

6 **Do you specialize in certain cuisines or types of menus?** Although they may claim to handle all types of weddings, caterers usually specialize in certain receptions (smaller versus larger, finger hors d'oeuvres versus full sit-down dinners). Some caterers may have chefs who specialize in certain cuisines (Continental, Southwestern, Indian, etc.)

7 **Where is the food prepared?** Will you need additional kitchen facilities at my site? Make sure these details are confirmed by the caterer to prevent any last minute surprises.

8 **When is the menu "set in stone?"** How close to the wedding can we get and still make changes in the menu? Trust us, there will be changes. Different family members, friends and relatives will add in their two cents on the perfect wedding menu.

9 **How is your wait staff dressed?** The key here is professional attire. Don't assume the wait staff will be wearing tuxedos (the exception is hotels that always have uniformed servers).

10 **For cocktail or buffet receptions, how often will the food be replenished?** Will the servings per guest be limited? Who makes the decision on when to stop serving?

11 **Given the style of my reception, how many waiters do we need?** For seated receptions, one waiter per 16 to 20 guests is adequate. For buffet or cocktail receptions, one waiter per 25 guests is standard.

12 **How is the charge for labor figured?** Is the clean-up (dish-washing, etc.) extra?

13 **How much does a dessert table cost?** Is the wedding cake price included in the package? Dessert or Viennese tables are popular in the Midwest and in parts of the Northeast. Be sure the cost of a dessert table is clearly identified.

14 **What are your cancellation/postponement policies?** Since catering is the biggest expense area, confirming this aspect would be prudent.

15 **Do you have a liquor license?** How is the cost of the beverages calculated? What brands of liquor will be served? Most caterers offer both "premium" (or "call") and generic or "house" brands. Can you taste the house brand of wine? If you plan to serve alcohol, you'll want the caterer to carefully explain what brands you are buying and how the cost is calculated. Per drink charges are often the most expensive, although per bottle charges can be just as costly.

16 **Are you familiar with my reception site?** If not, will you visit it with me? For off-premise caterers, don't assume they know your facility. Confirming details such as the kitchen facilities and the clean-up rules are very important if you want to get your security/damage/cleaning deposit back from the reception site. The site will hold you responsible for any damage or rule violations by your caterer.

17 **Do you receive any commissions from services you recommend?** Caterers may recommend bakers, florists or musicians but watch out! Some take "commissions" (we call them kick-backs) from the businesses they recommend. Don't just take their word—thoroughly check out any services before contracting.

18 **Will you guarantee price estimates?** Many caterers raise their prices at the beginning of the year. Since we urge you to plan in advance, your reception may be several months away. Our advice: negotiate a price guarantee in writing (or at least a cap on future increases). Most caterers will be willing to do this to get your business. One couple we interviewed in Colorado learned this lesson the hard way—the site they booked raised their prices 15% just weeks before their event. Their wedding budget was thrown into complete disarray.

Top Money-Saving Secrets

1 **Find a site where you can bring in an outside caterer.** Outside caterers are not only more affordable but many times offer higher-quality food and beverage service than caterers at hotels or other sites. The big savings come in lower overhead. Outside caterers may let you buy liquor at wholesale, provide rentals at cost and basically provide more food for the dollar. Best of all: outside caterers usually don't have lots of "nickel-and-dime" charges.

2 **Hold the reception in mid-afternoon.** A wedding reception at one or two in the afternoon will be much less expensive than evening affairs. Why? Because guests will probably have already had lunch, they won't be expecting a six-course, sit-down meal.

3 **Go ethnic.** Surprisingly, certain ethnic cuisines are affordable alternatives to traditional wedding fare. Chinese, Mexican, Italian and barbecue are crowd pleasers and, happily, 20% to 30% less than fancier, haute cuisine. Dress up an ethnic buffet with food stations (a design-your-own quesadilla bar or pasta station, for example) that lend some pizzazz to the meal. Instead of an open bar, tie in affordable alcohol alternatives (a margarita machine for a Mexican buffet, bottles of Chianti for an Italian meal) to save even more money.

4 **Consider a wedding brunch or luncheon.** Ever been to a restaurant and noticed the exact same menu is less money at lunch than dinner? The same rule often holds true for wedding receptions. Brunch or breakfast is often less expensive because the food/beverage items are less pricey than what's served at dinner. Portions are also smaller too, as is alcohol consumption.

5 **Have a dessert reception.** Why not skip all those other boring courses and cut to the chase: have a dessert-only reception. A Chicago bride told us how she pulled that off: her late evening ceremony (9 pm) was followed by a reception for 200 guests that featured a lavish buffet of desserts. On the menu: a fondue of fresh fruits, torts, cheesecakes, an ice cream bar, and favorite dessert recipes from relatives, along with the traditional wedding cake. An espresso bar with flavored coffees provided refreshments. Since there wasn't a full meal served, she saved $2000. (To avoid any confusion, it's appropriate to add on your invitation or reception card "Dessert Reception Following.") This tip might work best at a civic or independent site where you can bring in your own catering; facilities with large catering minimums (hotels, country clubs) may balk at this concept, especially during peak wedding months.

6 **Avoid Saturdays, if you can.** Some caterers have reduced rate-packages for Fridays and Sundays with 10% (or more) discounts. (The only bummer: some rental places may charge *extra* fees or overtime charges to deliver on Sundays.) Another way to save: some caterers have discounted rates for off-peak times of the year like April or November. One groom in New York City told us their reception site on Long Island had an off-peak rate that saved them $16 per guest for the very same menu. By moving their wedding date back one weekend, they were now in the "off-peak" zone—and saved 20%. A tip: most sites don't advertise their "winter season discounts." You have to ask.

Alcohol Alternatives

With the soaring cost of booze and worry over drunken driving, many couples are looking for alternatives to the standard-issue open bar at receptions. In San Diego, one wedding we attended featured an espresso bar with a selection of flavored coffees. Other couples are forsaking hard liquor for bars that serve a selection of micro-brewed beers, sparking waters, and other creative ideas. Go to any wedding in San Antonio, Texas and you'll probably see a frozen margarita machine humming away.

7 **Negotiate.** Yes, you can haggle with most caterers and reception facilities. Those written menus aren't cast in stone. If the caterer gives you a proposal for $38 per guest, ask what he or she can do for $30. If a competitor offers you a great freebie, ask if the facility will match the competition. Like all negotiations, you want to be reasonable and recognize that your leverage to get a good deal may depend on the date/time of year for your wedding.

8 **Avoid "budget-busting" menu items.** Certain food items are extremely expensive and can bust your budget. Two common examples are shrimp and beef tenderloin, while chicken is almost universally affordable. If you still want to have a "budget buster," get creative. Can't afford cocktail shrimp? Go for shrimp toast or a shrimp salad. Another tip: stay with fruits and vegetables that are in-season. Trying to get chocolate-dipped strawberries in December will cost you a pretty penny.

9 **Choose items that aren't "labor intensive."** Certain hors d'oeuvres may be made of simple ingredients but require painstaking labor to assemble. For example, hors d'oeuvres like "Boursin cheese piped into Chinese pea pods" take a long time to prepare since the cheese has to be hand-piped into the pea pods. Caterers pass along that labor cost to you.

10 **Tell them it's a family reunion.** As we mentioned in the reception site chapter, you can save money by telling a caterer that the event your planning is a "family function" (reunion, anniversary, etc). That way, you get to see the "regular" menus, which (surprise) may

REAL WEDDING TIP

Yeah, it's a family function! That's the ticket!

A Boston bride emailed this story about using our "family function" tip when approaching caterers: *"The tip to approach the reception sites as a 'family function' made an incredible difference in options for food and drink at the site we chose. We are getting the reception for $35 per person instead of their 'bridal package' of $70 per person! Turns out the site had a ten-page itemization for food and drink if you wanted a function, but a two-page brochure for weddings. This way, we had more information to CHOOSE what we wanted instead of having to go with their idea of what a wedding should be."*

be much less expensive than the "bridal packages." See the Real Wedding Tip on the previous page for more details.

11 **Forget the "bridal packages."** Most contain pricey items you don't need. One conference planner (who was also a bride-to-be) gave us this tip: it may be much more affordable to buy items like hors d'oeuvres *a la carte*. A good rule of thumb is eight to ten hors d'oeuvres per guest (less if your reception is outside standard meal times). If you've got 100 guests, then you need 800 to 1000 pieces of hors d'oeuvres. Our reader said she saved 25% by ordering a la carte (100 egg rolls, 200 beef skewers, etc.). Remember that what's considered an hors d'oeuvre can vary from region to region. In the Northeast, these may be tiny items (like cheese puffs) served during a cocktail hour before a sit-down dinner. In the South, they may be more substantial selections ("heavy hors d'oeuvres") eaten with a knife and fork that take the place of dinner.

12 **For buffet and hors d'oeuvres receptions, have the caterer's staff serve the items** instead of letting the guests serve themselves. This will control the amount of food served (and hence, the cost). When guests serve themselves, the food always seems to go much quicker (wonder why)!

13 **Buy your own liquor, if possible.** While most hotels, catering halls and country clubs don't let you do this, other sites may permit you to buy your own liquor. The savings of buying liquor at or near wholesale prices will be tremendous (perhaps a 50% to 70% off "retail" prices). Ask the caterer if they will refer you to a good wholesaler in your area. When you buy by the case load, you can normally negotiate lower prices than retail. Some liquor suppliers may even let you return unopened bottles for full credit. (Check to see if they will allow the same return of unopened beer and wine bottles; some may not allow returns because of damage that might occur when beer or wine is chilled and warmed). Wonder what wines are best buys? Check out the *Wall Street Journal's* "Weekend Journal" section—each Friday they review and rate a selection of wines, most of which are very affordable. The Journal's excellent advice is also available for free on the web at wine.wsj.com. One note of caution: beverages must be chilled prior to the reception, so plan ahead.

14 **Provide your own bar service.** In some cases, "free-lance" bartenders are cheaper than the caterers' own staff. If the caterer allows you to have your own bar service, do a cost comparison between the two options. On the other hand, some caterers may not allow free-lance bartenders because of liability concerns. What about having a friend or relative tend bar? We don't recommend tapping Uncle

Joe to do bar service. An amateur will waste more in booze than you'd save in bartender fees; skilled bartenders are more efficient at the task.

15 **Don't move those hors d'oeuvres!** Having hors d'oeuvres passed on silver trays may look elegant but watch out! One Florida wedding planner told us sites there charge exorbitant prices for "passed hors d'oeuvres." The more affordable alternative is to keep them stationary—scattered about the room at "stations" in chafing dishes. Of course, these exorbitant prices aren't the rule everywhere. A Wisconsin wedding planner says there is no premium price for passed hors d'oeuvres in her area; as a result, she highly recommends them to keep guests from over-indulging at a buffet table. The bottom line: compare costs for these two options carefully to get the best deal.

16 **Steer clear of course overkill.** For sit-down dinners, do you really need to serve both hors d'oeuvres and an appetizer? Or soup and salad? Some brides eliminate a dessert course and let the wedding cake suffice. Another money-saver: DON'T offer a choice of entree at sit-down dinners. Some sites will charge a premium for this option.

17 **Slash the alcohol bill.** If you still want to have that traditional open bar, there are a couple ways to save money. First, use only house brands instead of pricey "call" brands for hard liquor. If you're having a cocktail hour, serve affordable hors d'oeuvres to lower alcohol consumption (people drink less when they're munching cheese puffs). Finally, close the bar early, say an hour or so before the reception ends. Have less expensive soft drinks or punch available for the rest of the reception. Another idea: some hotels and catering halls offer flat-rate packages for beverages. Instead of being billed per drink ordered, you pay a flat fee per guest. This might be a more affordable alternative.

18 **Hire a student.** Got a culinary school in town? See if you can hire a student(s) to cater your reception. A bride in Illinois

---

Do-it-yourself ideas

If you are planning to cater your own wedding, consider the vast troves of recipe ideas on the web. A good example: About.com. Their wedding section (weddings.about.com) has an excellent archive of links to *hundreds* of web sites with appetizer, entrée and cake recipes. Another source: The Food Network (www.foodtv.com) has a large free recipe section. And we can't forget about Martha. MarthaStewart. com has two areas of interest to brides and grooms—"weddings" (which has advice on everything from cakes to favors and receptions) and "cooking" (recipes and more recipes).

called the Cooking Hospitality Institute of Chicago (312) 944-0882 and found graduate students will do her wedding for a fraction of what "professional" caterers charge. Sometimes these schools have their own restaurants, which might be another contact point.

19 **Go for a keg.** A keg of beer is equal to about SEVEN cases of beer. The bottom line: you save about 50% on beer if you use a keg instead of bottles. Worried a keg will give your reception all the ambience of a college frat party? Don't worry. Most caterers can hide the keg behind the bar and use a carbon dioxide tapper system to draw the beer. Another caterer trick: boxed wine. Pour boxed wine into carafes and you'll save 50% over bottled wine. Avoid having multiple selections of wine available on tables; that adds dramatically to costs since much of it is wasted.

20 **Just do a champagne toast.** Even the cheapest champagne is very expensive—bubbly has the highest cost per portion than even a mixed drink using premium liquor. Offering champagne through-out the entire evening is a budget buster for most couples. A better alternative: just do a champagne toast. Or skip it altogether.

Biggest Myths about Catering

MYTH #1 *"Maybe you can settle an argument I'm having with my mother. If I invite fewer guests, will my catering bill will go down dramatically?"*

Well, yes and no. Obviously, fewer mouths to feed will have an impact on your total bill. However, if you invite fewer guests, the price *per person* may go up. Why? That's because a large part of the per-person price caterers quote you is "fixed." Fixed costs include the caterer's overhead, kitchen facilities, etc. No matter how many guests you invite, caterers still have to pay these administrative expenses. Hence, you're paying for more than just the food. In a sense, most caterers have an unwritten base price or minimum that engaged couples must pay—no matter how many guests they want to invite.

MYTH #2 *"Buffets are always less expensive than sit-down dinners."*

This is one those great debates that has no one right answer. The bottom line: the cost of a reception is often *what* you serve rather than *how* you serve it. Hence a basic sit-down chicken dinner will be cheaper than a fancy buffet with shrimp, sliced beef tenderloin and other pricey dishes. Conversely, a five-course lobster dinner may cost several times more than a simple buffet with hors d'oeuvres like fruit, cheese and mini-sandwiches.

We've noticed that caterers tend to steer couples toward the type of reception they do most often. Hence, a caterer who frequently does buffet receptions will tell you a sit-down dinner is too expensive. In the Northeast (where sit-downs dinners are most common), caterers will advise just the opposite.

Of course, you can combine both types of receptions if you prefer. A "seated buffet" is set up like a sit-down dinner, with tables and chairs for every guest. The salad or first course is served at the table by waiters, while the main dishes are served buffet style.

MYTH #3 *"Given the expensive prices caterers charge, you get the feeling these guys make big, fat profits off weddings."*

Gosh, it may be hard to believe, but most don't. Profits only range from 8% to 15% of the total bill. In the past few years, food and insurance costs have soared for most caterers. Don't shed too many tears for them, though. Since the average business only earns a 5% profit on sales, caterers' profits aren't all that bad. Different caterers make more

---

Deals at Wholesale Clubs and Gourmet Supermarkets

Liquor prices too much for you to swallow? Full-service catering charges too high to stomach? Consider two alternatives that offer great deals: wholesale clubs and gourmet supermarkets.

Popping up in most major cities, wholesale clubs like Sam's, Costco and BJ's offer cut-rate prices on everything from electronics to groceries. Best of all, some of the clubs have fully stocked liquor departments where you can buy in case quantity at fantastic discounts. We visited a Costco and found prices 15% to 30% below regular liquor stores. Name brands of wine, beer and spirits were available in big quantities. If you're hiring a caterer who will let you purchase your own liquor, be sure to get a quote from a local wholesale club.

To find a location of a wholesale club, look at their web sites: Sam's (www.samsclub.com), Costco (www.costco.com) and BJ's(www.bjswholesale.com)

While many wholesale clubs have been adding liquor and groceries, supermarkets have remade themselves into "gourmet markets" with full-service catering departments. We've spoken to brides who have found affordable catering options for small at-home receptions at a local gourmet supermarket—and they found the quality to be excellent. Many markets also have pastry chefs on staff who can whip up a respectable wedding cake. With full-service floral departments as well, some markets offer an affordable one-stop shopping service. Prices for catering, cakes and flowers tend to be about 10% to 20% below retail.

money in different areas. For off-premise caterers, the biggest revenue area is the food. For on-site or in-house caterers (like hotels), the biggest money-maker is the alcohol.

MYTH #4 *"Aren't plastic plates more affordable than glass?"*

Nope. In many cases, the cost of renting glass is actually almost as affordable as using plastic! Besides looking nicer, glass doesn't have the negative environmental impact caused by throwing away plastics. Ask your caterer to do a cost comparison between plastic and glass.

MYTH #5 *"Guests always drink and eat more at weddings than any other party."*

This myth is used by caterers to justify higher prices for weddings than other types of parties like corporate events, retirement parties and the like. We don't buy it. Why? Almost any host today (whether bride or corporate party planner) buys catering packages based on consumption. That is, you buy 100 pieces of a hors d'oeuvre, 125 chicken dinners, etc. Most bars are billed on consumption (per drink, etc). Therefore, when a caterer says they charge more for weddings because guests are pigs, it rings hollow to us. Why is the same chicken dinner for a wedding 30% more than a corporate party?

Helpful Hints

1 **Make sure the catering representative who planned your reception will be there the night of the wedding.** Hotel catering staffs are frequently guilty of not showing up to make sure everything is right. If you contract with a smaller, off-premise caterer, make sure the owner is there. Obviously, the owner may not be able to be at your wedding reception every minute, but there should be a clear chain of command in case a problem arises.

2 **Have the caterer prepare you a going-away package.** Believe it or not, you probably won't get to taste any of the food at your reception. You'll be too busy shaking hands, giving hugs, posing for pictures, etc. Considering the amount of money you're spending, ask the caterer to prepare a going-away package with a sample of the evening's menu (don't forget to include the cake!). You and your fiancé will probably be starved when you leave the reception!

3 **Carefully budget food and liquor amounts.** No, guessing how much food or beverage you should budget for a reception is NOT an exact science. For hors d'oeuvres, one caterer suggested to us to budget 8 to 10 hors d'oeuvres per guest for a one hour cocktail reception. A Wisconsin wedding planner provided us with this rule of thumb to budget how many drinks guests will consume at an open bar: 2.5 drinks the first hour, 1.5 drinks the second hour and one drink per hour thereafter. Hence, for a four hour reception, you should budget five drinks per guest. Wow! Do people really drink that much at wedding receptions? No, Pattie told us. Remember that you are charged for the number of drinks *ordered*,

REAL WEDDING TIP

Tips on tipping

Boy, this is a perennial question—who do you tip? How much? First, understand that many wedding vendors (the caterer, limo, etc.) add a *mandatory* gratuity to the final tab. As a result, you don't *have* to tip anyone. However, if you believe an individual staffer has gone "above and beyond the call of duty," it may be nice if you slipped them an extra $20 or more. A server who tracks down a missing special dietary meal for a relative, a limousine driver who makes a special return trip to your house to retrieve an errant bridesmaid, a catering manager who works miracles with a cake that's collapsed— these are examples of extraordinary service that you may want to reward with an extra tip. You may also give a tip to the band or disc jockey if they turn in a stellar performance.

We've noticed there are some regional differences when it comes to tipping. Brides in the Northeast (particularly Long Island, New York and northern New Jersey) tell us it's standard practice to "grease" all wedding vendors with a $25 or $50 tip on the day of the wedding. Some bridal merchants can be darn pushy about this; one Long Island bride told us she was informed by her photographer that he expected her to tip his *assistant* 10% of the bill. And the catering manager told her that even though a labor charge was built into her $60 per plate reception, an additional tip would be nice. Our take on that: it's rude for a vendor to demand a tip, either for themselves or their workers. We say ignore them.

If you really want to give a tip, give it *directly to* the worker(s). One waitress who works for a catering hall in Cleveland told us their staff *never* sees extra tips that are paid with the final tab. Apparently, the owner of the facility pockets these as extra profit. Hence, don't give that tip to the owner or maitre'd—hand it directly to the people you want to receive it. And there's no law that says you have to give cash: consider handing out gift certificates or a bottle of wine as a thank you to wedding vendors.

not consumed. "So, when Uncle Joe can't remember what he did with his nearly full drink, he figures it's 'free' and he just gets another one," Pattie said. One scam that inflates liquor tabs: waitstaffs that clear half-full glasses before guests can finish them. As you'll read later in the Pitfalls to Avoid section, this is but one way some sites can boost the beverage bill.

Pitfalls to Avoid

Pitfall #1 Frozen Food.
"We went to a friend's reception last weekend at a hotel. I know the bride spent a lot of money, but the food was just so-so."

In our opinion, too many sites like hotels rely too much on frozen food. Bought in bulk, frozen versions of mini-egg rolls and mini-quiche are mainstays on some reception site menus. Obviously, its cheaper (and hence more profitable) to buy these items frozen and quickly warm them in chafing dishes than to painstakingly make the same items from scratch. The problem? Besides obviously tasting "frozen," caterers who use frozen food often aren't any less expensive than those who hand-make food from scratch ingredients. If the food at your reception is one of your high priorities, shop carefully for a caterer who doesn't use shortcuts.

Pitfall #2 The infamous cake-cutting fee
"Boy am I steamed! The reception site I chose for my wedding said they would charge me $1 per person to cut my wedding cake. After spending thousands of dollars on food and liquor, I think they're trying to wring every last nickel from me!"

WE COULDN'T AGREE MORE! Boy, this is our #1 pet-peeve with caterers and reception sites. Some of these guys have the audacity to charge you a ridiculously high fee to cut your wedding cake. Ranging anywhere from 50 cents to $3 per guest, this "fee" supposedly covers the labor involved to cut the cake, as well as the plates, forks, etc. The real reason some reception sites charge this fee is to penalize you for bringing in a cake from an outside baker (instead of having the site bake it for you). Even more amazing are some sites that don't even bake wedding cakes themselves but still charge cake-cutting fees! Talk about abusive—these fees are pure greed!

We say if you are spending hundreds or thousands of dollars on food and liquor, the caterer or reception site should NOT tack on $100 to $400 more just for the privilege of cutting and serving the wedding cake! First of all, you are already paying a mandatory service gratuity to have a staff present at the reception. Hence, the cake cutting fee is double-charging. Secondly, do you really think they pay the cake-cutter $100 to $400 for 30 minutes of work? We suggest you try to negotiate away this charge—don't forget that everything is always negotiable.

(Note: some caterers or sites try to sneak in the cost of serving coffee into the cake-cutting fee. We suggest you tell the caterer to forget the cake-cutting fee and just price the coffee out separately. If the site still insists on a cake-cutting fee, try to negotiate a flat fee, say $50 or $75, instead of a per guest charge.)

Another inflated price we've discovered: the cost of punch. One hotel in the West charges brides and grooms a whopping $35 per gallon of punch! Since a half gallon of Minute Maid Fruit Punch goes for $2 to $3 at grocery stores, you can see how outrageous this stuff can get.

PITFALL #3 CORKING FEES AND THE LIQUOR THAT RUNNETH OVER.

"My friend had her reception at a country club that seemed to push liquor on the guests. Every five minutes, they went around to the guests and pitched more drinks. I also understand they charged the couple for every bottle that was opened! Isn't this a bit excessive?"

Not only excessive but also quite expensive. When couples are charged based on the number of $20 bottles of wine or champagne that are opened, one mad staffer with a corkscrew can inflict heavy financial damage. Such charges (called corking fees) are perhaps one of the biggest cost pitfalls of any wedding reception. That's because couples must pay for any opened bottles whether or not they were poured! Think you can just re-cork the bottles and bring them home? Think again—most sites prevent the removal of liquor from the premises.

In a different twist on the same problem, some sites push drinks on guests when the bar is "open" (i.e., the engaged couple pays for each drink). Why would sites or caterers do this? BIG PROFITS! Liquor is the biggest money-making area for sites like hotels and catering halls, and hence the temptation to push booze or open unneeded bottles is too great for the greedy.

The solution to the corking fee pitfall is to give the caterer or reception site a limit on the number of bottles they can open. Tell them to confer with you before they go beyond that limit.

Another version of this scam surfaced in California. We spoke with a former employee of a catering company who admitted they brought empty bottles to receptions. Since the liquor charges were based on the number of empty bottles at the end of the evening, the caterer was able to make a killing. We recommend you count the bottles at the beginning of the evening and again at the end. If there are 100 full bottles at the start, there better not be 125 bottles (80 empty and 45 full) at the end.

Sites can also inflate the liquor tab by picking up half-full glasses, forcing guests who have just returned from the dance floor to go back to the bar to get something to drink. One wedding planner we spoke to suggested couples should explicitly tell catering managers to make sure the waitstaff is not overzealous in clearing half-full glasses. If you see specific examples of this behavior, you should be able to negotiate a 10% to 20% reduction in the beverage bill.

Pitfall #4 Gratuitous gratuities and sales taxes from hell

"When we saw the final bill for our reception, the facility charged us a 'gratuity fee' on everything including the room charge! Is this fair?"

Many facilities look at the gratuity as "extra profit," not something that is paid to the staff. One bride in California called in the above story, where the facility was charging an 18% gratuity on the *room rental fee*, of all things (this worked out to an extra $300). In our opinion, the gratuity should only be charged on the food and beverage. (We should note in some states it is illegal to charge a mandatory gratuity on the liquor tab—as an alternative to the gratuity, facilities often charge "bartender or bar set-up fees.") Placing a gratuity on other charges (like room rental, valet parking, coat check) is price gouging.

Another similar rip-off is the "double-charging" of labor. In Denver, Colorado, for example, many caterers charge both a gratuity and a "labor fee." While the staff generally gets the gratuity, the owners usually pocket the labor charge. As a result of this double-charging, couples are being socked with an effective 25% gratuity rate on receptions—an outrage in our opinion! (No, double charging for labor isn't illegal, but it still stinks).

What about sales tax? In some states, food and beverage is taxable. A few cities or counties even slap sales tax on labor charges like the gratuity and other services. Since the sales tax rate can be 5% to 10% in some cities, this can add to the bill in a hurry. Be forewarned: some brides have told us that their sites have slapped sales tax on items like room rental that were clearly *not taxable*. Why? Maybe it's just sloppy bookkeeping. Or they may be pocketing the tax to pay for that Mercedes parked out front. If you have any questions on what's taxable and what's not, check with your local city or county government (listed in the white pages of your phone book).

The state of California (always on the forefront of taxing everything that moves) has an inventive way of viewing this controversy. California law draws a distinction between a voluntary "tip or gratuity" and a "service charge," which is mandatory. Basically, the state determines that voluntary tips are NOT subject to sales tax—but mandatory service charges (those 19% whoppers charged by California hotels) are. Adding insult to injury, the state also considers such items as corking fees and cake cutting charges as mandatory (and hence, taxable).

The best advice: watch out for all these sneaky charges and taxes. Be sure to question any item that looks strange.

PITFALL #5 PRICE RISE SURPRISE!

"I booked my reception site a year in advance and we agreed on a certain price per guest. One month before my wedding, the catering manager informed me of a 20% price increase and pointed to the fine print in their contract. Is this fair?"

Our office has received several complaints from brides and grooms who believe they were stung unfairly by "surprise" price increases. Ironically, these couples may be tripped up by their own advance planning—they booked their wedding site so far in advance that the facility won't guarantee a price for food and liquor.

Instead, these couples received a written proposal and contract that included a "price escalation" clause. This enabled the site or caterer to raise the price with little or no notice. Obviously, that can be a painful lesson for brides and grooms who get socked with unexpected extra costs.

Certainly, the best course of action is to get a firm price guarantee. If that's not possible, try to negotiate a "reasonable" price increase cap in the contract—paying a small 5% increase isn't fun, but it's much better than being surprised with a 20% whopper.

Also look out for clauses that let the caterer substitute food items. Insist in the contract the caterer get your written approval first before any changes to the menu are made. You want to be reasonable, of course. While a sudden frost in Florida might change your plans for Mimosas, you don't want your caterer or reception facility to start making wholesale substitutions to the menu without your approval.

PITFALL #6 DO-IT-YOURSELF NIGHTMARES

"My family did all the catering for my sister's wedding. What a disaster! When we arrived at the reception site, the doors were locked so the food had to sit out in our hot cars. The potato salad spoiled and over 100 guests got sick from food poisoning."

Yep, that's a true story from a reader in Corpus Christi, Texas. While it's an extreme example of what can go wrong for those who want to go the do-it-yourself route, there are some important lessons—consider how BIG this task is before taking the plunge. Do you have time to prepare that much food? What about the delivery/set-up and refrigeration of the food before the reception?

If you want to do-it-yourself, you may want to compromise: have a restaurant cater the food. Or pick up prepared items from a grocery store or deli. Yes, this isn't as cheap as whipping up 400 canapés yourself . . . but it may be smarter in the end. Instead of serving the food from plastic trays or containers, dress up your buffet with some nice rented serving pieces.

Ever hire a professional photographer before? Probably not—that's why we hope this chapter will be helpful. This country has over 27,000 wedding and portrait photographers, making it a daunting task to find the perfect one for you. From key questions to important pitfalls to avoid, this chapter will give you a clear and concise guide to finding a great photographer at an affordable price.

What Are You Buying?

When you hire a professional wedding photographer, there are three main areas where your money goes:

1 Candids: These are the pictures taken at the wedding and reception that are assembled into an album for the bride and groom. Photographers often assemble candid packages for the parents (referred to as parent's albums) and gifts for attendants (usually two or four pictures in a gift folio). Note that parent's albums (usually 20 to 60 pictures) and gift folios are extra and are not included in our average photography tab.

2 Albums: Most photographers offer a wide selection of albums to hold the candids. The best are Art Leather, Leather Craftsman and Capri. Unfortunately, they are also the most expensive and are sold only by professional photographers. Art Leather albums (more on these later in the chapter) are guaranteed for a lifetime. With Capri or Leather Craftsman albums, the pictures are mounted to the pages, which are permanently bound in the album. Some photographers skimp by using cheap, vinyl albums with plastic-covered pages. We'll explain later why these cheaper albums can damage your pictures.

If you are looking for something different, see if your photographer can order Waterhouse albums—these stunning hand-bound albums are made of natural fibers and hand-torn papers and covers. Prices run $200 to $400, depending on the size and number of pages. You can see samples on their web site at www.waterhousebook.com or call them at 860-526-1296 for a dealer near you.

3 Portraits: Pictures taken prior to the wedding day fall into this category. A bridal portrait is a formal portrait of the bride in her wedding gown. Particularly popular in the Southern U.S., bridal portraits are taken in an indoor studio or on location typically four to six weeks before the wedding. An engagement portrait is a more informal picture of you and your fiancé. This portrait is often used to announce your engagement in the local newspaper.

Two expenses are involved with portraits: the sitting fee and the portrait itself. Sitting fees are a charge for the photographer's time and range from $50 to several hundreds of dollars. The most popular print size is 16x20 and this can cost $100 to $500 depending on the photographer and city.

Photography customs and traditions vary greatly across the U.S. and Canada. For example, in Sacramento, California, many couples have a formal portrait taken *after* the reception at one of the area's many parks. In the South, a formal portrait of the bride taken a month before the wedding is often framed and displayed at the reception. Several Colorado photographers bring studio-quality lighting systems to the wedding in order to do portraits of the bride and groom before the ceremony. A new trend for portraits: virtual backgrounds. Some photographers are using computer-generated backdrops to add sizzle to their portraits. The bride stands before a green background onto which a computer generated image is projected.

Average total costs: In most U.S. cities, the average tab for professional wedding photography—you might want to sit down—is $1500.

We should note that lower-cost rural areas may be less than that. A recent survey by Kodak put the national average of wedding photography at $969 in 1999 . . . and that was up from $740 (or 30%) in 1991. While we suspect that figure might be a bit low, any way you cut it, wedding photography is pricey.

So what does that buy you? That figure just covers your album of candid coverage at your wedding and reception. Keep in mind if you add all sorts of extras (parent's albums, bridal portraits) or if you hire a "celebrity" photographer in a larger city, you could spend several times more than the average ($2000, $4000 and up).

No matter where you are, however, the process of selecting pictures is relatively the same. We should note that photographers don't usually talk in plain English, so here are three typical terms you will come across and their simple translations:

♥ **EXPOSURES:** Basically this is defined by every time the camera goes click. At least 150 to 200 exposures are taken at the typical wedding and four-hour reception. Be careful of packages that limit the number of exposures below that level.

♥ **PROOFS:** Exposures are developed into proofs. The proofs are often 5x5 pictures from which you choose the final prints that will appear in your album. Unretouched, the proofs chronicle all the pictures that the photographer took at your wedding. Photographers often have packages that guarantee selection from a certain number of proofs. This can range from 80 proofs for small packages to over 200 for the largest. A new trend for proofs is to go digital; some photographers let you view proofs on a computer monitor. The advantage here is lower cost, since the proofs don't have to be printed. The downside? You can't take them with you or show them to relatives. While the web would be an obvious solution to that problem, most photographers aren't that sophisticated yet.

♥ **PRINTS:** The proofs are enlarged into final prints. For photographers who use medium format cameras (we'll explain this later), popular enlargement sizes are 5x7, 8x8, 8x10 and 10x10. The final prints are assembled into the album. (As a side note, some photographers offer to sell you the proofs, either individually or incorporated into the wedding album). As you'll read later, we recommend purchasing an album package that includes 60 to 80 prints to adequately tell the wedding story. Some of those pictures (say 10 to 20) would be enlargements, that is 8x10 or 10x10. The balance would be the smaller 5x5 or 5x7 prints. Exactly how many enlargements you want is a personal preference, but extra enlargements obviously tend to add to the final tab.

Okay, so now you know the basics of what you are buying. But how do you find a competent, yet affordable, professional wedding photographer in the first place?

Sources for Finding a Photographer

Photographers generally fall into two categories, commercial and portrait. While commercial photographers work for advertising agencies and other industrial clients, portrait photographers concentrate on weddings, special occasions, and (as you might guess) portraits. The best wedding photographers are those who specialize in just weddings and portraits, with several years of experience. They should do at least ten to 15 weddings per year. Here are three sources to find the very best wedding photographers:

♥ **RECENTLY-MARRIED COUPLES.** Yep, word-of-mouth referrals are your best bet for finding the best photographers. Ask them how happy they were with the photographer and final prints. Was there anything they would change?

♥ **WEDDING COORDINATORS AT CEREMONY AND RECEPTION SITES.** What an incredible resource! These people have seen hundreds of wedding photographers come through their door. Ask them who they thought were the best. Of course, their impressions are limited to the photographer's behavior at their particular site. Site coordinators rarely see the final photo album. Nevertheless, their opinions are valuable.

♥ **BRIDAL SHOWS.** These shows (sponsored by local bridal shops and reception sites) often have several exhibits by local photographers. Be aware that these shows may feature young or new photographers who are looking to build their business. Unfortunately, bridal shows also tend to showcase large photography studios whose quality can vary greatly from associate to associate (we'll discuss these studios later). Keep your eye on the local paper for shows in your area.

Where not to look. Unfortunately, the phone book is *not* a good source for wedding photographers. Many of the best wedding photographers do not invest heavily in this type of advertising. In fact, many don't advertise at all, working exclusively by word-of-mouth referral. Some photographers will also put an album of their work in local bridal shops. However, whose work is displayed has more to do with politics than merit. Another place that is a poor source: wedding advertising publications. Most good photographers avoid having anything to do with them.

Brides in Cyberspace: What's on the Web?

The web can help with wedding pictures in several ways. First, you can search for a photographer. Second, you can put your wedding pics on the web for guests to see them and order reprints. Let's look at each use in depth:

♥ To find a photographer, we suggest one of two sites: THE PROFESSIONAL PHOTOGRAPHERS OF AMERICA (www.ppa.com) and WEDDING AND PORTRAIT PHOTOGRAPHERS (www.eventphotographers.com). Each let you search for local photographers by city, zip or area code.

♥ Getting your wedding pictures online is simpler than ever. Of course, most folks have two types of wedding photos—those snapped by guests and others taken by a professional photographer. Let's look at each type:

1 **Guest pictures.** Did your guests use single-use cameras (discussed later in this chapter) to help you fill out the candids from your wedding? If so, getting these pictures on the web is relatively easy. When you drop them off for developing, most processors given you an option to get digital images like AOL's "You've Got Pictures (pictures.aol.com) or Kodak's Photonet. Then simply send your guests an email with the info on how to access the photos. Another source: Photoworks.com, which scans and stores your pictures online at no additional charge.

Other options to share your photos with guests include free sites like PictureTrail (picturetrail.com), Zing (zing.com) and PhotoPoint (photopoint.com). Most let you password-protect your photos so only your friends and relatives can view them. The only bummer? You have to do the scanning yourself with these sites. If you don't have a scanner, sites like Our-Album.net will do the scanning for you. This costs about $200 for 15 images.

Of course, if you are tech-savvy enough, you can post an online album yourself. Most internet service providers (ISP's) give you a certain amount of server space to upload files, including pictures. You just scan the pictures, FTP them to your ISP and create HTML pages that let your friend and relatives view them. If all that went over your head, then it might be best to leave this to some of the services listed above.

2 **What about the professional pictures?** In recent years, several online photo web sites have launched to help professional photographers sell reprints. Some examples include Collages.Net (www.collages.net), Club Photo (www.event.clubphoto.com), ShotsOnline (www.shotsonline.com), Photozone (www.photozone.com), and Photo-Relfect (www.photoreflect.com). See Figure 1 on the next page.

Figure 1: PhotoReflect.com is one of several companies hoping to sell wedding picture reprints online.

All of these services work much the same way. A photographer uploads the pictures to the site, which creates a password-protected site for your wedding. You email guests with the site address and password. Guests can then view the pictures online and order reprints right from the site. Most of these sites are free to photographers; they make their money by taking a cut of the reprint revenue.

A few caveats: while some sites have interactive features like guest

Proofless Studios: How Some Photographers Use the 'Net to Speed the Delivery of Wedding Albums

In the ancient days of wedding photography (like before 1995), brides and grooms first had to look at dozens of printed "proofs" to assemble their albums. Trying to judge what a picture would look like cropped or enlarged was difficult—and the wait to get the proofs and the final album sometimes stretched into weeks.

New digital technologies have made this process quicker and easier, for both photographers and consumers. Thanks to digital proofing and online ordering systems, final albums can be delivered to couples in a matter of days, instead of weeks or months.

Here's how it works: after the wedding, a photographer sends his film (most still shoot on film versus digital cameras) to a lab. The lab scans the film negatives and creates digital pictures which are downloaded by the photographer off the 'net—all in a matter of days, not weeks. Next, the photographer uses a software program like ProShots (www.proshots.com) or Montage by Art Leather (an album company) to create your album. Then, the pictures are shown books, all of the sites do not let you print or email the pictures to others. If you try to save the image to your hard disk, a watermark that says "proof" appears on the image. And beware that some photographers mark-up the reprint prices to sell online. If you or your guests plan to purchase more than a single print online, you might consider contacting the photographer directly for a better price.

Understanding Wedding Photographers: Some Basics

As you shop for a good wedding photographer, there are three key areas that you must always keep in mind:

1 Equipment. Obviously, the quality of equipment the photographer uses is directly related to how good your wedding pictures will look. No matter how talented and personable the photographer is, the resulting pictures will be a disappointment if he or she uses an inferior camera.

"I visited a wedding photography studio yesterday that said they use 35 millimeter cameras. They claimed the pictures look just as good as others shot with more expensive cameras. Is this true?"

Not exactly. To understand why, let's look at the two types of cameras mainly used for wedding photography: 35 millimeter and medium format cameras.

---

to you. Most photographers will create a slide show (on a big screen or computer monitor) with all your photos. Then you are presented with a suggested album layout (again on computer), complete with suggested enlargements, mattes, crops and so on.

Some photographers even give you a CD-ROM for you to take with you of the proofs or suggested album. As we mentioned earlier in this chapter, other photographers are using online reprint web sites to let your guests view and order pictures off the 'net. The days of passing around a proof book are numbered.

We expect more studios to go "proofless" over the next few years as digital cameras proliferate.

One caution to this "proofless" system: some photographers try to up-sell you by presenting a virtual album of, say, 100 pictures when your package just had 75 pictures. Photographers know showing you the possible album with all the enlargements and extra pictures convinces many consumers to pony up more money. If you want to stick with your budget, tell the photographer to construct the proposed album with the number of prints in your package and no more.

♥ **35 MILLIMETER CAMERAS:** Most of us are familiar with these widely-available cameras. There is quite a debate in the professional photography community when it comes to which (and what type of camera) is best. Some professional wedding photographers shun 35mm cameras because of their small negative size. Since some wedding photos are blown up to 8x10 or larger, this negative can produce pictures that are grainy. Other photographers also say 35mm pictures look flat and the colors are not as vibrant.

Photographers who are fans of 35mm point out that the quick action of the shutter on 35mm cameras lets them take more candid-style pictures (so-called photojournalism-style). They also say the equipment and film has improved dramatically in recent years, closing the quality gap with more expensive cameras. What about the problem of grainy blow-up pictures? They claim that most couples don't request pictures blown up bigger than 8x10, the upper limit on 35mm pictures for acceptable quality.

Kodak's Wedding CD

Leave it to Kodak to come up with a cool product that combines photography and technology—their new "Wedding CD" is a great example of how digital technology can be used to get more out of your wedding photographers.

Here's how it works: your photographer requests that his local lab make a Kodak Wedding CD of 100 of the best images from your wedding. The photographer pays the lab about $50 for this service; studios charge consumers $100 to $300 retail (or 10% of the package price) for the CD. Some photographers give this CD away for free if you order enough traditional pictures.

The CD lets you re-size, crop, colorize and print the pictures. You can email them to friends and relatives or export the pictures to Adobe PhotoShop. Don't like your wedding pictures in color? Change them to black and white with a simple keystroke. You can also enhance the photos with features like borders or word captions—or put the photos to use as greeting cards or on a web site. Best of all, the pictures are kept in an archival format that will be safe for decades.

To read more about this, go to Kodak's web site at www.kodak.com. The specific address with the info on the Wedding CD is www.kodak.com/global/en/professional/products/portraitCD/weddingCD.shtml. See the next page (Figure 2) for a picture of the Wedding CD web site.

♥ **MEDIUM-FORMAT CAMERAS:** The main distinction between medium format cameras and 35mm is their negative size: a medium format's square negative is usually $2^1/_4$ by $2^1/_4$. This provides much clearer photos when prints are enlarged. Medium-format cameras produce pictures that have richer depth, warmer colors and sharper contrasts than 35mm cameras. (To be technical, the warmth of a photograph is determined by the amount of flash light. However, medium-format cameras deliver pictures with more color saturation than 35mm. Color saturation relates to the richness of color in the print).

The Hasselblad is apparently the Mercedes of medium format cameras. This camera (which was the one NASA used on the moon for astronaut snapshots) is incredibly popular among the best wedding photographers, apparently for the beautiful pictures it takes. Another popular medium-format camera is the Bronica.

We should note in passing that there are also several larger-format cameras that produce even bigger negatives (and hence, greater color saturation) than standard medium-format. Cameras such as the Mamiya RB67 are considered the ultimate camera in this category. That camera takes a negative that is 6cm by 7cm.

One final tip about cameras: the best medium format cameras for weddings have a "leaf" shutter, instead of "focal plane." This enables flash-fill outside in the bright sun and prevents the bride's white dress

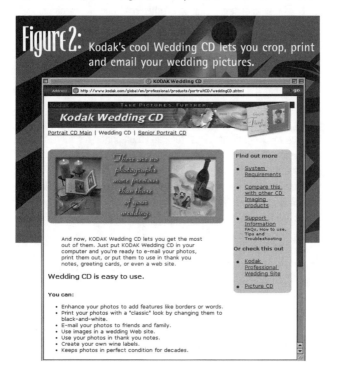

Figure 2: Kodak's cool Wedding CD lets you crop, print and email your wedding pictures.

from washing out," a professional photographer in New Jersey told us. The leaf shutter allows a photographer to properly balance shadows. Most medium format camera makers sell both types of shutters, so it might be worth it to ask the photographer which type he uses.

♥ **DIGITAL CAMERAS.** Yes, they are all the rage with techies, but digital cameras still aren't used widely by wedding photographers. Why? Megapixel digital cameras have come a long way in quality and storage capability, but most wedding photographers still use old-fashion analog film cameras. The reasons are somewhat murky, but we've noticed wedding photographers are a conservative bunch that have been slow to react to the digital age. Most tell us they have too much invested in their medium format and high-end 35 mm cameras to experiment with digital, especially since shooting weddings is a high-stakes business with little room for error.

Nonetheless, expect to see more and more photographers switching to digital in coming years. Not only are the cameras ultra-lightweight, but also most have LCD screens that let photographers instantly view their work and adjust lighting conditions accordingly. One of the first things photographers learn with digital cameras is that it is easier to work with a underexposed image than overexposed (that's the opposite of film). Why? Software can compensate for underexposed pictures and fix other glitches that previously required expensive manual re-touching.

Of course, digital cameras pose other challenges for photographers. First, they have to become comfortable with image manipulation software like Adobe's PhotoShop or find a lab that can process the digital pictures (most labs still work with just film). Then you have to output the pictures to a professional-type printer. Most inexpensive inkjet printers produce pictures that lack "archival quality"—that is, after a few years, the pictures start to fade even if printed on high-quality photo stock paper. That's being remedied by a new generation of printers that promise archival quality; we saw a demo of just such an Epson printer recently and we're impressed with the quality of photographs that were produced.

Even if your photographer still prefers film cameras, they still might use digital technology to let you view proofs digitally on a computer screen (see earlier in this chapter for details). And some photographers are starting to give out copies of proofs on CD-ROM's. See the following box on this trend.

"Well, now I'm confused. Should I hire a photographer who uses a 35mm or medium format camera?"

The key is to look at the pictures. As we'll discuss later in this chapter, there are several ways to evaluate photographs and some key questions to ask the photographer.

Also, consider the *style* of wedding photography you want. If you'd like a heavy emphasis on candid or spontaneous pictures, a photographer with a 35mm might be a best bet. Traditionalists who like a more posed look or who want to enlarge pictures for portraits should insist on a photographer who shoots on medium-format. Since most formal bridal portraits are enlarged to 16x20 (or larger), these should always be shot with a medium-format camera.

Why do some wedding photographers use 35mm cameras? One reason: money. 35mm cameras suitable for wedding photography cost several hundred dollars. Medium format cameras cost several *thousand* dollars—each. For example, a completely outfitted Hasselblad (camera, lenses, lights, flash) can cost from $10,000 to $15,000. Obviously, amateur photographers opt for the cheaper 35mm when they are starting out. What's most disgusting, however, are large studios that use low-quality 35mm cameras in order to cut corners. While the studio makes a few extra bucks of profit, engaged couples are left with inferior-looking photographs.

Of course, some professional photographers PREFER 35 mm cameras because they are smaller, less obtrusive and enable more of that hip "photojournalist" style. One such photographer told us she uses a Leica RangeFinder, which is sort of like the Hasselblad of small format cameras. "It looks like a toy but it costs a fortune ($3000 for a body and lens) because the lens are so great. This makes it perfect for shooting during the ceremony, toasts or other quiet private moments. It is also great in low light because it can be handheld at slower shutter speeds." Her point is well taken: negative size and image sharpness is not everything. Capturing the moment as it happens may be more important and smaller format cameras provide that flexibility: "From my point of view, a big camera, a big flash, and an assistant or two to hold them just makes the photographer intrusive," the photographer said.

Just as important as the camera is the lighting equipment. Lighting equipment and techniques often separate the amateurs from the pros. Amateurs will use only a flash mounted on the camera—the resulting pictures are flat and of poor quality. Professional wedding photographers will use a powerful flash placed about 45 degrees to the side of the subject. The resulting light provides shadows and depth. Some photographers will add one or more flashes aimed at the background. Photographer Mark Spencer of Mountain View, California told us he even puts light behind posed groups and dancing couples to give his pictures additional depth.

Who holds all these extra flashes? Usually it's an assistant. Pros have one at their side the entire day. Not only does the assistant hold the additional flashes, but he or she also makes sure the photographer doesn't miss any detail. In Dallas, Texas, we found one expert photographer who brings *two* assistants to each and every wedding.

2 Skill: Equally as important as having a high-quality camera is knowing how to use it. Photographing a wedding takes a tremendous amount of skill. This is not something that can be taught in a classroom. Only by actually going out there and clicking the camera can anyone learn how to be a good wedding photographer.

Skill involves not only knowing where to stand to get the best shot of the couple as they are showered with birdseed, but also how to coax a reticent flower girl into that perfect pose. The best wedding photographers learn how to work around adverse lighting conditions and, perhaps, adverse relatives.

The only way to tell a wedding photographer's skill is by looking at many albums of their work. After seeing hundreds of wedding albums, we are convinced that you can tell the skilled pros from the unskilled amateurs. One key: posing. Does the photographer creatively pose his or her subjects or are they lined up against a blank wall (like police mugshots)? And not every church looks like the Sistine Chapel—the best photographers deal with ugly backgrounds with creative posing and lighting.

One last caution about skill: don't believe studios that tell you that every one of their associates is trained in the same style. This has to be the biggest lie told by wedding photographers. True, studios may have a professed quality standard that they strive for but what matters most is the talent and skill of the individual photographer who will actually photograph your wedding. Despite the smooth sales pitch, quality can vary widely from associate to associate.

3 Personality: Besides professional equipment and the skill to use it, great wedding photographers also must have great people skills. This isn't nature photography where the photographer patiently sits out in a field for six hours waiting for that perfect photo of the yellow-finned butterfly. Wedding photography involves real people.

Obviously, this doesn't come as a surprise to you, but apparently this is news to some wedding photographers. Communication is key. Besides a sixth sense for good pictures, photographers must be persistent in getting the shots the engaged couple requests. Controlling large crowds of unruly bridesmaids and groomsmen for a group shot can be trying on even the best of nerves. Wedding photographers walk a fine line between being gentle conductors and absolute dictators. In the latter case, some fall victim to director's disease: barking orders at the bride and groom (or their guests) and turning the wedding and reception into a military exercise. (One good question to ask a photographer's references: how did they treat your guests? Were they polite and professional?).

Photographers must also work with other bridal professionals at the wedding, especially the videographer. Clashes between these two vendors can be nasty; we'll talk about this later in the chapter.

Remember that you will spend more time with your wedding photographer than any other merchant. For example, you won't see your florist or baker during or after the wedding. Not only do you meet with the photographer prior to the wedding, he or she will follow you around the entire wedding day. Then, you may spend several more hours with him viewing proofs and ordering prints. Make sure you like this person. We mean you need to *really* like this person. If anything makes you the slightest bit uncomfortable, consider hiring someone else.

Getting Started: How Far in Advance?

Obviously, photographers can only be at one place at one time. This limited capacity leads to a spirited competition between brides to book the best photographers. Once you reserve the ceremony site (and therefore confirm your date), consider shopping for a photographer. While some photographers can be had on short notice (a few weeks to a couple of months), booking nine to 12 months in advance of your date is prudent. That way you won't have to settle on a third or fourth choice. During the wedding season in your town, prime dates will go quickly.

Step-by-step Shopping Strategies

♥ **Step 1:** Once you have booked your ceremony site, contact three to five wedding photographers you have identified by using the sources we listed earlier in this chapter. Make an appointment with each studio. Request to meet the actual photographer who will be available on your wedding day.

♥ **Step 2:** On your visit, view as many pictures as possible from the photographer's past work. Be sure that you are looking at the photographer's own work, not a compilation of the studio's greatest hits. Also, ask to see a proof book from a recent wedding.

♥ **Step 3:** While looking at the work, decide if the pictures strike an emotional chord with you. Is the posing natural or do the subjects look uncomfortable? Are the pictures in-focus and well-framed? Check for any over or underexposed prints—a common problem among amateur photographers. Look to see icing details in wedding cakes and delicate lace in bridal gowns—if these subjects look washed out then the pictures are overexposed. Also check out the various poses a photographer uses. Are there any you'd like the photographer to mimic for your wedding?

♥ **Step 4:** Ask to see photos taken under low-light conditions, especially if you are planning to have a candle-lit ceremony. This is good measure of the photographer's skill, since low-light photography is a technical challenge for even the most experienced.

♥ **Step 5:** Ask the photographer the questions we list later in this chapter. Get a good reading on the photographer's style and personality.

♥ **Step 6:** After visiting with several photographers, pick the one you think offers the best quality for the most affordable price. Be sure to compare prices on an apples to apples basis, accounting for differences in package sizes and prices. Don't let any photographer pressure you into a quick decision.

♥ **Step 7:** Once you make your decision, get a written contract from the photographer. Before signing it, take it home and read it thoroughly. A good contract should specify:

The name of the actual photographer who will be at your wedding.
When the photographer will arrive and how long he or she will stay.
A minimum number of proofs to be provided.
The exact number of prints and the type of album.
The exact dates the proofs and the final album will be delivered.
Provisions in case the photographer gets sick or can't make the wedding.
A specific schedule with due dates for deposits/final balance payments.
Any additional charges for travel time, overtime costs, or other fees.

♥ **Step 8:** A few weeks before the wedding, set up another meeting with the photographer to go over details. Discuss your expectations of the photography and clearly state the types of pictures you want. Identify on a written list any special friends or relatives that you want photographed. The more explicit your instructions to the photographer, the better the odds your wedding photography will meet your high expectations. Frankly, you're paying a ton of money to this person so the least they can do is take the pictures you want. Bring a copy of this list with you to the reception. After taking all the time to make this list, you want to be prepared in case the photographer forgets his or her copy. Also: consider assigning a friend or relative to the photographer to help identify the folks on your list.

♥ **Step 9:** In Chapter 15: Last Minute Consumer Tips, we recommend you pick a trusted friend or relative to be a surrogate bad cop. This person ensures all the vendors are doing their job correctly, while letting you enjoy your wedding day. Introduce the photographer to your bad cop early on the wedding day so the he or she knows whom to turn to for help when trying to take all your requested photos.

Questions to Ask a Photographer

1 Who exactly will be photographing my wedding? This is perhaps the most important question to ask. Don't settle for vague answers like "one of our expertly-trained associates will do your wedding." Avoid wasting time by making sure your appointment is with the actual photographer, not the studio's marketing representative or wedding consultant. Another good question to ask: does the photographer have an assistant who comes to weddings? This helps a photographer concentrate on the event instead of worrying about his equipment, tripod placement and so on.

2 Can I see a complete album from one wedding you photographed? By viewing a complete album from one wedding, you can see how the photographer tells a story from beginning to end. Even better: try to look at several complete albums.

3 Can I also see a proof book from a recent wedding? This is the best way to see what you are buying. Proof books are an unedited and uncensored look at what you will receive after your wedding. Good wedding photographers probably have at least one proof book that is waiting to be picked up—ask to see it.

4 Describe to me your philosophy and approach to wedding photography. Ooo, this is a good question. Sit back and listen to what they say. How active a role do they take in the direction of the day's events? Obviously, some photographers may have a canned speech for this question, but you can shake them up by asking good follow-up questions.

5 What is your shooting schedule during a wedding? When do you arrive and what is your general order of shots? How long do the traditional pictures after the ceremony take? This is a real controversial area of wedding photography. See the The Great Before or After Controversy discussion later in this chapter.

6 What is the balance between posed and candid shots? Some photographers prefer to stage most pictures by formally posing the subjects. Ask the photographer's opinion about whether pictures should be posed or candid. A recent trend in wedding photography is photo-journalism. Here the photographer documents the wedding as it happens without any formal posing.

7 How many exposures will you take at my wedding? Is there a limit on the number of exposures or your time? Be careful of photographers who limit the number of exposures or time. Too many times we have seen weddings shift into fast forward because the photographer's clock was running out. Limiting the number of exposures is also a problem since it restricts the possible choices for your album. About 150 to 200 exposures should be taken to provide enough choices for an album with 60 to 80 prints (our recommendation to adequately cover the day's events).

8 **Do you bring any backup equipment?** What will you do if you are sick and unable to shoot the wedding? Cameras (even expensive ones) are just machines. Sometimes they break. Good photographers should have backup cameras and lighting systems ready in case of a mechanical problem. Having an associate on call in case of emergencies is also prudent.

9 **Can I see the actual album that comes with my package?** A favorite trick of wedding photographers is to show you their past work lovingly bound into leather albums. Then they forget to mention to you their packages come with cheaper vinyl albums with plastic-covered pages. And, oh yes, after the wedding, the photographer slips in that the leather albums are available at an extra fee. Besides the deceptive nature of this practice, some vinyl albums with plastic pages are also problematic since the chemicals in the plastic can damage the prints over time. (Some plastic is okay if it is of archival-quality; that is, free of damaging chemicals). Insist on seeing the actual album that is mentioned in the package before you sign the contract. For more on albums (and one popular brand, Art Leather), see the box later in the chapter.

10 **Describe to me the most difficult wedding you ever photographed. How did you handle it?** We love this question. It can be fascinating to see what the photographer defines as difficult.

What size album should we get?

Most photographers offer two sizes: a 5x5 album or an 10x10. The latter holds both small and large prints. If you have a choice, go for the larger album. Even if you don't purchase enlargements from them photographer, you may want to include a "memory" page at the front of the album with your wedding invitation and other momentos. These won't fit into a small album as easily. What about all those guest candids you might get as well? It's probably best to put those in a different album, separate from the professional pictures. We'll discuss a mail-order source for albums later in this chapter.

11 **How long will you keep the negatives?** If money is tight, don't purchase a large number of prints right after your wedding. Instead, buy the minimum now and wait a year or two to finish out the album. Most photographers store negatives for a few years after the wedding and will be happy to do reprints later when you have more money. The photographer who shot our wedding called us five years later and offered to sell us the negatives for $1 each (an offer we accepted) you may want to ask how long the photographer will store the negatives, whether you'll have an option to buy them and so on.

12 **If you shoot with a digital camera, will the prints be of archival quality?** Digital pictures printed on regular ink-jet printers will start to fade after just a few months. We'll discuss this issue more in the Pitfalls section later in this chapter; suffice it to say, be sure to confirm how your pictures will be printed if your photographer uses a digital camera.

13 **If you shoot with black and white film, do you do your own developing of the pictures?** A photographer who does his own in-house processing of black and white film is able to get the contrast just right. Many photographers we interviewed insist such in-house processing is the only way to insure black and white photographs to look just right. Interestingly enough, this doesn't seem to be a big deal with color film (most photographers send this out to a lab for processing).

14 **How soon will my photographs be ready after I submit my order?** You might be surprised how slow photographers can be when it comes to delivering a final album—sometimes measured in MONTHS not weeks. Photographers who value customer satisfaction should always quickly process albums and reprints. Another measure of customer service: how quickly are your phone calls returned? Messages should be returned within one business day. Taking days to return a simple voice mail is a red flag.

Top Money-saving Secrets

1 **Get married any time other than Saturday evening.** Many photographers offer discounted packages for weddings held during Saturday afternoon or any other time of the week. Savings typically range from 10% to 20%. As a side note: some photographers charge extra to work on Sundays, although that is the rare exception. We find this kind of strange: some brides report that photographers tell them Sunday is "family time," but if you want them to work they charge an extra fee. If Sunday really was family time, why work at all?

2 **Hire a photographer who works out of his or her home.**
When you walk into a photography studio in a fancy office complex and see all that plush carpeting and furniture, who do you think pays for all that? That's right, you do. No one has ever explained to us how designer wallpaper translates into great wedding photography. Our advice: seek out a photographer who works out of his or her home. Quite simply, the lower overhead of a home studio/office is often passed along in the form of more affordable prices. Believe it or not, after visiting with 200 wedding photographers, we found some of the best work was from home-based professionals. Savings here can range from 20% to 40% off our photography average.

Art Leather Albums: The Inside Story

Elmhurst, New York-based photography album maker Art Leather (www.artleather.com) seems to have a lock on the bridal market—if you visit a handful of photographers, odds are you'll see their albums. In business since 1925, Art Leather sells *only* to professional photographers. Here's a look at some of their offerings.

♥ FUTURA ALBUMS. Introduced in 1986, this is Art Leather's most popular line of wedding albums. The covers come in three varieties: Vinahyde, Aristohyde and Top Grain Cowhide (that is, leather). And, no, we're not making those names up.

Vinahyde is the cheapest, with *wholesale* prices (that is, the price the photographer pays Art Leather) at about $37 for a large size album that holds pictures up to 10x10. Aristohyde is the middle price point, at about $50. Want leather? A cowhide cover runs $170 (once again, at wholesale).

And that's just for the *cover*. Inside each Futura album are a series of gold-edged inserts that hold the prints. These slip (and lock into) the spine of the cover. Inserts are about $4 to $5 each at wholesale. Then add in the picture mats, which cost the photographer about 50¢ to 75¢ each.

So, lets add it all up: a large Futura album with a Vinahyde cover and 20 inserts (40 8x10s or 160 5x5s) would *wholesale* for about $140. That would retail for $280 or more.

♥ PERMA-BOUND ALBUMS. These albums feature pages with permanently mounted pictures (by contrast, the pictures are slipped into inserts in the Futura albums). Interestingly enough, the prices for Perma-Bound albums (covers, inserts) are just about the same as

---

3 **Skip the extra frills.** Forget about the extras that photographers will suggest you buy. Gift folios (pitched as the perfect gift for wedding party members) are fluff at $50 a pop. Bridal and engagement portraits are expensive extras. Instead, if you really want a portrait, take a candid from the reception and have it enlarged to a 16x20. You'll save the sitting fee (anywhere from $50 to $300) and the print is often less expensive too. Forget about ordering a frame from the photographer; this service is grossly overpriced. Instead, go to your favorite framing store.

4 **Hire a professional for the ceremony only.** Then let your guests capture the reception candids with their own cameras or

Futura. But we've noticed some photographers will charge higher prices for Perma-Bound albums, which do look fancier than Futura's.

♥ **THE MEZZO ALBUM.** These less expensive albums feature simpler pages (no gold edges) and covers. Photographers pay about $20 to $45 for a Mezzo cover; inserts are $1 to $3 each.

♥ **IMAGE BOX.** Introduced in the last couple of years, the Image Box is designed as an add-on that lets you display the best images of your wedding. Basically, it is a box that holds 12 to 24 mattes that are unbound (so they can be individually removed from the box). The box itself is $57 to $98 (again, wholesale prices photographers pay) for a vinyl cover or $147 to $254 for a "distressed leather" cover. The mattes are $4 to $6 each.

♥ **EXTRAS.** Art Leather sells a surprising number of extras and accessories for their photography albums. Want a gold oval frame (for a picture) on your album cover? That's another $7 at wholesale. How about a panorama photograph that runs across two pages in the center of your album? That's another $10 to $15. What about your names and wedding date (or monogram) printed on the album cover? That's $5 per line.

Besides albums, the other big part of Art Leathers business is gift folios. These cost the photographer anywhere between $4 and $15 each, depending on the size.

You can get more info on Art Leather (as well as preview some of their new products) on their web page at www.artleather.com. Art Leather does not sell directly to the public, however.

single-use cameras (see tip below for more information). Many engaged couples don't realize photographers offer a ceremony-only (two hours or less) package for small weddings. Of course, there is no law that says couples must have a small wedding to use this package. A no-frills ceremony-only package might run $300 to $500, depending on the photographer. One bride in Ohio told us she found a ceremony-only package there from a reputable studio for just $450 that was $1000 LESS than their five-hour plan. Obviously, prices will vary depending on the city you are in, but you can expect a savings of anywhere from 40% to 70%. (Note: beware of studios that might assign less-experienced photographers to shoot the ceremony-only packages.)

5 **Get your guests involved.** Supplement a professional photographer's pictures with shots taken by your guests. Kodak has a great deal on single-use (also known as disposable) cameras: The Wedding Party Pack has five cameras with built-in flash (call 800-242-2424 for a dealer near you). The retail is about $50-$55 but we've seen it for as little as $43 at K-Mart and other discounters like Sam's Club. Since each camera has 15 exposures and it costs about $4 to develop each roll, your total cost is $65 for 75 pictures (only 86¢ per picture). Fuji has a great deal too—the Wedding Cam with built-in flash is $12 for 24 exposures. We found a Fuji 4-pack (96 exposures) for just $48. With the developing cost about $6 per roll, your total cost is $73 for 96 pictures (just 76¢ per picture).

You can also shop online for single-use cameras. The Ultimate Online Wedding mall (stores.yahoo.com/ultimatewedding/discam.html) sells wedding single-use cameras for a little as $5.95 each for orders of 10 or more. C&G Disposable Cameras (www.cngdisposablecamera.com) offers free shipping on orders of five or more cameras. This site sells their 27 exposure camera with flash for $6.75 each.

One tip: be sure to place a small sign near the single-use cameras asking them to be returned at the end of the evening. That way guests don't think the cameras are a party favor! (If this worries you, an alternative to the single-use camera trick is to just buy film for several guests you know will have cameras.)

Should these cameras replace professional photographers? Of course not. Instead, we suggest hiring a professional photographer to cover the ceremony and let the guests snap away at the reception (they'll probably get pictures your photographer wouldn't take anyway). In your album, you can mix the candids taken at the reception with the professional pictures.

Worried about the quality? Pictures from single-use cameras have dramatically improved in quality the last few years. If you still have doubts, buy yourself a camera and do a little experimenting. Is there any difference among the brands of single-use cameras? We've noticed the bridal magazines are stuffed with ads from mail order companies offering single-use cameras (one offers a 27 exposure camera for $10 with free developing). We'd suggest sticking to the name brands (Kodak, Fuji) unless you can confirm the quality by shooting a few of these generic cameras first. With professional photographers charging as much as $10 to $25 for a single print, single-use cameras offer an affordable way to hold down the photography bill.

6 **Buy the album somewhere else.** Chances are you will get a photo album as a gift. If your budget is tight, forget the fancy leather album. If the photographer includes the cost of the album in the package, ask him or her what the discount would be for an album-less package. The retail price of an album from photography studios ranges from $150 to $400. Where can you find a great album for your wedding pictures without spending those kind of bucks? Check out the Real Wedding Tip on the next page for a mail-order source. Another hot trend for wedding pics: scrap-booking. Many arts and crafts stores like Michaels (www.michaels.com) and Hobby Lobby (www.hobbylobby.com) have jumped on the scrap-booking bandwagon, offering a myriad of supplies, albums and ideas to the do-it-yourself crowd. Check their web sites for free projects and supply lists.

7 **Consolidate your orders to take advantage of quantity discounts.** Okay, you've decided which pictures you want but hold it! Now your parents want a few extra prints. And Aunt Bea wants an 8x10 of you and your spouse exchanging vows. By consolidating several small orders into one large one, you may be able to take advantage of quantity discounts offered by your photographer. Also, you'll be able to avoid the service charges some photographers slap on orders after the bride and grooms album is delivered. One photographer we interviewed charges an extra 20% service fee on such reorders. In addition, we found several photographers who offer discounts if you turn in your order within a certain number of days after the wedding. Read the fine print.

8 **Buy the proofs at a discount.** What do photographers do with all those nice 5x5 proofs of your wedding? Apparently, not much. That's why you can sometimes negotiate to buy ALL the proofs for one low price. One bride in Atlanta bought 100 proofs for just $350. She then used them to fill in spots in her albums and as gifts for friends.

9 **Get a bid from PrimeShot.com.** This web site (www.primeshot. com) has built a network of "certified photographers" in most cities that shoot weddings and other corporate events. Their prices are probably about 20% to 30% less than other studios, given our research. The cool part: your pictures are available to view online three days after the event. And you can meet with the photographer before your wedding to discuss the event. You can submit a request for a quote on wedding photography by going to the web site; after you fill out a form, a PrimeShot.com staffer then contacts you with a bid a few days later.

10 **You get the film packages.** You just pay for the photographer's time; at the end of the evening, you get the film and deal with the developing. Obviously, these packages can be big money-savers—even if you pay a photographer $100 to $200 per hour for their time, the result is much less than what complete album packages run. But ... there are some pitfalls to this strategy, which we'll discuss later in this book.

Biggest Myths About Photography

MYTH #1 *A photographer I visited told me he has won several awards for his portraits. Should I be impressed?*

Not necessarily. To understand why, lets look at how photographers win these contests. According to an article in a professional photography magazine, some photographers hire models to pose for these portraits and then take hundreds of exposures to get just the right pose. Then, an army of professional retouching and airbrushing artists are used to enhance the image into an award-winner. The final work presented before the judging panel [bares] little resemblance to the original print or negative, the article stated, adding that many award-winning photographers create exceptional prints specifically for competitions, while exerting little effort toward producing the same caliber of images for customers. That's why you need to see examples of actual wedding albums, not just the glossy prints produced to win competitions.

MYTH #2 *I always see those photography specials advertised by big department stores. You know, the ones for $19.95 that include several dozen prints. Shouldn't wedding photographers be similar in price?*

Sorry to say, but that isn't true. Stores that set up these portrait specials hire an amateur to shoot 35mm pictures in a high-volume operation. Unfortunately, professional wedding photography ain't cheap. The time involved in shooting a wedding is one big factor. Weddings take hours of time, shooting on location with expensive professional equipment.

MYTH #3 *The best bridal portraits are those that are mounted on canvas.*

Yes and no. Studios like to pitch canvas-mounted portraits as top-of-the-line, but there is a catch. In fact, a bride in Alexandria, Virginia alerted us to this rip-off. She spoke with a professor of photography who does *not* recommend canvas-mounted portraits for a couple of reasons. First, in order to be mounted on the canvas, the print must be peeled. As a result, the portrait may crack and reveal the canvas beneath. Second, canvas-mounted portraits must be oiled periodically to preserve the print. And guess who pockets these hefty re-oiling fees? You guessed it, the photographer. All in all, the extra expense of canvas may not be worth the hassle.

Helpful Hints

1 **Photographers pricing methods may be as easy to understand as the federal income tax code.** We are not quite sure why this is. One possible explanation is that photographers want to give you maximum flexibility in choosing prints, albums and portraits. The only problem is that every photographer approaches pricing with a different philosophy that ends up confusing you, the consumer.

Another, more Machiavellian explanation is that photographers want to make comparison shopping more difficult. The lack of a pricing stan-

REAL WEDDING TIP

Mail-order albums can cut costs

Our favorite catalog for photo albums is Exposures (800) 222-4947 (web: www.exposuresonline.com). Their 48-page color catalog features albums, frames and accessories you wont find anywhere else. For example, a brocade photo album adorned with a silk tassel and faux pearl stud is $80. The album comes with one set of ten photo pages (which hold up to 80 pictures). Most Exposure albums use album pages made from archival quality mylar which does not contain chemicals that damage pictures. Other albums are scrapbook-style, where you use old-fashioned photo corners to mount pictures to the acid-free pages, separated by protective tissue. The Printemps is a hand-made, leather-bound, scrapbook-style 50 page album with leaf impressions on the cover for $95. Other scrapbook albums from Exposures cost $50 to $90, not cheap but much less expensive than albums from professional photography studios. You can also add in invitations, newspaper clippings and other mementos from your wedding. Exposures frames and other accessories are equally intriguing—great gifts for bridesmaids, friends and other relatives.

dard makes it very difficult to compare apples to apples. Instead you have one photographer who offers a complete package with an album of 50 8x10s for $800 and another has an a la carte system. The only way for you to make sense of this is to try to equalize the prices, in the same way the grocery stores often display the price per ounce of certain products. We do this by asking ourselves So how much does a four-hour package with 50 5x5s and 20 8x10s in an Art Leather album cost? This package provides adequate coverage for most weddings.

2 Watch out for personality clashes. One common problem: photographers and videographers who step on each other's toes. Since both are trying to document the wedding, there can be conflicts. One such clash occurred at a wedding in Wisconsin, where a photographer ordered a video company NOT to shoot any of the formal picture sessions. He claimed the formal poses of the bride and groom were his protected copyright images. Of course, that's nonsense. But . . . you may want to play it safe and tell the photographer you plan to have a videographer at your wedding—and find out how they can both work together without grabbing for each others throats.

3 Consider going with a woman-owned photography studio. Yes, men have dominated the profession of wedding photography for years. The only women at studios were secretaries or the wives of photographers who came along as assistants. Fortunately, today more and more women are actually behind the camera. While they may be harder to find, we suggest giving women photographers a look-see. Yes, we realize good wedding videography isn't dependent on the gender of the photographer . . . but we can't help but notice how many woman photographers seem better at capturing the emotional aspect of weddings on film. Perhaps this because sometimes the guys are caught up in the technical end of photography, missing some of the emotion while focusing on f-stops. We know that might be an over-generalization, but don't overlook women photographers just because they are outnumbered 10 to 1 at local bridal shows.

Pitfalls to Avoid

PITFALL #1 BAIT AND SWITCH AT LARGE PHOTOGRAPHY STUDIOS AND CELEBRITY PHOTOGRAPHERS.

My friend who recently got married contracted with a well-known, large studio to do her wedding. Everyone was shocked when the photographer arrived—the studio had sent out a person who had never shot a wedding before! The pictures were a disaster! How can I prevent this from happening to me?

Bait and switch is probably the biggest consumer complaint with wedding photographers. Unfortunately, some large studios bait engaged couples with a great reputation only to switch them by delivering less-than-great wedding photography. How does this happen? Basically, some studios farm out their weddings to poorly-trained associates or (even worse) stringers. Stringers are free-lance photographers who are often amateurs working on the weekend for a few extra bucks. The work of these photographers can be far inferior to professional wedding photographers.

A famous photographer in our town has taken many pictures of celebrities. Since the studio also does weddings, I assume my fiancé and I will get the same high quality photography.

Don't bet on it. Here's how it works in this case: every city in the U.S. probably has at least one celebrity photographer who attracts engaged couples to her studio based on her famous name. So who does the wedding photography? Instead of the famous photographer, weddings are often assigned to a no-name associate or a stringer. Hence, couples are baited into the studio by the famous photographer and then switched to a less-famous associate. While an associate may do good work, this is obviously deceptive since couples are duped into paying a hefty premium for celebrity photography, then often get much less.

Solution: You can prevent these problems by doing one simple thing: make sure the name of the actual photographer who will shoot your wedding is specified in the contract. Most importantly, *before* you sign the contract, meet with the actual photographer who will do your wedding and view several albums of his or her work. Don't let the studio show you a few slick sample albums and feed you the line "all our associates are trained in the same great style." Remember your wedding pictures are dependent on who is behind that camera, not a fancy name that's embossed in gold on the studios stationery.

PITFALL #2 HIDDEN CHARGES.

I really liked my wedding photographer. Yet, when the final bill came in, we were charged an extra $200 for travel time at $3 a mile! When we protested this fee, the photographer pointed to the fine print in his price list. And if we didn't pay the extra fee, he said he wouldn't give us our pictures!

Beware of fine print or hidden charges for travel time, over-time, special handling and other services. Sometimes, these fees are mentioned only in fine print on the price list, not your contract. One photographer charged an out-of-town bride a $500 penalty fee when she returned her proof book three days late, thanks to a delay at the post office.

This is why we recommend taking the photographer's contract home first and reading it thoroughly before signing. As we mentioned earlier in the catering chapter, you can request a change in the wording of any clause that makes you uncomfortable. Be wary of any requirements that may be unreasonable and ask for an adjustment to fit your needs.

PITFALL #3 SMALL PACKAGES AND HEAVY SALES PRESSURE.

I contracted with a photographer for one of his small wedding packages that had 20 8x10s in an album. After the wedding, the studio tried to pressure me into buying more prints than the original package-at those high reprint prices! My only problem—I never realized how many more pictures I would want for my album! Help!

The Great Before or After Controversy

Ever attended a wedding where it seemed like the bride and groom took forever to make it to the reception? Where were they? Was their limo hijacked by a UFO? More than likely the bride and groom were hijacked by a wedding photographer who took an amount of time equivalent to the Creation of Heaven and Earth to do the after-ceremony pictures.

So what exactly are the after-ceremony pictures? Basically, these are pictures of the bride and groom with the officiant at the altar, with the bridesmaids, with the groomsmen, with the whole bridal party, with their various relatives, etc. Also, since some churches restrict photography during the actual ceremony, several events from the ceremony (exchanging rings, lighting of the unity candle, the kiss, etc.) may be re-staged for posterity. All told, we are talking quite a few pictures here.

Photographers often mislead couples about how long this process takes. Sometimes photographers sound like a cartoonish version of Name that Tune. (Yes, Bob, I can take those after-ceremony pictures in 20 minutes. Well, Bob, I can do those same pictures in 15 minutes.) In reality, we have known several couples who took one to two *hours* to make it to their reception thanks to the after-ceremony photo session.

Of course, some bright person recently came up with a solution to this problem. Hey, why not do all those pictures *before* the ceremony? The only problem: this would require the bride and groom to see each other before the ceremony on the wedding day. OH NO! How can you break such a sacred superstition? they screeched.

Well, lets take a closer look at the prohibition of seeing each other before the ceremony. As far as we can tell, this started back in the year 1008 A.D. when all marriages were arranged and brides and grooms didn't see each other until the wedding day. Keeping the bride and groom separate was intended to prevent Thor the Viking (the groom) from running away in case Freya the Bride was not the beautiful Viking goddess he was promised. Or vice versa.

Ah, this is a popular deceptive practice by wedding photographers. Here, the studio attracts wedding business with low package prices like "Just $495 for complete coverage and an album with 20 8x10s!" Sounds like a great deal? No, it isn't. That's because most weddings generate dozens of great pictures—photographers often snap 40 to 50 pictures before the ceremony even begins!

The result is that most albums need at least 60 to 80 prints to adequately tell the story of an average wedding. Of course, photographers are well aware of this and realize couples will want to order many more pictures than those packages with just 20 prints. The result is that the $500 package ends up costing $1000, $1500, or even $2000 by the time the total order is placed. We have talked to photographers who admit

Today, brides and grooms not only know each other before the wedding, they also probably share the same tube of toothpaste. It seems a little silly that you wouldn't see your fiancé the day of the wedding when you were just sharing the same pint of Ben & Jerry's 24 hours earlier.

Furthermore, brides today are taught to believe that the groom stands at the end of the aisle and looks down toward his beautiful bride, all the while thinking Wow! Isn't she beautiful? Aren't I lucky? In reality, most grooms are thinking Thank God she's here. Now we can get this over with.

We're not trying to take away from this special moment but there are several advantages to doing the after-ceremony pictures before the wedding (i.e., seeing each other before the ceremony):

♥ **Everything is perfect:** Hair and makeup are fresh prior to the ceremony and hence those important pictures will capture you at your best. After the ceremony, all the hugging and crying can alter that perfect face, hairdo, etc.

♥ **You can leave immediately after the ceremony for the reception:** You will have more time seeing relatives and enjoying the party you spent so much effort (and money) planning.

Here's Our Recommendation: Get to the ceremony site two hours before the wedding. After everyone is dressed, clear out the church with just the groom at the head of the aisle. Then, with appropriate music playing, the bride emerges and walks down the aisle. After this initial meeting, all the formal group pictures are taken before the guests arrive.

Or here's another variation: in a private room at the ceremony site, have the bride and groom meet prior to the ceremony. Here, you and your fiancé can exchange gifts, marvel at each other's dapper appearance, gaze at the gown, etc. What's especially nice about this approach is that you actually get 15 minutes alone, just you and your fiancé. For the rest of the day you'll be surrounded by friends, relatives, and that ever-present photographer. On a day that's supposed to celebrate your relationship, its ironic that most brides and grooms have their first private moment in the car *leaving* the reception—after the whole shebang is over.

this deceptive practice is commonplace. Some studios even make matters worse by adding some heavy sales pressure after the wedding to increase the size of the order.

The most blatant example of this practice was one studio we visited that offered a package for $995 which included just 40 5x7s. The price list then went on to say that brides and grooms may purchase additional 5x7s or 8x10s to create a more complete story. Those additional prints cost $12 for a 5x7 and $20 for an 8x10. *Each.*

You can prevent this practice by selecting a package that offers the amount of coverage that will realistically tell the story of your wedding. For small weddings (under 100 guests with a short reception), this might be just 40 to 60 prints. Most will require 60 to 80 and some large weddings (with big bridal parties and long receptions) may require 100-plus prints.

In Milwaukee in 1998, a photographer was criminally charged with violating deceptive trade practice laws after several couples alleged he tried to pressure them to buy more wedding photos—if not, he refused to give them any pictures at all! The photographers defense: he was an artist and the couples needed to buy "more pictures" ($1000 worth) because that was the only way to show their complete wedding story. While that guy was an obvious scam artist, it points up that even if you have a written contract for a reasonable number of pictures, you can still get heat from a photographer who thinks *his* artistry demands more of *your* money.

The bottom line: be prepared for at least some sales pressure when you select your wedding photos. Don't get hooked by low-price packages that only give you a minuscule amount of actual pictures.

PITFALL #4 UNREASONABLE TIME LIMITS.

I recently attended a wedding where it seemed like the reception moved at the speed of light. Apparently, the photographer was in quite a hurry.

We can't tell you how many weddings we've seen where the reception looked like a sped-up film because the photographer's clock was ticking. After researching this book we now know why: photographers often sell packages with unreasonable time limits.

For example, we interviewed one photographer whose main package had only two and half hour's coverage. Since most photographers start their coverage one hour before the ceremony and because the ceremony itself can take up to one hour (including those pesky after-ceremony pictures), this would leave just 30 minutes to cover all the reception activities! No wonder the bride and groom seemed in a frantic rush to cut the cake, throw the bouquet, toss the garter, and so on! Instead of enjoying the reception, the couple was racing to get everything on film before the photographer's clock expired.

You can prevent this from happening to you by selecting a package with reasonable time limits, or better yet, no time limits at all. In the latter case, the photographer stays at the reception until both of you leave. However, some photographers argue their time is precious and want to impose some time limit. In that case, select a package with at least four hours coverage for an average wedding. You'll need more coverage (perhaps five or six hours) if you have a long ceremony or a large wedding party (all those pictures take more time).

Of course, it shouldn't come as a surprise to you that those same photographers who have those unreasonable time limits also offer overtime at a pricey charge per hour!

We should note that a close kin to this pitfall are photographers who limit the number of exposures they take at a wedding. Ask the photographer about any such limits before you sign a contract.

PITFALL #5 GREATEST HITS ALBUMS.

I visited a photographer who only showed me an album with pictures from several weddings in it. Shouldn't this person have shown me more work?

Yes. This problem is what we call the Greatest Hits Album. Even lousy photographers can occasionally take good pictures. In order to convince you of their excellence, these photographers compile all those greatest hits into one album. Obviously, you are only getting a tiny glimpse of their work.

When you visit a potential photographer, try to see as much work as possible. The best photographers should have sample albums that chronicle one wedding from beginning to end. This allows you to see how the photographer will tell the story of your wedding. Another helpful album to look at is a proof book. Unedited and uncensored, proof books will let you see what the photographer can (and can't) do.

PITFALL #6 FRIENDS AND RELATIVES.

A friend of mine decided to let her uncle, who is a shutterbug, photograph her wedding. What a disaster! His flash didn't work for half the pictures and the other half weren't that exciting anyway.

As most brides and grooms realize, having friends and relatives do various part of your wedding can save you a tremendous amount of money. While you might have a talented aunt who can help alter your gown and a helpful friend who bakes great cakes, you may want to draw the line at the photographs.

Photography is typically high on everyone's priority list and its no wonder—the pictures are all you have left after the wedding. Investing the money in professional photography is a wise choice. Trying to save money by using an amateur is tempting but we say resist the urge—at least when it comes to your ceremony, the most important pictures of the day. Well-meaning friends and relatives who are amateur photographers often bite off more than they can chew when they shoot a wedding. Adverse lighting conditions and other technical challenges can vex even the most talented amateurs.

If you are on a tight budget and can't afford a professional photographer, consider some of the money-saving tips mentioned earlier. Specifically, hire a professional for the ceremony only and have friends and relatives cover the reception with their own cameras or single-use cameras you provide.

Also be aware that many photographers' contracts specify that they must be the only photographer at the ceremony or reception. They claim that friends who snap pictures of the bride and groom compete with their work and equipment (their flashes may set off the photographers flash prematurely). Ask your photographer about any such prohibitions.

Pitfall #7 You get the film packages.

I met a photographer at a bridal show who told me that he can save me money by giving me all the film after the wedding. Then I go and get the pictures developed. Is this a good deal? What's the catch?

The catch is that you have to develop the film, which in most cases is from a medium format camera and much more complicated that it sounds. Unlike 35mm film (which you drop off at Target and then a day later—POOF! You have pictures!), medium format negatives must be developed by professional labs. These labs produce negatives that must be cropped and masked to make final prints. We won't go into more detail on cropping and masking, but we can say that we did this for some publicity pictures and it was quite challenging.

The other main problem is dealing with the lab. As a consumer, you may not know the photo-speak that photographers use to communicate with the lab. For example, many labs offer two choices: less-expensive machine prints or custom prints, which include touch-ups and artwork. We found communicating with the lab that did our publicity pictures dif-

The Package Game: Are you bronze, silver or gold?

Those cutesy names used by photographers to describe their packages aren't by accident. Many studios cleverly use psychological tactics to get couples to spend more. For example, some photographers use precious metals for package names: from bronze (the least expensive) to gold (top of the line). But what bride and groom just wants "bronze" wedding pics? Isn't daddy's little girl worth at least silver or gold?

Our advice: don't get caught up in all the clever marketing. Just pick a package that meets your needs and forget what the photographer calls it!

ficult. Furthermore, you have little leverage over the lab in case the developed pictures have quality problems, since you are a one-time customer.

Of course, these problems are lessened if your photographer shoots a "you get the film" package with a 35 mm camera. Still, you don't want to trust your wedding pics to K-Mart, so you might end up at a professional lab anyway to insure quality development.

Most professional photographers do not sell their negatives (at least not initially after the wedding). Their argument: what incentive does the photographer have to correct any problems if the last you see of him (or her) is when he gives you the film at the reception? Unless you have an intimate knowledge of professional photography development, you may want to steer clear of these get-the-film packages.

PITFALL #8 HERE TODAY, GONE TOMORROW?

My friend took some pictures of our wedding with his digital camera. We printed these out on an ink-jet printer and they looked great—UNTIL they started to fade just six months later! What happened?"

Here's a nasty surprise for those who like to be on the bleeding edge of technology—digital prints that are here today and gone tomorrow. Today's ink-jet printers produce prints that will start to fade after just six months. After a year, the image might be gone. Contrast this to conventional wedding photographs, which can last a generation or more when printed on special archival paper.

Fortunately, ink-jet printer manufacturers are working on a solution to the disappearing ink. Both HP (www.hp.com) and Epson (www.epson.com) have been rushing to roll out printers with longer-lasting ink. The latest Epson models, for example, have ink that will last six to 26 years, depending on the paper used. The company is also targeting professional photographers with new large-format printers that produce prints that can last 100 years when printed on special paper.

Sure, you can always output a digital photo again if the first print starts to fadeout . . . but that's a hassle. If you decide to have a friend take digital pics (or hire a professional photographer who shoots with a digital camera), a word to the wise: confirm the subsequent prints will be of "archival quality." Find out what type of printer that will be used to output the pictures and go to that manufacturer's web site to confirm how long the images will last.

PITFALL #9 PADDING THE BILL BY SPLITTING GROUPS

Our photographer insisted on NOT taking any big group pictures; instead all the relatives were shot in small groups. Was this done to increase his total bill?"

Yes, it is, in our opinion. One photographer admitted as much in a trade newsletter for professional wedding photographers: "By shooting the family in group shots, you are eliminating the possibility of extra sales. Taking (separate) groupings of relatives will produce as many as six portraits sold rather than the usual single group picture. It is almost forcing the parents to buy all of them rather than just the big group."

The same photographer also advised his fellow shooters that "grandparents are the real money makers." He makes sure to include the grandparents in many shots, knowing this increases resales. "God willing, all the grandparents are alive and still married," said the photographer since this adds to the profit dollars.

Trends

♥ **ODD ANGLES, BLURRY SHOTS, OFF-CENTER COMPOSITIONS.** That's how the *Wall Street Journal* described the hip trend of photo-journalistic wedding photographers. And they're right: these aren't your mothers wedding pictures. From celebrity photographers in Beverly Hills to the average wedding shooter in Des Moines, what's in is off-beat pics. What's out? Stiff, formal posed photographs. Instead, couples opt to make fun of their professions (a county prosecutor bride and her highway patrolman groom posed in handcuffs) and generally go for a lighter touch.

♥ **BLACK AND WHITE PHOTOGRAPHY:** Yes, its back. Some couples are rediscovering the contrast and beauty of black and white photography. We've seen several truly striking albums that mix black and white and color photography—à la *The Wizard of Oz.*

Special Touches to Make Your Photography Unique

1 **Add a memory page to your album.** This is a page at the front of the album with a copy of your invitation. We've seen couples add a few of the dried flowers from the bride's bouquet and some lace from the bridal gown to this page.

2 **Personalize your wedding photography.** Instead of an engagement portrait in a studio with a boring blue background, have the picture taken at a special location. Perhaps the place you first met or had your first date. Obviously, photographers will charge a little more to go on location (perhaps $50 to $150) but it is a nice way to personalize the portrait.

3 **Chronicle your engagement with pictures.** With your own camera, document the wedding process (trying on gowns, tasting cakes, visiting various reception sites) from the proposal to the big day. Undoubtedly, you will receive a photography album as a gift, so here's a use for it. Add your honeymoon pictures in the back to complete the album.

It's the centerpiece of your reception—all eyes will be on your wedding cake. But how do you get one that tastes as good as it looks? We'll explore that issue, plus give you nine money-saving tips to cut your cake costs. And what about that mysterious white icing you see on so many cakes? We'll explain the secret ingredient that bakers use to make white icing white, plus three other pitfalls to avoid.

What Are You Buying?

Wedding cakes have come a long way over the years. Once a dry, white tasteless confection with globs of sugary icing, wedding cakes have metamorphosed into gourmet desserts that are truly "to die for." Across the country, we have found a dazzling array of gourmet flavors and high-style designs that turn the pedestrian wedding cake into a culinary work of art. No matter how fancy the design, however, there are four basic elements to a wedding cake:

♥ **THE CAKE, ITSELF.** Traditionally, wedding cakes were vanilla-flavored confections. However, today anything goes. Gourmet cakes are the rage today, with options like you'd see from a four-star restaurant or top pastry chef.

♥ **THE FILLING.** In addition to cake flavor possibilities, many bakers also offer a variety of fillings. Fillings used to be fruit jams or buttercream icing, but have expanded today to include liqueurs, fresh fruit, custards and mousses. The traditional wedding cake has two layers of cake with one layer of filling in each tier. Lately, we've seen more European torte-style cakes: confections with four or five layers of cake and filling. This torte-style cake tends to be richer than an American-style cake.

♥ **THE FROSTING AND DECORATIONS.** The options for wedding cake icing are numerous. Some bakers opt for the traditional buttercream icing (to which liqueurs are often added) while rolled fondant or marzipan is also popular. Whipped cream icings and meringue icings are yet more options. No longer are you limited to the typical white icing; many brides want their cakes tinted to match the bridal party colors or merely prefer the antique look of an off-white icing.

Wedding cake fads come and go like fashion. In the 1970's and 80's, hip brides had wedding cakes adorned with gurgling fountains and plastic tiers. The taste of the cake was secondary, if not ignored completely. In the 1990's, simpler weddings ushered in the simpler wedding cake, more likely adorned with fresh flowers than plastic brides and grooms. At the start of the 21st century, cakes are changing again—this time to make a "personal" statement for the bride and groom. Other folks are following the trends set by cake diva Martha Stewart (more on this later). Wedding cakes are expected to both look AND taste good today.

♥ **DELIVERY AND SET-UP.** Another element you are buying is the delivery and set-up of the cake. This means the actual engineering of the cake with its several layers, possible separations (or stacking if you prefer the tiers to sit one on top of the other) and decoration if you want flowers and greenery. Rental items like the columns and plates for separating tiers are another cost. Some bakers have actually made a special stand for their cakes which they rent to couples for the day.

Average total costs. What's our favorite scene from the Steve Martin remake of *Father of the Bride?* It has to be Martin's character's shock at cake prices. After Martin Short's wedding consultant says that $1200 is a reasonable price "for a cake of this magnitude," Martin rejoins: "Franc, a cake is made of flour and water! My first car didn't cost $1200!" To which, Short replies: "Welcome to the 90's!"

Yes, they are just made of flour and water, but the average wedding cake still runs hundreds (if not thousands) of dollars. Cakes are typically priced per serving. We peg the average wedding cake at $525 for 175 guests—that's about $3 a slice. But, as Steven Martin learned, cake prices can be much higher. We noticed Palm Beach, Florida bakers expect $5 a serving for their creations, while the going rate in Massachusetts can range up to $15 a slice! In Boston, the wedding of a dot-com executive featured a cake with six individually lit waterfalls with lily pads, flowers and the words "to the love of my life" written in red icing on the cake. Cost: $8200.

Of course, cake prices in the real world are less than what folks in Boston or New York City pay. We noticed in Nebraska the average cake goes for $1.50 to $3 per serving. The average in Ohio is about $3 a slice.

The average deposit for a wedding cake can range from $50 to 50% of the total bill. The balance is due usually a week or so before the wedding.

Trends

What's new with wedding cakes? Here is a round-up of the latest trends:

♥ IN A WORD: FONDANT. Icing, that is—this hip look has been boosted by Martha Stewart. But there are some important caveats with fondant icing. We'll talk more about this in the pitfalls section.

♥ DECONSTRUCTION. The standard wedding cake used to be stacked layers. No longer. In North Carolina, bakers put cakes on separate "floating" cake stands of varying heights.

♥ CHOCOLATE WEDDING CAKES. Who said a wedding cake had to match the bride's dress?

♥ GIFT PACKAGES. Tiffany started this trend a few years ago when they featured a wedding cake that looked like stacked gift packages, all festooned in colorful icing wrapping paper.

♥ "MINI-CAKES." *In Style* magazine touted this trend in a recent wedding issue. Here each guest gets an individual wedding cake instead of a slice of a larger cake. Since these are all the rage at celebrity weddings, you can be assured the price is high. In Boston, bakers sell elaborately decorated minicakes for $10 a pop! In Manhattan, mini cakes can run $15 to $20 each. We don't quite see what all the fuss is about—isn't a mini-cake simply a cup cake by any other name?

♥ **Dr. Suess.** Oh, the places cakes can go! Symmetrical cakes are out; asymmetrical is in. A baker in Boston created a wacky "Dr. Suess" cake with eccentric angles, lopsided corners and other Cat in the Hat-inspired images.

♥ **And now, from California: Neon colors.** Yep, brides in Southern California seems to be snapping up wedding cakes in lime green and day-glo orange. Triple berry cake (yellow butter cake with three layers of fresh berries with cream) is a hip flavor.

♥ **Different flavors in different tiers.** If you can't decide between flavors, some bakers make it easy for you—they'll whip up a different flavor for each tier.

Sources to Find an Affordable Baker

There are three types of bakeries that do wedding cakes. Here's a breakdown:

1 **Cake factories/grocery stores.** Better know as commercial bakeries, these folks bake and deliver over ten cakes per Saturday. These businesses may be less personalized than the other two types of bakers. Grocery stores fall into this category, too.

2 **Reception sites and/or caterers.** Quality is sometimes great, sometimes not.

3 **Small bakers and pastry chefs.** These are the hardest to find, but often the best and most creative cake bakers. Some work out of their home; others are pastry chefs that might also have a small cafe business.

Here are our sources for finding great bakeries:

♥ **Florists.** Because they often work with bakers to help coordinate the floral decorations, florists may have great contacts.

♥ **Photographers.** Since they attend many receptions, photographers see the best and worst creations of local bakeries. They also often hear praise or criticism about cakes from guests.

♥ **Reception sites.** Besides helping set up the cake, as well as serving it, catering managers notice whether guests like the cake or not.

♥ **BRIDAL SHOWS.** Most bakeries offer samples of their cakes at bridal shows, so here's a great opportunity to taste without any pressure to buy.

Brides in Cyberspace: What's on the Web?

♥ You gotta love the web. Where else can you find a home page for the **INTERNATIONAL CAKE EXPLORATION SOCIETÉ** (www.ices.org), an association of cake bakers? Check their links section to find local chapters and baker's home pages. Also click on the newsletter link, which features pictures of creative cake designs (see Figure 1 below).

♥ **SUGARCRAFT.COM** has just about every supply for the do-it-youselfer, including edible pearls made of gum paste. "The prices are great," says a reader who emailed this tip.

♥ **WILTON** (www.wilton.com) is the undisputed leader in cake decorating supplies. Their crisply designed web site is fun to visit, complete with an on-line store and a "recipes and ideas" section. The latter featured a half dozen wedding cakes, complete with instructions, needed supplies and a picture of the final product.

♥ The web is also a great place to find small artisans that make cake toppers. If you don't like all the cheesy wedding cake toppers you see in discount stores, check out **PORTRAITS IN CLAY**, created by Burlington Vermont artist Adele Dienno (www.portraitsinclay.com). This company creates "fine heirloom sculptures" that are individually designed and

Figure 1: The International Cake Exploration Societé has a web site (www.ices.org) with all sorts of wedding cake pictures.

July 2000 Cake Photographs

fabricated in porcelain. Okay, this isn't cheap at $350 and up but it *is* unique. And a keepsake you can hand down in the family.

Getting Started: How Far in Advance?

Because bakeries can make more than one cake on a Saturday, brides may only need two to four months to plan. With some of the large commercial bakeries, you may even need less time (as little as a week's notice). Popular bakeries and popular dates may require more advance planning (between three and six months) and you may want to do this part early anyway to get it out of the way. You will need to know how formal the wedding will be and have a general idea of the number of guests you will have. You can finalize this number later, when the guest count becomes more concrete.

Step-by-step Shopping Strategies

♥ **Step 1:** Before visiting a baker, you will need to have a general idea of the number of guests invited. Final exact numbers won't be required until a week or two before the wedding date; this will allow you to get a basic price for a cake. Also, knowing your wedding colors will help guide the baker.

♥ **Step 2:** Given the resources above, identify two to three bakers who have skill levels and style ideas to fit your needs. Make an appointment with them and ask if you can have a taste test. Time the appointment to make it easier for the baker to give you a sample (like Friday while they are decorating cakes for Saturday weddings).

♥ **Step 3:** At the baker's shop, be sure to look at *real* photos of their past cake designs. Some bakeries use standard cake-design books and tell brides they can make anything from these publications. Be skeptical. It is preferable to see actual photos of what they can do!

♥ **Step 4:** Given the size of your reception, ask the baker for a proposal or estimate of the cost of a cake based on one or two of their styles. Also ask for suggestions on how much cake to buy. The amount of cake to order will depend on several factors: if you will be having a groom's cake or sweets table; how much other food you will be serving (sit-down dinner vs. hors d'oeuvres); the time of day; and the size of the slices (paper thin up to birthday cake size). Some bakers think a wedding cake slice should be four inches wide; others think just two inches.

♥ **Step 5:** Make sure you taste a sample of their cake. There is no substitute for having actually tasted it before buying. If a baker doesn't offer taste tests, you should be very cautious. You may have to buy a small six-inch cake from the baker in order to get a taste, but we prefer bakeries that offer free samples—these are usually the best.

♥ **Step 6:** Choose the baker and ask for a signed proposal detailing the design, flavors of both cake and filling, any rentals (like columns or stands), delivery and set-up fees, and deposit information. Don't forget to have the date, place and delivery time clearly written on the proposal. If you are planning far in advance, you may have to adjust the number of servings you will need—find out the last possible moment when you can change numbers.

♥ **Step 7:** Confirm any last-minute details and pay the balance on the cake a week or two before the wedding.

Questions to Ask a Baker

1 **Do you have any photos of previous designs?** The idea is to see the bakery's actual work, not to look through generic picture books with designs they may never have created.

2 **Can we have a taste test?** You may have to wait for a day when they are making cakes, but the best bakeries will offer free taste tests.

3 **Are there any extra charges?** Some bakeries prefer to break down the charges for almost everything. These items may include: fillings, complex decorations, silk or fresh flowers, delivery, set-up, cake plates and columns, and more. Find out exactly what these items will cost and get a written proposal.

4 **Who will decorate the cake with fresh or silk flowers?** If you prefer this type of decoration, find out how the flowers will be provided and who will decorate the cake. Some bakers can purchase the flowers and decorate it themselves. Others will get the flowers from your florist. In some cases, the florist is totally in charge. (Another tip for flowers intended for cake decoration: make sure you pick blooms that have not been sprayed with pesticides or preservatives).

5 **How far in advance is the cake prepared?** This may be a delicate question to ask, but you will want to know how fresh the cake is that you are buying. Almost all bakers must bake the cake a few days prior to the wedding, then freeze it before applying the decoration. Of course, no one wants to have a cake that has been frozen for more than a week. Unfortunately, some high-volume bakeries may do just that.

Top Money-saving Secrets

1 **Do the cake "switcheroo."** Here's a clever way to cut costs. Instead of buying a huge wedding cake to feed your guests, get a small cake for photos. After the pictures, wheel that cake into the kitchen . . . and have the caterer cut up sheet cakes in the kitchen. Out comes slices of cake for the guests, who probably won't know the difference (a slice of cake looks like a slice of cake, right?). But you'll notice the difference in your wallet. Sheet cakes cost 75% less than wedding cakes (as little as 50¢ a serving). Why? Much of a wedding cake is the decoration, which sheet cakes omit. This trick gets you the best of both worlds—a nice wedding cake for photos and the ceremonial cake cutting, while giving your guests some cake as dessert at a price that doesn't break the bank.

2 **Pass on your caterer's cake offer.** Many banquet halls, hotels and caterers will suggest you buy a wedding cake from them. Do they bake the cakes? Nope, they go to an outside bakery and order one of their cakes—and then mark it up to sell to you! Avoid the cake mark-up and contract directly with a baker. One caveat: some sites won't let you bring in an outside cake, so check first. Others slap brides with a "cake cutting fee" ($1 to $ 2 per guest) to discourage the use of outside bakers. We discuss this rip-off in our catering chapter; try to negotiate away this fee.

3 **Go simple and decorate with flowers.** All those fancy cake decorations (from gum paste flowers to fondant icing) cost a fortune. A better money-saving strategy is to get a plain, basic cake and decorate it with flowers. Blooms are more cost-effective than a baker slaving away for hours to create an icing masterpiece. Use the bridesmaids bouquets to decorate the cake's base. And use our flowers-at-wholesale from the 'net tip from Chapter 5 to buy roses on the cheap to complete the look. You'll save 25% to 40% by going plain and dressing it up with flowers. And the cake will look just as beautiful for photos.

4 **Order less cake than the number of people.** If you have a sweets table or groom's cake, consider fewer servings. Also if you will be eating a heavy sit-down meal or have a crowd that doesn't eat a lot of sweets, consider cutting back.

5 **Choose an independent or out-of-home baker.** This could mean as much as $1 to $2 difference in cost per serving. Out-of-home or small bakeries often have lower overhead which they pass on to brides. Caution: Local health laws may prohibit bakers from operating out of their home. Each city is different, so you may want to check with your local health department.

6 **Skip the anniversary cake top** (see pitfalls later in this chapter for more details).

7 **Roll the sides in nuts.** One bride emailed us an interesting story—she found wedding cakes from her favorite bakery were $4.50 a slice. But . . . if she opted for a cake with sides rolled in nuts, the price was $1.50. The complete story is in the Real Wedding Tip on this page.

8 **Hire the teacher.** A bride in Iowa phoned in this tip. She called a local crafts store to see if they had cake decorating classes. They did—and she hired the teacher to do her wedding cake. She estimated she saved about 30% off what a commercial bakery would have charged her for a similar cake.

9 **Consider off-beat places for cakes.** For example, Wal-Mart isn't exactly the first place brides think to look for wedding cakes. But one reader emailed us she found this deal: "My wedding cake was just $110! That's right—$110 for a 3 tier cake that feeds about 100 people! The new Wal-Mart Superstore in my town has everything including a bakery. The wedding cakes are beautiful and very affordable."

REAL WEDDING TIP

That's nuts!

Here's one way to save money with wedding cakes, from a reader in San Francisco:

"Since I have a favorite bakery that sells reasonably priced cakes, I assumed their wedding cakes would be too. Wrong! They were $4.50 a slice! Eek! But when I tried to cut costs, it was difficult. I made it clear that they didn't need to make frosting ribbons and roses, didn't need to have a balancing act with stacked tiers on little pillars, etc. But that made no difference in price. Why? Because, they explained, the majority of the labor to make a wedding cake is in getting the frosting smooth on the sides of the cake. Their wedding cakes are frosted, frozen, re-frosted to smooth, re-frozen, and so on. And the labor is most of the cost. So, we ended up buying our cakes with the sides rolled in nuts for $1.50 a slice. That way they don't have to have smoothly frosted sides, we don't have frostbitten cake, and we save a bundle. I just hope none of our guests have severe nut allergies . . ."

Biggest Myth of Wedding Cakes

MYTH #1 *"At every wedding I've ever been to, the wedding cake was tasteless and dry. It's impossible to find a good-tasting cake."*

Wrong. This fallacy is based on all those tasteless white cakes with Crisco-based icings that wedding guests remember from years past. Today brides and grooms can have a cake that tastes as good as it looks.

Pitfalls to Avoid

PITFALL #1: THE REVENGE OF MARTHA: CAKES THAT TASTE LIKE SAND PAPER! AND COST MORE!

"I fell in love with a cake design from Martha Stewart's magazine that featured rolled fondant icing. My baker warned me the cake will taste terrible! Not to mention cost 30% more. What's up?"

Martha sure makes pretty cakes, but look out—her current fave (cakes with rolled fondant icing) has some major drawbacks the diva of domesticity forgets to mention.

First, taste. Yes, fondant iced cakes have the ultra-hip smooth finish but don't ask how it tastes (some folks think fondant tastes too sweet; others say it is like eating gum paste). To understand why fondant lacks in the taste department, consider how it is made. Developed in the mid 1980's by British and Australian pastry chefs as a replacement for rock-hard royal icing, fondant is a mixture of sugar, gelatin and corn syrup. The result is a doughlike pastry. All the labor that goes into making and rolling out fondant onto cakes (not to mention hand-tinting) means higher prices—most bakers charge at least $1 extra per serving for fondant cakes. That's a 30% hike over average prices.

If you have your heart set on the fondant look, consider a couple of tips. Ask your baker to add a layer of buttercream frosting under the fondant to add flavor (guests can knock off the fondant icing and still have cake and icing below). Also, consider fondant look-alikes. One Texas baker mixes buttercream and cream cheese to give a fondant look with better taste.

PITFALL #2 ANNIVERSARY CAKE TOPS

"The baker I visited told me that 'of course you will want to save the top tier of the cake for your first anniversary.' This sounds like a silly tradition!"

Yes, we agree. Saving the top of the wedding cake to eat on your first anniversary is a common tradition in many areas of the country. This entails having mom or someone else remember to take the top home, wrap it very carefully, and put it in your freezer. Even supposing you have room in your freezer, the taste of the cake after 12 months may leave much to be desired. In fact, if you serve the cake at your wedding instead, you may be able to save 10% to 20% off your bakery bill—a much better deal than a stale year-old cake! If you want to follow this tradition, we recommend calling up your baker in a year and buying a small, freshly-made cake to celebrate with on your first anniversary.

PITFALL #3 MYSTERIOUS WHITE ICING.

"We attended a wedding last weekend that had a beautiful wedding cake. But, when we tasted the cake, there was this terrible, greasy after-taste. Yuck! What causes this problem?"

The answer lies in what makes white icing *white*. Well, a key ingredient in icing is butter—which creates a problem for bakers. Most butter made in the US is yellow, which gives icing an off-white or ivory color. To get pure white icing, bakers must use expensive white butter (imported from Europe). Unfortunately, some bakers use a less expensive short-cut to get white "buttercream" icing—they add white shortening like Crisco. Yuck! That's why some cake icing has a greasy aftertaste. If you want white icing, you might ask your baker how they make their icing white. For example, some bakeries offer a meringue icing (made from egg whites), while others do fondant, a paste of sugar, water and corn syrup that's rolled over the cake. Both achieve a white look without the Crisco.

PITFALL #4 WELL-MEANING FRIENDS AND RELATIVES.

"My aunt has offered to bake my wedding cake. She's good at baking basic cakes but isn't a wedding cake much more complicated?"

That's right. Offers like this are made with the best possible intentions but, if accepted, can be disastrous. Baking a wedding cake is far more complex than baking a birthday cake from a Betty Crocker mix. The engineering skills required to stack a cake and keep it from falling or leaning are incredible. Unless you have a friend or relative who is a professional baker or pastry chef, politely refuse their offer. Consider telling them you've already contracted with a baker to make your cake if you don't want to offend them.

PITFALL #5 EARLY DELIVERY AND COLLAPSING CAKES.

"My baker delivered my cake nearly five hours before my reception. In the interim, someone or something knocked the cake over and destroyed it! How could I have prevented this?"

This is a problem that often occurs when large bakeries deliver many wedding cakes on a single Saturday. The cake is dropped off (and set-up) hours before the reception and left unattended. As you can guess, Murphy's Law says that an unattended wedding cake is a collapsed wedding cake. No one at the reception site may admit to knocking it over but you can imagine how "things happen" during a wedding reception set-up. Prevent this problem by insisting the baker deliver the cake within two hours prior to the reception. You may want to coordinate with the catering staff to limit any scheduling snafus. Be sure someone (the catering manager, a maitre d', etc.) is there when the cake is delivered so they can keep an eye on it.

Unique Ideas

1 **Ethnic Traditions.** Many couples incorporate ethnic traditions into their wedding cake. For example, traditional French wedding cakes are actually cone-shaped confections made of cream-filled puffed pastry stuck together with caramelized sugar. Guests serve themselves by merely grabbing a cream puff from the cone!

2 **Different flavors in different tiers.** Can't decide between Italian Cream, mocha chip and carrot cake? Why not try all three in different tiers of your cake?

3 **Cheesecake.** Ah, here's an unique idea we are particularly fond of: cheesecake wedding cakes. Available in many different flavors, cheesecakes can be frosted with cream cheese icing (to look more like a traditional wedding cake) or left plain and decorated with fresh fruit or flowers. Yum!

Disappearing Deposits

Julie Jauregui Holloway e-mailed us this interesting story about a disappearing deposit—a good lesson for all brides. "Our baker charged us a $75 deposit for the lucite tiers used with our wedding cake—he told us we had one month to return them or we'd lose the deposit. Well, after the wedding, we had our maid of honor drop them off since we'd be on our honeymoon. Unfortunately, she forgot about the deposit and didn't ask for any money back. The bakery also wouldn't give her a receipt. Well, you can guess what happened next—we got back, asked the bakery for the money and they claimed they gave it to the maid of honor. It took three visits to the bakery before the manager agreed to refund our money."

Lights! Camera! Money! Wedding videos are an expensive newcomer to the bridal market. In this chapter, we cut through the technical mumbo-jumbo to give you a practical guide to finding an affordable yet talented videographer.

What Are You Buying?

Basically, there are two things you are buying when you hire a videographer: the cameraperson's time, and the video itself.

♥ **THE CAMERAPERSON'S TIME.** Many videographers will charge you for their time first and foremost. Most offer packages with a time limit of three, four, or more hours. Overtime is charged on an hourly basis. Some videographers will charge a flat fee for the whole wedding and reception; others offer "multi-camera" shoots as an extra option.

Besides hiring a cameraperson for a certain amount of time, you are also buying his or her talent and personality. As with photographers, it is very important to find a videographer who is not only skilled at camera work but is also easy to work with. You will be working with him as much as with the photographer.

And, of course, the videographer's investment in equipment is important—we'll discuss this later.

♥ **THE FINAL PRODUCT.** The most important item you're buying is the video-tape. There are several types of tapes (or styles of videographers) available:

Raw footage. This tape simply starts at the beginning of your ceremony and runs, uninterrupted, to the end of your reception. There is no editing or post-production graphics. Raw footage videos are the least expensive option, typically offered by amateur videographers. Professionals more likely will offer one of the next two options.

Edited "in camera." This type of video also does not have post-editing or added graphics. However, the videographer edits your video "in-camera." This means the cameraperson shuts off the camera during any uninteresting moments or rewinds and tapes over any unnecessary footage. If done by a professional, this option can work very well. It will usually be moderately priced in comparison with other types of tapes.

Post-edited. This type of tape is usually the most expensive because the videographer spends the most time on it. Videographers "post-edit" a tape after the wedding and reception. During this production, the videographer will take raw footage, cut out the boring parts (if there are any!), smooth the transitions, and add in titles and music. Some videographers add still photos (baby pictures, honeymoon photos) to give the tape a truly personal feel. If you have multi-camera coverage, post-editing blends the footage from several cameras to make for a more interesting tape. We've even seen tapes with special effects similar to those seen on television newscasts. Many videographers charge an additional hourly fee for post-editing, while others may have packages which include editing and special effects.

Highlights. In addition to tapes that cover the entire wedding and reception, some videographers offer brief highlight tapes that condense the day's events into a short montage that is 10 or 20 minutes long. Set to music and crisply edited, these tapes are perfect when you don't want to torture your friends with the full-length version of your wedding video.

Copies. Most wedding video packages include one copy of the video tape. Extra copies often cost more; however some videographers have packages that include copies for parents.

Average total costs: The average wedding video costs about $1000, although prices are all over the board depending on what you get. In small towns, a one-camera, unedited video could cost as little as $500. The mid-range in most cities, $750 to $1500 will buy you a one or two camera shoot, some editing, music and a few copies. Want to go whole hog? You could pay $2000, $3000 or even $5000 for a complete "movie" of your wedding, shot with multi-camera coverage and heavily edited with added music, titles and other special effects.

In general, more money buys you more camera coverage (two versus one camera) and extra frills like special effects, highlight montages and artsy editing.

In recent years, videographers have started to get creative with selling all sorts of add-ons, like a "love story" (a five to 20 minute video that reinacts how you met, the proposal, etc.). The extras can start at $800 and go up from there, depending on how elaborate they are. Another option: the "retrospective" which is a post-wedding video where the bride and groom reminisce about the day (see the Trends section later in this chapter).

Most videographers require a deposit for one-third to one-half of the contract amount to book a date. Some require another one-third payment on the day of the wedding with the balance due when the completed tape is picked up.

We should note one troubling trend with videographers and deposits: increasingly, we see video companies demanding complete payment UP FRONT, weeks before the wedding. Obviously, we have a problem with that. When a videographer receives ALL their money before your wedding, there is no incentive for them to deliver the final product on time. We prefer a small balance that remains to be paid until the tape is delivered—try to negotiate this point if a videographer demands total payment up front.

Sources to Find a Videographer

Wedding videography is a relative newcomer to the bridal market. Only in the 1980's did the videotaping of weddings really take off. Yet, finding a good videographer can still be a challenge. Here are some of the best sources:

♥ **RECENTLY-MARRIED COUPLES.** These folks can give some of the best advice about videographers. Look at friends' videos to decide what styles, editing and extras you might want.

♥ **PROFESSIONAL ASSOCIATIONS.** The Wedding and Event Videographers Association International (WEVA) offers a toll-free line at (800) 501-WEVA or (941) 923-5334 for brides to call to get a referral to local videographers. They have a web site at www.weva.com as well. WEVA has nearly 4000 members internationally. (We do have some concerns about WEVA; see the following box for details). Another source: the Association of Professional Videographers (209) 653-8307; web: www.avp.to. Finally, you can also check with national videographer franchises like Video Data Services (800) 836-9461 or (716) 381-9240 (web: vdsvideo.com). With over 200 franchises, Video Data Services has been in business since 1978.

♥ **TELEVISION STATIONS.** Many camerapersons at TV stations moonlight on weekends shooting weddings. They may have access to high-tech editing and special effects computers. In Ft. Worth, Texas, for example, one of the most popular videographers for weddings is the chief videographer for the NBC affiliate. One tip we heard from a reader: when you call a TV station, bypass the receptionist and ask to speak directly to a cameraperson. Why do this? Some stations don't like their camerapeople moonlighting at weddings and instruct receptionists to tell callers that this service isn't available.

♥ **WEDDING PHOTOGRAPHERS.** This can be a good source. Photographers

The dark side of WEVA?

We have mixed feelings about recommending brides contact The Wedding and Event Videographer Association (WEVA) for referrals to local videographers. While WEVA has done a good job at helping educate videographers and improve the quality of wedding videos, some of the association's activities have been questionable if not outright anti-consumer.

First, WEVA holds numerous "town meetings" and even a national convention for videographers. One common theme at these get-togethers: videographers need to RAISE their prices. WEVA's thinking here is that the profession of wedding videography is sullied by amateurs who offer cheap-o prices. The mantra of "raise your prices" is repeated again and again on WEVA's online message boards (which are hidden from view of brides).

Our take on this: while it is understandable that a trade association like WEVA wants to improve the professionalism of its industry, advocating such fee hikes smacks of price-fixing. The Federal Trade Commission has ruled that such collusion by trade associations runs afoul of anti-trust laws, so WEVA is skating on very thin ice.

Our second beef with WEVA: their web site offers a "Member Referral Service" that promises to pair you with a videographer but has some hidden pitfalls for consumers. Brides and grooms are supposed to fill out an on-line form that asks for your name, email, wedding date, city and state. All that's fine, of course. But the problems begin when WEVA asks for your ceremony and reception sites and the number of guests.

According to private emails posted on WEVA's industry-only message boards, videographers use this info to then "cherry-pick" customers. If you put down the fanciest church or hotel down as your sites, the videographers leap at your business. Not so if you plan a small wedding, where you'll be singing the country tune "If the phone don't ring, it's me!"

will be able to recommend good videographers they've seen at other weddings. Occasionally, photographers and videographers have conflicts at weddings. You can avoid this by choosing two people who have worked together before. Don't, however, feel obliged to use a photographer's suggestion without checking out the videographer carefully to see if he or she fits your needs. Another caveat: some photographers have video divisions, so, of course, they will recommend themselves to do the video. Of course, just because you hire the photographer doesn't mean you must go with their video package—check out other videographers before you make a final decision.

♥ **CEREMONY SITE COORDINATORS.** These folks often have first-hand knowledge about videographers since they are responsible for reciting the rules to camerapersons. Site coordinators can recommend people familiar with the site who are also easy to work with. And they may also hear back from brides about how good (or bad) the finished video is.

Brides in Cyberspace: What's on the Web?

Party Shots
Web: www.partyshots.com

What it is: On-line photo album captured from videotape.

What's cool: If you can get film developed in one hour and pizza delivered in 30 minutes, why does it take FOREVER to see pictures or video from your wedding? To the rescue comes Party Shots, a web site that uses captured stills from your wedding video to create a cyber photo album. Your videographer selects the images, transfers them to a computer and uploads the images to the web in a matter of hours. The day after your wedding, you get a 'net video album with cover page, 50 pictures and an interactive guest book. We saw several sample "party books" and were impressed—the images are high quality and the site is easy to navigate through.

Needs work: The price of Party Shots ($149 to brides and grooms) is a little much, especially since Party Shots only charges videographers $20 per album (plus the videographer's time to post the pictures on the Internet, of course). It would be nice to have an index page with thumbnails of all the photos—instead, you get a non-helpful index with a text listing of the photographs by number (pic1, pic2, etc.). Another drawback: as of this writing, only two dozen videographers nationwide offer this service, most of whom are in New York and other parts of the Northeast.

Understanding Videographers: Some Basics

When shopping for a professional wedding videographer, keep in mind these five elements:

1 **Lighting.** As with photography, lighting is key to a good video. Often, existing room light is not bright enough to get a good picture. In the past, videographers would need to flood a room with light in order to get good video, spoiling the ambiance of a candlelit reception hall.

Well, we have good news on this front. Advancements in technology have led to new professional video cameras that are sensitive enough for use with only available room light. If they do require any extra light, videographers can use smaller, low-wattage lights that are less distracting and still get good video.

2 **Sound.** Especially during your once-in-a-lifetime wedding ceremony, it is vital to get perfect sound on your video. Thanks to high technology, great video sound is possible without the use of giant boom microphones hanging over your head.

There are basically three ways to capture sound at the ceremony. The least effective is through a "boom" microphone. This is attached to the video camera and often picks up every sound in the room, including your vows. If you don't want to hear your seven year old nephew Joey squirming around in his seat and fidgeting, the boom microphone is not for you.

The next option is the "hard-wired" microphone. This type of microphone has a wire which connects it to the camera. The other end, typically a small clip-on mic, is attached to the groom's lapel, the official, the podium or the kneeling bench. This may not be ideal for some weddings, especially if there is a lot of movement during the ceremony. The sound quality is usually average to good.

The final (and most common) option is a "wireless" microphone. This microphone sends sound to the camera via a radio transmitter (about the size of a small Walkman) attached to the groom's waist.

One caveat: wireless microphones that are "low band" may pick up interference from police radios or other radio equipment. "High band" microphones, on the other hand, can weed out most interference and produce a clean, clear "I do" on your tape.

Remember that audio is as important as video. When looking at sample tapes, listen for rough transitions or conversations that are cut off. Sloppy audio can keep you from following the sequence of events on the tape. Another clue: check to see if the audio is in sync with the video.

3 **Equipment.** *"All this video camera stuff is so bewildering—I hear there are Super VHS cameras, digital cameras, Hi-8 . . . I'm so confused! I can't even program my VCR! Help!"*

Well, you're on your own with the VCR. But we can help you to understand the different cameras used for wedding videography.

The majority of wedding videographers shoot on Super VHS tape, an analog format that provides more lines of resolution than regular VHS.

These tapes are dubbed down to regular VHS for your final tape so they can play in an ordinary VCR. Other videographers use Hi-8 cameras (8mm) or one of the new digital cameras.

Digital is the big new thing for video professionals—the format lets videographers easily edit video and add special effects. Eventually, digital video cameras will enable an easy transfer of wedding videos to DVD's and to the web (although this is still in its infancy). But . . . most videographers haven't gone digital yet, thanks to the high price of such equipment (a $30,000 editing system, anyone?) and other technological hurdles.

No matter what format they use, the actual cameras most videographers use are far different (and more expensive) than the kind of camcorders you see at Best Buy. Most are professional-grade (or "prosumer"), which provide a sharp picture and vibrant colors. Today's prosumer cameras use advanced computer technology to produce better video.

The best professional cameras use "three-chip" technology—a separate computer chip to process red, blue and green colors. Unfortunately, these cameras are also quite expensive ($5000 to $15,000). As a result, fewer than half of all videographers use them. The balance use "one-chip" cameras.

Is it bad for videographers to use single-chip cameras? No, many combine single-chip cameras with Super-VHS or Hi8 tape to provide very crisp video. Are you confused yet? Well, in the next section, we'll try to explain why Super-VHS and Hi8 formats have become so popular.

What about industrial cameras? This category includes broadcast-quality cameras used by TV stations. These ultra-high priced cameras need bright light to produce good video and, hence, are rarely used by videographers who shoot weddings. Perhaps they're just overkill.

So, what does this all mean? Well, don't get bogged down in this technical mumbo-jumbo. What makes this even more challenging is the fact that video technology (cameras and formats) changes so quickly. The key is to look at the final product—the camera skills of the videographer are just as crucial as the type of equipment he or she uses.

4 **The Videotape** "Will a video shot on a digital camera work on our regular VCR?" "Can I get my wedding video on DVD?"

One key point to remember: no matter what type of camera your videographer uses (Super VHS, Hi-8, Digital), in most cases he or she will simply end up giving you a plain VHS tape. That's because videographers realize most folks have plain old VRC's at home. Yes, we realize all this video jargon may seem like a techno-torture test. But bare with us as we try to make sense of this.

The latest craze for consumer electronics is DVD players. Videographers have realized this too and are now beginning to offer DVD's as an option for wedding videos.

DVD's have two key advantages over plain old videotape: first they are more "archival" than videotape, which can be susceptible to heat, dust and other problems. Theoretically, DVD's might be better to preserve a video than tape. Another advantage: sharper pictures. As anyone who's watched a movie on DVD versus videotape, DVD's offer much better picture quality (as well as the ability to search, skip forward and other nifty features).

Of course, there are some problems with DVD's. We'll discuss those later in this chapter in the Pitfalls section. And what if your videographer doesn't offer DVD's but you just have to have that? Several companies will do the transfer from videotape for you, albeit at a steep price. We found one, Dallas Digital Transfer (214) 336-6292 (web: www.dallasdigitaltransfer.com), who offers to transfer one hour of video tape to DVD and provide three copies for $389.

5 **Camera Angle** *"Some sample videos I've viewed show the bride and groom only from the back or from strange angles in the church. Is there any way I can avoid such problems?"*

Some of the responsibility for these strange angles and shots belongs to the church or synagogue you choose. Many don't allow the videographer to move once the bride begins her walk down the aisle. They may also assign the cameraperson to a particular part of the sanctuary (like the back balcony). This is why it is important to check with the policies of your ceremony site. Also, you can ask the clergy if your

Wedding Videos: the good, the bad and the ugly

View a few wedding videos and you'll see quality that's all over the board. Yes, there are some wedding videographers who do truly stunning work. And, there are others that should stick to taping high school choir performances. After viewing literally hundreds of wedding videos, here are some points that separate the good from the bad:

♥ **GOOD:** The best videos have a mix of close-ups and far-away shots. You'll see plenty of TV-style production tricks, including shots that "link" one scene to another. The best videographers also bring a small ladder to make sure their shots aren't blocked by the back of guests' heads.

♥ **BAD:** Jerky movements and too-fast pans are signs that a videographer who needs to go back to video school. We've also seen bad videos where the video and audio portions were not in sync (they looked like the dialogue in a bad Kung-Fu movie). Another bad wedding video sign: the cameras in a multi-camera shoot are all focused on the same image.

videographer can get a better view (they might respond more to a bride and groom's request than that of the cameraperson).

It is crucial to have your videographer visit the ceremony site before the wedding (even attending the rehearsal) to see where he or she will be setting up. This advanced preparation may help avoid those camera angle problems. Be aware that some videographers will scout out the ceremony site for free—others charge a fee.

Many videographers today offer multi-camera shoots with two or even three cameras at the ceremony. So does that mean you have to pay three camerapeople to shoot your wedding? Not always. Some of these cameras may be remote-controlled from the back of the church. The different views are edited together on the final tape to provide a much more interesting video than single-camera coverage.

Getting Started: How Far in Advance?

As with photographers, good professional videographers can book months ahead of the date. Popular summer months are often spoken for by January or February in many major metropolitan areas. In New York City, videographers are commonly booked up to two years in advance! We recommend you hire your videographer six to nine months before the wedding (as soon as or even before you book a photographer).

Step-by-step Shopping Strategies

♥ **Step 1:** Using the sources discussed above, make appointments with two to three video companies. Ask to see a demonstration tape or a tape of a recent wedding. If you contact a studio with several associates, make sure you will be meeting with the person who will videotape your wedding. As with photographers, each videographer's style is different, so meeting the actual cameraperson is key.

♥ **Step 2:** See the sample or demo tape of each company. View more than just "highlight" tapes—ask to see complete weddings. Even better, ask if they can show you any wedding videos shot at your ceremony/reception site.

♥ **Step 3:** Check for sound quality and lighting—are there any awkward moments? Make sure you can hear the vows. This is the most important aspect of the video—isn't the exchange of vows the whole reason you are planning this wedding and reception anyway? If the lighting is extremely bright, guests may squint or turn away. You want everyone to feel comfortable so watch this aspect carefully.

♥ **Step 4:** If this is an edited tape, ask yourself if the editing is smooth and professional. Does the tape have a home-movie feel or a raw-footage quality? Or is it seamlessly edited with a smooth flow? Is the video enjoyable or boring? Decide if the special effects (if any) add to or detract from the video.

♥ **Step 5:** Make sure the personality of the cameraperson is pleasant. If you don't feel comfortable, shop for another videographer.

♥ **Step 6:** Get references from previous customers. Ask these recent brides if they were satisfied with their tapes. Did they meet their expectations? If they had to do it over again, would they choose that same company? How did the videographer deal with adverse conditions? Did they bark orders at guests or members of the wedding party? Checking references here is especially important since many video companies are still new to the business world and some lack professional track records.

♥ **Step 7:** Once you have decided on a videographer, get a signed contract. Specify the date, time, place, editing and other issues. Make sure they note any preferences too: will there be any interviews, for example.

♥ **Step 8:** Meet with your videographer again closer to the wedding date to discuss any special people you'd like on your tape. It may even be a good idea to draw up a list of names. Also go over the sequence of events and talk about any changes or additions.

Questions to Ask a Videographer

1 **Will you attend the rehearsal? Are you familiar with my ceremony/reception site?** These are critical questions since the videographer must determine the best angle, lighting options and sound needs for each site. Many ceremony sites have specific rules about where the videographer can set up. Some sites may also present sound or lighting challenges—the more familiar he or she is with the site, the better.

2 **Exactly what will the final product look like?** Find out how long the tape will be and what type of editing or graphics will be done. Often we've seen demo tapes with music synced to the action, fancy script graphics and even dissolves or other effects. Then we've been informed that all those options are extra on top of the package price. Watch out for these tactics.

3 **Who exactly will be shooting my video?** Again, remember that some companies, especially in busy summer months, may send out

unskilled amateurs (or stringers) to some of their weddings. Meet the actual videographer and see their work before booking. Unfortunately, some studios only assign their best camerapeople to the highest-priced packages.

4 **Are there any photographers in town that you have had difficulty working with?** The fit between photographer and videographer is critical—if they don't work together as a team, the scene may get ugly. Unfortunately, it may be difficult to get a truthful answer here since many videographers don't want to offend you or bad-mouth local photographers.

5 **Explain your general wedding shooting schedule.** This way you can find out what they do before the ceremony, whether they do interviews or not and how they expect the evening to run.

6 **Will I get the master tape and how many copies come with the package?** The master tape is the original tape. Some videographers keep this and give you copies just as photographers keep your negatives. If you want the master, shop for a videographer with a different policy. As for tape copies, they are usually extra. Plan ahead for this additional expense. The cost per copy could range from $20 to $80—or more. One note on master tapes: as technology evolves that lets consumers record their own DVD's, we expect more videographers will be keeping their masters to avoid unauthorized duplication of their work. In the past, if you copied a master onto another VHS, there was a noticeable decline in quality. With DVD's, that doesn't happen—and that fear will drive some videographers to drop master tape sales.

7 **Do you have back-up equipment? Do you edit your own work? Do you offer a guarantee?** Back-up equipment is a critical issue—the best videographers have back-up equipment with them at the ceremony/reception sites, not in a van or office across town. Even if it takes just a few minutes to run out to a vehicle, you can miss important moments. Another point to ask about: what happens if the videographer gets sick? Do they have a substitute cameraperson who can cover the event?

8 **Will you take a little time to educate me about video production?** This is a trick question suggested to us by Bill Kronemyer, a New Jersey videographer. Bill told us you're not looking for a technical lecture but insights into the videographer's philosophy. The videographer should acknowledge that each wedding is different—and be honest about the shortcomings of his or her work. "Beware of the person who doesn't or can't explain things to you. Or one who thinks he's the greatest on earth. Deep down, he is probably insecure. Picking a down-to-earth 'realist' is often a better bet than a 'braggart.'"

9 **Tell me about a wedding where something went wrong. How did you handle it?** This is a great question for all wedding merchants, not just the videographer. The wrong answer: "nothing bad has ever happened on a wedding shoot." Come on—weddings are attended by human beings who make mistakes. Professionals roll with the punches and still produce an excellent product. One common area for problems: the photographer. See the box below for more info on this perennial problem.

10 **When will my video be ready for pick-up?** Most professional videographers offer some kind of post-editing for their video packages. Even though digital cameras and editing equipment makes this process go quicker, it still takes a LONG time to get your final tape. The average is about eight to 12 weeks after your wedding! One videographer we interviewed takes six MONTHS to deliver the final tape. Be sure to ask so you are not surprised.

Top Money-saving Secrets

1 **Use a professional to tape the ceremony only.** Many professional videographers offer discounted "ceremony-only" packages costing anywhere from 40% to 60% less than complete packages (roughly $250 to $500). For the

---

Photographers and Videographers: The Balkans of Bridal?

Sometimes videographers and photographers behave like the Hatfields and the McCoys—and it usually is the bride and groom that suffer.

To understand why these so-called professionals sometimes act like guests on Jerry Springer, it is important to understand the roots of this feud. For years, the only person who documented a wedding was the photographer. This cushy role insured a steady stream of clients and profits. During the 1970's, video came on the scene and things haven't been the same since.

Some photographers view video as a major threat to their livelihood. Despite the fact that most weddings today are *both* videotaped and photographed, this feeling still dominates the photography profession. Photographer paranoia kicked into even higher gear in recent years when video went "digital" and videographers began talking about selling "digital stills" as prints to their customers. Most videographers and photographers realize the day when just one professional takes both digital video and still pictures is not far away. And that means "someone" is going to lose out on the lucrative bridal "memories" market.

reception, consider asking friends and relatives to bring their cameras to shoot footage. Note: beware that some studios use their least-experienced videographer to shoot the "ceremony-only" packages. Confirm who will be your videographer and view their work before booking. Other studios may refuse to do ceremony-only bookings unless they aren't booked for a full wedding that day.

2 **Have a friend tape your wedding.** Only as a last resort! If you choose to go this route, make sure your friend or relative has a tripod (to avoid those wobbly shots) and plenty of extra batteries. Frankly, this is not our first choice to saving money with wedding video. First, your "friend" who has to shoot the wedding will be stuck behind a camera for most of the day, missing out on all the fun. And while digital video cameras have improved the quality of home-made wedding videos in recent years, it still takes skill and effort to shoot a great video. Most amateurs simply don't have the camera skills.

3 **Use iMovie.** If you go the do-it-yourself route, see if a friend has a newer iMac DV. These computers come with Apple's ingenious iMovie software (it's free) that lets you whip up professional-looking videos (with special effects, editing, music and titles) in just minutes.

Hence, the bridal vendor version of Celebrity Death Match. Photographers complain that videographers interfere with their ability to capture the event on film—all the lights, boom mics and other video apparatus make photographers cringe. A typical battleground is the formal "posed" pictures that are taken of the bride and groom before the wedding. These are big money-makers for the photographer and they jealously guard this turf.

Some photographers go as far as trying to ban videographers from taking video of the formal posed picture sessions; they argue (somewhat unconvincingly) that their unique posings of the bride are their copyrighted images.

Videographers, for their part, claim that photographers try to sabotage their video by blocking shots and other sleazy tricks.

So, what's a bride and groom to do? First, make sure you tell the photographer you plan to have the wedding videotaped. If they turn red and start spouting obscenities, then it might be time to find a different photographer. And be careful to look through a photographer's contract carefully to make sure there are no restrictions on what can be videotaped. Photographers should learn to co-exist with videographers, for the sake of everyone's sanity.

4 Negotiate lower rates for less-popular wedding days/ months. It never hurts to ask.

5 Ask the videographer if they will do a scaled-back package for less money. Fewer bells and whistles (post-editing, special effects) mean less time for the videographer. Ask them if they can work out a "special package" that meets your budget.

6 Request a volume-discount for tape copies. If you need several copies, the video company should be able to offer you a volume discount off their normal prices.

7 Use multi-camera coverage only at the ceremony. While it's a nice luxury to have two or three cameras to cover the wedding ceremony, it may be overkill at the reception.

8 Use your company's video or photo department. Some large corporations have in-house photo or video departments. This can be a good money-saving strategy—some of these same experienced camerapeople free-lance on the weekends at much lower rates than you'd find in the bridal market.

9 Check the next town over. Not surprisingly, we found the most expensive videographers were the ones in big cities. By contrast, video companies in smaller towns or outlying suburbs often charge 20% to 40% less. And most videographers are willing to travel 50 to 100 miles one way to a wedding without an extra charge. So try to look at the next town over to save. The only trade-off: videographers in smaller towns usually offer fewer perks and choices for fancy video effects. But if that doesn't matter to you, go for the savings.

10 Consider a weekend warrior. About half of all wedding videographers are part-timers, so called "weekend warriors." Since wedding videos aren't their full-time job, they often charge less than their full-time competitors. Are these videographers any less professional? Nope, weekend warriors can produce just as professional a tape as full-timers. Just check their references carefully and view several demo tapes of actual weddings to make sure the part-timer is up to the job.

Biggest Myths About Videography

MYTH #1 *"We had a friend videotape our wedding. The tape was just OK—there were several parts that are out of focus and shaky. Our friend said we could just get that fixed."*

Don't count on it. You just can't "fix" a bad video that's blurry or missing audio parts. The best you can do is cut out the bad parts and try to piece it together. We've heard quite a few horror stories from couples who had a well-meaning friend or relative tape their wedding, only to end up with a disaster.

MYTH #2 *"I watched my friend's wedding video and found myself straining to hear the couple say their vows. We're writing our own vows and we really want to be able to hear what we say to one another on our video. Is it true that it's impossible to get clear sound on a video?"*

Sound quality depends heavily on the type of microphone. We recommend the use of a high-band wireless microphone attached to the groom's lapel. This type of microphone will overcome the disadvantages discussed earlier that come with boom microphones and hard-wired mics. If you can't find anyone with a wireless high-band microphone, listen carefully to the sound quality on sample tapes and decide who offers the best sound.

Some videographers today use multiple microphones to capture audio at the ceremony. The best companies even mix the audio "live" at the site, adjusting the volume level during the ceremony to make sure the best possible tape is made.

MYTH #3 *"I saw one sample tape that had interviews of the guests on it. I thought the interviews were kind of embarrassing and the guests seemed uncomfortable. Do I have to have interviews on my tape?"*

The answer is an obvious "no." We've seen several tapes where a good friend had too much to drink and related a sick joke. In another case, a guest suddenly had a microphone shoved into her face and made a few boring comments that didn't need to be saved for posterity.

Well this doesn't have to happen in your video. First, if you don't want any interviews, be specific with the videographer—especially if he or she has these segments on sample tapes. But if you do want interviews, choose a package that will allow you to edit out any embarrassing comments made by your guests. And don't forget to specify what kind of interviews you want. One couple we talked to asked their videographer to only interview relatives. Another couple specified interviews of only guests who really wanted to speak on the tape. These precautions should help you avoid the "video from hell."

Helpful Hints

1 Choose a package with enough time to cover the event. A four to six hour package should provide enough time to capture a typical wedding (allow more time for sit-down dinners or receiving lines). If you think your reception will go over, ask about overtime availability and charges. Some packages end when the cake is cut while others run to the reception's end. Ask when overtime kicks in—if the cake is cut an hour late? What if the bride gets to the church 45 minutes late? Confirming the exact conditions that lead to overtime charges is important.

2 Many uncontrollable factors can affect the quality of your video. For example, church P.A. systems can interfere with low-band wireless microphones. Another problem may be caused by your officiant or site coordinator. At one wedding we attended, the priest requested the videographer stand in a certain spot. The videographer thought she would have a good view of the couple's faces. However, the priest then decided to hold the entire ceremony with the couple facing the congregation. This left the videographer taping their backs for the entire wedding!

We feel its best to try to keep a sense of humor about these uncontrollable events. Having the videographer attend the rehearsal should also cut down on surprises.

Pitfalls to Avoid

PITFALL #1 DVD PROBLEMS

"I purchased a DVD copy of my wedding video, only to find it would NOT work in my DVD player! What went wrong?

Yes, you've just experienced the bleeding edge of technology—incompatible DVD formats. While the technical discussion of why this happens is beyond the scope of this book, brides and grooms should realize that DVD technology is very young and evolving. As of yet, there is no one standard for recording DVD's, hence the possibility that the DVD your videographer whips out may not work on your DVD player. A word to the wise: get the videographer's promise in writing that his DVD will work with your player.

PITFALL #2 "DIRECTOR'S DISEASE"

"I was a bridesmaid in a friend's wedding recently and I was very shocked at the behavior of the videographer. He kept ordering everyone around, telling us what to do. Is there a way to avoid this problem at my own wedding?"

Occasionally, we've run into an inexperienced wedding videographer who suffers from that strange malady known as "director's disease." These camerapeople tend to expect weddings and receptions to conform to some sort of script for an all-star movie production. Instead of simply capturing the day as it happens, they try to direct the actors (bride and groom) in a performance (the wedding).

In many ways, however, a wedding is a videographer's nightmare—unscripted and unrehearsed, things often happen spontaneously. Experienced videographers will have discovered this fact and (hopefully) will adapt to each fun, yet frantic event on your wedding day. If you check references carefully and ask former brides about this aspect, you can avoid a videographer infected with "director's disease."

Pitfall #3 Missing key events
"One of my friends complained that her wedding video was missing one of the events of the evening she thought was most important: her brother giving the toast. I don't want anything to be missed at my wedding. How can I prevent this?"

The bouquet toss, garter throw, toast and cake cutting among other things, are of paramount importance to most brides and grooms. Your videographer should at least be around for these events at your wedding. Amateurs and unseasoned professionals have been known to miss them—be sure to check with references.

To be fair, we should note a videographer does not typically tape EVERY moment of your wedding and reception. Some videographers even leave before the event is over.

When you hire a professional, you should also meet with him or her prior to the wedding to discuss those things you want in your video. Be specific and have him write your preferences down. Any key events you want covered should be clearly detailed in writing. Also bring him a list of important people you want in your video. Have a copy of this list with you at the wedding.

Pitfall #4 Big screen TVs.
"My wedding video doesn't look very good on my parent's big-screen TV. It looked fine on our 19" TV—what's the problem?"

The problem: some big screen TV's use a projection process to get the picture onto the screen. Unfortunately, this process causes a video's resolution to suffer. In other words, most videos (including movies) may look fuzzy on a big-screen TV. Don't blame the videographer for this problem!

Pitfall #5 Deceptive demo tapes.

"We saw this video company at a bridal show. They were playing a demo tape that looked great. When we asked them where it was shot, however, they sheepishly told us it wasn't really their work. What gives?"

Some franchised video companies will give their new franchisees generic demo tapes to help drum up business (since the fledgling company may not have examples of their own work yet). Confirm the tape you are seeing is actually their work. While every new videographer has to start somewhere, we'd recommend he not learn the ropes at your wedding.

Pitfall #6 Nickel and dime charges

"One video company in my area advertises a super-low price for wedding coverage. When I met with them, however, there were several 'additional charges' that inflated the package price."

We've heard this complaint from several of our readers. In Wisconsin, for example, we discovered a video company that charges extra for each microphone ($50 a pop). And, wouldn't you guess it, the videographer recommends *lots* of microphones. Other additional charges could include exorbitant fees for editing, music, graphics, special effects and tape copies. The best tip to avoid this is to get "apples to apples" bids from several companies. Don't be fooled by super-low prices that seem too good to be true.

Pitfall #7 Overtime surprise

"At our wedding, the slow caterers forced our videographer into 'overtime.' Unfortunately, he didn't inform us about this until 30 minutes into overtime—and then he said we couldn't get any of the footage after his time expired unless we coughed up another $100!"

Yes, overtime can be a thorny issue. While that four-hour package seems adequate, unforeseen events (a pokey photographer, a slow caterer) can make you run out of time in a hurry.

Our advice: find out what the overtime charges would be *in advance*. Get in writing that you will be notified 15 minutes BEFORE overtime will begin, so you can make a decision on whether to go forward or not. While we don't expect you to keep a constant eye on your watch during your wedding, it would be smart for a friend or relative to help make sure the photographer or videographer's clock isn't about to expire.

Some sleazy videographers (and photographers) make a bad situation worse by using hard-ball tactics to sell more overtime. Like in the above example, some will shoot for an extra 30, 40 or 50 minutes beyond the contracted period of time—and then refuse to give you the video (or pictures) for that time UNLESS you cough up the extra cash.

We say overtime issues are a two-way street. If the videographer has a strict policy on overtime, inform them the time they spend eating dinner (a meal you probably will pay for) is NOT on the clock. In fact, any significant time spent not shooting (such as the time it takes to drive from the ceremony to the reception) should not be counted toward your package limit.

Trends

♥ **WEB CASTING.** Did your grandmother miss the wedding? Soon your videographer will be able to upload a highlights montage to the 'net so your grandmother can watch the streaming video on her PC. Okay, maybe the word "soon" should be replaced with "some day." Before streaming video becomes a reality, broadband access to the 'net must reach most homes in the US (now it's in just a small fraction). But it might not be long before you can share your wedding video with others.

♥ **VIDEO "PRINTS."** As more videographers use digital video cameras, we are seeing an increase in companies selling video stills. No, they aren't as sharp as the photographer's prints, but the stills may be a good option if the photographer missed a key shot. Most videographers are selling them for $10 to $15 for a 5x5.

♥ **TV THEME OPENINGS.** One Toronto videographer produces elaborate TV-style openings for his wedding videos. Sample: the bride, groom and bridal party clown around in a park during a pre-wedding shoot that's edited to look like the opening for "Friends." Or the "Brady Bunch." Another videographer uses a GroomCam—a small camera the groom carries around to catch various shots, which are edited into the videographer's footage. And still another videographer uses a "steadi-cam" for fluid movement shots like those in movies. Want to spice up those guest interviews? One video company we met uses "Chroma Key" technology (like TV weathercasts) to project footage of the wedding behind guests as they talk about the bride and groom.

♥ **RETROSPECTIVE PACKAGES.** Here's an interesting twist on wedding video: why not do a post-wedding interview where you reminisce about the wedding? Take that footage and cut-in "flashback" scenes of the wedding and you've got the "retrospective," a new video add-on that some videographers are selling. The price: $850 to $1500—that's *in addition* to the regular wedding video package. The retrospective interview is usually done the morning after the wedding (when memories are fresh) or after the honeymoon.

♥ **DIGITAL EDITING.** Instead of editing on analog tape, cutting-edge videographers now edit tapes digitally on high-end computer workstations. This speeds the process and gives the videographer more flexibility in editing images. Another trend: better mic technology. New wireless mics have less interference problems and new "plug-on transmitters" can turn any mike into a wireless mic. These can be hidden in podiums to capture the ceremony vows or in the DJ equipment to capture the night's audio.

♥ **SPLASHIER GRAPHICS.** These new and constantly improving techniques make tapes less like home movies and more like Hollywood productions. Some unique additions we've noticed include dissolves and fades and even a technique called posterization (which freezes the picture and "colorizes" it). Adding still photos of your childhood at the tape's beginning and snapshots of your honeymoon at the end provides a complete video "album" feel to your tape. Of course, all these goodies tend to push up the price of wedding videos.

♥ **MULTI-CAMERA SHOOTS.** More and more videographers are using multi-camera shoots to capture the ceremony. Thanks to remote controlled cameras, however, this doesn't mean you have to have multiple camerapeople, which will inflate the final tab.

♥ **COMBINATION PHOTO/VIDEO STUDIOS.** Some photography studios have the attitude "if you can't beat 'em, join 'em" when it comes to video—many are adding "video divisions." Whether this involves sub-contracting out to another video company or actually having a "staff videographer," photographers have seized on the video trend as a lucrative side-line. Of course, just because the studio offers excellent photography doesn't mean they know beans about video. Be skeptical. Shop for each service as if they were separate companies.

♥ **FOILING TAPE PIRATES.** In the last few years, videographers have started using new technology to prevent couples from copying their wedding tapes at home. How? Video companies can encrypt their videos with a signal that scrambles the video when you try to copy it, similar to the technology that's used on rental movies to foil tape pirates.

We notice quite a bit of hypocrisy on this issue, however. Videographers who jealously guard *their* copyright are often the same folks who'll use pop songs as background music on their tapes. And trust us, they are not paying a royalty to Elton John or any other artist for their copywritten compositions. We've even seen videographers who brazenly use snippets of pirated Disney animated movies on their wedding tapes.

Chapter 12

ENTERTAINMENT

From harpists to dance bands to DJ's, choosing music for your wedding and reception can be challenging. In this chapter, you'll learn inge-nious ways to find your city's best musicians. We'll also take an in-depth look at the controversy between bands and disc jockeys (no, it has nothing to do with Napster) as reception entertainment.

What Are You Buying?

♥ CEREMONY MUSIC. From royal weddings to simple civil ceremonies, music has been an integral part of weddings for thou-sands of years. However, the role music plays varies from religion to religion. The main issue is the differ-ence between liturgical and secular music. Basically, liturgical music fea-tures sacred words from the bible, while secular music does not. Policies about what is and what is not appro-priate will vary from site to site.

Nevertheless, most churches have a staff organist or music coordinator who will help you with selections. Organists charge a fee based on the amount of time needed to rehearse, learn new pieces, etc. Other musicians (such as soloists, pianists or harpists) may also be employed for the ceremony. Ceremony music can generally be broken down into three categories:

1 The Prelude. Typically 20 to 40 minutes prior to the ceremony, prelude music sets the mood. Even if you don't have specific pieces in mind for the prelude, you can tell the organist/musicians your preferences for happy, upbeat music or perhaps more somber, quiet pieces. Sometimes an eclectic mix of different tempos and musical styles is a nice compromise.

2 Processional/Recessional. Processional music heralds the arrival of the bridesmaids and, later, the bride to the wedding ceremony. At the end of the ceremony, recessional music is basically the music everyone walks out to. Typically, the slower processional has a more regal and majestic feel than the quicker-paced recessional music. Sometimes, different musical selections are played for the entrances of the bridesmaids and the bride. Or the same piece can be played at a different tempo as the bride enters the ceremony site.

3 Music during the ceremony. Soloists or the congregation's choir are often used during this part of the ceremony.

Average total costs: Most ceremony musicians charge $50 to $150 per musician per hour. Some may have two to three hour minimums. When you hire ceremony musicians, the only thing you may need to supply is sheet music for unfamiliar pieces. If you're having a string quartet, don't forget to provide chairs without arms so they can bow!

♥ **Reception Music.** Ah, now the party starts! Whether you plan to have only soft background music for listening or a raucous rock and roll bash, there are several aspects to what you're buying. For listening music, a harpist, string quartet or guitarist may do double duty (playing at both your wedding and reception). If dancing is preferred, you have two basic choices:

1 Bands. When you hire a live band to play at your reception, you are contracting for a particular set of musicians to play a specified period of time. Most bands require periodic breaks throughout the evening and union rules may mandate break times. Bands provide everything (from instruments to the amplification system), but your reception site may need to provide a piano. Sometimes bands throw in a free hour of light cocktail music while guests dine. A specific repertoire of music is often implied in the contract—the best reception bands play a wide variety of music to please everyone's preferences.

So how much does a band cost? The price for four hours on a Saturday night can range from $500 to $5000. The key variables are the number of musicians and the popularity of the band. The majority of four-piece bands in major metropolitan cities charge $750 to $2000 for a four-hour reception (the lower figure is for smaller metro areas; the bigger number for the largest cities). Want a seven-piece orchestra? Or a locally famous club band? Expect to shell out $3000 to $5000 . . . or more. Deposits for a band can range from nothing (which is rare) to one-third down.

2 **Disc Jockeys.** When you contract with a DJ, you basically get one DJ (plus, perhaps, an assistant), an entire sound system and a wide variety of music on CD's, albums or tapes. Some DJs will add specialized lighting (colored spots that pulse to the music, for example) for an extra charge. Also extra may be rare or unusual song requests (such as ethnic music). A few pricey DJs may offer karaoke.

DJs are much less expensive than bands since, quite simply, DJs require less manpower. The average price for a professional DJ for four hours on a Saturday night can range from $300 to $1000. Most DJs in metropolitan areas charge $400 to $600 for a typical reception. Less experienced DJs may charge less than $400, while in-demand club or radio DJs command higher fees than average. Of course, always add to those costs for high-price areas like New York City. One bride there said DJ's in Manhattan are going for $500 to $1300 for five to six hours of music. Deposits roughly average $100.

Average total costs: Overall, couples spend about $1000 on the average for music at the ceremony and reception. If you live a big metro area like New York or LA, you can double or triple that figure. What inflates entertainment costs in big cities are minimums. One Chicago bride told us bands there often have an eight-person minimum—that is, the bandleader insists on having eight musicians on stage. That inflates costs. The Chicago bride told us prices there are $3500 to $6500 for popular wedding bands.

Sources to Find a Good Entertainer

Every major metropolitan area probably has a plethora of good wedding entertainers. The only problem is finding them. Ceremony musicians, reception bands and DJs typically keep a very low profile, choosing to work by word-of-mouth referral. Many of the most successful bands don't advertise their services. So how can you find these people?

♥ CEREMONY/RECEPTION SITE COORDINATORS. For ceremony music, the wedding coordinator at your ceremony site may be able to suggest a few names of harpists, soloists, trumpeters, etc. Music directors are also another source since they have worked in close contact with local musicians. For reception music, the catering manager at your site will undoubtedly have heard a wide variety of bands and DJs. Ask who really kept the crowd hopping. See the pitfalls section later in this chapter for a disadvantage to using this source.

♥ **INDEPENDENT CATERERS.** If you are having your reception at a site where you are bringing in a caterer, you may ask that caterer for entertainment suggestions. They usually can provide a referral to several entertainers.

♥ **WEDDING ANNOUNCEMENTS IN THE LOCAL PAPER.** Here's a sneaky way of finding good entertainers. Some local newspapers print wedding announcements that often list the names of the musicians that played at the ceremony or reception. Call the ceremony or reception site to find out how to contact the musicians.

♥ **MUSIC SCHOOLS AT LOCAL UNIVERSITIES/COLLEGES.** Many students who are talented musicians pick up extra bucks by performing at weddings and receptions. A nice plus: most are more affordable than "professional" musicians. Be sure to get a contract from them, however. Also make sure the student will be dressed appropriately.

♥ **MUNICIPAL SYMPHONY ORGANIZATIONS.** Most symphony musicians moonlight by playing at weddings and receptions. Call your local symphony for any leads.

♥ **ASSOCIATIONS.** Looking for a DJ? Call the American Disc Jockey Association (301) 705-5150 (web: www.adja.org) for a local referral.

♥ **THE UNION DIRECTORY OF LOCAL MUSICIANS.** Most cities have musicians' guilds or unions that publish a directory of members. If you know a musician who is a member, this directory may be a good source. However, in some parts of the country (like California), musicians that specialize in weddings are often not members of the local union.

♥ **AGENTS.** Last but not least, many bands and some DJs are booked through agents. Larger agents may book a wide variety of entertainers that specialize in weddings and receptions. In some cities dominated by unions, agents may be the only way to book a band. There are several advantages and disadvantages to using agents, which we will discuss later in this chapter in the spotlight "Secret Agent Man: Helping Hand or Scum of the Earth?"

Brides in Cyberspace: What's on the Web?

The Internet is awash in wedding and reception music info—here's a look at some of the best sites to search:

♥ PRODJ (www.prodj.com) has a great search engine to find a local DJ. You pop in the city or state and it will pull up DJ names. We searched for Cincinnati and found an amazing 22 prospects, complete with a paragraph description of each company, contact info and email link. ProDJ also has articles on selecting a DJ, a list of the Top 25 first dance songs and links to other related web sites. (See Figure 1 below)

♥ WEDDING TIPS (weddingtips.com/wtfavori.html) this site tracks the current top 30 "first dance" songs played at weddings and provides other music suggestions as well.

♥ THE CEREMONY MUSIC RESOURCE page (www.castle.net/~energize/CMRP/) contains song lists—and on-line song files you can download to hear snippets of the music! CD resources and links to other wedding music web sites round out this helpful site.

Figure 1: ProDJ.com's web site has extensive DJ listings. This search for Houston turned up 68 DJ's!

Welcome to ProDJ.com Event Planning

Address: http://www.prodj.com/ep/index.html

Event Planning
DJ Search   Advice   Wedding Assistant   Other Sites

Visit ProDJ.com's
Event Planning Advice Area

DJ Briefs Houston, Texas

Full Interactive Brochures
(Click On Their Names To See Their Sites)

Sound Minded Entertainment - Houston/Austin, TX

Mix Wiz DJ Association - Houston, TX

DJ Connection - Houston, TX

Mini Pages
(Click On Their Names To See Their Sites)

Avery Entertainment - Houston and SE Texas

Your DJ - Houston, TX

Standard Listings

WWWA Productions Mobile DJ Service - Houston, TX - Providing the best overall value in the Houston area. Standard package includes high tech lighting, sound, and an enormous music library. Collection includes Top 40, Dance/Club, Trash Disco, 80's,Good Time Oldies, and some country favorites. Been in the business for over 7 years. All occasions (Weddings, corporate parties, college parties). Requests are always welcomed. Will beat any price with identical setup. Call (713) 266-4722 or e-mail to john_chen@bigfoot.com

♥ THE ULTIMATE WEDDING SONG LIBRARY (www.ultimatewedding.com/songs/) has over 400 selections to help you plan your reception's playlist. You can search for first dance songs for the bride and groom, father and daughter, mother and son, etc. The cool part: Some of the music selections have sound clips you can listen to.

Getting Started: How Far in Advance?

Don't leave the music for your wedding and reception to the last minute. For ceremony music, you must give the organist time to learn and practice a special request. Meeting with the organist a month or two in advance will smooth the process.

For reception music, many of the best bands and DJs book up months in advance. In general, three to six months is enough time to book an entertainer in smaller towns and for "off-peak" wedding months. In the largest metropolitan areas, popular dates (the summer months and December) book up anywhere from six to twelve months ahead.

So what if you only have two months left to plan? Don't panic. You may get lucky and find a good band or DJ with an open date. It just may take a little more legwork.

Step-by-step Shopping Strategies

Ceremony Music

♥ **Step 1:** Find out your ceremony site's policy about wedding music. Realize that houses of worship often have varying policies about what is considered "acceptable" wedding music. For example, music like the "Wedding March" is not allowed at some sites because it's deemed too secular.

♥ **Step 2:** Meet with the music director of your ceremony site several weeks before your wedding. If you need to bring in musicians, use our sources to find three good candidates. Interview the musicians and discuss your ideas for the ceremony music.

♥ **Step 3:** Ask to hear samples of various selections. If you're getting married at a church, ask the music director if you can attend a wedding ceremony. Listen to how certain pieces sound on the organ or other instruments.

♥ **Step 4:** If you hire outside musicians, get a written contract specifying the date, time, place and selections of music. Find out if the musicians/organist will come to the rehearsal (and if there is any fee for this).

Reception Music

♥ Step 1: As soon as you have your wedding date confirmed, start your search for an entertainer. Decide what type of music fits your reception. Some important considerations include:

A. The time of day of your reception—For example, in the afternoon, few people feel like putting on their dancing shoes. Perhaps a good choice here would be a guitarist to play soft background music. But, hey, it's your reception so choose the music you want.

B. The ages of the guests—You can't please everyone but selecting a band/DJ that plays a wide variety of music will help keep everyone dancing.

C. The size of the reception—Typically, the "reception music axiom" says the larger the crowd, the bigger the band you need to keep the event hopping. In reality, a four or five-piece band can play a reception of 500 guests as easily as 200 guests. Do what your budget allows and don't get talked into a certain size band because you have X number of guests. For DJs, the size of the crowd may determine whether extra speakers/amplification are needed.

♥ Step 2: After deciding on the type of music you want, identify three good bands/DJs using our sources list. Call each of them on the phone and ask the questions we outline below. Ask to see them perform at an upcoming reception. Is it tacky to ask a band/DJ to visit them at someone's else's wedding. We don't think so. See the following box pm the next page for more on this topic.

♥ Step 3: When you visit the reception, don't go during dinnertime. Instead plan to stop in later in the evening around 10:30 when the dancing gets going full swing (ask the band or DJ for a suggested time to visit). Look for three key factors:

A. Is the band/DJ correctly reading the crowd? In other words, are they playing the right music for the guests at the wedding? Is anyone dancing? Are they ignoring one generation?

B. How much talking does the band leader/DJ do? Is this amount of chatter helping or hurting the reception? Do you like their announcing style?

C.   Is the band/DJ professional? Are they dressed appropriately? Is the volume at a good level or a deafening roar? Is the entertainer varying the tempo, mixing fast and slow selections?

♥ **Step 4:** After you preview as many entertainers as time allows, select the band/DJ you want. Get a written contract that includes the specific date, hours and place as well as the price and overtime charges. Also get the names of the exact musicians who will be there and the instruments they will be playing. If necessary, specify what dress you want the band members/DJ to wear. Finally, have specific sets of music written out such as your first song, special requests, etc. You may even want to attach a song list to the contract.

♥ **Step 5:** Remember that the better you specify the music, the more likely you'll get the music you want at your reception. Don't be ambiguous here by saying you want just "rock" or "dance music." Identify specific artists and songs and then star your favorites. For some artists,

"The Tackiest Wedding Book I've Read So Far!"

That was a comment from a reader of this book posted in a review on Amazon (fortunately for our fragile egos, most of the rest of the reviews on Amazon are better than that). What was this person so upset about? Our suggestion that you ask the band or DJ to see them perform at another wedding before booking. "Think about it," the reader wrote "how would you feel if a complete stranger showed up at your wedding reception to review the band/DJ you were paying to entertain you? As far as I'm concerned, the band/DJ can do their advertising on their own time!"

Well, let's take a look at this issue. First, we suggest the entertainer get permission of the bride and groom BEFORE a prospective client visits their reception. Second, if you do visit someone else's wedding, use some common sense. Dress appropriately and stand in the back of the hall. No eating or drinking, of course. You are there to just observe the band or DJ for a short time.

And, there is a quid pro quo here. If you visit a reception to check out a band, the same band might ask permission for another couple to do the same at your wedding—and we don't see any problem with that, of course.

Yes, there are some bands and DJ's who refuse to let couples see them perform before booking. We think that is the bigger concern—we wonder what they are trying to hide.

specifying a certain time period may be helpful (do you want old Sting or more current Sting songs?). Don't forget to clearly mark the song you want for a first dance.

♥ **Step 6:** Meet with the bandleader or DJ a couple of weeks before the wedding to go over the evening's schedule and any last minute details. Meet them at the site if they're unfamiliar with it to gauge any needs or problems.

Questions to Ask an Entertainer

Ceremony Music

1 What is the ceremony site's policy on wedding music? Does the church/synagogue have staff musicians or soloists? What is the fee? Don't assume anything is free.

2 **Does the church have any restrictions on the music I can have at my ceremony?** This is a particularly sticky area since some sites may have numerous restrictions on what is deemed "acceptable."

3 **Do staff musicians require extra rehearsals if I bring in outside musicians too?** Will there be an extra charge for rehearsals?

4 **Who exactly will be performing at my ceremony?** Especially when you hire outside musicians, confirm the exact performers who will be at your wedding.

5 **How familiar are you with my ceremony site?** Obviously this question is only for outside musicians. Inform them of any restrictions the site has on music. A pre-wedding meeting at the site might be a good idea in case there are any logistical questions (electricity, amplification, etc.)

Reception Entertainment:

1 **Who exactly will be performing at my wedding?** Be very careful here. The biggest pitfall couples encounter with bands/DJs is hiring one set of entertainers and getting another set at your wedding. See the Pitfalls section later in this chapter for strategies to overcome this problem.

2 **For disc jockeys, do you have professional equipment?** Novice DJs are most likely to use home stereo equipment from Radio Shack. While that's nice for a living room, it may not work in a large reception site. Experienced DJs have professional equipment (amplifiers,

mixers and speakers like you'd see in a club) that produces crisp sound and has enough power to fill up the largest ballroom. Another question: do you have back-up equipment? CD players can break; speakers blow out—make sure the DJ has a plan to fix any problem.

3 How do we choose the music? A simple but critical question. How open is the band leader/DJ to letting you select the evening's music? Do they want you to submit a song/artist list? Some bands/DJs will interview you and your fiancé to find out your musical preferences. If the entertainer is evasive about this question or replies that they "have a standard set they always play," you may want to look elsewhere.

4 Can we see you perform at a wedding? The best way to gauge whether a band/DJ is worth their asking price is to see them perform live. Most entertainers should let you attend an upcoming reception, with the permission of that bride and groom, of course. We've talked to some couples who feel uncomfortable attending a stranger's party. See the box earlier in this section for tips on this. If you can't see the band/DJ live, you might be able to view a video or listen to a demo tape (see the pitfalls section for drawbacks to this suggestion). Another smart idea is to call a few recently married couples for references. Ask the reference if there was anything they would have changed about the evening's entertainment.

5 How many breaks will you take? Will you provide a tape to play during those times? Instead of having silence during a band's breaks, consider playing a tape of dance music to keep the reception hopping.

6 Does the price include background music during dinner or cocktails? Some bands and DJs throw in a free hour of background music during dinner. One bandleader we met said he always throws in a free hour of cocktail music. Besides being a nice freebie for the bride and groom, this gives the entertainer an opportunity to scope out the crowd. Then, when the dancing begins, the band is better attuned to the music guests want.

Top Money-saving Secrets

1 Get married any other night than Saturday. Okay, we realize that this is not a popular alternative but few people realize bands/ DJs often give a 10% to 20% discount for Friday or Sunday weddings.

2 **Get married during the "non-peak" wedding season.**
Obviously, this varies from region to region, but generally entertainers offer discounts for particularly slow months like November and
January. Entertainers that would normally sit idle during these slow
times might be willing to knock 5% to 15% off their regular rates. Ask
and ye shall receive.

3 **Don't get married in December.** This is an absolute no-no.
Corporate and private Christmas/New Year's Eve parties push up
the demand for entertainers and (surprise!) up go the prices. One popular band we interviewed regularly charges $1450 for a typical reception.
However, dates in November and December go for $2500 and (are you
sitting down?) New Year's Eve goes for a whopping $4500.

4 **Hire a DJ instead of a band.** DJs charge an average of 60% less
than most live bands. If your parents can't stand the thought of
recorded music at your wedding, a possible compromise could involve
incorporating live music at the ceremony and then a DJ at the reception.
We'll examine the pros and cons of bands and DJs later in this chapter.

5 **If you're on a really tight budget, make tapes to play at the
reception.** Many reception sites already have a sound system. By
using your own stereo equipment and CD collection (or borrowing from
friends and relatives), you can record an evening's worth of entertainment for pennies. Besides your time, the only costs are for the tapes.
Some tech-savvy brides and grooms have taken this one step further—
they download MP3's from the 'net and burn their own CD's to use at
the reception.

6 **Select a band with fewer musicians.** Prices for bands are
often scaled to the number of musicians. Fortunately, today's
technology enables a four-piece band to sound like an orchestra (or at
least a larger band). That's because synthesizers and drum machines
can add a string section to a ballad, a horn section to a swing tune or
even Latin percussion to a salsa song. We met one pianist who uses a
computer and keyboard to simulate a several piece band for receptions.
Another band we interviewed augments a live drummer with a drum
machine to add a complex percussion track to current dance songs.
Fortunately, couples today don't have to pay for an extra percussionist
or horn section to get the same sound.

7 **If the DJ doesn't have the ethnic music you want, borrow it
from the public library.** Many public libraries have an extensive
collection of music (from polkas to Santana) all available to the public

on loan. This is a cost-effective way of getting the music you want at a price you can afford.

8 **Use a band member to play cocktail music.** As we mentioned earlier in this chapter, some bands throw this in as a freebie. Or they may offer you a cut-rate since they are already there.

9 **Consider hiring student musicians from a local university or college.** As we mentioned earlier in this chapter, many stu-

---

REAL WEDDING TIP

The Smart Way to Hire Student Musicians

Recent bride Melissa Martinez had a unique perspective to share on how to hire student musicians—she works for the music department at Rice University in Houston, Texas. Here are her thoughts: "I get at least 8-10 calls per month from brides looking for cheap entertainment. It's amazing how abusive some people can be when I say that I can't help them. I am not a booking agent, and I can't make a student take the job offered. I can only pass on information as I receive it. And some people try to take advantage of student labor. One person offered $25 for a six-piece jazz combo to play for a four-hour reception! That's total, not a piece!"

"Our jazz instructor is a professional musician whose talents are well known in Texas. Occasionally I will pass on names and numbers to him to handle, since he knows better than anyone which students can handle a job. Sometimes he offers his own services. Once again, I will get calls asking why I referred them to him, because he is too expensive, or he doesn't play the right kind of music, or he wanted a contract . . . I don't know if many music administrators have the same problems that I have, but it IS a problem. Is there any way that brides can be told not to harass us innocent working types?"

Here's Melissa's advice for brides-to-be: *"The couples who have had the best results in my experience have been the ones who come in person to the music or band department with a printed notice of what they are looking for, with all pertinent information also listed, and a number to contact or a time/location for auditions. Students see these on bulletin boards or on job postings, take them down and photocopy them, and follow through far more frequently than on phone messages."*

dents charge 20% to 30% less than so-called professional musicians. If you go this route, be careful to audition the musicians before signing a contract. For more on how to do this, check out the Real Wedding Tip on the previous page.

Biggest Myths About Entertainers

Myth #1 *"I'd never consider having a DJ at my daughter's wedding. All DJ's are unprofessional, dress sloppily and play disco music."*

We often hear this refrain from parents. Yes, its true that most DJ companies owe their entire existence to John Travolta and his infamous white suit. The good news is that most DJs have moved beyond disco and, with sophisticated equipment and a broad music repertoire, have become a credible threat to live bands. We'll discuss the pros and cons of DJs in "Canned vs. Fresh: Should you have a DJ or a band at your reception?" on the next page.

Myth #2 *"For our reception, we've decided to hire a great band that plays in several local clubs here. Is this a good choice?"*

Be careful. A great club band does not necessarily make a great wedding reception band. The main reason is variety. Playing a wedding reception requires musicians to be "jacks of all trades." Not only must they play Sarah McLachlan and Barenaked Ladies for the bride and groom but they must also satisfy Mom's and Dad's request for Elvis and Grandma's request for Glenn Miller. Switching between the Rolling Stones and Benny Goodman can be vexing for even the best bands.

While good club bands may feature competent musicians, they often play to a narrow audience. For example at one wedding, we saw one great club band that did excellent covers of 60's standards. While the bride and groom and their friends loved this music, the parents and grandparents stood in the back of the room for most of the evening.

Of course, you can't please everyone all the time. However, bands should play music for *all* the generations present at a wedding. Before you hire that great club band, make sure they have a wide repertoire encompassing many musical eras.

Helpful Hints

1 **For ceremony music, remember that sheet music is often written for instruments other than a church organ.** Hence, give the organist plenty of time to transpose and rehearse the piece so it's perfect by the wedding day.

2 **Should you feed the band/DJ?** Obviously, this is up to you. You may not want to provide a meal to each band member at a $75 per plate sit-down dinner. However, at least try to arrange with the caterer to provide them with some snacks or sandwiches. Remember that bands/DJs have to be at the reception a long time, and a well-fed entertainer performs better than one with an empty stomach (the same goes for the photographer and videographer). Of course, the flip side of this argument is that entertainers can often figure out how to pay for their own meals the other six days of the week, so why do you have to feed them at your wedding? Whatever your decision, inform the band leader/DJ about food arrangements before the wedding.

3 **Tracking down obscure ethnic music.** Unfortunately, the local record store rarely stocks ethnic music today. Hence, DJs may find it challenging to locate certain songs. A better solution may be to let them borrow your family's records or tapes. Specifically point out the songs you want.

SPOTLIGHT:

Canned vs. Fresh:
Should you have a DJ or a band at your reception?

DJs are often the Rodney Dangerfield of wedding reception music—they just don't get any respect. For example, we've read many other books on weddings that don't even mention DJs as an entertainment alternative. Instead, *Emily Post's Complete Book of Wedding Etiquette* suggests "a full orchestra" complete with a "string section for soft background music before the dancing starts." We don't know about you, but hiring a 40-piece orchestra with accompanying string section was just a teensy bit out of our wedding budget.

According to Emily Post, if you're having a small, informal wedding, "a record player provides adequate and lovely music." Nowhere are the words "disc jockey" mentioned. Even more disturbing is the venerable *Bride's Book of Etiquette* which, after talking at length about the merits of "small orchestras" at wedding receptions, says "taped, pre-recorded music is a good alternative when live music is not available." Of course, instead of mentioning DJs, the book suggests you "ask a music buff friend to pre-mix your selection on one long-playing tape."

Hey! What's going on here? Do the etiquette fanatics who write this drivel just have their collective heads in the sand? Or is there a conspiracy to deny the existence of DJs? If all these wedding experts are convinced that only live orchestras are appropriate for wedding receptions, then explain to us why disc jockeys dominate reception music in most major cities.

Well, let's take a look at why DJs are so popular. According to a recent survey in *Bridal Guide*, 64% of all brides choose a DJ—that's much more than those who hire a band (22%) or have no music at all (14%). Of course the number-one reason is cost—DJs cost only $300 to $500 for an evening, compared to the $1000, $2000 or $3000 fees bands demand. With the cost of a wedding soaring, couples are obviously opting for the affordable alternative.

Perhaps a more subtle reason may be the state of pop music today. Almost all the dance music you hear on the radio is augmented by complex keyboard and percussion tracks. For a live band, trying to reproduce this music is perilous at best and embarrassing at worst. Sure, bands can play Glenn Miller and Johnny Mathis rather realistically, but many reception bands we've heard make every modern tune they attempt sound like "New York, New York."

To their credit, DJs have also cleaned up their act in recent years. Many companies are now professionally run businesses with tuxedo-clad DJs and professional sound equipment. This is a far cry from the late 1970's, when less-formal DJs spun mind-numbing disco hits complete with throbbing disco lights. Of course, disco is still with us (under the new label of "dance music") but many DJs diversified their music collection to include rock, country, and rap, as well as the hits from the 50's through the 90's.

In fact, musical versatility is one of the top reasons couples choose DJs. Since most weddings feature several generations of guests, a good mix of music is a must. While some bands play a variety of music, many are most proficient at one or two musical genres. The lack of variety is one of live bands' biggest disadvantages.

Another plus for DJs: they never take breaks. Most DJs play music continuously, unlike bands which need to take breaks every hour. Just when the crowd gets into a particular groove, the band shuts down for five to ten minutes. Obviously, this can kill the mood. With a DJ, the beat never stops until the party ends.

So what does Emily Post suggest if you want continuous music? Hire two orchestras, so one can play while the other is on break! No, we are not making this up.

Of course, we could rattle off a million advantages of DJs over bands, but that wouldn't faze those hard-line etiquette gurus. With their noses firmly planted in the air, they'd say something like "only live music such as a combo or orchestra is appropriate for a proper reception."

Still, bands do dominate in some areas, especially in cities with a thriving live music scene (i.e., New Orleans, some East Coast cities, etc.). Also, bands are still the most popular choice for those large "society" weddings.

Sure, we admit that watching a live band crank out "Louie, Louie" is more visually interesting than seeing a DJ play the same song via a CD. All we are saying is don't get bullied by the etiquette police into hiring a band when a professional DJ might fit your musical (and financial) preferences better.

Pitfalls to Avoid

Pitfall #1 Bait and switch with bands and DJ's

"My fiancé and I saw this great band perform at a friend's wedding so we hired them for ours. At our reception, different musicians showed up and it just didn't sound the same."

This is perhaps the #1 problem brides and grooms have with their reception entertainment. We've known some agents and bandleaders who play "musical chairs" with backing musicians—sometimes known as "pick-up bands." Here a group of musicians are thrown together at the last moment ... and the lack of rehearsal shows. You might hire a certain "name brand" band but then the bandleader substitutes some different (and possibly inferior) musicians at your reception. Hence, you don't get what you paid for, that is quality entertainment. Large DJ companies with several crews are also guilty of this tactic. You can prevent this deceptive practice by specifying in a written contract the exact musicians/DJ you want at your wedding. Stay away from agents, bandleaders or DJ companies who won't guarantee the entertainers who will be at your reception.

Pitfall #2 Chatterbox band leaders and DJs

"We recently attended a wedding where the band leader incessantly talked to the crowd. No one found this constant chatter amusing and it detracted from the elegance of the reception."

Band leaders and DJs often have their own "schtick"—a certain routine they do at a wedding. How "energetic" you want the band to be is your call since, of course, it's your money. Don't be surprised by a chatty band/DJ. See them perform at another reception before you sign that contract. If you have any doubts, ask them about the amount of talking and tell them what you believe is appropriate for your reception.

Pitfall #3 Deceptive demo tapes.

"We heard a demo tape from a band that sounded great. But later we saw the same band live and boy was it disappointing! What happened?"

Some demo tapes are produced in studios where a battery of sophisticated electronic equipment can make the weakest band sound like a stadium headliner. Add a little reverb to the vocals and clean up the guitar with some equalization and poof! Instant superstar band! In the harsh reality of a live performance, however, none of these studio tricks can save a lousy band. Listen to the demo tape for "style," not production quality. Beware the slick demo tape and try to see the band perform in person.

We heard about a twist on this scam from a bandleader in Boston. We call it the "Milli Vanilli syndrome," after the 1980's band that faked their albums through creative lip-synching. Some bands don't just "clean up" their demo tape in a studio, but use *entirely different* musicians to record the tape! That's right, the band pictured on the videotape is *not* the one that has recorded the soundtrack, just like Milli Vanilli.

PITFALL #4 KICKBACKS AND "REFERRED" LISTS.

"My wedding site recommend a musician who turned out to be lousy! Meanwhile, several great musicians in my town are nowhere to be found on their 'recommended list.' What's going on here?"

A problem with some wedding site coordinators (as well as catering managers at reception sites) is kickbacks. Believe it or not, some of these folks demand "fees to be listed on the site's "recommended list" of musicians. A harpist in Northern California told us this unscrupulous practice is rampant there. Ask the coordinator if they take fees from recommended musicians. If you don't get a straight answer, be careful.

PITFALL #5 DISCO MAY BE HAZARDOUS TO YOUR HEALTH

"I went to a wedding last weekend where the DJ had a fog machine. That was cool, except it left a slippery residue on the dance floor—several folks lost their footing!"

Disco effects (fog, strobes, pulsating lights) might be fun in a night-club, but sometimes they can be hazardous at a wedding reception. Examples: fog machines that leave a slick film on the dance floor. Excessive use of strobe lights can cause seizures among elderly guests. And watch out for that bubble machine—the soap solution that's used for bubbles can stain the delicate fabric of your wedding dress. (If you use wedding bubbles as a send-off substitute for rice, make sure the solution is non-staining).

Trends in Wedding and Reception Music

♥ **NEW TECHNOLOGY.** CD's, MP3's and digital tapes have enabled DJs to provide crystal clear sound, replacing scratchy vinyl and mediocre cassette tapes. In the live music world, bands now have access to increasingly sophisticated computerized synthesizers and drum machines. With these computers, bands can add a phalanx of horns or a dash of strings to their "basic" sound, enabling them to compete better with a DJ in music reproduction.

♥ **DJs ARE REPLACING BANDS AT MANY RECEPTIONS.** Perhaps it's the cost. Or better technology. Whatever the reason, bands are losing the wedding market to DJs in most towns.

♥ **ETHNIC MUSIC AND BANDS.** Mariachis are chic in the Southwest, while a good Polka band is still in vogue in the Midwest. Couples are not only celebrating their own family heritage but also reflecting a new cultural diversity. One recently married Anglo couple in Miami had a Caribbean-flavored reception complete with a salsa band. When their caterer asked why they selected this theme, the couple responded that this was the music they grew up with.

♥ **AT THE CEREMONY, THE "WEDDING MARCH" IS BEING REPLACED BY A WIDER VARIETY OF CLASSICAL AND MODERN MUSIC.** This is partly due to some churches forbidding this song on religious grounds. To others, the song has become too clichéd.

Special Touches to Make Your Wedding/Reception Music Unique

1 **Personalize the wedding and reception music with your favorite songs.** Incorporating special songs that have personal meaning for you and your fiancé is a great way to make your celebration unique. Before the wedding, give the band leader/DJ a list of special requests.

2 **Instead of standard organ music, consider different musical instruments.** The combinations here are endless. Many couples enjoy harp and flute duos, while others attest to the regal splendor of a single trumpeter. Classical guitar as well as violin are beautiful alternatives, too.

3 **Use ethnic music to celebrate family heritage.** Several weeks before the wedding, talk over the possibilities with your

band/DJ. Some songs may take a band time to rehearse or a DJ time to track down.

4 **If you're unsure about classical music for your ceremony, consider checking out a local library.** Many have extensive music selections (including wedding music) you can borrow to see what might work for your wedding. Looking for a special song to dedicate to parents? Mikki Viereck of New Traditions Music (800) 447-6647 has crafted "A Song for My Son" from the CD New Wedding Traditions ($20) in response to requests from couples for a "mother-to-groom" song. Mikki has four CDs (single song CDs are $10) which include other weddings songs (including a "Father's Song") as well as instrumental and country versions of her songs.

Secret Agent Man:
Helping Hand or Scum of the Earth?

So, what exactly is an entertainment agent? People in these businesses function as middlemen between bands or DJs and consumers. An agent's primary activity is booking bands and DJs at various engagements—in return they receive a commission. The standard commission is 15% of the band's regular performing fee. Now, the power of agents varies from city to city. In cities with stronger musicians' unions, agents tend to proliferate. In general, we've found agents more likely to dominate older cities such as New York and Chicago rather than sun belt towns like Atlanta and Dallas.

Agents cite several reasons for their existence. First, they can more effectively market the bands to engaged couples by pooling their resources. Also, many bandleaders (who have other daytime jobs) hate the paperwork associated with deposits, contracts, etc. Agents do all the legwork and remove the administrative hassles.

Fine, you say, but what can an agent do for me as a consumer? Well, agents provide "one-stop shopping," enabling you to make one call and get information on a wide range of bands and DJs. If you are in a hurry or just aren't aware of the entertainment options in your area, an agent can certainly help. Agents don't charge you a fee for their services, instead they collect a commission from the bands.

As you might imagine, some entertainers are less than enthusiastic about giving agents a 15% cut of their salary. Many of the entertainers we interviewed for this book held unanimously negative opinions about agents. And, frankly, we've met some agents who were in desperate need of a personality transplant. Other agents make used car salesmen look like Mother Teresa.

The main gripe we have with agents is their lack of "product knowledge." Too many just book a band or DJ without giving thought to whether their music is appropriate. Other agents deny brides and grooms the right to preview the band/DJ at a wedding before booking— a cardinal sin in our view.

Another major factor in this controversy: many bands say off the record they will give brides and grooms discounts off their regular rates if they book them directly. For example, one band told us they would knock off 15% (which, of course, is equal to the agent's commission) from their $2000 normal reception rate—that's a savings of $300, no small potatoes.

Agents respond to our criticism by claiming they can save brides and grooms money. One agency told us they can "get a lower price because they do a volume of business with a band, whereas a band leader contacted directly can get very greedy." Furthermore, agents claim that legitimately professional bandleaders will keep their prices the same—whether the booking comes directly from the couple or through an agent.

Well, we've "mystery shopped" dozens of bands and DJs and have yet to find any entertainer quoting a fee over their "regular rates." Agents gave us no special discount deals and we often found many professional bandleaders who offered a quiet discount when approached directly.

So what should you do? Try to book a band/DJ directly if you have found them from one of our sources listed above. If you need help, call an agent. Be careful to check out any band/DJ the agent recommends before you sign that contract. You might even call the local Better Business Bureau to check on the agent. Most importantly, meet the band to talk over the music, scheduling, and other reception details.

How do you get the best deal on a limo? What the heck is wedding insurance? Do you really need a wedding consultant? This chapter gives advice on these and more bridal topics. Plus, we'll examine online gift registries, wedding rings, and honeymoon bargains.

Limousines: Getting to the Church on Time

What is it about limos? Sure, a limo is a special treat for most folks—but many brides find a limo ride is the road to hell. The complaints? Late limo. No limo. Stinky limo. You name it, we've heard it.

And it's not just limo companies that target the bridal market—we've heard plenty of complaints about all sorts of limos from other consumer advocates. The industry seems rife with sleazy operators and questionable tactics. Here's our advice on how to book a limo without getting taken for ride:

What Are You Buying?

♥ THE LIMOUSINE. A stretch limousine has several basic amenities such as an extra long body, plush carpeting, a stereo, possibly a TV, sunroof and telephone, and a privacy window. More luxurious models have been known to contain even a hot tub or other interesting amenities.

Of course, there is no law saying brides and grooms must be driven to their reception in a limo. Non-traditional forms of transportation include horse-drawn carriages, antique cars and even buses or trolleys.

♥ **The Driver.** Every type of transportation you hire will include a driver. The driver should be dressed appropriately, either in a dark suit and chauffeur's cap or a black tuxedo.

Average Cost: Limousines will cost approximately $60 to $150 per hour. Usually, they have a three hour minimum rental time, with the total cost for the car between $180 and $450 per car per evening. The driver is paid with an additional mandatory gratuity of about 15% to 20%. The price you pay for a limo depends on the type of car—basic stretch limousines are less than Rolls Royce or Excalibur packages. For non-traditional transportation, the cost usually starts at $100 an hour and goes up depending on the vehicle you rent.

Sources to Find Transportation

Some sources include the Yellow Pages under "Limousines," "Carriages-Horse" or under "Wedding Services." By all means ask a recently married friend for recommendations and look for information about transportation companies at bridal shows. Another creative idea: scan the phone book for classic or antique car clubs. These non-profit groups of car buffs may have members who'll rent out their vehicles by the day.

Brides in Cyberspace: What's on the Web?

♥ **Limos.com** lets you search for a limo in the US and Canada by following just a few steps. Pick the location, type of car and service you want and bingo! You get a list of local limo companies, complete with contact info, web site links and more. You can even request an online quote. We also like the fact that Limos.com notes which companies are members of the National Limousine Association.

♥ Jeff & Nancy Ostroff are a recently married couple who have put together a web page (**BridalTips.com**) of their hard-won consumer knowledge about all things bridal. Their section on hiring a limo (web: www.bridaltips.com/limo.htm) is a great example of their clear, concise advice. From there, you can explore other topics, from gowns to gift registries.

Getting Started: How Far in Advance?

For most limousine companies, you may not need to start looking until a month or two before your wedding date. If limos are popular in your area and you have a wedding date in the busy summer months, consider planning three months in advance. For carriage companies, you may also have to plan farther in advance because the demand is greater and the supply limited.

Step-by-step Shopping Strategies

♥ **Step 1:** Using the sources mentioned above, identify two or three companies that offer the transportation you need.

♥ **Step 2:** Find out what type of vehicle you will be hiring. See if you can visit the company and see the cars or carriages. Get details on available options, minimum required hours and the cost per hour.

♥ **Step 3:** Visit the company and check out the vehicles. See how clean the cars are and what amenities they have. Find out who will be driving the car and what they will be wearing. Don't just rely on a phone call to book a limo—seeing is believing.

♥ **Step 4:** Consider calling the National Limousine Association (800) NLA-7007 (web: www.limo.org) to find out if the company you want to hire has adequate insurance and is licensed. These folks can give you that information or at least inform you of how to find it for yourself.

♥ **Step 5:** Choose the company you like the best and get a contract detailing the car you like, date, pick-up times and any special requests. As you get closer to your wedding day (say a week before the event), call to remind them of your date and time. Clearly identify arrival times and other special requests IN WRITING. Another smart tip: get the vehicle license number for the car you are reserving IN WRITING. That helps prevent a last-minute substitution of a substandard vehicle.

Questions to Ask with Limos

1 **Will we be able to bring champagne?** Will you provide us with ice and glasses? Some companies will allow you to bring alcohol while others will even supply it. In some areas, it is illegal for the company to provide the alcohol, but they will bring ice and glasses for BYOB. Don't rely on the limo company to provide any champagne—it usually is the cheapest stuff they can find.

2 **Who will be the driver?** How much is the gratuity for the driver? Typically, you aren't given a choice about how much the gratuity will be. Gratuities range from company to company, so check around before you book.

3 **Do you have any discounts available?** As we mentioned above, many companies will discount their service for week nights. Other discounts may be available if you hire more than one vehicle or if you hire them for longer time periods.

4 **Do you specialize in weddings?** Those companies that do may have special bridal packages or other freebies. Confirm the basic amenities of the car.

5 **How many vehicles do you own?** Small companies may only have a handful of limos. If things get busy, they might contract out the cars and drivers from other services—that's a major problem. If you go with a smaller limo company, make sure you get IN WRITING a promised car the service actually owns and the driver you expect. Even better: get the owner to agree to do the driving.

6 **How much is overtime?** Even the best laid plans can go awry. Make sure you know what overtime rates will be and get that in writing. That way the driver won't just make up a high overtime charge on the fly.

Top Money-saving Tips

1 **Call a funeral home.** Yes, you read right—call a funeral home for a great deal on a limo rental for your wedding. Now, we should say right off the bat that this sounds nutty, but it does work. And we are not talking about renting a hearse from the funeral home but a limo they normally use to shuttle relatives back and forth. We heard about this bargain from recent bride Stephanie Kampes in Drexel Hill, PA. She priced regular limo companies at $275 for three hours, plus a 15% gratuity. "Then I called a reputable funeral home and was surprised with the price!" Apparently, this funeral home rents out it's standard stretch limos during down times (Saturday night must not be a big time for funerals). The cost? $125 for the evening. "This may sound rather morbid, but it works!" she said. "While they don't have hot tubs or TV's, funeral homes have lovely limos!" While not every funeral home rents out limos for weddings, it's worth a try.

2 **Find a transportation company with a short minimum time requirement.** Most companies require you to hire them for a minimum of three hours. You may be able to find someone who is willing to require only an hour or two-hour minimum, thus saving 30% to 60%.

3 **Rent a trolley!** A bride in Trenton, NJ called in this great idea—she found a company that rents a 30-seat trolley for four hours for $715 (which includes a gratuity for the driver). We found trolley companies in other cities that had even lower rates (look in the phone book under "Weddings Services," "Limousine Rental" or "Buses-Charter/Rental"). If you're having a large wedding party and don't want to rent a fleet of limos, this might be a smart idea.

4 **Consider a "pick-up/drop-off" service.** Instead of having the limo driver wait outside the church during the ceremony, simply hire a limo to pick you up after the ceremony and go to the reception. Often this will cost you much less than hiring someone for three hours.

5 **Have your wedding on an off-night.** Some companies offer deals for brides having weddings during the week.

6 **Rent a luxury car.** Many car rental companies rent Cadillacs and Lincoln Continentals for as little as $50 to $100 per day. While you'll need to find a driver (perhaps a friend or relative), this is a big savings over a limo. A bride in Turnersville, NJ rented a white Corvette for $179 for her wedding transportation. And that fee was for 24 hours!

The Limo Driver Terrorist

A bride-to-be in Atlanta Georgia wrote us with this limo scam story—her sister-in-law fell victim to the "early arrival/over-time" surprise rip-off. How does this scam work? First, she wrote, "the limo showed up at the bride's house over 30 minutes early. The driver was insistent that the bride and her mother finish dressing and ride to the church, which they did. After the wedding and after all the guests left the ceremony site for the reception, the driver boarded the wedding party into the limo. He then informed the couple 'the limo is on overtime' and demanded $60 before he would take them to the reception."

"Since neither wedding gowns nor bridesmaids dresses have pockets (another bad idea), the groom and best man frantically scraped together the ransom. The limo company reluctantly refunded part of the additional charges only after several unpleasant telephone calls during the next few weeks." How can you prevent this from happening to you? First, if the limo arrives early, don't get in it, no matter how insistent the driver is. Realize that the moment you step inside, the driver's clock is running. Try to pay any overtime fee or deposit by credit card—then you can dispute the charge later if you feel you were mistreated.

7 **Consider hiring a "regular limo."** These are regular luxury cars—
not the stretch variety. Many limo companies offer these cars at
reduced rates. Another tip: ask if the limo company has discounts for
slightly less fancy limos (like those without window tint).

8 **Hire a corporate limo company.** Companies that specialize in
limos for executives and business travelers sometimes have better
deals than limo companies that target the bridal market. Why? Corporate
limo companies can get really lonely on the weekend and hence discount
their rates. One bride told us she saved 35% by going this route.

9 **Don't say the word "wedding."** Bridal packages at limo companies always seem to be more than corporate rates. You might want
to leave the word "wedding" out of your discussion with a limo company at first just to make sure you see ALL their rates. Negotiate for a better rate if the bridal package is 30% more than the regular rates.

Pitfalls to Avoid

PITFALL #1 COMPANIES THAT DON'T SHOW UP.
This is one of the biggest problems with limousine compa-
nies. We recommend you check with the Better Business
Bureau in your area if you have any questions about a limo service.
Checking with the city agency that licenses limousines will also determine
whether the company you are considering meets local requirements.

PITFALL #2 WE DON'T OWN THE CAR!
Some limo companies advertise they carry exclusive brands like Rolls
Royce. The problem—they don't actually own the car, they just contract
for it from another company. As you can imagine, this is a major cause
for limo headaches (such as cars not showing up) since the company
doesn't have control over the vehicle. Bottom line: if the company does-
n't own the car you want, don't book them.

Wedding Rings

The good news about wedding rings is you can buy a beautiful band
in just about any budget range. Unlike other goods and services you're
purchasing for the wedding, there is a plentiful supply of jewelry stores
and other sources to find rings. For example, in our town of 100,000
people, we have just one bridal dress shop, but over 40 jewelry sources
(from chain stores in the mall to independent shops and custom jewelry makers). The plentiful supply means you'll probably find something to
fit your budget and style.

What Are You Buying?

What does a set of rings cost? Couples spend on average $1000 for wedding bands, according to a recent article in *Kiplinger's Personal Finance Magazine*. Yes, that's $500 per ring! Prices range from as little as $50 for a plain 14K gold ring to $1000 (each) or more for a heavy, solid platinum ring.

What does 14-karat mean? That number refers to the purity of gold in the ring—and that's just one factor that influences a ring's value. Here are the five key aspects to keep in mind when ring shopping:

♥ **GOLD PURITY.** The "karat" is a term that refers to the purity of the gold. 24-karat (24K) gold is pure, 100% gold. Wedding rings also come in 18K, 14K and even 10K gold. 18K has 75% gold (25% other metals), 14K is 58.5% gold and 10K has a mere 41.6% gold. Which is best? There are trade-offs to each karat class. While 18K has a higher gold content, it's also softer (and perhaps more susceptible to damage). By contrast, 14K is harder and wears better—and it's less expensive.

♥ **PLATINUM IS HOT!** Half of all wedding rings sold today are platinum—that's up from nearly nothing five years ago. Why is platinum so hot? Well, platinum is very dense, which makes the ring feel more substantial. The metal is also very strong, a plus for holding stones like diamonds (which are set-off dramatically by platinum's pure white coloring).

Of course, you're going to pay for that. A white gold ring that's $170 would cost $800 for platinum. One consumer tip: ask the jeweler if the platinum ring is pure platinum. Since platinum rings are so pricey, yet so popular, many mall jewelers have begun offering water-downed rings with just 65% to 75% platinum (the balance is other metals) to sell at a lower price point. Rings should be stamped with their purity; 95% pure platinum rings are best.

Platinum's popularity has been a double-edged sword lately. Limited supplies and surging demand has pushed prices for platinum wedding rings up 40% or more in 2000. At the same time, designer brands like Scott Kay and Christian Bauer have been heavily advertising their pricey creations in bridal magazines; that has led to a bigger market for so-called "designer" rings.

♥ **STYLE.** Consider color. While pure gold comes only in one color (yellow, as you might guess), gold can be combined with other metals to form different colors. A 14K white gold ring is a mix of gold (58.5%) plus copper, nickel and zinc. In order to cover over any yellow tints, white gold rings are often coated with rhodium, a metal that's a member of the platinum family. In addition to color, the style of the ring also refers to its shape. Rings can be either flat or half-round—a dome-like or curved appearance.

♥ **WIDTH.** Ring width is measured in millimeters (mm). Most woman's wedding bands are 2 to 5mm, while men's are 4 to 7mm. Of course, the wider the ring, the more expensive it is. Other widths are also available.

♥ **FINISH.** Just like the icing on a wedding cake, a ring's finish can range from simple to ornate. Like the shiny look? Then choose a high polish ring, instead of a matte finish. Rings can have monograms, diamond cut patterns and other finishes. A milgrain edge is popular today—that's an ornamental border on the edge of the ring that resembles a string of tiny beads. Want diamonds in your wedding ring? You can have stones that encircle the band or just on top.

Top Money-saving Tips

1 **Go for a 14-karat ring.** Yes, it has less gold in it than 18K or 24K rings, but this is also an advantage. As we mentioned above, 14K gold is harder and wears better than higher-karat rings. And, best of all, it's much less expensive.

2 **Check out pawn shops.** Divorces and other financial mishaps often lead folks to pawn their wedding rings. As a result, pawn shops have an incredible selection of jewelry at very good prices. Another good bet: estate sales (usually advertised in newspapers) often feature rings and other jewelry.

3 **Comparison shop.** Which place has the best deals on wedding rings—mall stores or independent jewelers? Well, there is no one answer. Sales, special deals and other events may make one jeweler temporarily less expensive than another. Make sure you're comparing "apples to apples" with rings (same width, gold purity, etc.).

4 **Don't forget about antique stores.** One bride called us with this incredible bargain: she found a platinum wedding band from the 1920's at an antique store. The ring, which had a half-carat diamond and sapphires, cost her $700. She had it appraised at $1400.

5 **Go mail order or surf the web.** See the Spotlight: Best Buy below for a discount mail-order source for wedding rings.

6 **Consider the new synthetics.** If you have your heart set on a diamond wedding ring but your wallet can't handle diamond prices, consider new synthetic alternatives. One option: Moissanite (www.moissanite.com), a diamond look-alike that is made by Charles & Covard (a lab that fabricates man-made gemstones). A one and a third carat Moissanite ring runs $990; a similar-size and quality diamond would run you $4500. The only bummer: Moissanite is only available at certain jewelers (check their web site for a dealer near you); some states only have a small number of Moissanite dealers.

SPOTLIGHT: BEST BUY

WEDDING RING HOTLINE
(800) 985-7464 or (732) 972-7777; www.weddingringhotline.com

Tired of the high prices of mall jewelry stores? Like the prices but not the styles of discount, catalog showrooms? Well, we found a great alternative: The Wedding Ring Hotline of Englishtown, New Jersey.

Owner Mitch Slachman has been in the business since 1983 and has developed a loyal clientele in New York and New Jersey. The Wedding Ring Hotline not only carries Mitch's custom designs, but also the styles of leading designers' lines as well. If you see an advertisement for a name-brand ring or have the style number, you can get a price quote.

And talk about good deals—The Wedding Ring Hotline's prices are 25% to 33% below retail on most designs. Or Mitch can custom design a ring for even bigger savings. Wedding Ring Hotline's retail showroom (under the name Bride & Groom's West) in Englishtown, New Jersey has over 1000+ styles on display. (It's best to call for an appointment).

If you don't live in that part of the country, you can call for their color catalog (or surf their extensive web site). We saw an impressive number of styles, from monogrammed bands to diamond-studded rings. A simple 4mm plain band in 14K white or yellow gold starts at $62. Most simple styles in 14K gold are in the $30 to $250 range. Want platinum? For a man's solid platinum ring that would sell for $1200 retail, Wedding Ring Hotlines' price would be $600 to $700. A woman's (2mm) plain platinum ring would be about $165 (compare at $400 or more). Call for price quotes on 18K gold and other rings.

Another cool part to the Wedding Ring Hotline: they also sell designer brands like Scott Kay and Christian Bauer (among others) at attractive prices. So if you see a ring advertised in a bridal magazine, call them first to get a price quote before you pay a hefty mark-up at a retail store.

The Wedding Ring Hotline takes all major credit cards and has a 30-day 100% money-back guarantee if you're not happy. There's also no sales tax if you live outside New Jersey, a big money-savings as well.

More web sites for diamond rings:
♥ DIAMOND CUTTERS (www.diamondcutters.com) has an excellent tutorial on buying a diamond. Check out their "tricks of the trade" section (in the articles area) to learn what rip-offs to avoid when diamond shopping.

♥ **Diamond Grading** (www.diamondgrading.com) has an extensive FAQ on diamond buying as well as a chat group and other helpful info.

Further reading. As you've noted above, this section just addresses wedding bands. We assume you already have a diamond engagement ring. Yet, if you're more interested in learning how to purchase diamonds and colored stones, there are three excellent books to read (all are available on Amazon.com or in bookstores):

♥ **Engagement & Wedding Rings: The Definitive Buying Guide for People in Love** by Matlins, Bonanno, Crystal (1999, $16.95, Gemstone Press 800-962-4544, 802-457-4000).

♥ **The Diamond Ring Buying Guide: How to Spot Value & Avoid Rip-offs** by Renee Newman (1996, $14.95, International Jewelry Publications, PO Box 13384, Los Angeles, CA 90013).

♥ **How to Buy a Diamond : Insider Secrets for Getting Your Money's Worth** by Fred Cuellar (2000, $14.95, Sourcebooks Trade)

If you have access to the Internet, check out Jim Kokernak's "Frequently Asked Questions (FAQ) about Diamonds." This 16-page guide includes sections on finding a jeweler, the basics on diamonds, how not to get ripped off and more. You can find this FAQ at the http://www. rpi.edu/~kokerj/diamond/diamond.html.

Dubious items: Wedding Insurance, Name Change Kits

What's the silliest bridal accessory we've discovered? Would you believe lucky pennies for $5 each? Yes, that's what a company in Texas was selling—a penny wrapped in tulle and tied with a ribbon. If that wasn't enough, we found another catalog selling "lucky six-pence" for $12. Last time we checked exchange rates, a six-pence was worth, say, ten pennies. What a deal, eh? Here are some more dubious items.

♥ **Wedding insurance.** Do you need wedding insurance? Fireman's Fund/R.V. Nuccio (800-ENGAGED, web: www.rvnuccio.com) offers a policy that protects you in case of cancellation of the wedding, lost photos, damaged bridal attire, lost gifts and personal liability for bodily injury or property damage at your wedding and reception. Premiums start at $195. So, should you buy? Well, *Money Magazine* picked wedding insurance as a great example of insurance you really don't need, pointing out that the skimpy coverage doesn't justify the hefty premiums. We have mixed feelings about this insurance—if your reception site requires you to purchase liability insurance, this might be an affordable alternative. If your spouse is in the military and you worry a surprise overseas deployment may scuttle the wedding plans, this insurance may also help. Of course, read the policy carefully to catch all the fine print.

♥ **WATCH OUT FOR NAME CHANGE RIP-OFFS.** Don't fall victim to any of the "name change scams," where companies promise they'll handle your name change for a fee. Authorities have been cracking down on such rip-offs and recently arrested a Las Vegas couple who tricked thousands of women into paying them for services the Social Security Administration offers for free. The couple ran a business that mailed out letters to help brides change their names on their Social Security cards for a fee of $15. Yet forms for that purpose are available to the public free of charge from local Social Security offices (check the web at www.ssa.gov or the government listings in your local phone book for locations).

Bridal Shows: Fun Afternoon or Highway to Bridal Hell?

If you need a good laugh, attend a local bridal show in your town. If you aren't convinced that the wedding "industry" is a joke, this is the place to give your cynical side a booster shot.

Basically, most bridal shows attempt to stage a fashion show (we use the word "show" here very loosely) and a trade fair. The latter consists of various booths with displays from merchants with names like "Brides 'R' Us" and "Fred's Professional Wedding Photography." Like sharks smelling blood in the water, these merchants crawl out of their subterranean homes and swim circles around brides, passing out little gifts like potpourri balls, which will emit such a pleasant perfume that it will take you three months to get the smell out of your purse.

The fashion show is the alleged bait to get you (the consumer) into their (the merchants') clutches for two hours of unabashed commercial plugs. During this fashion show, you will actually see live and in person many of those hideous bridesmaids gowns that you only thought existed in the bridal magazines and in the backs of closets. After hearing the announcer say for the twentieth time, "Here's a lovely taffeta design with PUFF SLEEVES" you'll probably be able to actually feel your teeth grind.

What's most interesting about these runway shows is the realization of how far removed the bridal apparel industry is from reality. If you look closely, you'll notice the "new design for this year" looks suspiciously like one from a wedding you attended in 1993.

After the show and the non-stop commercial plug-a-thon (yes, Bob, we'd love to thank Burt's Wedding Chair Rental for providing the chairs you're sitting in today! Aren't they just lovely! And they're just $3.95 plus deposit!), you have time to walk around the booths and chat with local merchants. Many of these merchants will lunge at you from their booths and shove a brochure in your hand while simultaneously complimenting you on how LARGE your engagement ring is—all with a look of sincerely feigned sincerity. While visiting a recent bridal show, we were struck by the sheer ingenuity of wedding entrepreneurs who have invented brilliant ways to separate you from your money.

Perhaps the best known bridal show operator is Bridal Expo, based in that state known for bridal bliss, New Jersey (just ask Bruce Springsteen). Bridal Expo mounts this massive multi-media show that admittedly is much more polished than the typical dog-and-pony show put on by locals. Slickly choreographed, Bridal Expos are thick with plugs for the Official Sponsors.

What's most hysterical about the Bridal Expo is that these folks from New Jersey think that the world is simply dying to see what newest horror the New York bridal designers are trying to heap on us consumers. At one show in Denver, we couldn't help but notice the crowd audibly guffawing at several bridal gowns that some designer must have dreamed up in his Manhattan office during a bad acid trip.

The biggest scam at all these bridal shows are the so-called door prizes. As you enter, most bridal shows will ask you to register for A FREE EXCITING HONEYMOON TRIP TO IRAQ. Of course, besides your name and address, the "registration card" will ask for your phone number, fiancé's name, yearly income, birth place, blood type, and so on. As you wander around the booths, the wedding merchants will ask you to fill out entry forms for such tantalizing door prizes as "A FREE NAPKIN (WHEN YOU PURCHASE $1000 WORTH OF PICTURES)!"

As you fill out the forms, you'll noticed the merchants and show organizers will barely be able to keep the drool from dripping down their shirts in sheer excitement. That's because this whole prize thing is a big sham—what these bridal shows really want is your phone number and address. Then they can call you frequently at dinner time to inform you that they have a BIG SPECIAL this month and that if you sign up NOW you won't be killed by their bridal death squad.

Yes, bridal merchants pay hundreds of dollars to do these shows and THE BIG REASON is that list of brides, all neatly alphabetized with their home phone numbers, wedding date, bank account numbers, and more. Many brides are alarmed to find after attending a bridal show that they must buy a six-foot mailbox with forklift to handle the volume of mail that will give new meaning to the word junk.

The lesson? If you've got an afternoon to kill and would like to overdose on sugar from 67 cake samples, then a bridal show may be for you. But, if you value your privacy, be careful out there. Nothing says you have to give these shows or merchants your real address or phone number.

Wedding Consultants

Wedding planners have been satirized in movies, lionized by bridal magazines—and generally ignored by brides. Once a fixture of weddings in the 1950's, wedding consultants were hunted to near extinction in the 1970's when weddings were less formal affairs usually held on a beach.

As weddings have become more complex and formal events, professional wedding consultants have made an impressive comeback. We should note, however, that there are several types of wedding consultants. Many people who work at bridal shops or retail florists call themselves "wedding consultants." In addition to helping the bride with their own specialty, these folks pass along referrals of other bridal professionals. While they may be helpful, these are not the wedding consultants we are referring to in this section.

We define a "professional wedding consultant" as an independent business person who, for a fee, helps plan and coordinate the entire wedding. They don't actually bake the cake or sew the gown—this is done by outside suppliers. In a sense, a wedding consultant is like a personal shopper. Or as some planners have discovered, like a low-paid waitress.

So How Much Do Wedding Consultants Cost?

Most charge an hourly fee or a percentage of the wedding budget. For example, one consultant we met charges a 15% fee on wedding expenditures. So, if you spend $20,000 on a wedding and reception, you then write out a check for $3000 to the consultant. Other party planners we met charge a flat hourly fee ($75 per hour, for example) no matter what your budget. Many consultants offer different levels of help—coordinating just the rehearsal and wedding ceremony costs a small fee, while planning the whole affair from the ground floor up will run you much more.

Sources to Find a Consultant

♥ CALL A PROFESSIONAL ASSOCIATION. June Wedding (702) 474-9558 (www.junewedding.com) will give you a referral to a local bridal consultant (their membership is mostly in the Western US). Another group is the Association of Bridal Consultants (860) 355-0464 (www.bridalassn.com).

♥ ASK YOUR FRIENDS. The best planners work by word-of-mouth referrals.

Questions to Ask a Consultant

1 **Exactly how do you work your fees?** Do you accept commissions or finder's fees from other bridal

merchants? See the Pitfall section below for more information on this practice. Ask the consultant to clearly explain his/her fee schedule.

2 **How will you incorporate my tastes into the wedding?** If the consultant will be doing the majority of the legwork, ask them how they will account for your tastes. Will they get your approval at various stages in the planning process?

3 **How long have you been a consultant? How many weddings have you planned?** This is a key question. Many "consultants" we've talked to were far too inexperienced to entrust the planning of a $20,000 wedding. Some have been in business for less than a year or so. We recommend you trust your wedding only to a seasoned professional with at least three years minimum experience. Sure, consultants with less experience can still plan and coordinate a beautiful wedding—but be careful. You don't want someone "learning the ropes" on your big day. Other related questions: How many weddings do you do in a year? On a typical weekend?

4 **Are you certified?** If the bridal consultant belongs to a professional organization, that's nice . . . but, it's even better if they've been certified or accredited. Check out the organization that certified the planner to insure they are in good standing—and ask how they certify consultants (education, experience, license requirements).

5 **Do you have five vendor referrals?** Yes, you want to check with past clients of the consultants. But, go one step further: ask for referrals from five wedding vendors they work with all the time (photographers, florists, etc.). You'll get an idea of the caliber of the consultant's contacts by the names they provide.

6 **Will you provide regular written updates?** Communication is key—you should be updated on the planning at regular intervals.

7 **Can you work within our budget?** Yes, that's the $64,000 question. Sure, you may not have a firm grasp on what the budget should be, but a good consultant should be able to estimate what the wedding you want will cost. If the consultant can't work within that budget, ask if you can hire them on a "per meeting" basis. Many planners offer this "limited service" option, which enables couples to tap the planner's expertise without paying full price.

Special thanks to Robbi Ernst of June Wedding for providing some of the questions to ask listed above.

Pitfalls to Avoid with Wedding Planners

PITFALL #1 KICKBACKS AND VENDOR REFERRAL FEES

"I visited a wedding consultant who recommended I buy my wedding gown from a particular bridal shop. Later, I learned the shop paid her a commission for recommending me. Is this legitimate?"

Well, it certainly isn't ethical. This points up a central problem we have with some less-than-professional consultants. In a clear conflict of interest, some consultants collect "finder's fees" or "commissions" (read: kickbacks) from other bridal merchants on the products and services they recommend to brides. So who are they representing—the bride or the merchants? We don't believe a consultant can negotiate effectively for the bride when they receive a kickback from bridal merchants. If you use a consultant, make sure the consultant clearly identifies how they get paid.

PITFALL #2 PERCENTAGE-BASED FEES MAY ENCOURAGE GREED.

"One bridal consultant told me she could save me hundreds of dollars. However, her fee is based on a percentage of the money I spend. Where is her real incentive to save me money?"

Of course, a professional consultant relies on word-of-mouth referral for new clients. If they don't deliver what they promise, word will spread quickly. However, we do agree that a conflict exists here: when their income is based on how much money you spend, less-than-ethical consultants may feel the temptation to encourage lavish spending. Or at least, the incentive to save you money comes in conflict with their bottom line. Realize that all consultants do not charge a percentage-based fee—others charge flat fees or hourly rates. This might be a better alternative.

PITFALL #3 COUNTERFEIT CONSULTANTS.

"I called a so-called 'wedding consultant' from the phone book. Instead of offering a consulting service, she pitched me on her wedding chapel and reception site."

Yes, many "all-in-one" wedding companies deceptively advertise themselves as wedding consultants. Don't be fooled—these businesses aren't interested in consulting on your wedding. They just want you to book their wedding and reception site, photography and so on.

PITFALL #4 LACK OF REGULATION.

"I contacted a wedding consultant to talk about my wedding. Boy was I surprised! This person knew nothing about weddings. Aren't these guys suppose to be licensed?"

Unfortunately, very few laws regulate wedding consultants. When you think about it, wedding consultants are quasi-financial planners—they advise people on how to spend money. Big money. Unlike other financial planners, however, there is very little regulation. Anyone can call themselves a wedding consultant—and sometimes it seems like everyone is. Some cities do require wedding consultants or party planners to be licensed. In most areas, however, the industry is left to police itself. Consider hiring a consultant who is a member of a professional association. Many require their members to subscribe to a basic ethics pledge. Other groups offer on-going training through seminars and workshops.

Advantages of Consultants

♥ **BRIDAL CONSULTANTS CAN SAVE YOU TIME.** If you and your fiancé are working too many hours to plan your wedding, you may find a wedding consultant to be worth the expense. Frankly, planning a wedding is very time-intensive. Realistically evaluate your schedules and time commitments to decide if you can handle it alone. Brides planning large and expensive wedding may find consultants a necessity.

♥ **LONG-DISTANCE WEDDINGS MAY REQUIRE SUCH HELP.** Planning a wedding in another city is quite challenging. Having a local bridal consultant to coordinate the details may be prudent.

♥ **SEASONED EXPERTS MAY BE ABLE TO NEGOTIATE MORE EFFECTIVELY, GETTING YOU A BETTER DEAL.** Now we aren't talking about novices here but wedding consultants with years of experience. These people are on a first-name basis with catering managers and other bridal professionals. Some consultants are tough negotiators who can make sure you get the best price. Other consultants claim that other bridal professionals have a vested interest in doing their very best work for their clients—if they don't, they may lose future business. We are not sure to what extent these claims are true but we do believe one thing: a talented, experienced consultant may be worth the extra expense.

Disadvantages of Consultants

♥ **THE "PROFESSIONAL ORGANIZATIONS" FOR BRIDAL CONSULTANTS AREN'T THAT PROFESSIONAL.** Unlike other fields, most bridal consultant associations don't have rigid standards for membership. Printed up business cards that say you're a wedding consultant? Have a pulse? That's enough for some wedding planner associations. Their main business is selling "home study" courses that are of dubious value.

Other groups are better—June Wedding (702) 474-9558 (www.junewedding.com) is probably the best-run professional organization of the bunch. Director Robbi Ernst teaches on-going training courses for both new and experienced wedding planners. And June Wedding takes a strong position on the kickback issue; they advise members to NEVER take vendor referral fees.

So what does this mean for you? While it's a good sign if the bridal consultant you've discovered is a member of one of these groups, don't assume they are all-knowing "experts." Check references and ask some tough questions to weed out the amateurs.

Gift Registries

Bridal gift registries have been around in various forms for over 50 years and it's no wonder: they offer convenience for both the guest and bride. Last year, the wedding gift industry racked up $17 billion in sales of china, salt and pepper shakers, toasters and a gazillion other items.

Yet, for all the promise, registries are among the bigger complaint areas for brides and grooms. Just about everything that CAN go wrong has happened with these so-called "convenience" services—items that are out of stock for what seems like a decade, surly clerks, high prices and more. We'll discuss all of the sordid details in Pitfalls to Avoid later in this section.

For years, the bridal registry biz was dominated by big department stores. These stores offered gift registries for a limited selection of china, crystal, flatware and so on. Fortunately, this all began to change in the 1980's and 90's when discount stores and specialty chains added gift registries, giving couples more choices.

Yet, the biggest news of all in recent years is the advent of the online gift registry. The marriage of the gift registry (essentially a database, of course) with the web (open 24 hours, 7 days week) promised to give both couples and their guests new convenience. Now, you can register for gifts at 3am in your pajamas, see what items your guests are buying and even change the registry as your wedding draws near. Like everything with the 'net, however, much of this has been more hype than reality so far.

On the plus side, there are more competitors than ever in the gift registry biz. Newcomers like TheKnot.com are battling with established department stores for the online gift registry market and the biggest winner so far is the consumer. We'll review the best sites to register on line next.

Brides in CyberSpace: What's on the Web?

Wedding Channel (formerly DellaWeddings.com)
Web: www.weddingchannel.com or weddings.della.com
What it is: The largest online wedding gift registry
What's Cool: Despite its teething troubles (see the next page for details), we have to give The Wedding Channel/Della the award for the

best wedding gift registry. Hands down, this site has the most going for it of all in the category.

Della (formerly called Della & James) was founded in 1998 and got its name from the O'Henry short story "The Gift of the Magi." (The characters Della and James in the story gave up their most prized possessions to buy gifts for each other). In 2000, Della merged with the Wedding Channel, which already was building a sizeable gift registry of its own.

Della has an impressive group of backers that have pumped $45 million into launching the site, including Amazon.com, Neiman Marcus, Crate & Barrel and Williams Sonoma. All in all, the site has 30 stores with their registries online, including Dillards, REI, Restoration Hardware, Gumps, Sharper Image and more. Even better, Della lets you register at local stores in a limited number of cities (Boston, Chicago, Dallas, Los Angeles, New York, San Francisco and Seattle) on line from your computer as well. The Wedding Channel's registry boasts many Federated Department stores, including Bloomingdales, The Bon Marche, Burdines, Goldsmith's, Lazarus, Macy's, Rich's and Stern's. (As we went to press, the Wedding Channel was planning to merge both Della and its own registry into one massive site set to debut in Fall 2000).

You can register one of two ways: in the store or online (at least with some stores). The Wedding Channel/Della has an excellent series of tools in case you need help, including a product guide, checklist and even an interactive "consultant." The latter asks you about your lifestyle, cooking needs, how you spend your weekends and other issues before recommending several items.

Like all online registries, you can view and modify your registry online. The site lets you track which gifts are sent and (allegedly) emails you when guests make purchases. The prices are the same at Della as in the store; the site also promises to honor all sale prices.

Needs work. Online gift registries wow brides with the promise of all sorts of techno-wizardry. Wouldn't it be cool to get an email letting you know a guest purchased a gift the moment it happened? That way you could get a head start on all those thank you notes and maybe even adjust your registry to add in new items if needed.

The email feature was one of Della's promised cool features. Yet, a *Wall Street Journal* reporter who tested this service found it lacking—despite numerous purchases, there were no emails. Della claims this glitch happened because the items were back-ordered or the retailers didn't notify Della of the purchases yet. (The reporter's advice: check the site instead of relying on email notifications). Another bummer: Della.com promised brides they could register at local stores and have those items listed online. The reporter for the *Journal* spent several hours at Gumps picking out crystal and china, only to later discover that all guests could view or buy online from that store was gift certificates. Della.com promises the local store gift option will be online sometime in mid 2000. But why did the site promise that in the first place before it was ready to deliver?

Beyond those problems, we still don't like the "announce" feature of sites like Della. The company promises to "tastefully inform your guests about your registry or wedding page through our complimentary guest notification service. We'll help you keep your friends and family up-to-date on your plans." Translation: Della will send your guests an email pitching them to buy gifts. Sorry, that's just plain tacky.

♥ **Other online gift registries.** TheKnot.com is the Wedding Channel's big competition in the registry field. The Knot has 10,000 gift items on its site, but is not affiliated with any major department store. That's the Knot's biggest disadvantage: your guests MUST go online or dial a toll-free number to order, instead of visiting a local store. On the plus side, the Knot has several "registry short-cut starter lists," with suggestions for couples who are "adventurous," "casual," "gourmet" and so on. Even if you don't register here, those lists might be a good place to get ideas.

Pitfalls to Avoid with Gift Registries

PITFALL #1: OUT OF STOCK!

"We registered for a china pattern, but when guests made their purchases, we found the items were out of stock! And we'd have to wait three MONTHS for delivery."

Yes, stores are famous for letting you register for items that have long been out of stock. Then when you go to pick up the items, you get the bad news—thanks to a back-order, come back in several WEEKS or MONTHS to get the items. A word to wise: BEFORE you register, check the stock status of items you want. If the store doesn't stock many of the items, it could be a recipe for frustration.

PITFALL #2: SEASONS CHANGE.

"We thought we'd be smart if we registered six months in advance of our wedding, only to learn that by the time the wedding rolled around, some of the items we wanted were long gone!"

Sometimes, it DOESN'T pay to plan ahead. Registering too early can be a problem—items change, get discontinued, go on back-order or worse as time rolls by. Our advice: wait until two or three months before your wedding to register for gifts. Sure, you can do shopping before that, but don't actually create the registry until closer to the wedding. Guests don't start buying gifts until right before the wedding, so you aren't making anyone's life difficult by waiting.

PITFALL #3: SIXTEEN SALT AND PEPPER SHAKERS

"Hey! I thought the gift registry was supposed to stop duplicate gifts? We registered and STILL got three toasters, four blenders and other duplicates!"

Theoretically, when your guests buy a gift from a registry, a computer sitting in a climate controlled room somewhere in Delaware is supposed to SUBTRACT that item from your list. That way, your Aunt Mable doesn't buy you that sixteenth salt and pepper shaker set. Yet, note we used the word "theoretically" in that first sentence. The reality: sometimes clerks still have to hand-enter your gift items into a computer . . . and those clerks forget. Or the registry fails to get updated for a myriad of reasons only a computer tech knows. Expect glitches and deal with a store that has good customer service to handle such problems.

PITFALL #4: CHANGES, WHAT CHANGES?

"We registered with a department store that promised we could see our registry online. Yet when we went to the web site, all we could do was SEE it. No changes were allowed!"

That's right. Some department stores have put their gift registries online—but that only means you VIEW the registry and guests can buy items online. Want to change an item? Update a quantity? You'll still have to go into a store to do that. The Wedding Channel/Della has a chart on their web page that shows you what their "partners" allow as far as registry changes. (See Figure 1 below). While we expect most stores to let you work hi-tech wizardry on your registry from the web some point in the future, that point may be a few years off.

Figure 1: Register carefully with Della.com—not all of their partners let you review, create or edit gift registries online.

@ DellaWeddings – Your Account

What you and your guests can do at Della Weddings...

	review registries created in-store	create and edit registries online	purchase gifts
Chiasso		•	•
Crate and Barrel	•		•
Dean & DeLuca		•	•
Dillard's	•		•
Gump's	•	•	•
Neiman Marcus	•	•	•
REI		•	•
Restoration Hardware	•	•	•
Williams-Sonoma	•	•	•
Wine.com		•	•

Money Saving Tips with Gift Registries

1 **Price shop BEFORE you register.** Don't assume one store has the lowest prices just because they give you a "low price" guarantee. That usually means they will refund you the difference if you find a better price. Before you register, visit at least three different stores to get an idea about prices, policies on returns and other details. Be aware that "sale prices" at one store may be higher than the "everyday low price" at another.

2 **Consider lower-price alternatives.** No, you don't have to just register at a department store. Off-price retailers like Home Depot and Target have moved into the bridal registry biz in recent years and offer a great alternative. Remember that not ALL of your guests can buy $200 gift items at department stores; giving them a wide option of items at different price points in several stores is smart.

3 **Get sale guarantees in writing.** Department stores are famous for running numerous sales throughout the year. Unfortunately, some "forget" to give you or your guests the discounted price when purchasing a gift or items to fill-out your registry. Double check the registry's promises regarding sale prices and verify purchases to make sure you get the best price.

4 **Go for a discounter to fill in purchases.** Get 7 of 8 place settings you wanted? Want to fill in the final items? Consider buying china and tableware from a discounter. Michael Round (800-4mround; www.mround.com) is a Washington DC-area store that sells china, silver, and crystal at prices that are 25% off retail. Best of all, the store is an authorized dealer for all the name brands it carries.

5 **Buy a house.** Who says you have to register just for household goods? Register for a mortgage so your guests can give you the gift of homeownership. The US Department of Housing and Urban Development has a bridal registry that lets you accumulate a down payment for a home through an account with a qualified bank. Over 30 lenders nationwide participate in the program. For more info, call 800-CALLFHA or look on the web at www.hud.gov/bridal.html.

Honeymoons

What are the best honeymoon deals? How can you hurricane-proof your honeymoon? Where do you go online to save? We'll explore these and other tips in this section.

What are you buying?

The average honeymoon costs $3000, although there are honeymoon trips for all sorts of budgets. On the dirt cheap end, close-to-home get-aways can be had for under $1000. Conversely, a week's stay on a posh Caribbean island can be double or triple the "average" honeymoon budget.

Remember the golden rule of honeymoon shopping: NEVER PAY RETAIL. Honeymoons are an $8 billion business and we'd guess 90% or more of honeymoons are sold at prices that are discounted off the "brochure price," "rack rate" or other stated rate.

What are the most popular sites? Travel agents say Hawaii, Jamaica, Mexico and Orlando are the top honeymoon destinations. Cruises are also at the top of the list.

Sources to find honeymoon info

♥ THE NEWSPAPER. Yep, even though it is low-tech, the travel section in your Sunday paper is a good starting place for honeymoon planning. You'll see what vacation packages are available in your area, what sales might be on and more.

♥ TRAVEL AGENTS. A few do still exist and if you can find a good one, they can be invaluable. Savvy agents know which hotels have the most romantic views and which tour operators are most reliable. Sadly, it is hard to find a decent agent these days, much less one that is a "honeymoon expert." Ask friends and co-workers if they know good agents.

♥ THE WEB. If there is one thing the web is great for, it's travel. From discount airfare sites to official tourism bureaus for far flung locales, the web can't be beat. We'll go over some of our favorite 'net spots for deals later in this chapter.

Money Saving Tips with Honeymoons

1 Go "off-season." Discounts of up to 40% can be had on lodging and airfares when you travel in the so-called off-season. But just when is the off-season? It depends on the location. See the following chart for details.

2 Try the shoulder seasons. If you don't want to go to a tropical island in the heat of summer, consider the "shoulder seasons." These are times in between the peak and off-peak seasons. For example, in the Caribbean, packages in the weeks after Easter and between Thanksgiving and Christmas can be great deals. Ask an agent if the destination you want has any shoulder season deals.

WHEN IS THE OFF SEASON?

You can save big when you take a honeymoon in the off-season. Here's a list of what's off when:

DESTINATION	OFF-SEASON
CALIFORNIA WINE COUNTRY	FALL MONTHS (SEPTEMBER AND OCTOBER)
ROCKY MOUNTAINS	SUMMER HAS GREAT DEALS AT SKI REPORTS; FROM EASTER UNTIL THANKSGIVING .
EUROPE	NOVEMBER THROUGH MARCH.
CARIBBEAN	MID APRIL TO MID DECEMBER. (BUT WATCH OUT FOR HURRICANE SEASON).
ORLANDO	AFTER EASTER TO EARLY JUNE. SEPTEMBER TO BEFORE THANKSGIVING AND THE MONTH OF DECEMBER UP UNTIL CHRISTMAS; JANUARY AFTER NEW YEAR'S DAY.
HAWAII/SOUTH PACIFIC	PRICES CAN BE SLIGHTLY HIGHER IN WINTER (ESPECIALLY THE CHRISTMAS HOLIDAY) BUT THEY DON'T CHANGE MUCH YEARROUND.

3 One word: Orlando. There are so many deals to Orlando and so much to do there (it's more than just Disney) that you can't go wrong. Many airlines offer $500 packages (per person) for a week in Orlando—that includes airfare, hotel and a car rental. One airline that offers such great deals is Southwest Airlines. Which brings us to tip number #4:

4 Two words: Southwest Airlines. This low-cost airline has expanded in recent years and now serves such honeymoon friendly destinations as Orlando, Salt Lake City (think ski vacation) and Ft. Lauderdale (a great jumping off point for a cruise).

5 Alternative airports. Low-fare airlines like Southwest tend to like smaller airports that enable them to avoid congested hubs. Hence you'll find lower fares out of Midway in Chicago than O'Hare. Always consider an alternative (usually smaller) airport when trying to save.

6 Plan in advance. The cheapest seats and hotel rooms tend to go first; booking several months ahead of time will ensure you won't have to pay premium prices for peak season dates.

7 **Don't plan in advance.** Okay, we know that contradicts #6, but think about it. There are many last-minute honeymoon options that can be steals. For example, later in this chapter we'll review a web site that offers cut-rate deals for cruises booked at the last moment. Tour company like Sun Trips (www.suntrips.com) also advertises deals on packages that depart within a month—check their web site or the travel section of your newspaper for details.

8 **Take an e-fare honeymoon.** Speaking of not planning in advance, many airlines now post super-low airfares for travel the following weekend. You leave on a Saturday and must return on a Monday or Tuesday—and you won't know where you are going until Wednesday before the honeymoon (that's when the airfares are posted). If you are adventurous, check out the web site SmarterLiving.com, which lists all the deals. An example: we checked the e-fares from Boston one weekend and found 34 deals, including $138 round trip to Ft. Lauderdale, $158 to New Orleans and $218 to San Francisco.

Hurricane proof your honeymoon

Most weddings (and therefore, honeymoons) are in the summer. And since most couples opt for a beach getaway, the temptation to hit the Caribbean is high. Unfortunately, so is the risk for hurricanes. While the hurricane season peaks in September, you can encounter a vacation-destroying tempest anytime from June to November.

So, what can you do to hurricane proof your honeymoon? Remember your ABC's. Not all Caribbean islands are in the high-risk zone for hurricanes—the "ABC" islands of the Dutch Antilles are a good example. Aruba, Bonaire and Curacao each have a 2% or less chance of getting whacked by a hurricane in each year. And here's another bonus: the summer "low season" produces some great deals to these tropical getaways.

For example, Caribbean Concepts (800) 423-4433 offers a week in Aruba from August to October for just $645 (includes air AND hotel) from Boston; $665 from New York or $739 from Dallas. Those prices are per person with a stay at one of the better resorts on Aruba, the Mill.

If you like diving, Bonaire is your island. A honeymoon here runs just $658 (per person) out of Miami or $774 from Newark with packages from Caradonna Caribbean Tours (800) 328-2288. For a more European feel, try Curacao. Several resorts are just $650 to $830 (for air and hotel) per person per week from Vacation Travel Mart (800) 288-1435 (www.vacmart.com).

Other destinations with very low hurricane risk include Margarita (an island off the coast of Venezuela; to book call Servitorus 305-381-9026), Panama and Tobago, the little sister to Trinidad.

9 **For destination weddings, see if the airline has a "bridal discount."** If you plan to take ten of your closet friends and/or relatives on a destination wedding, ask about discounts. US Airways and American offer a 5% to 10% discount on the lowest fare for wedding parties of ten or more. American even provides the bride and groom with a packet of airline "upgrade" coupons, car rental discounts and coupons for free drinks and headsets.

10 **Book early for peak times.** Be careful if your honeymoon corresponds with any peak travel times, like Europe in the summer, the Caribbean over the holidays, spring break in Orlando and so on. In those cases, booking early to get the best deals is prudent.

11 **Travel on off-days.** The slowest days for air travel (Saturday, Tuesday, Wednesday) often see the lowest fares. In contrast, fares tend to be higher on busy travel days like Thursday, Friday and Sunday.

12 **Follow the disaster.** A hurricane just hit a Caribbean island? Terrorists strike against a European country? Such events usually create tremendous bargains, as other travelers cancel their plans. Go against the flow for good deals.

13 **Bid on a bargain.** Many couples have found deals on Priceline.com and other travel auction sites. But beware: Priceline tickets often require bizarre schedules (6am departure, anyone?) and connections that leave you open for delays.

14 **Consider a consolidator.** The cheapest way to fly internationally is to check out travel consolidators, who buy blocks of tickets from airlines to re-sell at good prices. A good example: www.1travel.com.

15 **Tour companies.** Vacation package companies like Apple Vacations (www.applevacations.com) and Sun Trips (www.suntrips.com) book affordable vacations with charter airlines and decent hotels. These combined deals can be great steals—$400 per person for a week in Cozumel including airfare and hotel, for example.

Brides in Cyberspace: What's on the Web?

BestFares
Web: www.bestfares.com
What it is: The Mother of All Travel Deal sites
What's cool: Best Fares is probably the best source for unbiased info on travel deals, steals and more. Check out their "News Desk" (www.

bestfares.com/travel_center/desks/newsdesk.asp) for a massive archive of airfare, hotel and vacation specials. Look for "Snooze Alarm" deals, which are low-fare specials that airlines only offer for a small time. Best Fares chronicles all the airlines fare sales and more.

Needs Work: Unfortunately, the News Desk is just arranged chronically; you can't search for deals by destination or any other feature. Instead, you scroll through window after window to scan headlines for different deals. Some deals are for "Members Only" ($59.90 for one year).

Here are several more web sites that offer honeymoon deals:

♥ **THE DAILY AUCTION** (www.thedailyauction.com) has incredible deals to Europe. The auctions are held two days a week and feature airfares from Lufthansa and hotels deals from Hilton. How great are the deals? How about two tickets (for a week's stay) from Detroit to Paris for $420? That's total for TWO TICKETS, not each. Other deals we saw were Philadelphia to Berlin for $410 for two tickets and Boston to Zurich for $230 for one ticket. Most of the trips posted are for certain days about a month out from when you travel. You must leave and depart on certain days and stays run seven to ten days.

♥ **SPUR-OF-THE-MOMENT CRUISES** (800) 343-1991, web: www.spurof.com has last-minute specials from cruise lines. Samples: $773 for an inside cabin for a nine-night Alaska cruise. Or try a week long cruise in the Caribbean for just $499 per person.

♥ **VACATION DIRECT** (www.vacationdirect.com) lists vacation rentals made available directly by owners. You can rent a guest cottage, villa or condo anywhere in the world. The site enables you to search by location, event or interest/activity. You deal directly with the property owner, saving money by eliminating any agent fees.

So many islands, so little time

If you want to head to a tropical getaway for an island, the Caribbean offers plenty of options. But what is best for different interests? Here are some thoughts:

Best Scuba: Cozumel and Bonaire.
Best Snorkel: Cozumel, St. Croix and Virgin Gorda.
Best Shopping: Bermuda, Bali.
Best Music: Jamaica.
Best Beaches: Aruba, Antigua and Barbados.
Best for food: Martinique, Guadeloupe, Curacao.
Best for Eco Trips: St. John, US Virgins.
Best Upscale: St. Maarten, St. Bart's, Nevis and Anguilla.
Best Volcanoes: Big Island Hawaii.

Canadian brides face some of the same challenges as their counterparts, with one exception: in a country as vast as Canada, how do you find local resources to plan a wedding if you're in Vancouver and the wedding is in, say, Toronto? Well, we found an excellent Canadian web site that covers just about everything that's bridal in the Great White North. Plus, we rate and review some of Canada's best home-grown bridal designers and invitations catalogs.

Bridal gowns

The average bridal gown in Canada sells for $700 to $1000 Canadian. When you factor in the exchange rate, this works out to about $500 to $700 —that's about the same as brides spend in the US, give or take a hundred dollars.

How does that compare to total wedding expenses? In Canada, the average wedding is about C$10,625, so the bridal gown is about 10% of total expenses. That's somewhat higher than the US, where the dress accounts for about 5% of marriage expenses. The average Canadian couple invites about 125 guests to the wedding—that's much less than the 175 guests invited to US weddings:

AVERAGE WEDDING COSTS IN CANADA

(all figures in Canadian dollars)

APPAREL	$700
FLOWERS	600
CAKE	400
RECEPTION	6300
PHOTOGRAPHY	900
VIDEOGRAPHY	750
INVITATIONS	125
MUSIC	850
TOTAL	**$10,625**

In other ways, the Canadian bridal market is similar to the US. The average engagement is 10.7 months and over half of the couples are paying for their wedding themselves. The average age of Canadian brides and grooms could have something to do with that statistic: the bride is typically 29, the groom 30.

Of course, there are important differences. The number of weddings in Canada each year is about 154,750 (according to 1999 figures). That contrasts to the US, with 2.4 million weddings annually. As a result, Canada's bridal "industry" is not as developed as the —and that's both good and bad news. On the upside, the less-lucrative nature of the Canadian market means scam artists are more likely to concentrate their efforts in the US. However, the smaller number of brides translates into a smaller number of wedding merchants. And less competition usually means higher prices and less selection.

Top Money-saving Tips

Yes, the average bridal gown in Canada costs C$700 to C$1000. Is that too much for you? Here are five tips to save money:

1 **Go mail order.** Discount Bridal Service, the mail-order discounter we mentioned earlier in this book, services Canada. While the company doesn't have reps on-site in Canada, you can order a dress by calling their Arizona office at (800) 874-8794 or (602) 998-6953. How much can you save? Well, Discount Bridal Service sells all those name-brand designer bridal gowns, bridesmaids dresses and accessories you see in the bridal magazines. The discount is typically 20% to 40% off the retail price. The only downside? You have to pay shipping, duties and

GST, which might make some of the savings disappear. On the other hand, DBS sells many designers that are not even distributed in Canada. Hence, if you see a dress during a shopping excursion to the US and you can't live without that gown, DBS may be the answer.

2 **Watch out for "designer dumps."** What happens when bridal designers have too many gowns and not enough customers? It's sale time! Yet, American designers don't want to sully their fancy, full-price image in the United States. So, they load up the truck and head north. The designers rent a hotel ballroom, take out ads that scream "MONSTER BRIDAL DRESS SALE! ONE DAY ONLY" and let the bargains rip. While there is no schedule to these sales, you might want to keep an eye on the papers to see if one comes to your town.

3 **Check out David's.** As we mentioned earlier in this book, David's is an off-the-rack operation that has dozens of outlets in the US. One is in Buffalo, New York (716) 834-6100, which told us they see quite a few brides who make the short trip from Toronto. David's periodically has $99 gown sales, but even their regular dresses ($300 to $600) are pretty good deals. (Since David's is growing rapidly, you may be able to find a store closer to you by calling 800-399-2743 or 610-896-2111; web: www.davidsbridal.com). Of course, cross-border shopping has its own drawbacks—call your local Revenue Canada office for duty information.

4 **Go for one of our "best buy" designers.** Affordable gown makers like Mon Cheri, Eden and Mori Lee are all available in Canada. For example, Mori Lee has extensive distribution in Canada (contact their Canadian distributor, Richman Group 416-789-9911 for a store near you).

5 **Dicker the price.** Off the record, Canadian bridal manufacturers tell us it is a buyer's market for wedding dresses in Canada. The plain fact: there are too many gowns chasing too few brides. As a result, shops are hungry for business and may make you a deal. While that doesn't mean they'll knock 40% off that dream dress, you might be able to negotiate a small discount . . . it can't hurt to ask!

Gown preservation

As you read earlier, there are lot of scam artists in the business of bridal gown "cleaning and preservation." Fortunately, we did find one honest person who does this in Canada—Forever Yours Bridal Gown Preservation in Toronto (800) 683-4696, (416) 703-4696 (www.gowncare.com). Owner Jerry Shiner's family has been cleaning delicate garments since 1933 and his company now specializes in bridal gown cleaning and preservation. Forever Yours charges a base price of C$200 to C$300, with a more specific price quote offered depending on the type of gown, detailing and so on. The process takes about six to eight weeks and the company offers pick-up and delivery across Canada. While the service is pricey, you're getting museum-quality preservation and tremendous care that insures beads and lace aren't damaged in the cleaning process.

Reviews of Canadian Bridal Designers

As a Canadian bride, you basically have two choices when it comes to selecting a bridal gown: imported or domestic. Many US designers have Canadian distribution (most notably Mori Lee and Demetrios/ Sposabella). Therefore, you can use the US designer reviews earlier in this book to gauge various styles and price options (although Canadian duties on dresses made in Asia may add slightly to the retail prices you see in Canada).

Of course, you can go domestic. Canada has a dozen or so manufacturers of bridal gowns and their reputation for quality is earning fans on both sides of the border. Unlike their US counterparts, most Canadian bridal designers actually make their gowns domestically. On the upside, the workmanship and construction quality is generally excellent, especially compared to the imports. On the downside, the price is usually higher (as you'll read below in more detail).

As a side note, many Canadian bridal manufacturers are attempting to expand their distribution in the US. In recent years, several Canadian designers debuted in the US and, while their distribution may be spotty at this point, expect to see more Canadian bridal gowns in the lower 48. Why? Well, NAFTA is one reason—the trade agreement recently lowered tariffs and duties on goods made in Canada that are imported into the US (and vice versa). A weak Canadian dollar has also spurred exports. Of course, another explanation is obvious: many Canadian designers are simply looking for new markets. Since the US has 15 times more weddings than Canada, the designers look to the US market as one of their few growth opportunities. They're hoping their quality gowns and clean styling will appeal to US brides, despite prices that can be high at times.

What follows is an overview of the best Canadian bridal designers. Note that the following prices are in Canadian dollars. At the time of this writing, prices for these dresses in the United States were quite similar to the Canadian prices.

Alfred Sung Shanghai-born designer Alfred Sung is sort of like the Ralph Lauren of Canada—pop across the border and you'll see the Sung name plastered on everything from luggage to sunglasses, perfume to socks. Given his success with evening wear, it wasn't too surprising when he licensed his name for a bridal line in the early 1990's. What was surprising was how successful it was: Sung (which is made by Toronto-based bridal maker Jai) is a smash hit, thanks to its contemporary styling. A typical Sung look is a plain gown with tiny hand-crafted flowers at the waistline, a touch of guipure lace or ribbon accents. The line is divided into two collections: Boutique ($600 to $700) and the Signature Line ($800 to $1600). Quality and construction is above average (all gowns are made in Canada), but we were disappointed with the fabrics, mostly polyester satin and organza. For dresses that top $1000, we'd expect to see more silk. *Sizes 4 to 20, with sizes 22 to 30 available only in the Signature line for 20% extra. For a dealer, call (800) 295-7308 or (416) 247-4628. Web: www.alfredsungbridals.com.*

Barbara Allin Toronto-based designer Barbara Allin's dress collection is a subsidiary of Allin Rae, a company better known for their ornate headpieces. We saw Allin's plain gowns at a recent trade show and were impressed. For $600 to $950, these are some smartly designed dresses. Fabrics included polyester satin and silk satin. One odd note: Allin doesn't put her name into the gowns. Instead, the gowns' tags reference her Canadian registered number (CA 18172). *For a dealer near you, call (416) 469-1098.*

Catherine Regehr Vancouver evening-wear designer Catherine Regehr had ten years of design experience creating couture gowns before she branched out into bridal in 1997. Her specialty: translating hot evening wear looks like slinky sheaths into bridal gowns. We saw Catherine's collection recently and thought it was on the mark—dresses are available in both polyester or silk fabrics and you can mix and match various tops with several skirt styles. Prices for a complete gown were $600 to $3000. *Sizing is rather limited (petite, small, medium and large). For a dealer near you, call 604-734-9339.*

Paloma Blanca See review earlier in this book in Chapter 2. In Canada, Paloma Blanca makes gowns under the name BB Couture.

Gordon Gordon has been in business since the 1970's and turns out dresses in the $800 to $1000 range. The looks are "simple and elegant," according to a representative we spoke to. A typical Gordon dress features a plain skirt and train and just a touch of beading or lace on the tight-fitting bodice. Fabrics include silk and duchess satin. Sizing starts at 4 and Gordon does offer large size dresses. Delivery takes four to six weeks, which makes Gordon one of the more speedy Canadian bridal manufacturers. *Call (905) 276-3399 for a dealer near you.*

Guzzo Looking for something daring? Check out some of the gowns from couture bridal dressmaker Guzzo. Designer Frances Guzzo has turned out bustier-style gowns since 1982 from her downtown Toronto retail "studio." And these gowns leave little to the imagination. An example? Try a strapless silk satin hand-beaded bustier bodice with a silk organza skirt for $3000. The gowns (which have been featured in Wedding Dresses and Modern Bride magazines) start at $2000, but many are near $3000. Most of the dresses are made of silk and all are custom cut (made to your measurements). *Delivery is 12 to 14 weeks. Call (416) 585-9820 (web: www.guzzobridal.com) to find a dealer near you.*

Ines Di Santo If we were to give an award for Canada's most flamboyant bridal designer, Ines Di Santo would win hands down. This Argentina-born Italian designer has a flair for the dramatic, accenting her dresses with tiny porcelain roses, Austrian crystals and intricate metallic embroidery. As you might expect, all this extravagance doesn't come cheap—most Ines Di Santo bridal gowns start at $2000 and range up to a whopping $4600. Yet you are getting value for the dollar; we saw the dresses at a recent fashion show and found the looks to be extravagant. All the fabrics are silk. In business since 1976, Ines has her own shop called Chez Moi in Woodbridge, Ontario (just outside Toronto). *Sizes 4 to 20 and a few petite sizes are also available. Call (905) 856-9115 to find a dealer near you.*

Justina McCaffrey Justina McCaffrey is our pick as the best bridal designer in Ottawa. Okay, she's probably the only bridal designer in Ottawa, but don't hold that against her. McCaffrey designed a women's evening wear collection for Creed's of Toronto before launching her own company in 1989. McCaffrey's all-silk bridal gowns feature slick European styling (that is, plain skirts and only minimal detailing on the bodices). The emphasis here is on the fabric (including silk brocade and dupioni), not extravagant beading and lace. The dresses sell for $1500 to $2000 in Canada, about $1700 to $2500 in the US. You can visit Justina McCaffrey's retail store in Ottawa or check out another bridal shop that carries her dresses (about dozen or so in the US). *Call toll-free (888) 874-GOWN or (613) 789-4336 to find a dealer near you. Internet: www.jmhc.com*

Madison Collection The best buy among Canadian bridal designers has to be the Madison Collection, a Toronto-based company that turns out beautiful dresses at affordable prices. With gowns that run $800 to $1400, you can find "European styling" and quality fabrics in a variety of fashion-forward looks. A good example is style 8864, a French satin jewel neckline with sleeveless bodice detailed with scattered pearls. The price: $800. Sizing is somewhat limited (sizes 6 to 20), but they will do "over-size" dresses for an additional 20% of the cost. The quality is top-notch. *Call The Richman Group at (416) 789-9911 for a dealer near you.*

Rivini Toronto-based Rivini's signature look is hand-crafted roses and delicate hand-beaded bodices. The company divides its gowns into fabric groups and offers such options as Austrian crepe, silk peau de soie and silk duchess satin. We saw the gowns at a recent trade show and were impressed with the clean, fashion-forward looks. One stand-out was an empire gown with beaded tank-style neckline, bias skirt and chiffon train for $1750. Other dresses ranged from $1250 to $3000. *Sizes range from 4 to 16. Call (416) 977-1793 to find a dealer near you.*

Invitations

Many of the mail order invitations catalogs we review earlier in this book ship to Canada. A prime example is Dawn, which markets extensively to Canada. Dawn's toll-free number for Canadian brides is 800-535-8586; or write to PO Box 2504, Winnipeg, Manitoba R3C 4A7. Here are two other choices:

Classic Canadian Weddings
To order call: (800) 833-6761
Or write to: PO Box 1761, Winnipeg, Manitoba R3C 2Z9
Canada's largest wedding invitations mail-order outfit, this company offers both traditional and contemporary designs. Orders ship within 48 hours. Besides invites, the catalog also sells a wide variety of accessories, including "Western cake tops," favors, memory albums and more.

Nicole
To order in English, call: 800-228-0486; Française: 1-800-465-1716
Write to: PO Box 1294, Station B, Mississauga, Ontario L4Y 3W5
or CP 477, Succursale Youville, Montreal, Quebec H2P 2V6
Nicole is Canada's only bilingual invitation catalog—you can order from it (and get your questions answered) in either English or French. Most of the designs are quite traditional; Nicole offers a low price guarantee. We were pleased with the samples we saw from Nicole; the paper quality and printing were above average, while the pricing was attractive.

Discount Invitations
To order: Call toll free at (888) 969-9394 www.discount-invitations.com
This site, in business since 1998, offers professionally printed invitations in two days for Canadian brides. A catalog is available, or you can see their invitations online. The styles we saw ran the gamut from plain cards to fancier floral creations and more. Discount Invitations claims to offer a 20% discount off Canadian invitations books and prints its prices in Canadian dollars. While their web site is a bit confusing and cluttered, owner Lano Tondu does provide personal service.

Photographers, Florists and other local vendors

Brides in Cyberspace: What's on the Web?

Wedding Bells
Web: www.weddingbells.com
What it is: Canada's coolest wedding web site.

What's cool: Trying to find a photographer in Edmonton? A florist in Winnipeg? Then, you need to check out this massive web site, run by Wedding Bells, a Canadian bridal magazine. Our search for reception sites in Calgary, for example, yielded an amazing 43 possibilities, from historic homes and local parks to four-star hotels. Each listing provides contact info and a descriptive paragraph that provided basic facts (capacity, special features, etc.). There's even a French version of the site for Quebec. Besides local wedding merchant info, other sections of the web site featured fashion news, Canadian bridal trends and traditions, etiquette issues and an email monthly newsletter with "fresh new ideas" that aren't on the web site.

Needs work: Since the site is so huge, it can be daunting to navigate. Check out the "table of contents" for a site map so you don't get lost. We would also liked to see more links to vendor home pages in the local resources section.

Other web sites to consider: We love the **Frugal Bride** (www.frugal-bride.com), which has some great money-saving tips and vendor recommendations, all with a Canadian focus. Another good site: **WeddingCanada.com**, which has regional vendor listings by province.

Cakes. The traditional Canadian wedding cake—the fruit cake—is out of favor as brides opt for more gourmet options. A baker in Mississauga told the *Toronto Star* recently that the only exception are Jamaican dark rum cakes, which are sometimes cut up in souvenir pieces for guests to take home. Otherwise, Canadian brides are going for mousse, fresh fruit or cheesecakes. Prices for a two-tier cake in Ontario start at C$190, while three-tier confections are C$295 and up.

What can you do to deal with these last-minute wedding crises? Here's our answers to a Bridal 911.

Okay, let's assume you're the perfect consumer. Instead of using cash or a check, you've put all the deposits on a credit card. All the agreements with each service are in writing. You've dotted all your "i's" and crossed all your "t's." But what if your wedding day arrives and, for example, the florist delivers dead flowers? Or the photographer sends a last-minute "stand-in"? Or the wrong wedding cake is delivered? Here are some thoughts on how to deal with such crisises.

Meet the Surrogate Bad Cop

No matter how careful you are, things can still happen at your wedding and reception that are not according to plan. That's why you need a Surrogate Bad Cop as an "enforcer" to fix last minute problems and correct wayward merchants.

Who can be a surrogate bad cop? Anyone you believe is trustworthy and reliable. This can be your best friend, your mother or a close relative. Of course, if you're hiring a professional wedding planner, they would play this role typically.

What does the surrogate bad cop actually do? **Their job is to make sure you enjoy your wedding.** While you're greeting guests and having fun, it's the surrogate bad cop's role to tell the florist to fix the flowers. Or track down the photographer. Or find out why the wrong wedding cake was delivered and see if it can be fixed.

In addition to major problems, the surrogate cop also handles any minor situations. One bride told us she was upset with the band she hired when the musicians launched into an unscheduled set of heavy metal music. While she was posing for pictures, the bride had her surrogate bad cop (her sister) talk to the band leader. She informed him of the band's mistake and said the bride had requested they change the tempo. And the band complied.

The Surrogate Bad Cop's Bag of Tricks

Any good enforcer needs the right tools at their disposal to do their job effectively. Here's a look into their "bag of tricks," a special folder/notebook that you give to them on the wedding day:

1 **Phone numbers of every contracted vendor** (business, home, cell, pager). Okay, it's Saturday night, the wedding is in one hour and the florist is nowhere to be found. You call the shop and, of course, it's closed. Now what? That's why you also need a home number for the key contact at every service. Even better: get cell and/or pager numbers as well. These numbers will be crucial if your surrogate needs to track down an errant florist, photographer, DJ, etc.

2 **Copies of each contract and proposal.** Let's say the florist has shown up, but she's missing several arrangements. Or a special orchid corsage for your grandmother. However, the florist claims you never ordered that. What can you do? Well, if you're smart, you'll put copies of every contract and proposal into your surrogate cop's bag of tricks. That way she can whip out the florist's proposal and tactfully point out that, yes, there is suppose to be an orchid corsage. Usually, florists carry a few extra flowers with them (or they can perhaps pop back to their shop and pick up the missing pieces). One hopes that you won't have to resort to producing written contracts to correct problems, but it's a nice back-up just in case. Also, it helps the surrogate bad cop figure out just what you ordered.

3 **Authority to act on your behalf.** This "invisible" tool is important. You must tell each service (photographer, florist, caterer, DJ, band, etc.) that this special person will be acting on your behalf during the wedding and reception. If your surrogate comes to the merchant with a request, they should know it is your wishes.

4 **Cell phone or pager.** Communication is key—making sure your surrogate bad cop has a cell phone or pager is critical to correcting problems quickly. Don't assume you'll have access to a phone at the ceremony or reception site. If you arrive at the church and the doors are locked, a cell phone will be a life-saver.

The Final Check-Up

A week or so before your wedding, you should set up a "final check-up" with each merchant and service. Whether it is an in-person meeting or by telephone, you should discuss the following:

♥ CONFIRM ALL DATES, DAYS, TIMES AND LOCATIONS. You need arrival or drop-off times from such services as the florist and baker. Be careful if you're not getting married on a Saturday—make sure the merchant knows your wedding is a Friday or Sunday. We've heard stories of "no-show merchants" who assumed all weddings are on Saturday. Don't forget to call the officiant—you can't get married without him or her.

♥ GET ALL THE PHONE NUMBERS WE MENTIONED ABOVE.

♥ TELL THEM THE IDENTITY OF YOUR "SURROGATE BAD COP." While you may not use those words exactly, let the companies know that this one special person will be helping you that day. They should treat any request from this person as your direction.

♥ CONFIRM THE ORDER. Now is the time to make sure that the florist can do bird of paradise flowers in your bouquet. Or that the wedding cake will be a certain flavor. Go over the menu with the caterer and fix any problems. Make sure they have your special requests in writing in their files.

♥ PAY THE BALANCE. Many services and merchants will require the payment of the balance due at this time. Try to pay by credit card.

Strategies for Dealing with Wedding Day Crises

Bridal 911 problems fall into one of three categories:

1 **Improper deliveries.** What can you do if the wrong cake is delivered or the caterer serves the wrong main course? While you (or your surrogate cop) may be able to contact the company before the start of the ceremony, there may not be enough time to fix the problem. Solution: ask the company to make an "adjustment" in your final bill. This doesn't mean you get the item for free—but a discount or partial refund may be in order.

2 **No shows/Late arrivals.** If the photographer is late, use the contact numbers to track him/her down. Solution: anyone who charges by the hour should make an adjustment in their bill if they run late. Or they may be able to make up the time by staying later.

3 **Inferior quality.** You were promised big, beautiful roses, but the florist has delivered half-dead, miniature roses. The DJ said he had an extensive collection of country music, but it turns out that it's just one Garth Brooks album. Honestly, there isn't much you can do on the day of the wedding if a company has deceived you about the quality of their products or services. However, after the wedding, you may want to dispute the charge on your credit card. If you paid by check or cash, you may have to take the merchant to small claims court to recover your money. Document the problem with pictures or video. Also, complain to the Better Business Bureau and your city/county's consumer affairs office.

Many so-called wedding "disasters" are due to the lack of written agreements or ambiguous contracts. You can stop this problem by simply getting everything in writing.

Another source of problems are "early deliveries." One bride in Texas told us about a wedding cake that was delivered *six hours* before her reception. As the hotel was setting up the ballroom, someone with a ladder whacked the cake. The lesson: don't have the flowers, cake or other items delivered *too early*. There's just too much of an opportunity for problems.

Finally, some goofs are due to a lack of organization on the businesses' part. Whether the mix-up is an honest mistake or an intentional fraud, it doesn't matter. As a professional, the vendor should act to correct the mistake or give you a refund. Sadly, not all wedding merchants are professionals and you must take steps to protect yourself as a consumer.

The Bottom Line

While there's no such thing as a perfect wedding, there is such a thing as a consumer-savvy bride and groom. With credit cards, complete written agreements and a well-armed surrogate bad cop, you can get the quality that you're paying the big bucks for at your wedding and reception.

After reading through all the tips and advice in this book, your first thought may be "Let's elope!" And, if you didn't question your sanity in this process at least once, we would be worried about you.

Of course, it's easy for us to sit here in our Ivory Tower and tell you that you need to keep your "perspective" while wedding planning. In truth, perhaps many married couples take perverse joy in seeing engaged couples go through the anguish of planning a wedding. It's almost like a boot camp for marriage: if you can survive this, then you are fit to join the rest of us on the other side of the fence of marital bliss.

Even if weddings are some sinister plot to initiate the single into the married world, this doesn't excuse the fact that the entire US wedding industry, your friends and relatives are trying to convince you that YOUR WEDDING DAY IS THE SINGLE MOST IMPORTANT DAY OF YOUR LIFE. And, of course, unless you get everything perfect, the wrath of the WEDDING GODS will be on your head.

We hope this book is useful as you plan your trip down the aisle. We sincerely appreciate your purchase of this book and we want to help you any way we can. If you have any questions about this book or just want to chat, see the "How to reach us" page at the end of this book.

In the face of all this, our message to you is quite simple: have a good time. Don't take this bridal stuff too seriously. Remember that you are planning a party to celebrate you and your fiancé's relationship. And, theoretically, people are suppose to have fun at parties. Even the guests of honor.

PHONE/WEB DIRECTORY

Wonder where these contact names appear in the book? Check the index for a page number. **Remember that many of these contacts do not sell to the public directly; the phone numbers are so you can find a dealer/store near you.** Refer to the chapter in which they are mentioned to see which companies offer a consumer catalog, sell to the public, etc. For space reasons, we omitted the "www." prefix in front of the web site addresses.

Contact Name	Toll-Free	Phone	Web Site
Introduction			
Alan & Denise Fields (authors)		(303) 442-8792	bridalgown.com
Jeremys		(415) 882-4929	
Shea Stadium reception site		(718) 565-4332	
2G Roses		(800) 880-0735	freshroses.com
EZ Bow Maker	(800) 311-6529	(865) 453-3060	
Michaels		(800) 642-4235	michaels.com
Miracle Bow		(301) 739-6314	offray.com
Wedding Invit. CD-ROM	(800) 621-3684		pcpapers.com
Apparel for the Bride			
The Wedding Channel			weddingchannel.com
The Knot			theknot.com
Romantic Headlines			romanticheadlines.com
Veils A La Mode			veilsalamode.com
August Moon Designs			bridalstuff.com
Federal Trade Commission		(202) 326-2222	ftc.gov
JCPenney's bridal catalog	(800) 527-8345		jcpenney.com
Trousseaux.com			trousseaux.com
Barenecessities.com			barenecessities.com
Bridesmart			bridesmart.com
Ebay			ebay.com
Fabric sources			
Hyman Hendler		(212) 840-8393	
Dulken & Derrick		(212) 929-3614	
Greenburg & Hammer	(800) 955-5135		
David's Textiles	(800) 548-1818		
Minnetonka Mills	(800) 328-4443		
The Fabric Mart	(800) 242-3695		
Fabric Depot	(800) 392-3376		
McGowen's		(908) 965-2298	
Milliners Supply			milliners.com
Vogue Fabrics		(847) 864-1270	
Bridal Couture (book)	(800) 258-0929		
Academy of Fashion	(888) 493-3261		

Making Memories	(503) 252-3955	makingmemories.org
Just Once (rental)	(212) 465-0960	
An Alternative (rental)	(888) 761-8686 (816) 761-8686	
Filene's Basement sale	(617) 542-2011	
Internet Resale Directory		secondhand.com
Nat'l Assoc. of Resale & Thrift Stores		narts.org
Nearly new Bridal		nearlynewbridal.com
Rummaging Thru N. Calif (newsletter)	(707) 939-9124	secondhand.com

Gown manufacturers

ABS by Allen Schwartz	(212) 398-0330	absstyle.com
Alfred Angelo	(800) 531-1125 (561) 241-7755	alfredangelo.com
Alvina Valenta	(212) 354-6798	alvinavalenta.com
Amsale	(800) 765-0170 (212) 971-0170	amsale.com
Bianchi	(800) 669-2346 (978) 738-9790	houseofbianchi.com
Bonny	(800) 528-0030 (714) 961-8884	bonny.com
Bridal Originals	(800) 876-4696 (618) 345-2345	bridaloriginals.com
Christos	(212) 921-0025	christosbridal.com
Demetrios/Ilissa	(212) 967-5222	demetriosbride.com
Diamond Collection	(212) 302-0210	diamondbridal.com
Eden	(800) 828-8831 (626) 358-9281	edenbridals.com
Emme	(888) 745-7560 (281) 634-9225	emmebridal.com
Eve of Milady	(212) 302-0050	
Forever Yours	(800) USA-Bride	foreverbridals.com
Galina	(212) 564-1020	galinabridal.com
Group USA		groupusa.com
Ian Stuart	(914) 369-6631	ianstuart.com
Impression	(800) BRIDAL-1 (281) 634-9200	impressionbridal.com
Jacquelin	(941) 277-7099	jacquelinbridals.com
Janell Berte	(717) 291-9894	berte.com
Jasmine	(800) 634-0224 (630) 295-5880	jasminebridal.com
Jessica McClintock	(800) 333-5301 (415) 495-3030	jessicamcclintock.com
Jim Hjelm	(800) 924-6475 (212) 764-6960	jlmcouture.com
Lazaro	(212) 764-5781	lazarobridal.com
Maggie Sottero	(801) 255-3870	maggiesotterobridal.com
Marisa	(212) 944-0022	marisabridals.com
Mary's	(281) 933-9678	marysbridal.com
Mon Cheri	(609) 530-1900	mcbridals.com
Monique	(626) 401-9910	moniquebridal.com
Monique L'Huillier	(310) 659-9888	moniquelhuillier.com
Moonlight	(800) 447-0405 (847) 884-7199	moonlightbridal.com
Mori Lee/Regency	(212) 840-5070	morileeinc.com
Paloma Blanca	(416) 235-0585	palomablanca.com
Priscilla of Boston	(617) 242-2677	priscillaofboston.com
Private Label by G/Ginza	(800) 858-3338 (562) 531-1116	privatelabelbyg.com
Pronovias	(516) 371-0877	pronovias.com
Robert Legere	(212) 631-0606	
Scaasi/Forsyth	(804) 971-3853	
St. Pucchi	(214) 631-4039	stpucchi.com
Sweetheart	(800) 223-6061 (212) 947-7171	gowns.com
Tomasina	(412) 563-7788	tomasinabridal.com
Venus	(800) 648-3687 (626) 285-5796	
Vera Wang	(800) 839-8372 (212) 575-6400	verawang.com

Discount Bridal Service	(800) 874-8794		discountbridalservice.com
Bridal Marketplace			bridalmarketplace.com
Bridsave.com			bridesave.com
GownsOnline	(408) 985-5594		gownsonline.com
NetBride			netbride.com
Pearl's Place	(504) 885-9213		pearlsplace.com
Priceless Bridal	(818) 340-6514		bargainweddinggowns.com
RK Bridal	(800) 929-9512		rkbridal.com
Wedding Expressions	(319) 753-5217		weddingexpressions.com

David's	(800) 399-2743		davidsbridal.com
The Gown Company	(212) 979-9000		thegowncompany.com
Jessica McClintock Company Stores			
South San Francisco			(415) 553-8390
Mont Clair, CA	(909) 982-1866		
Huntington Beach, CA			(714) 841-7124
El Paso, TX	(915) 771-9550		
Proteus' Discount Bridal Store	(415) 495-7922		
Jeremys	(415) 882-4929		
Bridal World Outlet	(619) 426-2100		
Alfred Angelo Company	(954) 846-9198		
JcPenney outlets	(800) 222-6161		
Affordable Bridal Warehouse	(602) 279-4933		

Container Store	(800) 733-3532		containerstore.com
I Do Veils book	(800) 295-0586	(440) 333-3143	

Apparel for the Wedding Party

BestBridesmaid.com			bestbridesmaid.com
Formals Etc	(318) 640-3766		formalsetc.com
An Alternative	(888) 761-8686	(816) 761-8686	
Dillards			dillards.com
Discount Gloves	(800) 479-4696		bridalgloves.com
Bloomingdales by Mail	(800) 777-0000		
Spiegel catalog	(800) 345-4500		
Talbot's catalog	(800) 882-5268		talbots.com
Chadwicks of Boston	(800) 525-6650		chadwicks.com
One Hanes Place	(800) 300-2600		onehanesplace.com
Discount Dyeables			discountdyeables.com
Outlet Bound			outletbound.com
Le Stella	(888) 626-7888		www.lestella
Alexia	(800) 235-0681		
Manufacturers			
After Six	(800) 444-8304	(212) 354-5808	aftersix.com
Alyce Designs		(847) 966-9200	alycedesigns.com
Bari Jay		(212) 391-1555	
Belsoie	(800) 634-0224	(630) 295-5880	belsoie.com
Bill Levkoff	(800) LEV-KOFF		billlevkoff.com
Champagne		(212) 302-9162	champagneformals.com
Dessy Creations	(800) 52-DESSY	(212) 354-5808	dessy.com
Jordan		(212) 921-5560	jordanfashions.com
Marlene	(800) 826-2563	(412) 243-7560	marlenesbridal.com
New Image	(800) 421-4624		newimagebridesmaids.com
Watters and Watters		(972) 960-9884	watters.com

Tux Express	(480) 991-6655	
Marrying Man.com		marryingman.com
Gingiss		gingiss.com
Etuxedo.com		etuxedo.com
4Tuxedos.com		4tuxedos.com
Men's Wearhouse		menswearhouse.com

Ceremony Sites

USA CityLink		usacitylink.com
Ibride		ibride.com
Places (book)	(212) 737-7536	

Flowers

Assoc of Spec Cut Flowers	(440) 774-2887	
Flint Hill Flower Farm	(301) 607-4554	
Flowersales.com		flowersales.com
International Floral Picture Database		flowerweb.com
C. O. D. Wholesale		codwholesale.com
Bliss' Floral Chart		www.blissezine.com/weddingfloral/
Elegant Cheesecakes	(650) 728-2248	elegantcheesecakes.com
Iluminations catalog	(800) CANDLES	illuminations.com
Linen & Lace	(800) 332-5223	linen-lace.com
Butterfly Celebration	(800) 548-3284	butterflycelebration.com
2G Roses	(800) 880-0735	freshroses.com
Get Fresh		getfreshwithme.com
Michaels Arts & Crafts	(800) 642-4235	michaels.com
Hobby Lobby	(405) 745-1100	hobbylobby.com
MJDesigns	(817) 329-3196	mjdesigns.com

Invitations

OurBeginning.com	ourbeginning.com
WedNet	wednet.com
Einvite	einvite.com
Catalog Orders Headquarters	catalog.orders.com
Costco	costco.com
Gaddis Design	gaddisdesign.com

Manufacturers

Carlson Craft	(800) 328-1782		carlsoncraft.com
Chase Paper		(508) 478-9220	
Checkerboard Invitations		(508) 835-2475	
Crane	(800) 472-7263		crane.com
Elite	(800) 354-8321		
Embossed Graphics	(800) 362-6773	(630) 236-4001	embossed.com
Encore	(800) 526-0497		encorestudios.com
Jenner		(502) 222-0191	jennerco.com
Pacific Thermo.	(800) 423-5071	(818) 998-2000	
NuArt	(800) 653-5361		
Regency		(717) 762-7161	regencythermo.com
William Arthur	(800) 985-6581	(207) 985-6581	williamarthur.com

Mail order catalogs

American Wedding Album	(800) 428-0379	theamericanwedding.com
Ann's Wedding Stationery	(800) 821-7011	annswedding.com
Creations by Elaine	(800) 452-4593	creationsbyelaine.com

Dawn	(800) 332-3296		invitationsbydawn.com
Dewberry Engraving	(800) 633-8614		
Evangel Christian Invitations	(800) 457-9774	(812) 623-2509	evangelwedding.com
Heart Thoughts	(800) 648-5781		heart-thoughts.com
Now & Forever	(800) 521-0584		now-and-forever.com
Precious Collection	(800) 537-5222		preciouscollection.com
Reaves Engraving		(910) 610-4499	reavesengraving.com
Rexcraft	(800) 635-3898		rexcraft.com
Wedding Traditions/Sugar & Spice		(800) 535-1002	wedding-traditions.com
Willow Tree Lane	(800) 219-1022		willowtreelane.com
Julie Holcomb Printers	(877) 877-8905		julieholcombprinters.com
Clover Creek invitations	(800) 769-9676	(802) 425-5549	
Invitesite			invitesite.com
Fine Paper Co		(626) 584-9804	
Dreamland Designs			dreamland-designs.com
Wedding Invit. CD-ROM	(888) 727-3772		pcpapers.com
Invitation Hotline	(800) 800-4355	(732) 536-9115	invitationhotline.com
Paper Direct	(800) 272-7377		paperdirect.com
Paper Journey	(800) 827-2737	(203) 744-2949	
Paper Showcase	(800) 287-8163		papershowcase.com
Favours Internationale		(781) 383-1065	
Hercules Candies	(800) 924-4339	(315) 463-4339	herculescandy.com
Tender Seed Co			tenderseedcompany.com
Nelson Trading Company	(800) 699-1859		nelsontrading.com
Moosie Wrappers			moosiewrapper.com

Reception Sites

Coors Brewery	(901) 375-2100
Minnesota Zoo	(612) 431-9215
Wedding Links Galore	weddinglinksgalore.com/sites.htm
Weddings newsgroups	news:alt.wedding, news:soc.couples.wedding
The Wedding Channel	weddingchannel.com

Catering

National Association of Catering Executives		nace.net
About.com		weddings.about.com
Food Network		foodtv.com
Martha Stewart		marthastewart.com
Sam's Club		samsclub.com
Costco		costco.com
BJ's Wholesale Club		bjswholesale.com
Cooking Hospitality Institute (Chicago)	(312) 944-0882	

Photography

Waterhouse Albums	(860) 526-1296	waterhousebook.com
Professional Photographers of America		ppa.com
Wedding and Portrait Photographers		eventphotographers.com
Photoworks.com		photoworks.com
Picture Trail		picturetrail.com
Zing		zing.com
PhotoPoint		photopoint.com
Our Album		our-album.net
Collages.net		collages.net
Club Photo		event.clubphoto.com

ShotsOnline		shotsonline.com
Photozone		photozone.com
PhotoReflect		photoreflect.com
Proshots		proshots.com
Kodak		kodak.com
The Wedding Photographers Network		theknot.com
Kodak Wedding Party Pak	(800) 242-2424	
Exposures catalog	(800) 222-4947	exposuresonline.com
Art Leather albums	(718) 699-6300	artleather.com
C&G Disposable Cameras		cngdisposablecamera.com
PrimeShot.com		primeshot.com

Cakes

International Cake Exploration Societe	ices.org
Wilton	wilton.com
Portraits in Clay	portraitsinclay.com
Nerd World	nerdworld.com/nw7657.html

Videos

Party Shots		partyshots.com
WEVA	(800) 501-9381 (941) 923-5334	weva.com
Prof. Videographers Network (So Cal)		pvn.org
Assoc. of Professional Videographers	(209) 653-8307	avp.to
Dallas Digital Transfer	(214) 336-6292	dallasdigitaltransfer.com
Video Data Services	(800) 836-9461 (716) 381-9240	vdsvideo.com

Entertainment

American Disc Jockey Association	(301) 705-5150	adja.org
ProDJ		prodj.com
The Ceremony Music Resource page		castle.net/~energize/CMRP/
The Ultimate Wedding Song Library		ultimatewedding.com/songs/
Song for my Son CD	(800) 447-6647	

Etcetera

Limo consumer tips		bridaltips.com
National Limo Assoc.	(800) NLA-7007	limo.org
Moissanite		moissanite.com
Wedding Ring Hotline	(800) 985-7464 (732) 972-7777	weddingringhotline.com
Engagement Rings book	(800) 962-4544 (802) 457-4000	
Diamond FAQ		http://wam.umd.edu/~sek/wedding.html
Diamond Cutters		diamondcutters.com
Diamond Grading		diamondgrading.com
Wedding insurance	(800) 364-2433	rvnuccio.com
Way Cool Weddings		waycoolwedding.com
Destination & Specialty Wedding Page		http://umich.edu/~kzaruba/wedding.html
June Wedding (assoc.)	(702) 474-9558	junewedding.com
Assoc. of Bridal Consultants	(860) 355-0464	bridalassn.com
Michael Round	(800) 4 MROUND	mround.com

Honeymoons

SunTrips	suntrips.com
1Travel.com	1travel.com
SmarterLiving	smarterliving.com
Carribean Concepts	(800) 423-4433

Caradonna Tours	(800) 328-2288		
Vacation Travel Mart	(800) 288-1435		vacmart.com
Servitours		(305) 381-9026	
Spur of Moment Cruises	(800) 343-1991		spurof.com

Canada

Wedding Bells			weddingbells.com
David's (Buffalo, NY)		(716) 834-6100	
Forever Yours (preservation)	(800) 683-4696	(416) 703-4696	gowncare.com

Bridal gown manufacturers

Alfred Sung	(800) 295-7308	(416) 247-4628	alfredsungbridals.com
Amici		(905) 264-1466	
Barbara Allin		(416) 469-1098	
Catherine Regehr		(604) 734-9339	
Gordon		(416) 593-0688	
Guzzo		(416) 585-9820	guzzobridal.com
Ines Di Santo		(905) 856-9115	
Justina McCaffrey	(888) 874-4696	(613) 789-4336	jmhc.com
Madison Collection		(416) 789-9911	
Rivini		(416) 977-1793	
Wedding Canada			weddingcanada.com
Frugal Bride			frugalbride.com

Invitations

Classic Canadian Weddings	(800) 833-6761	
Nicole	(800) 228-0486	
Discount Invitations	(888) 969-9394	discount-invitations.com
Wedding Bells		weddingbells.com

INDEX